TRUMPED!

A NATION ON THE BRINK OF RUIN . . .
AND HOW TO BRING IT BACK

DAVID A. STOCKMAN

NEW YORK TIMES BEST-SELLING AUTHOR OF **THE GREAT DEFORMATION**

TRUMPED!

**A NATION ON THE BRINK OF RUIN . . .
AND HOW TO BRING IT BACK**

DAVID A. STOCKMAN

❀ Laissez Faire Books

For Jennifer, Victoria, Rachel and Robert.

ISBN: 978-1-6212918-4-8 (print)
ISBN: 978-1-6212918-5-5 (ebook)

20 19 18 17 16   1 2 3 4 5 6 7

Published by Laissez Faire Books, 808 St. Paul Street, Baltimore, Maryland
www.lfb.org
www.agorafinancial.com

Cover and Layout Design: Andre Cawley

CONTENTS

PART 1

———

TRUMPED!
WHY IT HAPPENED

CHAPTER 1:

Flyover America's Decline and the Rise of Donald Trump

FIRST THERE WERE 17. THEN LITTLE MARCO, LOW ENERGY JEB AND LYIN' Ted were gone. At length, there was one. And now there is even a chance he may become president.

Donald Trump's wildly improbable capture of the GOP nomination and rise toward the White House is surely the most significant upheaval in American politics since Ronald Reagan.

Yet the rise of Trump—and Bernie Sanders too—vastly transcends ordinary politics. In fact, it reaches deep into a ruined national economy that has morphed into rank casino capitalism under the misguided policies and faithless rule of the Washington and Wall Street elites.

This epic deformation has delivered historically unprecedented setbacks to the bottom 90% of American households. They have seen their real wealth and living standards steadily deteriorate for several decades now, even as vast financial windfalls have accrued to the elite few at the very top.

In fact, during the last 30 years, the real net worth of the bottom 90% has not increased at all. At the same time, the top 1% has experienced a 300% gain while the real wealth of the Forbes 400 has risen by 1,000%.

That's not old-fashioned capitalism at work; it's the fruit of a perverted regime of printing press money and debt-fueled faux prosperity that has been foisted on the nation by the bipartisan ruling elites.

To be sure, the proximate cause of this year's election upheaval is similar to that in Reagan's time. Back then, an era of drastic bipartisan mis-governance generated an electoral impulse to sweep out the Washington stables.

Now, however, it is not just the Beltway political class that is under attack. The very foundations of American economic life are imperiled. What remained of healthy market capitalism in Reagan's time is no more.

It has been battered by 30 years of madcap money printing at the Fed. It labors under the $50 trillion of new public and private debt generated by that monetary eruption. And it staggers from the destructive blows of serial financial bubbles.

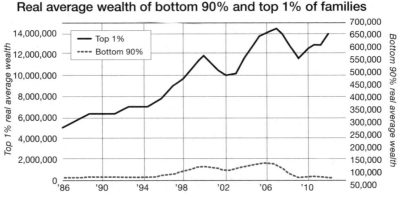

Real average wealth of bottom 90% and top 1% of families

These bubbles have self-evidently resulted in a destructive boom-and-bust cycle in the financial system, but also much more. Bubble Finance has drained productivity and efficiency from the Main Street economy and has channeled vast resources to speculators and wasteful malinvestments.

THE ECONOMIC ROT WAS GENERATED IN WASHINGTON, NOT BY OPEN BORDERS AND TRADE

Unfortunately, this policy-generated rot at the foundations of the U.S. economy has bred a profusion of public fears and scapegoats. Illegal immigrants, bad trade deals and the unfair mercantilist practices of China and many other foreign governments have taken the blame—especially in Donald Trump's campaign patter.

But these scapegoats are either irrelevant or just symptoms. The real problem is not free trade or free movement of people.

To the contrary, America's faltering economy was caused by the policy machinations of Washington, D.C., not at the illegal crossing routes on the Arizona border or the containership berths at Long Beach. For more than three decades, the nation's central bank has flooded the U.S. and world economies with too much free money (dollar liabilities) and Washington politicians have accommodated the Beltway racketeers and the country's huge entitlement constituencies with too much free booty.

So the real disease is bad money and towering debts. The actual culprits are the Wall Street and Washington policy elites who have embraced statist solutions, which aggrandize their own power and wealth.

That much, at least, Donald Trump has right. Throwing out the careerists, pettifoggers, hypocrites, ideologues, racketeers, power seekers and snobs who have brought about the current ruin is at least a start in the right direction.

Trump is directionally correct on another great matter as well. The American Imperium abroad has been a fiscal, foreign policy and moral catastrophe, as we outline in depth in Part 3.

When the Cold War ended 25 years ago, NATO should have been disbanded and Washington's vast war machine should have been drastically shrunken—even as the rest of the so-called free world was invited to share in the pursuit of peace and in shouldering the burdens of its own security.

But what we got, instead, were the Clinton/Bush/Obama wars of intervention and occupation. They have resulted in failed states, sectarian carnage and terrorist blowback, not a more secure America.

Worse still, political demagogues, including Trump, have fanned public fears that the barbarism Washington unleashed in Syria, Iraq, Libya, Yemen and elsewhere now threatens every city and town in America. That is a gross exaggeration, to say the least, as we demonstrate later in this book.

Yet there is absolutely no doubt that the arrogant and insular groupthink of the Imperial City is the cause of the murderous chaos that rages across the greater Middle East and beyond. Americans are fearful because Washington's reckless and destructive foreign interventions have not made them more secure; it has put them in harm's way.

So far, Donald Trump's solutions have been largely rhetorical, inchoate and often far too bellicose. But he has pinned the tail where it belongs. That is, on the imperial notion that America is the indispensable savior-nation and policeman of the world when Washington should be focused on America's homeland security first.

What made America great once upon a time, of course, were free markets, fiscal rectitude, sound money, constitutional liberty, non-intervention abroad, minimalist government at home and decentralized political rule.

Whether Donald Trump gets that part of the equation remains to be seen, and already there is much to suggest that he won't.

Then again, the GOP establishment has betrayed these principles entirely; the Democrats are clueless; and the mainstream media and punditry is overtly hostile.

So if the ideals of world peace, capitalist prosperity and constitutional liberty are to survive at all, it's up to The Donald.

Admittedly, that seems like cold comfort. There is much that is dark, disturbing and authoritarian about the Trump personality and candidacy.

But a nation that has been Trumped is a people coming back to life. Americans don't want to take it anymore. Instead, they want their existing rulers to take a permanent hike.

That's a damn good start, and it is the outlaw campaign of Donald J. Trump that has finally lit the flame of rebellion.

THE ESSENCE OF TRUMP'S APPEAL— FLYOVER AMERICA ISN'T WINNING ANYMORE

This book is no testimonial on behalf of Donald Trump's candidacy. Much of what he advocates is wrong-headed or downright reprehensible. But it does salute him as the rallying force for Main Street insurrection because the existing regime of Bubble Finance on Wall Street and statist aggrandizement in Washington threatens incalculable ruin.

In that context, we are mindful that in posturing as an anti-politician outsider Trump has also proven himself to be a rank demagogue. His scurrilous attacks, inter alia, on Moslems, Mexicans, minorities, women, political opponents and countless more are frequently beyond the pale—even by today's rudely partisan standards of public discourse.

Indeed, there has rarely been a political figure in American life who has emitted as much baloney, bombast, brimstone and bile as Donald Trump. And none has ever matched his narcissism and egomaniacal personality.

But that's not why he's succeeding.

The Donald's patented phrase that "we aren't winning anymore" is what's really striking a deep nerve on Main Street. His rhetoric about giant trade deficits, failed foreign military adventures and other short-comings of America's collective polity self-evidently touches that chord.

Indeed, Trump's appeal is rooted at bottom in voter perceptions that they personally are no longer winning economically, either. And as hinted at above and as we will further document in depth, the vast expanse of Main Street America has indeed been losing ground for the last 25 years.

What is winning is Washington, Wall Street and the bicoastal elites. They prosper from a toxic brew of finance, debt and politics.

We call this deformed system Bubble Finance. Its tentacles extend from the vast apparatus of Wall Street and the finance and asset management businesses it feeds to the venture capital hotbeds of Silicon Valley, Boston, New York City, Research Triangle, Seattle, San Diego, Austin and Denver.

It also includes to the LA branch of entertainment (movies and TV) and the San Francisco branch of entertainment (social media). Most im-portantly of all, it encompasses the great rackets of the Imperial City and its extensions and auxiliaries.

Indeed, Washington's unseemly prosperity arises from its sundry pre-cincts of debt-financed Big Government. The latter has been enabled, in turn, by the massive bond-buying campaigns of the Fed and other central banks.

These flourishing domains of statist hegemony include the military/industrial/surveillance complex, the health and education cartels, the plaintiffs and patent bars, the tax loophole lobbies, the black and green energy subsidy mills and endless like and similar K-Street racketeers.

By contrast, most of America's vast flyover zone has been left behind. When adjusted by an honest measure of inflation we call the "Flyover

CPI," real hourly wages are lower than they were in 1985, *and real median household income is down 21% from year 2000 levels.*

As we will show below, the US economy has not generated any new breadwinner jobs since the turn of the century. Real net business investment is 20% below its year 2000 level. And productivity growth is on the verge of extinction.

So it is no coincidence at all that the economic health and wealth of the bottom 90% of households has been slumping for decades. The plain fact is, the Main Street economy is failing, and failing badly.

Not so when it comes to the financial economy of Wall Street and its venture capital satcllites. The real net worth and incomes of the top 1% have soared owing to the fact that the stock market has been transformed into a gambling casino by the massive monetary intrusion of the Fed.

As will be more fully explored later, virtually free overnight carry trade funding, monetization of the public debt on a heretofore unimaginable scale and stock market bailouts and puts have generated vast ill-gotten gains from incessant leveraged speculation. These gains, of course, have not remotely trickled-down to Main Street.

Moreover, the wealth round trip of the bottom 90% depicted in the chart above was hardly real in the first place. The calculated levels of Main Street net worth temporarily rose owing to Greenspan's 15-year housing bubble. But that eventually culminated in the great financial crisis, meaning that what is left is mainly the mortgage debt.

In fact, Flyover America is buried in debt—$14.3 trillion of it. Household debt relative to income is still more than double its historical level.

Likewise, the companies most Americans work for have been strip-mined to the tune of trillions in order fund financial engineering gambits like stock buybacks and M&A deals rather than productive investments in plant, equipment and technology.

Finally, the taxpayers of Flyover America are already heavily burdened. Yet they have not yet begun to feel the further, massive tax increases that will soon be required to fund the Warfare State and Welfare State excesses of the ruling elites.

Indeed, three decades of rampant money printing, debt accumulation and serial financial bubbles have resulted in what we call the "Great Deformation."

In Washington, K-Street racketeering has usurped democracy. On Wall Street, speculation has extinguished honest price discovery and efficient capital allocation. In America's corporate C-suites, financial engineering and stock pumping have replaced productive investment.

What has emerged is a mutant state that is neither capitalism nor democracy. Soon 10,000 people will own a preponderant share of the wealth; 10 million people will live grandly off the droppings; 150 million will live off the state; and the rest of America will be left high and dry waiting for the house of cards to collapse.

That prospect explains why Trump is winning in Flyover America—even as it confirms why the bicoastal elites have gone postal on The Donald. The mess in America is their fault, and they are trying mightily to shift the blame.

But that shrill attack is also why voters believe Trump's charge that the system is rigged.

It surely is, and our purpose in the pages ahead is to show exactly how and what needs to be done to bring America back from the brink.

DONALD TRUMP'S CANDIDACY—THE GOOD AND THE BAD OF IT

In the next chapters we will document at length why the United States is a nation on the brink of financial ruin. Our purpose at this point, however, is to dispel any illusion that Donald Trump—the man and his platform— offers any semblance of a remedy.

In the great scheme of history, The Donald's role may be to merely disrupt and paralyze the status quo. And that much he may well accomplish whether he is elected or not.

For what is actually happening is metapolitical. The bipartisan ruling elites are being Trumped, as it were, by a populist uprising.

Their entire regime of casino capitalism, beltway racketeering and imperial hegemony is being unmasked. The unwashed voters are catching on to the "rigged" essence of the system, and have already become alienated enough to rally to outlaw politicians—like Bernie and Trump—peddling ersatz socialism and reality-TV populism, respectively.

To be sure, the metaphor of shock and awe and the idea of "regime change" have been given a bad name by Bush the Younger and his bloody henchmen. Yet there is no better way to describe Donald Trump's rise and role than with exactly those terms.

The current regime arose in the 1980s from Ronald Reagan's regrettable decision to rebuild the nation's war machine—along with the GOP's conversion to Dick Cheney's "deficits don't matter" fallacy and Alan Greenspan's ill-fated discovery of the Fed's printing press in the basement of the Eccles Building. Those deplorable, illicit and unsustainable departures from sound policy have subsequently morphed into the full-blown mutant state referenced above.

Its many deformations are undeniable. They include soaring public and private debts at home; the peace-destroying and fiscally crushing American Imperium abroad; serial financial bubbles that have gifted mainly the 1%; and rampant Beltway influence peddling and a PAC-based campaign finance system that amounts to money racketeering, among countless other ills.

This entire misbegotten regime is now well past its sell-by date; it's waiting to be monkey-hammered by an unscripted and uninvited disrupter.

For at least that role, Donald Trump is eminently qualified. He represents a raw insurgency of attack, derision, impertinence and repudiation.

He's the battering ram that is needed to shatter the polite lies and delusions on which the current regime rests. If he had been ordered from central casting for that role, in fact, it would have been difficult for Hollywood to confect anything close to the brash, egomaniacal rabble-rouser who now has the ruling elites in a fever pitch of sanctimonious reproach.

It is no wonder they are virtually screeching that he is "unqualified." Yes, Donald Trump is rude, impulsive and loutish to a fault.

That's why, in fact, his is unsuited for the establishment's job definition. That is, to preside over another four years of the kind of risible, kick-the-can fantasy-world that serves the interests of our Wall Street and Washington rulers.

The latter would have the left-behind legions in Flyover America believe that everything is fixed and that the financial crisis and the Great Recession were but a random and unrepeatable bump in the night that will never recur. As Obama blatantly fibbed at the Democratic convention, America is already great and America is already strong.

No, not even close. America is heading for a devastating financial collapse and prolonged recession that will make the last go-round look tame by comparison. We will present chapter and verse in the pages ahead, but suffice it here to say that the entire recovery is one giant Potemkin village of phony economics and egregious financial asset inflation.

It isn't even a mixed or debatable story. Beneath the "all is awesome" propaganda of the establishment institutions is a broken system hurtling toward ruin.

For example, during the month of July 2016, when the Democrats were convening in Philadelphia to confirm a third Obama term and toast 25-years of Bubble Finance, exactly 98 million Americans in the prime working ages of 25 to 54 years had jobs, including part-time gigs and self-employment. That compares to 98.1 million during July 2000.

That's right. After 16 years of the current regime we have 5 million more prime working age Americans and not a single one of them with a job. At the same time, the number of persons in households receiving means-tested benefits has risen from 50 million to 110 million.

Even as the economic wagon has faltered and become loaded with dependents, however, the financial system has grown by leaps and bounds. For example, during those same 16 years public and private debt outstanding in America has risen from $28 trillion to $64 trillion; the value of publicly traded equity has increased from $25 trillion to $45 trillion; and the net worth of the Forbes 400 has nearly doubled from $1.2 trillion to $2.4 trillion.

In a word, the U.S. economy is a ticking time bomb. Main Street economics and Wall Street finance have become radically and dangerously disconnected owing to the reckless falsification of financial markets by the Fed and Washington's addiction to endless deficits and crony capitalist bailouts and boodle. There is not a remote chance that this toxic brew can be sustained much longer.

Under those circumstances the very last thing America will need in 2017–18 when the brown stuff hits the fan is a lifetime political careerist and clueless acolyte of the state who knows all the right words and harbors all the wrong ideas.

Indeed, during the coming crisis America will need a brash disrupter of the status quo, not a diehard defender. Yet when the Dow index drops by 7,000 points and unemployment erupts back toward double digits, Hillary Clinton's only impulse will be to double down.

That is, to fire-up the printing presses at the Fed from red hot to white heat, plunge the nation's fiscal equation back into multi-trillion deficits and crank-out Washington's free stuff like never before. A combination of a Clinton White House and the devastating day of reckoning just ahead would result in Big Government on steroids.

It would also tilt the Imperial City toward war in order to distract the nation's disgruntled voters in their tens of millions.

After all, Hillary the Hawk has never seen a war she didn't embrace including Bosnia, Kosovo, Afghanistan, Iraq, Syria, Libya, Yemen, and Ukraine. Having fatuously likened Vladimir Putin to Hitler, she and her government in waiting are deeply invested in Washington's reckless and unnecessary confrontation with Russia, and are now even making the balmy claim that the Kremlin was behind the hacking of the DNC's trove of email gossip and skullduggery.

Indeed, her prospective war cabinet—including Victoria Nuland and Michéle Flournoy—is comprised of the actual architects of Washington's unprovoked NATO siege on Russia's own doorsteps.

So Hillary Clinton may be perfectly qualified to wonk and conciliate her way through the fantasyland jabber of *The New York Times* editorial boardroom. But that's the wrong venue entirely.

The next four years, by contrast, will not be a time when Washington connections, manners and an extensive official resume will count for anything at all. Nor will a facility for establishment double-talk about how Uncle Sam is riding to the rescue be a virtue.

In fact, the credibility of every financial institution along the Acela corridor will be in tatters. That includes the fiscal firemen of Capitol Hill, the money printers at the Fed, the IMF bailout brigades headquartered in D.C., the global banking cartels domiciled in NYC, the gambling houses and fast money hedge funds of Wall Street and the mutual fund combines of Boston.

In that context, Donald Trump's overwhelming virtue is that he is not Hillary Clinton. He may be lacking in policy tutorials, but so what?

At least Donald Trump does not carry a bulging 30-year-old bag of bad ideas. By contrast, Hillary's ideas—and those of the establishment for which she shills—about how to fix the coming economic and foreign policy crises are so unequivocally and irremediably bad that it is not possible that there is anything worse.

That's not to say that Donald Trump's economic policy ideas—to the extent that they are semi-coherent and describable—aren't plenty dubious. You can find much that is pretty awful in his public quips and bromides.

Indeed, if you are a "low-interest-rate man," as he claims to be, you are clueless about the central menace of our times: to wit, the rogue central banks and the massive falsification of financial markets that have resulted from their heavy-handed intrusion and money pumping.

If you don't want to touch Social Security and Medicare—ever—you have your head buried in the fiscal sand. On that score, even Trump's prodigious comb-over has disappeared below the surface.

If you think that fraud, waste and abuse have anything to do with the nation's suffocating national debt, you are not thinking at all; you are channeling Ronald Reagan.

If you think, in fact, that giant corporate and individual tax cuts will pay for themselves in higher economic growth you are also channeling Ronald Reagan; and you are also propagating a patently false GOP revisionist history of the 1980s budget debacle.

The Reagan tax cuts didn't come close to self-funding. The only reason that the national debt rose by a mere 250% on the Gipper's watch is that upwards of 40% of the original revenue loss was rescinded with tax increases later in his term.

If you think a $10 minimum wage is warranted, as apparently the GOP candidate does on alternating days of the week, you haven't meet any robots lately.

The minimum wage was always a jobs killer because it causes capital substitution for labor. Yet with today's breakthroughs in robotics a big minimum wage hike will literally ionize millions of low-skill jobs.

If you think a big public infrastructure program is needed to prime the economic pump, you don't understand federalism or even where productivity comes from.

The only genuine federal infrastructure responsibility is the Interstate Highway System, but that's generally in good shape already—and could be perfected with a modest hike in the gas tax. The rest of it is either pork or public works, and the difference can only be sorted out by local governments, affected voters and taxpayers who actually foot the bill.

Finally, if you think that the $8 trillion in cumulative current account deficits that the United States has run without interruption for the last 35 years is due to bad trade deals, you are essentially clueless as to why America is on the brink of economic ruin. The $60 billion we import from Mexico and $500 billion from China is a symptom of the nation's rotten regime of Bubble Finance, not its cause.

Unfortunately, Donald Trump appears to be an economic blank slate who can embrace any and all of the above errors and delusions. That's because his economics are purely glandular. Insofar as it is possible to discern, he has never been troubled by any kind of economic model or coherent philosophy at all.

But, alas, that is also his virtue. What needs to happen when the next recession and stock market plunge unfolds is exactly nothing. "Policy" is what is ruining American capitalism, and the corpulent bailout and pork-barrel state is it creating is what is eviscerating political democracy.

If Donald Trump is elected president, there will be no shovel-ready stimulus plan or any other economic policy fix within the first 100 days. Instead, there will be a gong show of such fury and fractiousness as to immobilize the Imperial City indefinitely.

If Hillary Clinton wins, the GOP-controlled House of Representatives will lapse into a partisan killing field for any economic tonics the White House may offer.

Either way, both ends of Pennsylvania Avenue will end up in political trench warfare. And either way, the Fed will end up even more paralyzed.

If it attempts negative interest rates to combat the coming recession, the savers and retirees of Flyover America will finally erupt with torches and pitchforks.

On the other hand, if it goes for another massive QE campaign, it will be an admission that $3.5 trillion of it was an utter failure. Even the Wall Street gamblers will stampede for the exits.

In a word, the historic virtue of Donald Trump is that win or lose, his candidacy means that the illicit Washington and Wall Street "policy" regime will finally come to a grinding halt.

The Great Liquidation of crushing debts, insanely inflated assets prices, rampant carry-trade speculation, debilitating malinvestments and unspeakable windfalls to the gambling classes will finally commence. And none too soon.

TWO SIDES OF THE STATIST COIN— TRUMP, PRO AND CON

Donald Trump's inchoate views on economics are a virtue mainly because he has not been schooled in the follies of bipartisan fiscal and monetary "stimulus policy." Essentially, the Beltway's incumbent practitioners of this misbegotten policy regime are statist advocates of CINO (capitalism in name only).

Not The Donald. Whether the business empire Trump claims to have built is all it's cracked-up to be (by him) or not, there is a secret sauce to it that the mainstream liberal journalists fails to grasp. They would find it downright frightening if they did.

To wit, Trump's incessant bragging about his business prowess and accomplishments is not merely or even mainly an unbridled and uncouth expression of egotism and self-absorption. Actually, it is a profession of

rudimentary faith—a policy conviction—that America's capitalist economy grows owing to what capitalists like himself create and foster, not
because of the "policy" interventions of the Imperial City's knaves, crooks
and scolds.

To some considerable degree, "making America great" is about unleashing the nation's capitalists again. It's an expression that prosperity is not
bestowed by the state but won by the kind of builders, investors, innovators
and workers that The Donald fancies to be the essence of Trump Inc.

To that extent, Donald Trump could be regarded as an incipient antistatist. While this might seem like an overly generous characterization, it
is a measure, alas, of the degree to which the bipartisan "policy" consensus
on economics has congealed around what is essentially a Keynesian axiom
of endless macroeconomic intervention and "stimulus."

To be sure, the GOP proposes to accomplish the fiscal stimulus side
of this task via "tax cuts" for business and "job creators" everywhere and
always. By contrast, the Democrats favor the targeting of "tax credits" and
spending increases to constituencies mainly inside the DNC political um-
brella such as education, Medicaid and green energy. Both are not loath
in the slightest, however, to charge-off the trillions of fiscal leakage to our
mountainous national debt.

And both parties are fully onboard, of course, with the massive fraud
that has become central bank policy both here and around the world.

Starting in the year 2000 with just a $500 billion balance sheet after
86 years of operation, the Fed has actually purchased $4 trillion of ad-
ditional Treasury debt and GSE securities since then and funded it with
credits conjured from thin air. This has been a monumental act of "something for nothing" economics in which the trillions Congress has wasted
on war and welfare have been financed with digital money magic.

So when it comes to economics, it is hard to see how Trump could
end up more statist than the bipartisan status quo. But the problem is
that Donald Trump has a domineering and authoritarian personality and
extreme penchant for believing in the efficacy of his own personal force
of action.

In fact, he undoubtedly fancies himself as Horatius at the Bridge, but the truth of the matter is that he seems to have far more tendencies toward the opposite. Namely, the proverbial man on the white horse.

For any constitutionalist, this should be a cause for concern during any season, but in the current fraught environment it's a clanging alarm bell. That is, a genuine capitalist like Trump is unlikely to see the state as a battering ram for economic recovery and prosperity. But when it comes to the issues of law and order and terrorism, his glandular impulses go all the wrong way.

Donald Trump, in fact, is also an incipient police statist. In that modality he offers himself as the "strongman" who will marshal all of the vast resources and coercive powers of the state to protect an allegedly imperiled and fearful citizenry from a wave of crime and terrorist attacks.

TRUMP'S ANTICRIME DEMAGOGUERY— DANGERS AND DIGRESSIONS

But unlike the Horatius of Roman lore, there are no Etruscan hordes of criminals or terrorists at the bridge of America's 19,345 towns and cities. Virtually 99.9% of them are safe, secure and peaceful almost all of the time—save for motorists reading their I-Phones on the freeways.

The purported crime and terrorism wave, in fact, is essentially a figment of the cable news version of reality TV, and most especially the CNN war channel and its perennial black versus blue & white race narrative.

Needless to say, Donald Trump has great difficulty distinguishing the actual facts on these matters from the simulacrum of reality conveyed by cable TV because he is a product of that very thing. Without his 11-year run on "The Apprentice," the nation would have been stuck with Clinton versus Bush redux.

On the purported domestic "crime wave" that rang-out from the rafters during the GOP convention in Cleveland, however, it's not even a close call. According to the FBI data, there has been an astonishing 50% reduction in the U.S. violent crime rate since the early 1990s.

That's not just a little bit of improvement or a heartening directional vector; it's a powerfully embedded trend and slam-dunk proof that the last thing America needs is a Washington led war on crime, and especially a White House pre-occupied with it.

Donald Trump is not only dead wrong about the purported crime wave, but in blatantly demagogueing the issue he is inflaming cable TV's black versus blue & white narrative. So doing, he actually fuels the establishment's specious argument that he is not qualified to be president because he is "divisive."

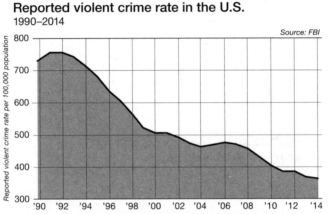

Reported violent crime rate in the U.S.
1990–2014

Source: FBI

The latter charge, of course, is too rich for words. What establishment economic and war policies actually do is to essentially pit the 1% against the 90%. Yet by foolishly flogging the crime card The Donald threatens to obfuscate the socioeconomic class divide that is at the heart of the real crisis which stalks the nation.

Yes, in selective cities like Chicago and Baltimore there has been a surge in violent crimes. But those are examples of the rotating exceptions, which, as the chart above proves beyond a shadow of doubt, have been more than offset by the overwhelming trend of sharply declining violent crime rates throughout the United States.

Yet Trump's anti-crime digression is not the half of it. The entire cable reality-TV narrative about police killings of civilians and the killing of officers on duty by criminals is entirely about goosing viewership ratings, not about rising homicide rates. In truth, there is no epidemic of either— just a massive, unwarranted, sensationalized and context-free surfeit of media coverage.

Regrettably, Trump has embraced—hook, line and sinker—the non-existent war on cops. Yet during the three years ending in 2014, the number of on-duty police officer deaths was lower than at any time since 1960!

And, as the chart below makes clear, well less than half of the 126 deaths in 2014 were due to the deliberate shooting of cops by criminals. A much larger portion was due to traffic accidents involving patrolman and other causes such as heart attacks—perhaps prompted by too many donuts in the line of duty.

Total U.S. police deaths on duty

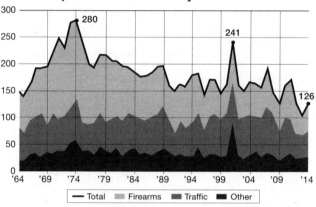

In fact, the actual rate of intentional, felonious killings per 100,000 officers has been plummeting for decades. During 2014 it was actually 71% lower than the year Ronald Reagan left office.

Nor can some run-rate blip extracted from recent months or a rash of headline events like the recent Dallas assassinations negate that truth. The police forces of America are not suddenly imperiled by cop-killers, and, in fact, police work is not even among the "top 10" most hazardous occupations.

There are about 750,000 police officers in the United States, so the above results for 2014 computes to about 17 deaths on the job per 100,000. That's way below logging workers at 128 per 100,000, pilots at 53 per 100,000, garbage collectors at 37 per 100,000 and even farmers and ranchers at 21.3 per 100,000.

That Donald Trump has chosen to pound the tables on this issue is indicative of his dangerous penchant for reality TV theatrics and his fundamental confusion between courageous and honest political leadership and further aggrandizement of an already overly strong central state.

Under any sound notion of federalism, in fact, community policing is a function for local and state governments, not the grandees and pooh-bahs of the Beltway.

Even were the crime rate stats not so dramatically favorable, full-throated demagoguery in behalf of America's police forces should have no place in a presidential campaign; and, more importantly, there is no reason whatsoever for Washington to even be involved in legislating criminal law and the operational machinery of its enforcement.

To the contrary, the places where most of the nation's violent crimes and assaults on law enforcement officers actually occur—a few dozen large urban areas—have not been helped by the Federal government at all. They have actually been put in harm's way.

Indeed, when viewed in longer-term prospective it is evident that the two pulses of gun-related police deaths in the last century were caused by Washington's follies—first Prohibition in the 1920s and then the federal "War on Drugs" incepting the 1970s.

Gun-related U.S. police deaths
Per 1M population, 1870–2015 (est.)

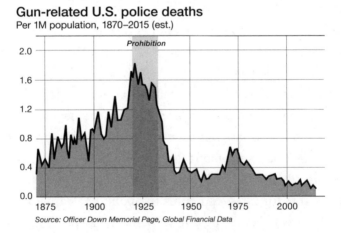

Source: Officer Down Memorial Page, Global Financial Data

To wit, abolish the federal "War on Drugs" entirely and turn the distribution of all currently banned "controlled substances" over to Phillip Morris and other law-abiding purveyors of legal poisons and a good share of even the criminal violence we do have would eventually disappear.

And that would especially be true if the prisons and jails were emptied of drug users and traffickers.

That's because in its infinite folly, the federal government and its state and local fellow travelers have incarcerated upwards of 1.0 million drug law offenders on the grounds that they are being punished while society is being protected.

That's balderdash. Society doesn't need any protection from vending machines, sidewalk emporiums or other legal forms of commerce that could readily distribute any drugs, which today are controlled by violent globe-spanning cartels and the vicious underground distribution networks they operate in local communities.

Likewise, the bulging prisons and jails full of drug offenders are not punishing anyone. To the contrary, they are taxpayer-funded trade schools for criminals.

In short, eliminate the federal drug and seizure laws and segue the drug business to the tobacco companies, banks and Colorado-style pot entrepreneurs and the trend in the chart below would head even closer towards zero per 100,000.

In fact, hugging the zero bound is exactly where this rate stands in England and numerous other outposts of civilization.

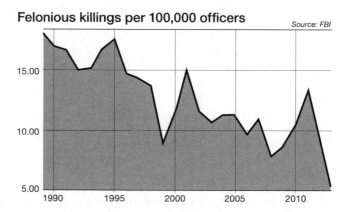

Felonious killings per 100,000 officers

Source: FBI

As to the other side of the coin, the cops in America are at once way over-militarized, and also way over-mandated with the enforcement of nanny- state laws that give them too many excuses to exercise lethal force against citizens. Very simply put, get them out of narcotics, prostitution, gambling and related social control missions and they will kill far fewer people. Furthermore, take back their armored vehicles and other military gear and they will have far fewer Rambo-tendencies.

Even then, excessive police use of force and unjustifiable killings are not a national epidemic, and do not require heavy-handed federal intervention. As the FBI computes it, the annual number of so-called "justifiable homicides" by police officers has been relatively constant at around 400 per year for nearly three decades.

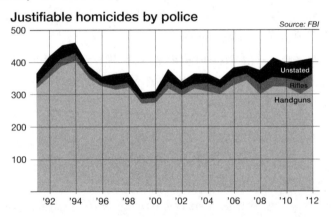

Even if the above numbers are suspect because the characterization as "justifiable" is largely police determined and reported, the chart below does not remotely justify the nightly derby of purported police violence by two of the most gullible empty suits in cable journalism—Anderson Cooper and Don Lemon of CNN.

Half the time they have the story wrong because purported "innocent victims" weren't all that, such as the Michael Brown case in Ferguson. Besides, the liberal media narrative vastly exaggerates the facts and fails to point out that if there is any fault to be ascribed, it is to the local sheriffs, police chiefs and city governments that are not doing their job of managing and disciplining the law enforcement officers under their command.

If Donald Trump must engage on an issue that isn't even among the "Top 10" imperatives with regard to cleaning the stables in the Imperial City let him heap a fusillade of tweets at the real culprits like Mayor Rahm Emanuel of Chicago.

Even when more objective and broader measures of police use of fatal force are considered, the cable reality news narrative doesn't really hold up.

The highest numbers reported are from a private tracking project called "Fatal Encounters." The number of civilian deaths by police for the 28 states for which there is "complete" data appears to have risen from about 350 annually in the year 2000 to 700 at present. But the problem with this version is that it makes no effort to distinguish between justifiable use of police firearms against threatening criminals and civilian killings, which should have never happened.

At the end of the day, the overwhelming message of the data is that there is neither crime wave nor eruption of police violence on either the giving or receiving end. Donald Trump is on a wild goose chase, yet it is precisely one that unwittingly serves the ferocious campaign of the ruling elites to discredit his candidacy.

TRUMP'S TERRORIST FEAR-MONGERING— RAUCOUS COVER BAND FOR THE WAR PARTY

Contrary to the spurious "morning in America" refrains of the Democratic convention, the nation is indeed heading for ruin. But that is not due to violent crimes or terrorist threats on Main Street. Instead, it is owing to the larcenous economic- policy crimes of the Imperial City—a matter that Trump's GOP convention narrative hardly mentioned.

There is a growing likelihood, therefore, that the Trump campaign will be entirely sidetracked from the core economic crisis of Flyover America. That's especially owing to The Donald's shrill remonstrations about the dangers of domestic terrorist attacks.

By contrast, after 15 years it is abundantly evident that the horrific attack of 9/11 was a complete fluke. It could have been readily thwarted by alert intelligence work, and even then it only happened because of the complicity of Saudi Arabian officials.

In fact, the San Diego-based Saudi handlers of 2 of the 19 terrorists received wire transfers of more than $75,000 from the Saudi ambassador's wife. We now know from the recently released 28 pages of classified text from the Joint Inquiry that at least one of the handlers—Omar al-Bay-oumi—was a Saudi agent. The report leaves little doubt that the Prince Bandar faction of the Saudi ruling family facilitated the murderous crime against 3,000 innocent Americans, which occurred on September 2001.

Since then, by contrast, there have apparently been no foreign government facilitations of organized terrorist attacks on the U.S. homeland, and mirabile dictu, there have been none.

In fact, during the period between 9/11 and the recent lone wolf, terrorist-inspired rampages in San Bernardino and Orlando about 70 times more citizens were killed by lightening attacks on America soil than by jihadist-oriented terrorists.

That's right. During that 14-year interval more than 425 civilians were felled by lightning, according to the National Weather Service, but there had been just six civilians killed by terrorists. Two were killed at the El Al counter at LAX airport in 2002 and four at the Boston Marathon attacks in 2013.

There were also five deaths from the unsolved anthrax attacks of 2001 that were not likely the work of terrorists, as well as the murderous 2009 rampage at Fort Hood and the killings at the Chattanooga military centers two years ago. But most Americans have never set foot on a military base nor do they have any risk of exposure to the special propensity for violence that may be kindled at facilities where ordinary humans are deliberately turned into killing machines.

Yes, Orlando and San Bernardino were clearly lone wolf(s) events that an oafish CNN war storm-chaser described as "do it yourself terrorism." But such random "inspired by" mayhem committed by mentally deranged and sociopathic killers like the three individuals involved in these episodes, as well as the recent killer-truck rampage in Nice, France, are not organized terrorism; they are the excrescences of the tiny margin of humanity who inhabit the dark netherworld of psychotic disorder.

So the best thing that 324 million Americans can do about that danger is to tune out every single word that politicians have to say about it—and most especially those of Donald Trump. As a New Yorker, he was clearly traumatized by the immediacy of 9/11 and has made civic, and now political hay, by ingratiating himself to two of the most rapacious municipal monopolies in America—the New York police and firemen's unions.

Still, for 99.99% of Americans the risk of being killed or injured by a jihadist lone wolf is lower than being struck by lightning. And most surely it is far less than their exposure to the periodic eruption of mass killings by the full universe of homegrown psychopaths and demented malcontents who strike for other reasons and with disturbing regularity.

Just in the last four years alone, 105 people have been killed and 100 injured by non-jihadist killing rampages in a dozen different cities from coast to coast. These included the recent events at the Colorado Springs Planned Parenthood clinic and the Roseburg, Oregon campus, as well as the horrific black church murders in Charleston SC last June, the madness at Newton CT elementary school in December 2012 and the slaughter in the Aurora CO movie theatre in July 2012.

Altogether there have been 26 incidents of non-jihadist mass killings since 9/11 including the Blacksburg, Va., campus rampage which resulted in nearly 50 deaths and injuries. About 425 Americans were killed or injured during these incidents of terror-crimes committed overwhelmingly by sick young men often harboring white supremacist or other hate-based motivations.

Worse still, the overwhelming share of so-called terrorists plots that have been intercepted by law enforcement turn out to be FBI stings, including two-thirds of actual FBI prosecutions. Indeed, many of the cases involving no count drifters and psychotics have been so egregious that it would almost appear that the FBI is targeting the mentally ill in order to justify its massive operations and budgets.

In justifying one of its more notorious sting operations, in fact, former FBI assistant director, and now CNN talking head, Thomas Fuentes, left nothing to the imagination:

> If you're submitting budget proposals for a law enforcement agency, for an intelligence agency, you're not going to submit the proposal that "We won the war on terror and everything's great," cuz

the first thing that's gonna happen is your budget's gonna be cut in half. You know, it's my opposite of Jesse Jackson's 'Keep Hope Alive'—it's 'Keep Fear Alive.' Keep it alive.

Would that both kinds of actual terrorism be expunged from the land: the hateful doings of the Syed Rizwan Farooks (San Bernardino) and the demented mayhem of the Dylann Storm Roofs (South Carolina). But there is virtually nothing that Washington politicians can do about either—*except most surely to not make it worse by trying to bomb, drone, invade and occupy the real jihadist kind of terrorism out of existence.*

After all, is it not evident after two decades now of jihadist style terrorism—whether quasi-organized, remotely inspired or lone wolf executed—that it is fostered by blowback from Washington's imperial mayhem?

Most especially, is it not evident that the terrible 21st century military violence Washington has inflicted on the Moslem populations of the Middle East is actually what breeds revenge and acts of terroristic retaliation?

The fact is, terrorism did not suddenly sprout up a few years ago from the teachings of a 1370 year- old religion, nor from a belated discovery in struggling Middle Eastern nations that they hate America's freedom, prosperity and materialistic culture.

No, as I will document exhaustively, jihadist style terrorism came to America only after Washington trained and armed the mujahedeen in the 1980s, waged unprovoked war in Saudi Arabia and Mesopotamia in the 1990s and fostered the anarchy of failed Middle Eastern states—from Afghanistan to Iraq, Syria, Yemen, Somalia and Libya—thereafter.

Needless to say, the worst of Imperial Washington's sins and crimes is its arrogant pretension that America is morally exceptional and therefore functions as the "indispensable nation" on the world stage. In fact, the American Imperium has been a bloody failure from Vietnam through Central America, Afghanistan, Iraq, Syria and now Libya for the second time, among countless others.

In that context, Donald Trump has the correct impulse—homeland security first and primarily mounted from these shores.

But in being lured into Washington's utterly false campaign of propaganda and lies about the threat of jihadist terror in the cities and towns of America—a campaign designed to justify the nation's unconstitutional $80 billion spy-state apparatus at home and its vast war machine abroad—the Trump candidacy is in danger of being stealthfully co-opted by the ruling elites.

The latter need to keep public fears of jihadist terrorism in high fever in order to justify their neocon agenda and extract from taxpayers—current and future—the horrific cost of the warfare state apparatus on which much of Imperial Washington feeds. Alas, based on the bellicose rhetoric which emanated from the Cleveland convention—such as Rudy Giuliani's hysterical terrorist fear-mongering —the Trump campaign appears to be stumbling into its appointed role as a raucous cover band for the War Party's more crafted headliners.

Were Donald Trump to end-up shilling for the War Party in a losing race it would be bad enough. That's because it would further intensify the public hysteria about terrorism that keeps the American Imperium alive—notwithstanding its blatant and chronic policy failures and its staggering cost.

But were he to actually win the White House based on his crude anti-Muslim and terrorist fear-mongering, there is little reason to believe that The Donald would permanently check this stump speech red meat into one of the YUUGE freezers at Trump Tower. Instead, he is likely to push his police statist propensities to new extremes of unconstitutional encroachment on what remains of personal liberty in America.

Needless to say, that would do nothing for Flyover America nor would it help to rejuvenate the nation's ruined main street economy.

In fact, it would lead right into the Ronald Reagan trap. Namely, the shunting of political capital into the pursuit of warfare-state fiscal resources and police state legal authorities to the complete neglect of attacking and removing the statist regulatory, fiscal, tax and monetary barriers to the revival of capitalist prosperity.

Nevertheless, I will summarize below and describe in more detail in the chapters ahead a way forward that could break the baleful anti-capitalist and anti-democratic regime of the Washington and Wall Street elites. The Trump campaign is already taking shape in the wrong direction, of course, but a roadmap back to the true mission that history beckons of it may not be entirely superfluous.

THE NEXT FINANCIAL CRISIS IS COMING SOON

Unfortunately, it is too late to reverse the tidal wave of system failure that has been brewing for three decades now. It will soon end in a speculator implosion.

Whether that crisis commences before November 8 or soon thereafter is largely immaterial. If the Trump campaign has the good sense to focus on the gathering economic storm clouds, it's the one thing that could catalyze an out-with-the-bums uprising across Flyover America on Election Day.

So let us reiterate our thesis even more vehemently. The idea that the American economy has recovered and is returning to an era of healthy prosperity is risible establishment propaganda. It's the present day equivalent of the Big Lie. It's the reason why Hillary Clinton's campaign to validate and extend the current malefic Wall Street/Washington regime is so reprehensible.

In fact, the natural post-recession rebound of the nation's capitalist economy has already exhausted itself after 84 months of tepid advance. Now, the massive headwinds of towering public and private debts, faltering corporate investment and productivity, Washington-based regulatory and tax-barriers and the end of an unsustainable central bank fueled global credit, trade and investment boom are ushering in a prolonged era of global deflation and domestic recession.

Indeed, the only thing that has really recovered from the epochal breakdowns of 2008–9 is the stock market averages, which are now at levels 3X the March 2009 bottom. But as we will detail in chapter 3, the market's current lofty valuation is an utterly artificial fiction of Bubble Finance.

In fact, the market would be heading for a hefty correction in any circumstance after being fueled for seven years with free money and massive liquidity injections by the central bank. But at a nosebleed 25X reported GAAP earnings, and after an 18% decline from their September 2014 peak already, the broad stock market is more over-valued than any time in history, including the peaks before 2008, 2000 and 1929.

So in the face of the fast oncoming domestic recession and deepening global deflation, Wall Street is set-up for the mother of all crashes. And what makes it so wicked is that the casino gamblers have been rescued by the Fed so many times since 1987 that they have no clue that the nation's monetary central planners are out of dry powder.

The reasons are explained in chapter 4, but suffice it here to say that when the stampede for the exits gets underway this time, and there are no monetary firemen at the ready, sheer bedlam will quickly ensue on Wall Street.

Likewise, there will be no possibility of a fiscal rescue, either. That's because during 84 months of the weakest recovery in history Washington has whiffed entirely on the fiscal front. Not a single thing has been done about the structural deficit and the fast approaching insolvency of the nation's massive social insurance system.

Indeed, when the $150 billion per year disability trust fund ran out of cash, the cowardly men and women of Capitol Hill merely authorized a raid on the soon to be insolvent OASI trust fund for retirees and their dependents.

Accordingly, as the eventuality of the next recession becomes impossible to deny, the updated budget projections will show a swift return to trillion dollar annual deficits even without any new "stimulus" programs. The Washington fiscal fireman will be hog-tied, and the insouciant breast-beating by Barack Obama about how he has tamed the Federal deficit will be reviled by his successors for decades to come.

It can be said with not inconsiderable certainty, in fact, that under current bipartisan policy and realistic economic forecasts at least $15 trillion will be added to the nation's current $20 trillion of public debt during the next 10 years.

That is, under economic projections for the world economy as it is, not as the latter day Keynesian devotees of Rosy Scenario who inhabit the Washington budget offices fantasize it to be, the federal debt ratio will approach 150% of GDP during the next decade. That means, in turn, that when interest rates eventually normalize—as they must if the monetary system of the world is to survive—debt service will soar to $1.5 trillion per year.

That happens to represent more than 6% of a prospective nominal GDP that has only grown at 3% annually for most of this century. Another description for that unsustainable equation would be a fiscal Doomsday Machine.

So there is a perfect storm of calamity brewing, and the rumbling sounds of its arrival are being heard by the plain people of America, even if the bicoastal elites remain clueless in their temporary world of Bubble Finance prosperity. Even as they harrumph and remonstrate against Trump's bombastic and politically incorrect style, they are missing entirely the profound economic grievances, which have brought Flyover America to the political barricades.

To be sure, The Donald could readily turn into every bit of the scorched earth marauder that the ruling elites are now shrieking about. If he manages to avoid being Goldwatered and actually takes up residence in the White House, we may end up with more of the police state demagogue who harangued the nation during the Republican convention and less of the capitalist insurrectionist who has given hope to tens of millions of voters left behind in Flyover America.

At this late hour, however, it is not even a case of paying your money and taking your chances. There is no chance at all if Hillary Clinton is elected.

There will be war. There will be a crash. There will be fiscal and monetary bedlam.

But there will be no recovery or anything, which passes for real capitalism and honest democracy in America ever again.

TEN GREAT DEALS FOR THE DONALD

But there is a sliver of hope. If Donald Trump is elected, eschews a law-and-order crusade and does not capitulate to the destructive policies of the Wall Street and Washington bicoastal establishment, there is a way forward. The political outlaw who considers himself to be the world's greatest dealmaker would need to do just that.

To wit, a President Trump determined to rid the nation of its mutant regime of Bubble Finance at home and failed interventionism abroad would need to make ten great deals.

A **Peace Deal** with Putin for dismantlement of NATO, cooperation in the middle east, strangulation of ISIS by the Shiite Crescent and a comprehensive worldwide agreement to end the arms trade and pave the way for general disarmament.

A **Jobs Deal** based on slashing taxes on business and workers and replacing them with taxes on consumption and imports.

A **Sound-Money Deal** to repeal Humphrey-Hawkins, end the Fed's war on savers and cash, abolish the FOMC and limit the Fed's remit to passively providing liquidity at a penalty spread over market interest rates based on sound commercial collateral.

A **Glass-Steagall Deal** to break up the giant financial conglomerates, limit the Fed's liquidity window to "narrow banks" that only take deposits and make loans and deny deposit insurance to any banking institution involved in Wall Street trading, derivatives and other forms of financial gambling.

A **Federalist Deal** to turn back most of Washington's domestic grant and welfare programs to the states and localities in return for a mega-block grant with a 30-year phase-out.

A **Regulatory Deal** based on an absolute four-year freeze on every single pending regulation, and then subjecting every existing statute to strict cost-benefit rules thereafter.

A **Liberty Deal** to get Washington out of the War on Drugs, criminal law enforcement and regulation of private conduct and morality.

A **Health Care Deal** based on the repeal of Obamacare and tax pref-
erences for employer insurance plans and their replacement with wide-
open provider competition, consumer choice and individual health
tax credits.

A **Fiscal Deal** to slash post-disarmament defense spending, devolve
education and other domestic programs to local government and claw
back unearned Social Security / Medicare entitlements benefits from the
affluent elderly.

And a **Governance Deal** to amend the Constitution to rescind Citizens United, impose term limits and establish public finance of all
federal elections.

What follows are the facts and analytics that demonstrate why America
is fast heading toward ruin under the existing policy regime, and why these
ten deals could establish the charter for a new way forward.

CHAPTER 2:

Why the Flyover Zone Is Hurting—
Bubble Finance Is Strictly
for the Bicoastal Elites

W E ARE NOW IN YEAR EIGHT OF THIS SO-CALLED RECOVERY. YET THERE are still 45 *million* people on food stamps—one out of every seven Americans. The median real household income is still 5% below its level in the fall of 2007 according to the BLS data. And it's more like 12% lower based on the more honest gage of inflation presented below.

Likewise, there are still only 71.3 *million* full-time, full-pay "breadwinner" jobs in the nation—nearly 1.4 *million* fewer than way back when Bill Clinton was packing his bags to vacate the White House in January 2001.

At the same time, we have had monetary stimulus like never before. There has been 93 straight months of virtually zero interest rates. The balance sheet of the Fed has been expanded by $3.5 trillion. For point of reference, that is 4X more than all of the bond buying during the entire first 94 years of the Fed's history.

So something doesn't parse, and that's to put it charitably. The truth is, the Fed's entire radical regime of ZIRP and QE constitutes a monumental monetary fraud.

It has not "stimulated" a wit the struggling Main Street economy of Flyover America. Instead, it has showered Wall Street speculators with trillions of windfall gains and gifted the bicoastal elites with a false prosperity derived from financial inflation and government expansion.

That perverse redistribution to the top of the economic ladder is the inherent result of massive central bank interest rate repression under conditions of Peak Debt. Stated differently, what amounts to a regime of Keynesian central banking has totally backfired.

In theory, cheap interest rates are supposed to work mainly through the credit channel of monetary policy transmission. Monetary "stimulus" is accomplished by inducing households to ratchet-up their leverage ratios in order to supplement consumption spending from current income with the proceeds of incremental borrowing.

For about three decades after the 1960s this Keynesian parlor trick more or less worked because U.S. households had unused runway on their balance sheets. But that ended when they reached Peak Debt on the eve of the financial crisis.

Since then, $3.5 trillion of money pumping by the Fed has not moved the collective household balance sheet of America a single dollar higher. Total credit market borrowings by households—mortgage, credit cards, auto loans, student loans and other borrowings—amounted to $14.2 trillion in late 2007. Nine years later that figure has hardly moved by a rounding error and now stands at $14.3 trillion.

So what has happened is that the Fed's massive injection of liquidity in the financial markets through QE and ZIRP has never left the canyons of Wall Street. The mechanics of this colossal failure will examined more completely in Chapter 4, but the essence of the result is straight-forward.

To wit, instead of stimulating household and business credit formation and thereby reflating Main Street consumption and investment, central bank credit flowed entirely into speculative carry trades, structured finance and corporate financial engineering. So doing, it massively inflated financial-asset values and turned Wall Street into a bubble-ridden gambling casino.

Herein follows an initial bill of particulars on how the resulting bi-coastal finance-based prosperity left Flyover America far behind. I show that the "recovery" narrative endlessly trumpeted by the Fed and its fellow travelers on Wall Street and in the financial media does not remotely reflect on the ground economic reality.

Instead, it derives almost entirely from a narrow band of badly flawed and thoroughly misleading labor-market indicators and other faulty "incoming data" from the Washington statistical mills. The financial-media headlines extracted from the latter, of course, have not changed the dismal reality on Main Street.

To begin with the most obvious example, consider the graph below on industrial production of consumer goods. It dramatically refutes the whole point of ultra-low interest rates, which are obviously designed to induce households to borrow and spend, and thereby trigger a virtuous cycle of rising demand, increasing production, more jobs and income and even more consumer spending. That's Keynes 101.

Yet after seven years of massive monetary stimulus, domestic production of consumer goods is still *9.1%* below its pre-crisis peak, and is actually at a level first reached in early 1999!

Never once in its constant blather about a steadily "improving" domestic economy has the Fed noted this fundamental rebuke to its entire ideology.

After all, if you are priming the pump with trillions of inducements for households to borrow and spend, why has consumer goods production remained in the sub-basement of its historical trend line and "recovered" at such a tepid rate?

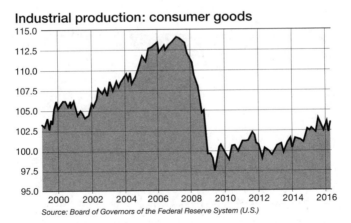

Industrial production: consumer goods

Source: Board of Governors of the Federal Reserve System (U.S.)

The disconnect between the mainstream recovery meme and the chart above is implicit in the latter's construction. That is, the industrial production index is a measure of physical output. Accordingly, it is not distorted by the flaws in the primitive measures of inflation published by the BLS.

3% COST-OF-LIVING INFLATION IN FLYOVER AMERICA MEANS SHRINKING REAL INCOME

That's crucially important because even the tepid measures of Main Street economic improvement ballyhooed by the establishment are based on "real" or "deflated" dollar values. But these deflators vastly understate the actual rise in the cost of living experienced by most of Flyover America, meaning that the advertised figures for "real" wages and incomes, for instance, are highly misleading and overstated.

In fact, constant dollar median household income—based on an accurate measure of inflation—is down 21% since the turn of the century. Working Middle America has never before had such a deep and sustained setback, even during the Great Depression.

The drastic deterioration of middle class living standards depicted below, of course, is heatedly denied by the ruling elites. Yet their disavowal is based on the flagrant manipulation of the inflation data by the BLS based on a pseudo-science called hedonics.

Real median household income

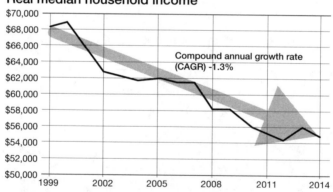

Supposedly, this adjustment to the actual sticker price of goods and services takes account of "quality" improvements like airbags on autos and higher speeds and functionality on computers. Then again, candy bars get smaller; fast food gets less nutritious; retail purchases, especially online commerce, require more and more unpaid "self-service" labor; and Chinese-made toasters go to the junk heap far faster than such appliances did decades ago.

Never mind. Hedonics was never meant to be scientific or balanced. In fact, it was a back door ruse to trim the cost of Social Security and other entitlement COLAs concocted by Alan Greenspan and George H.W. Bush's chief economists back in the 1990s. They eventually accomplished by statistical stealth some of the Social Security cuts that Ronald Reagan failed to obtain in the open arena of legislative action during the 1980s.

This is not speculation. I was there when the entitlement reforms failed and when the plan to shrink the inflation-measuring rod was hatched.

Consequently, the BLS's inflation index has become increasingly inaccurate. This hedonics distortion has been further compounded by the underweighting and mismeasurement of the four horsemen of inflation—food, energy, housing and medical—that absorb the preponderant share of Main Street paychecks.

As detailed below, those systemic errors have been remedied in what we call the "Flyover CPI." When median household incomes are deflated by this more accurate cost-of-living index, the reason Main Street feels it is being left behind becomes starkly evident.

In a word, the purchasing power of its wages and savings is being eviscerated. What had been $68,000 in today's purchasing power at the turn of the century is barely $55,000 today.

So when Donald Trump tells voters that the system is rigged, they have solid reason to concur. When he proclaims that America isn't winning anymore, they know he's talking about them.

And, yes, when he talks about the crooked establishment he strikes a chord, as well. Rigging the inflation rate with a sawed-off ruler may put lipstick on the official data, but it does not change the truth of steadily shrinking living standards on Main Street America.

WHY INCOMES AND WAGES ARE FALLING IN FLYOVER AMERICA

As we indicated, the persistent shrinkage of real wages and net worth in Flyover America is no accident or blemish of capitalism. It is a consequence of the Washington/Wall Street consensus in favor of printing press money, rock bottom interest rates and 2% inflation targeting. Together and at length, these misguided policies have buried Main Street households in inflation and debt.

Neither of these millstones is even acknowledged by the mainstream narrative because they have been essentially defined away. By the lights of the Fed and its Wall Street acolytes, in fact, debt has been christened a growth tonic while inflation is held to be a special form of monetary goodness that levitates economic output, incomes and jobs.

Alas, that's just plain old tommyrot. There is no case for siding with more inflation as a matter of policy and there is much history to warn us of the dangers of rampant debt.

With respect to the scourge of the ever-escalating cost of living, the chart below tracks our Flyover CPI, which includes heavier weights (66%) than the regular CPI (55%) for the four horseman of inflation—food, energy, medical and housing. It also incorporates a more accurate measure of market based medical costs and housing/shelter costs.

This Flyover CPI is a far more honest indicator of the actual cost of living pressures faced by Main Street households, therefore, than the sawed-off measuring rod used by the Fed called the PCE deflator less food and energy.

Needless to say, during the 29-year span since Alan Greenspan's arrival at the Fed in August 1987, most people have needed food, heating, transportation, shelter and medical care. The Flyover CPI, based on an accurate measuring of those necessities has risen by 3.1% per year during that period.

That relentless rise in living costs has not slowed down since the turn of the century, as shown in the chart below. Yet compared to the 3.1% per annum gain in the actual cost of living in Flyover America since the year 2000, the Fed's favorite measure has risen by just 1.7% annual.

The wedge between these two inflation measures is not just a statistical curiosity; it's a big deal and a trenchant commentary on why the Washington Beltway and Flyover America are two ships passing in the dark.

In fact, just since the turn of the century the actual cost of living on Main Street has risen by 40% more than acknowledged by the nation's purported guardians of price stability at the Federal Reserve.

That the political class in Washington and the speculators on Wall Street, therefore, are clueless about the deep economic distress afflicting Main Street America is not at all surprising. They think regular people are 40% better off than they actually are.

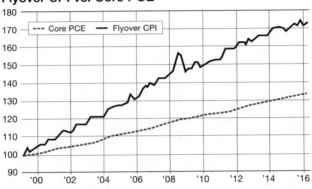

Flyover CPI vs. Core PCE

Indeed, this relentlessly increasingly cost of living explains the rise of Donald Trump more than anything else. The fact is, when the purchasing power of hourly wages is deflated by this honest measure of inflation, their buying power is 5% lower than it was 30 years ago. Wage earners are not winning anymore, not by a long shot.

SHRINKING MAIN STREET LIVING STANDARDS IS A DELIBERATE FEDERAL RESERVE POLICY

This baleful condition is directly attributable to the Washington and Wall Street policy regime. That's because the Keynesian central banking model adopted at the Fed after 1987 had it exactly upside down.

At the time and ever since, the dominant new force in the world economy has been export mercantilism in Asia and elsewhere. That eruption of vast new industrial capacity drained the Asian rice paddies of cheap labor, thereby emitting unprecedented deflationary pressures on global wage rates.

In the face of the "China price" on goods and labor, what was needed in America, therefore, was the very opposite of what Washington's Keynesian academics and policy apparatchiks delivered. *That is to say, under a regime of free markets and sound money there would have been high interest rates, domestic wage and price deflation, high savings rates and massive reinvestment in the nation's aging capital stock.*

Especially after Mr. Deng opened China's export drive by radically devaluing the yuan in 1994, the die was cast as more fully explained in chapter 5. But in essence, the only way that real labor incomes could have risen in the United States, in fact, is via a reduction in nominal wage rates off-set by an even faster rate of annual decline in the CPI and other costs of production in the domestic economy.

Needless to say, the Keynesian academics who dominate the Fed and the monetary policy narrative cannot even fathom that possibility because they are enthrall to the ancient texts of JM Keynes. The latter proclaimed that nominal wages are inherently "sticky" and can't adjust downward like other economic prices.

That was pure claptrap during the 1930s and ever more so today. "Sticky wages" only happen when there are state enforced union monopolies and employers are precluded upon penalty of jail from offering lower nominal rates to any willing takers.

Stated differently, the "sticky" wages hypothesis is a purely political proposition, not an economic truth. It was opportunistically embraced by statist redistributionists and the union movement alike.

For the latter it was a rationale for pure labor law protectionism. For the former is was a justification for workplace originated income redistribution, and then for Washington based monetary intervention to counter-act the loss of jobs and production that is the inherent result of artificially high labor prices.

In truth, there is endless evidence that wages aren't sticky—notwith-standing the rearguard action of unions and labor law protectionism. For instance, the North American auto industry cut fully loaded auto plant wages from $60 per hour to $30 per hour when Toyota and the rest of the transplants established production in Kentucky, Alabama and other right-to-work states in the South.

Indeed, in the absence of NLRB protectionism and labor practice harassment, and then the $85 billion taxpayer bailout of the UAW auto plants in 2008–2009, the lion's share of the U.S. auto industry would have moved from the Rust Belt to the South. Nominal wages would have been sharply reduced in the process.

The same is true with high-wage, unionized grocery stores. A huge share of the grocery store business has now migrated to the far lower nonunion hourly rates at Wal-Mart. Ditto for the migration of construction work from building trades union dominated firms to nonunion competitors.

At the end of the day, "sticky wages" is a euphemism for labor protectionism and the resulting state-enabled "sticky" and inefficient allocation of production and resources.

Nevertheless, from Greenspan forward the Fed was busy fueling domestic inflation on the false theory that rising nominal wages had to be "accommodated." So doing, the nation's central bank fatally undermined the competitiveness of domestic production and jobs on the basis of a theory that belongs in the Museum of Academic Crackpottery.

In Chapter 5 we will develop more fully the true rationale behind Donald Trump's apparent crude protectionism. But suffice to say that he is correct in insisting that Washington policy caused the massive off shoring of jobs and the resulting descent of real wages over the last 25 years.

For the most part and contrary to The Donald, however, that wasn't owing to bad trade deals. Instead, it was the inherent result of inflationary monetary policies that drove nominal wages to uncompetitive levels.

Moreover, even as Fed policies were off-shoring good paying jobs they generated a double whammy in Flyover America. That is, cheap interest rates enabled domestic households and business to borrow at deeply subsidized, uneconomic rates and spend the proceeds on even more imports—foreign purchases that were not being earned by American exports.

THE KEYNESIAN 2.00% FOOLISHNESS—WHY INFLATION IS BAD FOR FLYOVER AMERICA

In this context, there is another reason why the elites who make and communicate national policy couldn't be more wrong. Their wrong-headed

Keynesian model not only embodies a bogus theory about wage rates, but actually postulates that domestic inflation is a good thing.

We refer here to the Fed's 2.00% inflation target and the spurious claim from the Eccles Building and its Wall Street megaphones that there is actually a deficiency of inflation. In a world of the "China price" that is just plain asinine.

Worse still, it's based on the myth propagated by Bernanke and other modern Keynesians that nominal incomes among economic agents all march higher in lockstep as the central bank pursues its spurious 2.00% annual inflation targets.

In fact, there is no lockstep march or equitable inflation at all. The incomes and wealth of the bicoastal elites gain far more from financialization and asset inflation than they lose to the CPI, while slowly rising nominal wages in the flyover zones are relentlessly squeezed by too much inflation in the cost of daily living.

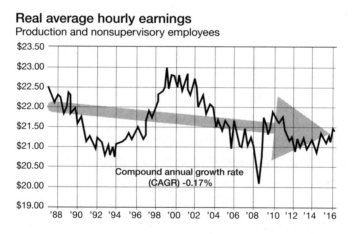

So Wall Street is winning and Flyover America is losing. There is a reason Donald Trump is resonating with the latter—and it's not just red neck racism and xenophobia, either.

It's the handiwork of the Washington/Wall Street corridor. Capitalist growth, dynamism and prosperity is being extinguished in America because it is being betrayed by a rogue central bank and the Washington politicians, Wall Street gamblers and tech sector bubble riders who prosper from it.

PEAK DEBT—WHY THE MAIN STREET PARTY IS OVER

Since the financial crisis there has been another significant jolt to household spending capacity in addition to the implicit shrinkage of real wages suggested above. Namely, most Main Street households have hit Peak Debt, meaning that their spending capacity is no longer being supplemented with incremental borrowings.

Needless to say, that is a dramatic change from the pattern of the previous 30 years as displayed in the graph below. In effect, the easy money policies of the Fed—especially between Greenspan's arrival in August 1987 and the 2008 financial crisis—induced the household sector to perform a giant LBO on itself.

So doing, it ratcheted up its leverage ratio from a historically stable rate of about 75–80% of wage and salary income prior to the 1980s to nearly 220% by the peak in 2007.

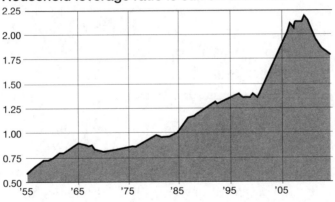

Household leverage ratio is still off the chart

Since then, the ratio has dropped significantly, but still remain far above what had been healthy levels prior to the post-1987 household-borrowing binge. This has been called "deleveraging" by the commentariat, but its true import has been totally obfuscated by the "all is awesome" meme.

Still, the untoward implication is hard to miss if you focus on something other than the monthly deltas. To wit, during the household sector's LBO between 1987 and 2008, total credit market debt outstanding erupted from *$2.7 trillion* to *$14.2 trillion* on the eve of the financial crisis or by 5.4X.

Since then, it has not increased by a single dime!

What that means is that we have a Say's-law economy, not the Keynesian one jabbered about by our monetary politburo and the mainstream financial media. Household consumption is now 100% dependent upon current production and income, and growth of the former depends upon expansion of the latter.

Needless to say, when the one time anomaly of bloated consumption based on rising leverage ratio comes to an end and the 70% of GDP represented by household consumption has to be currently earned, you have fish of an entirely different kettle.

Total credit market debt

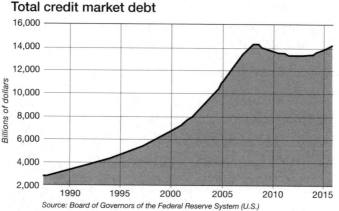

Source: Board of Governors of the Federal Reserve System (U.S.)

Stated differently, money pumping and artificially cheap credit no longer stimulates household spending because the latter are tapped out. A potent indicator of that truth is the fact that housing construction still remains in the sub-basement of history, notwithstanding the lowest real mortgage rates ever recorded.

Indeed, new starts of single-family housing units after all of this alleged "recovery" are still lower than at any time in the last 33 years, save for four months in the 1990–91 recession and during the recent financial crisis. Yet, historically the whole point of Keynesian money pumping was to stimulate mortgage borrowing and new housing construction.

The same lack of monetary stimulus efficacy holds true with respect to labor hours employed in the nonfarm business sector. And in this context, it needs be emphasized that in a gig and contract-worker based economy, the only meaningful measure of the quantity of labor employed is *hours, not "jobs."*

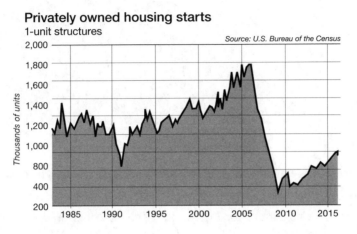

Privately owned housing starts
1-unit structures

As we will thoroughly document in a later chapter, in fact, traditional headcount based labor indicators, such as the monthly establishment survey's nonfarm payroll count, are essentially meaningless white noise.

By contrast, since the turn of the century labor hours in the nonfarm economy have advanced at an anemic rate of just 0.4% annually. That is only one-fourth of the 2.0% rate, which prevailed during the prior 16 years.

Needless to say, this radical growth downshift is not due to demographics. The adult population has actually grown from 212 million in 2000 to 253 million at present. And even when you set aside an additional 11 million retirees on Social Security, there are an additional 30 million potential workers, representing upwards of 60 billion labor hours on a standard work year basis.

In short, the chart below puts the lie to the alleged virtuous circle of Keynesian stimulus. There has been no pump-priming of consumption spending, production, jobs, income, and more of the same.

Indeed, the Fed's balance sheet has grown by *900%* during the last 16 years—from $500 billion to $4.5 trillion. By contrast, labor hours have risen by only *6.7% on a cumulative basis.*

There is self-evidently a big time blockage in the transmission mechanism.

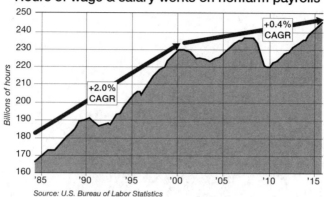

Hours of wage & salary works on nonfarm payrolls

Source: U.S. Bureau of Labor Statistics

The same is true for business investment spending, which is the vital building block for Main Street productivity and true gains in living standards.

The classic argument for Keynesian stimulus, of course, has always included the notion that businessmen are somewhat slow-witted. Therefore they are chronically in need of government inducements to increase capital spending. Apparently, the monetary central planners in the Eccles Building can espy opportunities for future profit that ordinary businessmen are too stupid to see.

Low interest rates were supposed to sharpen their vision. Presumably the record low rates on corporate loans and bonds during recent years should have accomplished that turbo-charging effect in spades.

But it hasn't. Bubblevision is always telling us about whatever tiny change in nonresidential business investment occurred or didn't occur during the most recent quarter. *What it never reports is the trend line of real net business investment after current period depreciation.*

The latter, of course, measures the capital resources consumed in the production of current GDP. Owing to the laws of arithmetic, this crucial measure of business sector health and growth—*real net investment*—cannot rise unless current period CapEx exceeds current capital consumption.

As shown on the next page, that has not remotely been happening since the turn of the century.

In fact, real capital consumption has risen by 53% over the last 16-years, while real net investment is down by 17%.

Real net fixed investment

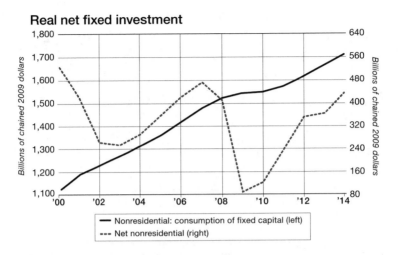

- — Nonresidential: consumption of fixed capital (left)
- --- Net nonresidential (right)

SUPPLY-SIDE DEFICIENCY VERSUS FINANCIAL ASSET INFLATION

There is plenty more evidence where these examples came from, but the larger point is clear. *The U.S. economy has a giant supply-side problem that can't be alleviated by demand-side stimulus. Accordingly, the economy of Flyover America continues to falter even as the ruling elites bask in the glow of rampant financial asset inflation.*

As we have demonstrated repeatedly, *monetary stimulus is a one-time parlor trick.* It only works when there is business and household balance sheet space left to leverage, thereby permitting spending derived from current production and income in the manner of Say's law to be boosted with spending derived from incremental borrowings.

Under conditions of Peak Debt, therefore, the Keynesian credit magic ceases to "stimulate" the Main Street economy. Instead, it never leaves the canyons of Wall Street, where it cycles in an incendiary spiral of leveraged speculation and the systematic inflation of financial assets.

The graph on the next page summarizes that story succinctly. The broadest measure of the stock market—Wilshire 5000 index—has *risen by 125%* since 1999.

The real median family income, by contrast, has *fallen by 7%* as calculated by the Washington statistics mills. *And by 21% when an adjusted for the true 3% per year cost of living rise is accounted for.*

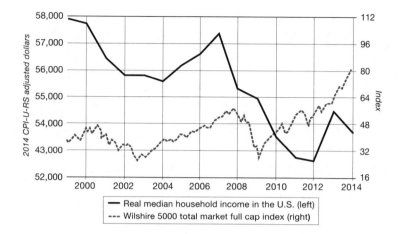

Stated differently, the bicoastal elites, who own most of the nation's financial assets or who feed off the financial system and a debt-swollen central state in Washington, believe themselves to be in the pink of prosperity. They do not understand, of course, that this is all a giant bubble, which at length will burst, in spectacular fashion, causing their own unearned windfalls to shrink in the process.

In the meanwhile, they may at least start to appreciate that the flyover zone of America has been left behind. The Main Street insurgency fueling Donald Trump's shocking rise to the top of the presidential race proves that much in spades.

CHAPTER 3:

The Warren Buffett Economy:
How Central Bank-Enabled
Financialization Has Divided America

DURING THE 29 YEARS AFTER ALAN GREENSPAN BECAME FED CHAIRMAN in August 1987, the balance sheet of the Fed exploded from $200 billion to $4.5 trillion. *Call that* a 23X gain.

That's a pretty massive increase—so let's see what else happened over that three-decade span. Well, according to Forbes, Warren Buffett's net worth was $2.1 billion back in 1987 and it is now about $73 billion. Call *that* 35X.

During those same years, the value of nonfinancial U.S. corporate equities rose from $2.6 trillion to $36.6 trillion. That's on the hefty side, too.

Call it 14X and take the hint about the idea of financialization. The value of these corporate equities rose from *44% to 205% of GDP during that 29-year interval.*

Financialization of U.S. economy
Corporate equities and GDP

Compound annual growth rate
MV corporate equities: -10.4%
GDP: 5.2%

Equities value % of GDP
1981: 44%
2014: 205%

Market value of corporate equities

Gross domestic product

Needless to say, when we move to the underlying economy, which purportedly gave rise to these fabulous financial gains, the X-factor is not so generous. As shown above, nominal GDP rose from $5 trillion to $18 trillion during the same 29-year period. But that was only *3.6X.*

Next we have wage and salary disbursements, which rose from $2.5 trillion to $7.5 trillion over the period. Make that *3.0X.*

Then comes the median nominal income of U.S. households. That measurement increased from $26,000 to $54,000 over the period. Call it *2.0X.*

Digging deeper, we have the sum of aggregate labor hours supplied to the nonfarm economy. That fairly precise metric of real work by real people rose from 185 billion hours to 240 billion hours during those same 29 years. Call it *1.27X.*

Further down the Greenspan era rabbit hole, we have the average weekly wage of full-time workers in inflation-adjusted dollars. In constant 1982 dollars, as calculated by the BLS's short ruler, that figure was $330 per week in 1987 and is currently $340. Call that *1.03X.*

Finally, we have real median family income. *At about $54,000 then and now, call it a three decade long trip to nowhere if you credit the BLS inflation data.*

But when you deflate nominal household income by our more accurate Flyover CPI per the last chapter, you end up at the very bottom of the Maestro's rabbit hole.

Median real household income went backwards! It now stands at just 0.8X of its starting level.

So 35X for Warren Buffett and 0.8X for working people. That is some kind of divide.

OK, it's not entirely fair to compare Warren Buffet's $70 billion gain to the median household's actual 21% loss of real income. There is some "inflation" in the Oracle's wealth tabulation, as reflected in the GDP deflator's rise from 60 to 108 during this period.

So in today's constant dollars, Buffett started with $3.8 billion in 1987. Call his inflation-adjusted gain 19X then, and be done with it.

And you can make the same adjustment to the market value of total nonfinancial equity. In constant 2015 dollars of purchasing power, today's aggregate value of $36.7 trillion compares to $4.5 trillion back in 1987. Call it 8X.

Here's the thing. In the context of a 0.8X Main Street economy, Buffett isn't any kind of 19X genius nor are investors as a whole 8X versions of the same.

The real truth is that Alan Greenspan and his successors turned a whole generation of financial gamblers into the greatest lottery winners in recorded history. They turned redistribution upside down—sending unspeakable amounts of windfall wealth to the tippy-top of the economic ladder.

ZIRP FUNDS WALL STREET GAMBLERS AND INFLATES FINANCIAL ASSETS, NOT THE MAIN STREET ECONOMY

These capricious windfalls to the 1% happened because the Fed grotesquely distorted and financialized the U.S. economy in the name of Keynesian management of the purported "business cycle." The most visible instrument of that misguided campaign, of course, was the "fed-funds," or money market, rate, which has been pinned virtually at the zero bound for the last 93 months.

Never before in the history of the world prior to 1995 had any central bank decreed that overnight money shall be indefinitely free to carry trade gamblers. Nor had any monetary authority commanded that the hard earned wealth of liquid savers be chronically confiscated by negative returns after inflation and taxes. And, needless to say, never had savers and borrowers in a free market struck a bargain on interest rates night after night at a yield of virtually 0.0% for seven years running.

Not only did the Fed spend 29 years marching toward the zero bound, but in the process it became addicted to it. During the last 300 months, it has either cut or kept flat the money market rate 80% of the time. And until the token bump of December 2015, it had been 114 months since the foolish denizens of the Eccles Building last raised interest rates by even 25 bps!

The Fed's addiction to the "easy button":
Rates falling or flat, 80% of the time since 1990

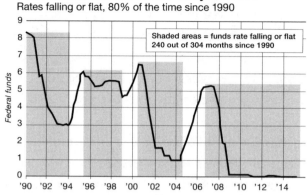

The simple truth is, the Fed's long-running interest rare repression policies have caused systematic, persistent and massive falsification of prices all along the yield curve and throughout all sectors of the financial market.

The single most important price in all of capitalism is the money market rate of interest. It sets the cost of carry in all asset markets and in options and futures pricing. It therefore indirectly fuels the bid for debt, equity and derivative securities of every kind in the entire global financial system.

Needless to say, when the cost of money is set at—and frozen at— zero in nominal terms, and driven deeply negative in after-inflation and after-tax terms, it becomes the mother's milk of speculation.

So an urgent question screams out. Didn't the obstinate zealots at the Fed realize that zero cost overnight money has only one use, and that is to fund the speculative trades of Wall Street gamblers?

The reason that ZIRP is of exclusive benefit to financial gamblers is straightforward. No businessman in his right mind would fund equipment, inventories or even receivables with borrowings under a one-day or even one-week tenor. The risk of fatal business disruption resulting from the need to precipitously liquidate working assets if funding cannot be rolled-over at or near the existing interest rates is self-evident.

Likewise, no sane householder would buy a home, automobile or even toaster on overnight borrowings, either.

And, yes, financial institutions experiencing the daily ebb and flow of cash excesses and deficiencies do use the money market. That's what the "Fed funds" market used to be until Bernanke and his band of money printers effectively abolished it in the fall of 2008.

But managing fluctuating cash balances does not require ZIRP—especially when most banks historically alternated between being suppliers and users of funds on practically an odd/even day basis. Cash balances in the financial system can be cleared at 0.2%, 2%, 5% or even 10% with equal aplomb.

So ZIRP is nothing more than free COGS (cost of goods sold) for Wall Street gamblers. It is they who harvest the "arb."

That is, the spread between the free overnight funding dispensed by the Fed and any financial asset with a yield or prospect of short-term gain. And, yes, if push comes to shove, these same fast money gamblers can ordinarily liquidate their assets, repay their overnight borrowings and start with a clean book the next morning—unlike business and household borrowers in the Main Street economy.

Stated differently, the Fed's ZIRP policy is a giant subsidy to speculators—and one that is made all the more egregious by an utterly foolish communications policy. In the name of "transparency" the Fed actually telegraphs, via such code words as "patient"—that there will be no rate increases without ample warning. In this case, at least for the following two meetings.

Accordingly, speculators don't have to worry about even one single dime of unexpected change in their carry cost. Nor are they ever inconvenienced by the losses that can result from needing to suddenly dump less than fully liquid assets (or liquidate options and other similar "structured finance" positions) in order to repay their overnight borrowings in the event of a sudden rise in the money-market rate.

The truth is that in an honest free market traders cannot earn windfall returns arbing the yield curve. The vigorish gets competed away. Likewise, asset prices and funding costs move independently, thereby causing return compression toward the time value of money and the risks embedded in each trader's specific book of assets and liabilities.

By contrast, the ZIRP market is completely dishonest and therefore deeply subsidized. And every Econ 101 student knows that when you deeply subsidize something, you get more and more of it.

In essence, by clinging obstinately and mindlessly to ZIRP, the Fed is just systematically juicing the gamblers, and thereby fueling ever greater mispricing of financial assets and ever more dangerous and explosive financial bubbles.

In fact, after 90 months of ZIRP, it must be truly wondered how supposedly rational adults can obsess over whether the another tiny smidgeon of a rate increase should be permitted this year or next, and whether the economy can tolerate a rise in the funds rate from 38 bps today to 63 bps when it finally does move.

The difference is utterly irrelevant noise to the Main Street economy. It can't possibly impact the economic calculus of a single household or business!

But then, again, the Fed doesn't serve the Main Street economy: it lives to pleasure Wall Street.

Having pinned the money market rate at the zero bound for so long and with such an unending stream of ever-changing and fatuous excuses, the occupants of the Eccles Building are truly lost. They do not even fathom that they are engaging in a word splitting exercise that is no more meaningful to Main Street borrowing, spending, investing and growth than counting angels on the head of a pin.

CAUGHT IN A TIME WARP—WHY THE FED KEEPS FEEDING THE GAMBLERS

So why does the Fed persist in this farcical minuet around ZIRP?

The principal reasons are not at all hard to discern. In essence, the Fed is caught in a time warp and fails to comprehend that the game of bicycling interest rates to heat and cool the macro-economy is over and done.

As further documented below, the credit channel of monetary transmission has fallen victim to "Peak Debt." This means that the Main Street economy no longer gets a temporary pick-me-up from cheap interest rates because with tapped out balance sheets most households have no further ability to borrow.

The only actual increases in household debt since the financial crisis has been for student loans, which are guaranteed by Uncle Sam's balance sheet, and auto loans, which are collateralized by over-valued vehicles.

Stated differently, home equity was tapped out last time and wage and salary incomes have been fully leveraged for years. So households have nothing else left to hock.

Accordingly, they now only spend what they earn, meaning that the Fed's interest rate manipulations—which had potency 40 years ago—have no impact at all today. In fact, it cannot be repeated enough: Keynesian monetary policy through the crude tool of money market rate pegging was always a one-time parlor trick.

Likewise, as documented in Chapter 2, the Fed's interest rate machinations have not, as per the traditional Keynesian model, induced the business sector to acquire incremental productive assets financed with borrowed capital. Instead, virtually the entire increase in business debt outstanding—and it is considerable, having rising from $10 trillion on the eve of the financial crisis to nearly $12.5 trillion today—has gone into financial engineering.

But stock buybacks, LBOs and cash M&A deals do not cause output to expand or productivity to increase whatsoever. They just bid up the price of existing financial assets, thereby further rewarding the ZIRP-enabled gamblers who inhabit the casino.

Still, notwithstanding the utter blockage of the credit channel of monetary transmission to households and businesses, our monetary central planners cling desperately to ZIRP. This obstinacy arises from the theory, apparently, that it might still do a smidgeon of good. Besides, ZIRP hasn't caused any consumer price inflation, or at least that's what they contend—so where is the harm?

Well, yes. Doing a rain dance neither causes harm nor rain. Yet there is a huge difference. Zero interest rates are not even remotely harmless. They amount to a colossal economic battering ram because they transform capital markets into gambling casinos.

So doing, they cause risk and long-term capital to be mispriced, generating an accumulating level of malinvestments and excess production capacity. And this is a worldwide condition because all central banks are engaging in the same game of financial repression.

As is now evident in the case of oil, iron ore, copper, consumer electronics, shipping and much more, vast excess capacity ultimately results in the collapse of boom time prices and profit margins. At length, a withering cycle of deflationary adjustment, profit collapse and plunges in new capital spending is set in motion.

So the traditional Keynesian model of Main Street "stimulus" is just not working, but beyond that our monetary central planners are trapped in a dangerous feedback loop. Having fueled the boom with cheap money, they now justify the prolongation of ZIRP on the grounds that they must use the same tool to ward off the deflation they caused in the first place.

At the end of the day, there is nothing behind the curtain at the Eccles Building. The spurious words clouds in the Fed's 500-word meeting statements, and hints about the next meeting's potential for hairline changes in the money market interest rate, or not, are of relevance only to the day traders and robo-machines in the casino.

Fed policy is designed to keep them rolling the dice. It rests on the delusional hope that the drug of ZIRP or near-ZIRP can keep the stock market averages rising and a trickle down of extra spending by the wealthy flowing into the reported GDP and job numbers.

FINANCIALIZATION AND THE BUBBLE AT THE TOP

These considerations make clear that it was neither a slightly lower trend rate of CPI inflation over the past 29 years nor an improvement in the art of central banking which has driven the core reference rate in the world financial markets—the 10-year U.S. Treasury note—down by 85%.

Greenspan, Bernanke and the rest of their central banker posse have been quick to take credit, of course, but never for what they have actually done. The stunning decline in the world benchmark cap rate is owing to the fact that central bankers flat-out falsified it.

They accomplished this by pegging the money market rate closer and closer to the zero bound, meaning that the cost of carry on repo was reduced to virtually nothing. This, in turn, enabled speculators to buy increasing amounts of government debt with tiny slivers of true capital, thereby turning the U.S. treasury bond market into a daisy-chain of collateral.

And a daisy chain it was. As a result of massive QE purchases, bond prices have had a huge artificial bid from the central bank printing presses as opposed to real money savers. These steadily rising bond prices meant that carry trade punters could capture both the current interest spread between the coupon yield and zero-cost repo, and also the holding period capital gain on the bonds.

In a word, the profit opportunity was so fabulous that speculative capital flowed into the staid sovereign bond markets like never before. Owing to this speculative capital inflow, traders were able to generate massive amounts of collateral-based repo credit, which funded even more demand for bonds and even higher prices.

In short, the sovereign-debt markets essentially became a giant confidence game. Government debt nearly financed itself by generating its own carry.

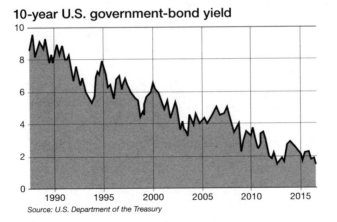

10-year U.S. government-bond yield

Source: U.S. Department of the Treasury

Once upon a time, of course, this wondrous bubble of ever rising bond prices couldn't have happened because the catalyst—massive QE—was correctly understood to be an outright monetary fraud. Yet during the last two decades monetary rectitude has vanished. The combined balance sheets of the world's central banks, in fact, have expanded from $2 trillion to $21 trillion.

All the while and without question, however, the central bankers had not repealed the law of supply and demand.

To the contrary, they had their big fat thumbs on the scale to the tune of nearly $20 trillion of "demand" for securities that was funded with fiat credits conjured from thin air, not from honest savings out of current production and income.

Needless to say, the resulting plunge in the yield of the 10-year treasury note shown above to what are completely false and unsustainably low levels caused two powerful distortions.

In the DM economies like the United States, it generated an enormous expansion of unproductive debt that funded excessive fiscal expansion, household consumption and business financial engineering. In the EM economies, it resulted in the systematic underpricing of long-term capital, thereby generating a tidal wave of malinvestments and excess capacity.

On the home front, two decades of price falsification resulted in a monumental financialization of the U.S. economy. The sum of business debt and nonfinancial market equity rose from about $12 trillion at the time of Greenspan's arrival at the Eccles Building to $93 trillion today. Accordingly, the value of debt and equity securities mushroomed from about 2.4X GDP to 5.4X.

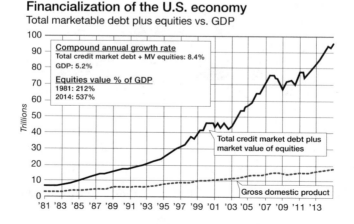

Financialization of the U.S. economy
Total marketable debt plus equities vs. GDP

HOW BUBBLE FINANCE WAS EXPORTED TO THE REST OF THE WORLD

At the same time, the Fed's financial repression campaign was exported to the rest of the world. The mercantilist export-based economies of east Asia and the petro-states, in effect, mopped up the Fed's excess emission of dollar liabilities through massive currency pegging operations and the accumulation of U.S. Treasury and GSE paper.

The staggering extent of the Fed's export of monetary inflation is shown in the chart below. In round terms, the collective balance sheets of the world's central banks have grown by 10X during the last two decades. There is nothing even remotely resembling this in all of recorded financial history—nor was it even imagined by the most rapid inflationists and monetary cranks of yesteryear.

Self-evidently, this monetary eruption did not happen in a vacuum. When central banks expand their balance sheets in today's fiat money world it has a double whammy impact. It can led to the expansion of both conventional bank credit and also to capital market based credit in the form of repo and other loans based on financial collateral as described above.

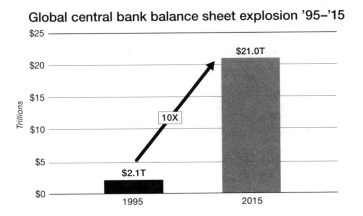

Global central bank balance sheet explosion '95–'15

As a result, the world economy was inundated by a veritable credit tsunami. During the last two decades total public and private debt outstanding on the planet has soared from $40 trillion to $225 trillion or by nearly 5.6X.

The compound growth rate of 9.0% annually was nearly double the growth rate of global GDP during this period, implying that global leverage rose in nearly parabolic fashion. In fact, the gain in total debt was nearly 4X greater than the gain in GDP.

Yet even that understates the level of risk and deformation embedded in these worldwide trends. That's because a goodly share of the GDP gains—especially in the vast Ponzi scheme of China and its supply base (as addressed in later chapters)—represented one-time fixed asset investment spending. But much of that will turn out to have been both unsustainable and economic waste which will have to be written-down or liquidated entirely.

Stated differently, the global credit tsunami funded massive over-investment in fixed public and private assets, but especially in China and the EM. The impact was a one-time acceleration of global economic activity that temporarily inflated current income and profits—phantom growth that goosed the value of financial assets even more.

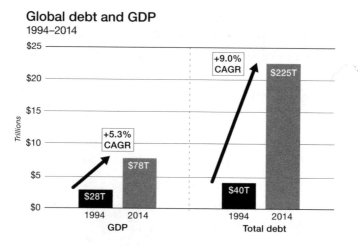

But this central bank fueled boom will ultimately be paid for in the form of a prolonged deflationary contraction. Then, trillions of uneconomic assets will be written off, industrial sector profits will collapse and the great inflation of financial assets over the last 29 years will meet its day of reckoning.

UNSUSTAINABILITY OF FINANCIALIZATION

There is no reason whatsoever to believe that the financial carrying capacity of the U.S. economy—or any other DM economy—has improved since the 1980s. And that means that soaring cap rates on financial assets are way overdone and unsustainable. At current nosebleed levels, neither stocks nor bonds are earning their valuations.

In fact, DM cap rates should have gone in the opposite direction in recent years. That is due to aging demographics, declining competitiveness versus the surging EM economies, dwindling rates of productivity growth and a dramatic increase in the leverage ratio against both public and private incomes.

All of these adverse macro-trends mean that the U.S. economy's ability to generate growth, incomes and profits has been significantly lessened. Accordingly, since the U.S. economy's ability to service debt and equity capital at an honest market rate of return has diminished, the logical expectation would be that the finance ratio to national income would fall.

In fact, once Greenspan took the helm and his apparently atavistic embrace of gold standard money melted-down under the Wall Street furies of October 1987, the finance ratio erupted. As shown below, it has never looked back and at 5.5X national income has reached a point that would have been unimaginable on the morning of Black Monday.

Stated differently, under a regime of honest money and market determined financial prices, the combined value of corporate equities and credit market debt would not have mushroomed by 8X—from $11 trillion to $93 trillion—during the past 29 years. For crying out loud, the nominal GDP grew by only 3.6X during the same span.

In effect, the U.S. GDP has been capitalized at a higher and higher aggregate financial valuation for no ascertainable reason of fundamental economics. And the standard mainstream argument that today's extremely elevated cap rates are warranted because interest rates are so unusually low is an especially meritless rationalization.

Those are not genuine economic rates. They are the artificial product of central bank financial repression and falsification. The cost of debt and money must inevitably revert to honest market levels or the central banks will simply destroy the monetary system.

Indeed, there is no reason why the 260% ratio of equity and credit market debt to GDP that was recorded in 1986 should have risen at all. At that point, in fact, Paul Volcker had completed his historic task of extinguishing runaway commodity and CPI inflation and had superintended a solid recovery of real economic growth.

Arguably, therefore, the U.S. economy was carrying about the right amount of finance. At that healthy ratio, in fact, today's $18 trillion economy would be carrying about $48 trillion of combined market equity and credit market debt, not $93 trillion.

In a word, the Greenspan era of central bank driven price falsification and monetization of trillions of existing assets has generated a $45 trillion overhang of excess financialization.

Financialization of the U.S. economy
All marketable debt plus equities % of GDP

HOW ST. WARREN BUFFETT RODE THE FED'S $45 TRILLION BUBBLE

Even when you purge the cumulative price inflation out of these gargantuan figures, the story does not remotely add-up. The above outlandish graph—which implies that real finance grew at 10X real median incomes—does not capture capitalism at work. Nor did the speculators who surfed upon this $45 trillion bubble harvest their monumental windfalls owing to investment genius.

Instead, it is the perverted fruit of Bubble Finance, and there is no better illustration of this bubble surfer syndrome than the sainted Warren Buffett.

The Oracle of Omaha is no genius and he did not invent anything, even a unique method of investing and allocating capital. He may have read Graham and Dodd as a youthful punter, but his nominal net worth did not grow from $2.1 billion in 1987 to $73 billion at present by following the old fashioned precepts of value investing.

Instead, he bought the obvious consumer names of the Baby Boom demographic wave like Coke and Gillette; had a keen facility for grabbing what he believed slower footed investors would also be buying later; appreciated the value of banks and other financial companies (like Goldman Sachs) that suckled on the public teat; and mainly rode the 29-year wave that caused finance to soar from $12 trillion to $93 trillion after Greenspan took the helm at the Fed.

Stated differently, under a regime of honest money and free market finance no mere insurance company portfolio manager could make 19X in real terms in 29 years. It can't be done purely through the money game.

Moreover, on the insurance side of the Berkshire Hathaway house, Buffett didn't invent any new products or services, either—except the standard gambit of paying claims as late as possible.

That's right. A 19X real gain in three decades can occasionally be achieved by inventors of something fundamentally new and economically transformative. Thomas Edison, Henry Ford and Bill Gates fit that mold, but not an insurance portfolio manager from Omaha.

The truth of the matter is that the better part of St. Warren's fortune was manufactured in the Eccles Building.

Even he backhandedly admitted as much in his famously unctuous and gratuitous letter thanking the Fed for bailing out the financial system (and his investment in Goldman, Well Fargo and other financial institutions) during the so-called "financial crisis."

The actual purpose of the Wall Street meltdown was to purge decades of speculation, leverage and excessive risk-taking—the very thing that Buffett thanked them for averting and which preserved his fortune.

And that's the evil of Bubble Finance. It not only transformed a competent and preserving manager of insurance company assets into an alleged investment genius, but also conferred on Buffett an utterly underserved reputation for financial expertise and wisdom.

In fact, the man is a statist windbag who constantly talks his own book. The very sound of it must cause his libertarian and gold-standard father and storied congressman from Nebraska, Howard Buffett, to roll in his grave.

CHAPTER 4:

The Case Against Keynesian Central Banking and Why the FOMC Should Be Abolished

The mythology of Buffett's purported investment prowess, however, is just emblematic of the larger narrative that obfuscates the destructive monetary regime that has been in place since Greenspan's ascension.

As the Fed and its Wall Street megaphones have it, the $45 trillion "bubble" identified in Chapter 3 is no such thing. Instead, it is held to be completely natural and a sign of long-term economic progress—even if this vast expansion of finance was interrupted by temporary meltdowns in 2000–2001 and 2008–2009.

These latter financial disorders, in fact, are purportedly not the fruits of the central banking regime at all, but are chalked off to exogenous factors and nonrecurring events. That is, the devastating financial busts since 1987 were allegedly owing to a mix of too much investor exuberance, too much deregulation, a one-time housing mania and a smattering of Wall Street greed and corruption, too.

And that's not to overlook some of the more far-fetched reasons for the two big financial meltdowns of this century. Foremost among these is the Greenspan-Bernanke fairy tale that Chinese workers making under $1 per hour were saving too much money, thereby causing low global mortgage rates and a runaway housing boom in America!

Needless to say, not only are these rationalizations completely bogus; but so is the entire underlying predicate for Keynesian monetary central planning.

To wit, the claim that market capitalism is chronically and destructively unstable and that the business cycle needs constant management and stimulus by the state and its central banking branch is belied by the historical facts.

Every economic setback of modern times, including the foundation events of the Great Depression—was caused by the state. The catalyst was either inflationary war finance or central bank fueled credit expansion, not the deficiencies or inherent instabilities' of market capitalism.

THE "AGGREGATE DEMAND' DEMAND" DEFICIENCY MYTH AND SAY'S LAW OF SUPPLY

Nevertheless, the Fed's model gives short shrift to the millions of workers, entrepreneurs, investors and savers who comprise the ground level economy and the billions of supply-side prices for labor and capital through which they interact and ultimately generate output, income and wealth.

Instead, the Fed focuses on the macroeconomic aggregates as the key to achieving its so-called dual mandate of stable prices and maximum employment. Essentially, the United States is held to be a closed economy resembling a giant bathtub. In the pursuit of "full employment," the central bank's job is to keep it pumped full to the brim with "aggregate demand."

As I shall explain below, however, the domestic macroeconomic aggregates of employment and inflation cannot be measured on an accurate and timely basis. Neither can they be reliably and directly influenced by the crude tools of the central bank, such as pegging the money market rate, manipulating the yield curve via QE, levitating Wall Street animal spirits via wealth-effects "puts" and various forms of open-mouth intervention such as "forward guidance."

For reasons mentioned in Chapter 3, of course, these Keynesian aggregate demand management tools did appear to work for several decades prior to the arrival of Peak Debt. But as I have indicated, that was a one-time monetary parlor trick. Households and other economic actors were repeatedly induced to "lever up" via periodic cycles of cheap-money stimulus, thereby supplementing consumption spending derived from current incomes with the proceeds of incremental borrowings.

That did goose "aggregate demand" but only on an intertemporal basis. That is, ever-rising household leverage ratios simply borrowed economic activity from the future; they did not generate new, sustainable wealth.

And now monetary stimulus doesn't work anyway because household balance sheets are fully leveraged relative to income. This cardinal reality is completely ignored by the central bankers, however, because they are in thrall to the primitive idea handed down by J.M. Keynes himself: namely, the notion that the capitalist business cycle is always running short of an economic ether called "aggregate demand." The latter is purportedly an *independent quantity* of household and business "spending" which *should be happening* in order to fully utilize domestic labor and business capacity.

The term *independent* needs special emphasis. Under the historical and sound economics of Say's law, aggregate demand is not independent; it is a derivative of production and income. It is what households and businesses choose to spend, rather than save, from current income and cash flow.

Prior to the confusions introduced by JM Keynes, most economists understood the common sense proposition that production comes first. In an honest and stable economy, it still does.

Accordingly, true "aggregate demand" never needs any help from the state and most especially its central banking branch. It will expand automatically and proportionately to the rise in current production and the increased application of the supply side factors, which make it happen.

That is, the true source of increased aggregate demand is more labor hours and improved productivity, increased entrepreneurial effort and managerial efficiency, greater savings and investment and more technological innovation and invention.

By contrast, today's central bankers—both those who lean toward the Keynesian texts and those who follow Milton Friedman's revisionist version—are statists. They claim to know that the actual level of "aggregate demand" derived from current production and savings is incorrect and chronically deficient.

This purported demand shortfall occurs, apparently, either because incomes are too low owing to underutilized labor and capital resources; or savings are too high owing to hoarding, lack of confidence or just plain stupidity among consumers and businessmen.

Accordingly, the job of the state—the fiscal authorities in the original 1960s Keynesian incarnation and since Greenspan essentially the central bank—is to supply this chronically missing quotient of "aggregate demand." Say's law of supply is thus superseded by the supposedly greater wisdom of central bankers.

Having divined the correct level of "aggregate demand", in fact, the central bank is then charged with making up the shortfall. This spending increase is accomplished by cutting interest rates or monetizing the public debt to order to foster increased borrowing, thereby supplementing spending derived from current production with the incremental proceeds of expanded credit.

At length, according to the Keynesian texts, the nation's economic bathtub becomes filled to the brim with just the right amount of "aggregate demand". Accordingly, labor is fully employed, industry operates at 100% of capacity, government coffers bulge with "full-employment" revenues and unicorns prance around happily throughout the land.

WHY "POTENTIAL GDP" AND FULL-EMPLOYMENT ECONOMICS ARE A CROCK

Here's the thing. The whole bathtub model of "potential GDP" and the associated state of "full employment" is a crock. It consists of a bunch of made-up roundhouse benchmarks that are absolutely meaningless in today's global, fluid and technologically dynamic economy.

This also means that the theoretical "aggregate demand" that is the target of Fed policy is a chimera, too. Unlike true aggregate demand derived from actual current production and income, the Keynesian central bankers' version is merely inferred from crude guesses about the theoretical production and employment capacity of the domestic economy.

In fact, these "potential GDP" and "full employment" benchmarks are not scientific in the least; they are little more than the econometric scribblings of Keynesian academics.

The results are so silly, primitive, constantly changing and logically superficial as to beg a basic question: to wit, if massive financialization and cheap money were not so convenient for Wall Street and Washington alike, would real adults actually take our Keynesian central bankers seriously?

I think not. Bubble Finance liquidity for Wall Street and endless monetization of the public debt for Washington is the veil of convenience that enables our monetary central planners to operate virtually without restriction.

Accordingly, the Federal Reserve soldiers on in a constant state of heavy-duty intrusion in the financial markets, including the lunacy of what is now 93 months of ZIRP.

The denizens of the Eccles Building are like the crazy man in the bus station waving his arms in a circular motion to ward off an elephant attack. In a similar manner, the FOMC fiddles with fractional changes in the money market rate under the delusion that it is making up the aggregate demand shortfall and thereby closing the gap between actual and potential GDP.

Well, let's see. Everyone knows this is a service economy. So how do you measure the potential output of a Pilates studio and whether its instructors, equipment and facilities are fully employed?

Should that computation be based on five or seven days a week and one, two or three eight-hour shifts of instruction per day—or something else? And what are the units of output—solos, duets and group sessions of one hour or more or less?

How about black car limo fleets and drivers? Now that Uber has arrived in so many cities with digitally dispatched service on demand, vehicle fleets do not spend half of their time sitting around waiting for clients anymore.

Huge latent fleet capacity has thus been liberated by technology in this instance, and in too many like and similar circumstances to even recount. For instance, what is hotel room capacity in a world of Airbnb, and do the owner-hosts who supply clean, equipped and serviced rooms count as "employed."

That is to say, "capacity utilization" is an utterly fluid and dynamically changing condition that cannot be even remotely fathomed in a globally traded, technologically dynamic, and service-focused modern economy. The whole idea of measuring potential output is a stupid throwback to the 1950s, when freshly minted Keynesian PhDs were looking for an excuse to practice their math skills.

Nor is full utilization of "labor" a serviceable proxy. As explicated further on, in a gig-based world, where labor is increasingly scheduled by the hour and according to computer-monitored demand loads, the traditional concepts of "unemployment" and "slack" labor resources are completely obsolete and immeasurable. When Janet Yellen mumbles about "slack," she might as well be talking about leprechauns.

Indeed, in a globalized market for labor, what counts is the price of labor (i.e. the wage rate) not the theoretical volume of unused bodies deemed to be "participating" in the labor force during any given month by the bean counters of the BLS.

If domestic labor is overpriced on the margin, which it surely is in the United States, then no amount of aggregate demand "stimulus" is going to put displaced textile and furniture workers back to work. Household spending on these items based on induced borrowing will actually end up being collected by overseas shipping lines and Chinese factories.

Worse still, when monetary central planning is practiced on a global basis, as it has been for most of this century, it causes enormous overinvestment in industrial capacity in the emerging-market world owing to the repression of capital costs. To take one example, China now has excess steel capacity—700 million tons—that is well more than double the entire steel industry of the United States and Europe combined.

That monumental excess capacity, built in less than two decades from cheap state-supplied credit, is now being dumped into the world steel market. This tidal wave of cheap steel amounted to 110 million tons last year and is growing rapidly, reflecting the desperate efforts of the red suzerains of Beijing to stabilize their out-of-control credit and construction bubble.

When it comes to fiddling with the monetary policy dials, therefore, the capacity utilization figure at any point in time for the U.S. domestic iron and steel industry—which produces less than 100 million tons per year in its entirety—is just plain noise. The level and price of steel and steel-containing product import volumes, and Commerce Department actions under the antidumping laws, are literally hundreds of times more important than 25 bps on the money-market rate.

The same is true of the automotive industry and most other durable-goods manufacturers. A 70-year-old $60-per-hour UAW auto assembly plant in Indiana limping along on a single shift is not merely under-utilized by 66% owing to a three-shift global best-use standard. When it is up against spanking new $20-per-hour assembly facilities elsewhere in the world, it is effectively 100% under-utilized from an economic-efficiency and return-on-capital perspective.

Nevertheless, these types of labor and industrial-capacity-utilization rates comprise the "potential GDP" benchmark on which the Fed predicates its incessant monetary pumping. It is the basis for over-riding Say's law and for postulating that "aggregate demand" is deficient and that the Main Street economy always veers toward underperformance, recession and worse.

No it doesn't. The claim of business-cycle failure and the need for relentless and plenary monetary-policy interventions in the financial markets designed to smooth and optimize it is a self-serving invention of central bankers and Keynesian economists. It's the founding myth on which their very power, livelihood and self-importance depends.

The truth of the matter, however, is that if production and income growth is slow or even non-existent, that condition everywhere and always is caused by supply-side barriers to advance, not the postulated shortfall of "aggregate demand".

So the business-cycle-failure story is complete nonsense. Cutting to the chase, the Humphrey-Hawkins Full Employment Act is one of the stupidest, most dangerous and anti-democratic laws ever enacted.

It amounts to a plenary delegation of power to a tiny unelected and unaccountable posse of monetary bureaucrats. Under the statute's enabling act remit, the latter are free to define its vague and purely aspirational goals—maximum employment and stable prices—anyway they wish.

Moreover, they are then further empowered to manipulate in hot pursuit of these arbitrary quantitative targets any and all financial prices—and to do so without standards or limits, and regardless of whether these rubbery targets for societal betterment are efficacious or not.

In plain English, 5.0% unemployment on the U-3 measure and 2.00% inflation on the core PCE deflator are economically meaningless targets. They are impossible to achieve through interest-rate manipulation and the rest of the Fed's tool kit, especially its wealth-effects "put" under the stock market.

Likewise, these so-called Humphrey-Hawkins targets have no discernible relationship to societal betterment. There is not a shred of evidence, for example, that wage workers are better off with 2% inflation than they are with 1%, 0.0% or any other arbitrarily chosen rate. And that's even truer when the inflation target is derived from a deeply flawed price index like the core PCE deflator and measured over a completely arbitrary, and usually unspecified, time frame.

THE FED ISN'T NEEDED TO COMPENSATE FOR BUSINESS-CYCLE FAILURE—MODERN HISTORY PROVES IT

So it needs to be reiterated: Forcing the macro-economy into adherence to these crude Humphrey-Hawkins policy targets is utterly unnecessary because the predicate that capitalism has a death wish and is prone to recessionary collapse is dead wrong.

In truth, that is a self-serving scary story peddled by the monetary central planners and their grateful Wall Street beneficiaries. I have addressed the myth of the foundation event—the Great Depression of the 1930s—at length in my book *The Great Deformation: The Corruption of Capitalism in America*. Suffice it to say that the modern Keynesian narrative has it precisely upside down.

The Great Depression did not stem from a fatal flaw of capitalism or the failure of the 1930–33 Federal Reserve to crank up the printing presses, or even Hoover's allegedly benighted dedication to fiscal rectitude and honest gold-standard money.

Just the opposite. The Great Depression originated in the excesses of state action—the massive indebtedness and inflation of the Great War and the easy-money credit bubbles of the Roaring Twenties—not to its supposed *deficiencies*.

Likewise, the post-war business cycles prior to Greenspan's accession were short-lived, well-contained and self-correcting. They too were owing to the errors of state action, not the inherent flaws of capitalism or an alleged business-cycle instability that threatened an unstoppable downward spiral.

Specifically, two of these recessions were temporary consequences of what had been red-hot war economies in 1953–54 (Korea) and 1969–70 (Vietnam). The first was self-cured by the inherent resilience of market capitalism and involved virtually no fiscal or monetary "stimulus" under the orthodox strictures of President Eisenhower and William McChesney Martin at the Fed.

Likewise, the post-Vietnam so-called recession hardly registered in the economic statistics——save for a 70-day auto strike. The latter wasn't even a business cycle, but a random shock from the complete shutdown of GM and its massive supplier base in the fall of 1970 at a time when GM was at its peak and occupied 45% of the entire US auto market.

Needless to say, that strike was eventually resolved by the parties involved, triggering a sold rebound immediately thereafter. There was no business cycle failure or threatened tumble into an economic black hole—nor did the fiscal and monetary authorities of the day do much to "stimulate" the natural forces of recovery.

By contrast, the two deepest recessions of the pre-Greenspan period—the 1974–75 downturn and the deep 1981–82 recession—were caused by a very evident villain. In those cases, you can pin the tail squarely on the donkey at the Federal Reserve itself.

As we also demonstrated in *The Great Deformation*, the mid-1970s boom-and-bust cycle was not caused by the 1973 post-embargo "oil price shock." To the contrary, it was the result of Fed Chairman's Arthur Burns' abject submission to Nixon's demand for a 1972 pre-election surge of the U.S. economy.

The obsequious and weak-spined Professor Burns, in fact, pumped reserves and new credit through the banking system at nearly a 40% annualized rate near its peak. It is that action which set the stage for the inflationary blow off in 1972–74 and which necessitated a sharp monetary braking action thereafter.

As to the deep plunge of the early Reagan era, the Mighty Volcker was at the helm, of course, only because Arthur Burns and his successor, the hapless golf cart manufacturer William Miller, had fueled a massive domestic credit expansion during the second half of the 1970s.

Accordingly, the double-digit inflation that Volcker brought to heal was manufactured by the central bank, not by the OPEC cartel, silver and copper speculators or greedy consumers, as Jimmy Carter had it at the time.

THE DEMISE AND REVIVAL OF FULL-EMPLOYMENT KEYNESIANISM

Moreover, as of Volcker's turn at bat, there was at least a possibility that Washington policy might escape from the thrall of Keynesian economics. That's because in its original fiscally oriented guise it had flopped miserably during the previous two decades.

It had been first installed on the fiscal side during the Kennedy-Johnson era, and was then embraced by Nixon himself when his itinerant policy groupie, George Schulz, professor of labor economics, persuaded him to adopt the full-employment budget concept.

The latter was pure Keynesian claptrap. In fact, it was the original incarnation of the hoary idea referenced above that the United States was a closed domestic economy resembling a giant economic bathtub, which needed to be filled to the brim with GDP for maximum societal welfare.

According to Schulz and his original band of business Keynesians, the job of the state was to mobilize aggregate spending via fiscal deficits and easy monetary credit. These spigots of state-fueled "aggregate demand" would then be held open until the economic-policy experts certified that potential GDP and full employment had been achieved and that the bathtub was full to the brim.

Mercifully, the primitive experiments with so-called full-employment stimulus during Johnson's "guns and butter" policies after 1965, and the Nixon-Burns money-printing spree of 1972–74 resulted in the 1970s catastrophe of stagflation. Accordingly, bathtub-based Keynesianism was on deaths door when Ronald Reagan arrived at the White House in 1981.

And the giant Reagan deficits notwithstanding, it was further buried by the roaring success of Volcker's hard-money policy and the Reagan's administration resolute refusal to consider anything that smacked of proactive fiscal or monetary "stimulus" during the dark days of 1982.

In this context, it needs be recalled that the giant Reagan deficits were structural, not cyclical forms of discretionary Keynesian stimulus. As it happened, they were owing to a planned tripling of defense spending and a tax-cut bidding war that got totally out of hand in the summer of 1981. The latter ended up reducing the permanent out-year revenue base by 6% of GDP compared to an original White House goal of 3.5%.

These were both policy errors in their own right, of course. But they involved no notion at all that capitalism needed the helping hand of the state in order to get back on its feet after a state-sponsored credit inflation had set it on its heels.

Then came the 1984 election campaign about morning in America, which was mainly harmless political bloviating. But the White House politicians could not leave well enough alone.

Soon there followed the disaster of the Plaza Accord of 1985, designed to trash the dollar and artificially stimulate domestic economic activity. And then on the heels of the Plaza Accord there transpired the real calamity: Ronald Reagan was tricked by Jim Baker and the Republican elders on Capitol Hill into forcing Volcker out of his job as chairman of the Fed. In Chapter 5 we will show that the double-talking, power-seeking, lapsed gold bug named to replace him, Alan Greenspan, brought Keynesian bathtub economics right back into the center of policy, and then doubled down during the 1990s.

Yet in the world after Mr. Deng's pronouncement that it is glorious to be rich and even more virtuous to export, the idea of a full-bathtub policy in a single country is absurd. Industrial capacity and labor are global and incessantly dynamic, meaning that the primitive measures of domestic-labor and business-capacity utilization published by Washington's rickety statistical mills measure nothing that is accurate or economically meaningful.

Thus, the utilization rate of the auto industry, as was discussed previously, might have been remotely relevant before 1980. Today it reflects a domestic-sales and production cycle that leaks like a sieve owing to the integration of the North American auto production base under NAFTA and the massive ebb and flow of export vehicles from Europe and East Asia.

So instead of a full bathtub of domestic employment and GDP, the Fed has generated a $45 trillion financial bubble since Alan Greenspan took the helm in August 1987. After 29 years, honest price discovery has been destroyed, thereby reducing the nerve centers of capitalism—the money and capital markets—to little more than gambling casinos.

This central bank-caused disabling of capitalist financial markets has been exceedingly counterproductive. Speculative rent seeking in the financial arena has replaced entrepreneurial innovation and supply-side investment and productivity as the modus operandi of the US economy.

In short, the pursuit of Keynesian business-cycle management and stimulus through central bank interest-rate pegging and massive monetization of existing public debt results in systematic falsification of asset prices, not "stimulus" of the Main Street economy. It amounts to monetary central planning for the perverse purpose of redistributing wealth to the top of the economic ladder.

THE FOLLY OF THE BATHTUB-ECONOMICS MODEL AND KEYNES' ODE TO HOMESPUN GOODS

As indicated above, the Keynesian bathtub model of a closed, volumetrically driven economy is a throwback to specious theories about the inherent business cycle instabilities of market capitalism that originated during the Great Depression. These theories were wrong then, but utterly irrelevant in today's globally open and technologically dynamic post-industrial economy.

The very idea that 12 people sitting on the FOMC can adroitly manipulate an economic ether called "aggregate demand" by means of falsifying market interest rates is an especially bad joke when it comes to those parts of "potential GDP" comprised of goods-production capacity and the measurement and mobilization of the potential labor force.

In the case of goods production, today's world of open trade and massive excess industrial capacity means that the Fed can do exactly nothing about domestic slack in the goods production sectors. As we have seen, whether the domestic steel industry's capacity utilization rate is 90% or 60%, for example, is a function of how much steel the Chinese are dumping on the U.S. market and how aggressive the Commerce Department is in imposing anti-dumping penalties—not 25 bps on the money market rate.

In the vastly oversized global steel market case and that of virtually all traded goods, it all depends upon the marginal cost of labor, capital and materials and the extent of state intervention and subsidization.

Indeed, the only thing that the denizens of the FOMC can do about capacity utilization in any domestic industry is to reread Keynes' 1930 essay in favor of homespun goods and recognize that it is they—not Donald Trump—who are the real advocates of protectionism!

As I detailed in *The Great Deformation*, the Great Thinker actually came out for stringent protectionism and economic autarky six years before he published the General Theory and for good and logical reasons that his contemporary followers choose to completely ignore.

Namely, protectionism and autarky are an absolutely necessary correlate to state management of the business cycle. Indeed, Keynes took special care to make sure that his works were always translated into German, and averred that the state-controlled economy of Nazi Germany was the ideal test bed for his economic remedies.

Eighty years on from Keynes' incomprehensible ode to statist economics and thoroughgoing protectionism, the idea of state management of the business cycle in one country is even more preposterous.

Thus, in the case of potential labor supply, the unutilized amount of labor (i.e. unemployment) is a function of the global labor cost curve.

Furthermore, labor is now employed in atomized form as hours, gigs, and temp agency contractual bits, not headcounts as toted-up by the Census Bureau's employment survey takers (or fakers).

In fact, the Census Bureau survey takers and the BLS numbers crunchers don't have the foggiest idea about how to compute the nation's potential labor supply. Nor do they know much of it is employed on any given day, month or quarter.

Accordingly, the Fed's apparent target of 5.0% on the U-3 unemployment rate is especially ludicrous. The denominator of that figure is a crock because it excludes 92 million adults not even counted as being in the labor force—of which only half are retired and receiving Social Security benefits (OASI).

At the same time, the numerator is way understated because it excludes not only all of the uncounted millions deemed not in the labor force, but also excludes millions more who are functionally unemployed, but are counted as jobholders if they work only a few hour per week. The computed result, therefore, is as good as pure noise as you are likely to find anywhere.

As I indicated earlier, in today's economy they only way to measure labor is on an hours basis because increasingly that how it is scheduled by employers. At the present time, there are 210 million adult Americans between the ages of 16 and 68—to take a plausible measure of the potential work force.

Accordingly, if we accept the convention that all adults are at least theoretically capable of holding a full-time job (2,000 hours per year) and pulling their share of society's need for production and work effort, that amounts to 420 billion potential labor hours in the US economy.

By contrast, only 240 billion hours are actually being supplied to the U.S. economy according to recent BLS estimates. Technically, therefore, there are 180 billion unemployed labor hours, meaning that the real unemployment rate is 43%, not 5%!

Yes, we have to allow for stay-at-home wives, students, the disabled, early retirees and coupon clippers. We also have drifters, grifters, welfare cheats, bums and people between jobs, enrollees in training programs, professionals on sabbaticals and much else.

But here's the thing. There are dozens of reasons for 180 billion unemployed labor hours, but whether the Fed is monetizing massive amounts of the public debt and pegging money-market interest rates at 38 bps or 63 bps doesn't even make the top 25 reasons for why these potential hours are unutilized.

What actually drives our current 43% pro forma unemployment rate is global economic forces of cheap labor and new productive capacity throughout the EM, and also dozens of domestic-policy and cultural factors that influence the decision to work or not.

In that context, schoolmarm Yellen's focus on the minutia of the BLS labor statistics in the pursuit of her campaign to fill up the bathtub of potential GDP is borderline loony.

For instance, the amount of unmonetized labor utilized in households and elsewhere is constantly changing depending on demographics, household composition, cultural values, economic pressures on family budgets, child-care costs and availability and much more. The Fed can't possibly keep up with this or take account of it in calibrating full employment.

That point was brought home way back in the 1970s during one of those periodic Washington debates about full employment. Legendary humorist Art Buchwald weighed in with a sure fire way to double the GDP and do it instantly.

That was at a time when most women had not yet entered the labor force and politically incorrect discussion was still permitted on the august pages of the *Washington Post*.

Said Buchwald: "Pass a law requiring all men to hire their neighbor's wife!"

That is, monetize all of the cleaning, cooking, washing, ironing, scrubbing and errands and shopping done every day in American households by unpaid spouses and get the monetary value computed in the GDP. And in the process, get homemakers factored into the labor force and their contribution to the economy's real output reflected in the labor utilization rate.

As a statistical matter—even though four decades of women entering the labor force have passed since Buchwald's tongue-in-cheek proposal—there are still approximately 75 billion unmonetized household labor hours in the US economy. Were they to be counted in both sides of the equation, our 43% unemployment rate would drop to 25% for that reason alone.

Needless to say, whether household labor is monetized or not has no impact whatsoever on the real wealth and living standards of America, even if it does involve important social-policy implications. But unmonetized household workers are absolutely part of the potential labor supply, and changes in their participation rate in the monetized economy is highly variable depending on almost anything you can think of except 25 bps on the Wall Street borrowing rate.

And the same thing is true for almost every other factor that drives the true hours-based unemployment rate. Front and center is the massive explosion of student debt—now clocking in at $1.3 trillion compared to less than $300 billion only a decade ago and virtually zero when Greenspan launched Bubble Finance.

The point is not simply that this debt bomb is going to explode in the years ahead; the larger point is that for better or worse, Washington has made a policy choice to keep upwards of 20 million workers out of the labor force and to subsidize them as students.

Whether millions of these debt serfs will get any real earnings-enhancing benefit out of this "education" is an open question—even as the answer leans heavily toward not likely in either this lifetime or the next.

But these 40 billion potential labor hours are now far greater in relative terms than under the stingy student subsidy programs, which existed in 1970 when Janet Yellen was learning bathtub economics from James Tobin at Yale. Stated differently, there is enormous "slack" in the labor force because the higher-education lobbies rule the roost on Capitol Hill, not because Janet Yellen and her posse rule the money-market rate.

Likewise, there are currently about 17 billion annual potential labor hours accounted for by Social Security disability recipients. Again, that is a much larger relative number than a few decades back, and it is owing to the deliberate liberalization of social policy by Congressional legislators and administrative law judges. The FOMC has nothing to do with this form of unemployment, either.

Then there are the billions of potential labor hours in the unmonetized "underground" economy. While the social value of work by drug runners and street-level dealers is debatable, it is self-evident that state policy—in the form of the so-called "war on drugs" and the DEA and law-enforcement dragnet—account for this portion of unutilized labor, not the central bank.

The same is true of all the other state interventions that keep potential labor hours out of the monetized economy and the BLS surveys. That starts with the Obamacare 30 hours per week threshold and goes from there to the minimum-wage laws and petty licensing of trades like beauticians, barbers, electricians and taxi drivers, among countless others.

Finally, there is the giant question of the price of labor as opposed to the quantity. And here it needs to be noted that "off-shoring" is not just about shoe factories and sheet and towel mills that went to China because American labor was too expensive.

Owing to the rapid progress of communications technology, an increasing share of what used to be considered service work, such as call centers and financial back-office activities, have also been off-shored on account of labor price.

Moreover, the process of direct wage suppression due to off-shoring of goods and services production has ricocheted into adjacent activities. That's because former holders of offshored jobs have been willing to accept lower wages in purely domestic sectors when push comes to shove.

Indeed, the cascade of the China "labor price" through the warp and woof of the entire US economy is so pervasive and subtle that it cannot possibly be measured by the crude instruments deployed by the Census Bureau and BLS.

In short, Janet Yellen doesn't have a clue as to whether we are at 30% or 20% or 5% unemployment of the potential adult labor hours in the US economy. But three things are quite certain.

First, the real unemployment rate is not 5.5%—the U-3 number is an absolute and utterly obsolete relic that belongs in the Smithsonian, not the Eccles Building.

Secondly, the actual employment rate of America's 420 billion potential labor hours is overwhelmingly a function of domestic social policy and global labor markets, not the rate of money-market interest.

And finally, under conditions of Peak Debt, the Fed is powerless to do anything about the actual labor-utilization rate, anyway. The only tub its lunatic money-printing policies are filling is that of the Wall Street speculators.

AN UNNECESSARY HISTORICAL DETOUR: THE CARTER GLASS "BANKERS BANK" VERSUS KEYNESIAN CENTRAL BANKING

If Warren Buffett and his ilk weren't so hideously rich, Main Street America would be far more prosperous. I must hasten to add, of course, that this proposition has nothing to do with the zero-sum anti-capitalism of left-wing ideologues like Professors Piketty and Krugman.

Far from it. Real capitalism cannot thrive unless inventive and entre-preneurial genius is rewarded with outsized fortunes.

But as we demonstrated in Chapter 3, Warren Buffett's $73 billion net worth, and numerous like and similar financial gambling fortunes that have arisen since 1987, are not due to genius; they are owing to adept surfing on the $45 trillion financial bubble that has been generated by the central bank Keynesianism of Alan Greenspan and his successors.

The resulting massive redistribution of wealth to the tiny slice of households, which own most of the financial assets, is not merely collateral damage. That is, it is not the unfortunate byproduct of continuous and extraordinary central bank "stimulus" policies that were otherwise necessary to keep the U.S. economy off the shoals and the GDP and jobs on a steadily upward course.

Just the opposite. The entire regime of monetary central planning is a regrettable historical detour; it did not need to happen because massive central bank intervention is not necessary for capitalism to thrive.

In fact, today's style of heavy-handed monetary central planning destroys capitalist prosperity. It does so in a manner that is hidden at first—because credit inflation and higher leverage temporarily goose the reported GDP.

But eventually they visibly and relentlessly devour the vital ingredients of growth in an orgy of debt and speculation.

To appreciate this we need to turn back the clock by 100 years—to the early days of the Fed and ask a crucial question. Namely, what would have happened if its charter had not been changed by the exigencies of Woodrow Wilson's foolish crusade to make the world safe for democracy in 1917?

The short answer is that we would have had a "bankers' bank" designed to provide standby liquidity to the commercial banking system. Moreover, that liquidity would have been generated not from fiat central bank credit conjured by a tiny posse of monetary bureaucrats, but from self-liquidating commercial collateral arising from the decentralized production of inventories and receivables on the Main Street economy.

That is to say, the 12 Federal Reserve Banks designed by the great Carter Glass in the 1913 act were to operate through a discount window where good commercial paper would be discounted for cash at a penalty spread above the free-market rate of interest.

The job of the reserve banks was to don green eyeshades and assess collateral based on principles of banking safety and soundness. So doing, they would enable the banking system to remain liquid based on the working capital of private enterprise, not the artificial credit of the state.

Accordingly, there would have been no central bank macro-economic policy or aggregate targets for unemployment, inflation, GDP growth, housing starts, retail sales or any of the other litany of incoming economic metrics. The curse of Humphrey-Hawkins would have never happened.

To the contrary, the level and rate of change in national economic output and wealth would have been entirely a passive outcome on the free market resulting from the interactions of millions of producers, consumers, savers, investors, entrepreneurs, inventors and speculators.

Stated differently, Washington's monetary authorities would have had no dog in the GDP hunt. Whether the macro economy slumped or boomed—and whether GDP grew by 4%, 2% or -2% would have been the collective verdict of the people, not the consequence of state action.

Likewise, honest price discovery would have driven the money and capital markets. That's because there would be no FOMC at the Eccles Building pegging the overnight interest rate or manipulating the yield curve by purchasing longer-term public debt and other securities.

In fact, under its original statutory charter, the Fed was not even allowed to own government debt or accept it as collateral against advances to its member banks.

That is a crucial distinction because it means that the Fed would not have ventured near the canyons of Wall Street nor have had any tools whatsoever to falsify financial-market prices. Speculators wishing to ply the carry trades and arbitrage the yield curve—that is, make money the way most of Wall Street does today—would have done so at their own risk and peril.

Indeed, the infamous "panics" of the pre-Fed period usually ended quickly when the call money rate—the overnight money rate of the day— soared by hundreds of basis points a day and often deep into double digits.

Free-market interest rates cured speculative excesses. The very prospect of a 29-year bubble, which took finance (credit-market debt outstanding plus the market value of non-financial corporate equities) from $13 trillion to $93 trillion, as occurred between 1987 and 2015, would not have been imaginable or possible.

Indeed, the great speculators of the day like Jay Cooke ended up broke after 10 years, not worth $73 billion after three decades.

Notwithstanding the inherent self-correcting, antibubble nature of the free market, defenders of the Fed argue the U.S. economy would be forever parched for credit and liquidity without the constant injections of the Federal Reserve.

But that is a hoary myth. In a healthy and honest free market, credit is supplied by savers who have already produced real goods and services, and have chosen to allocate a portion to future returns.

Indeed, the difference between fiat credit conjured from thin air by central banks and honest savings is the fundamental dividing line between Bubble Finance and healthy capitalist prosperity.

Needless to say, the claim that the economy would be worse off if it was based on real savings is the Big Lie on which the entire regime of monetary central planning is based. It is also the lynchpin of the Warren Buffett economy.

It is not surprising, therefore, that free-market finance is an unknown concept in today's world and that Carter Glass' bankers' bank has been lost in the fog of statist historiography. All of the powers of Wall Street and Washington militate against it.

HOW TO RESTORE HONEST CAPITAL MARKETS: ABOLISH THE FOMC

The approximate hour Janet Yellen spends wandering in circles and spewing double talk during her post meeting pressers is time well spent. When the painful ordeal of her semi-coherent babbling is finally over, she has essentially proved that the Fed is attempting an impossible task.

And better still, that the FOMC should be abolished.

The alternative is real simple. It's called price discovery on the free market; it's the essence of capitalism.

After all, the hotshot traders who operate in the canyons of Wall Street could readily balance the market for overnight funds. They would do so by varying the discount rate on short-term money.

That is, they would push the rate upwards when funds were short, thereby calling-in liquidity from other markets and discouraging demand, especially from carry-trade speculators. By contrast, when surplus funds got piled too high, they would push the discount rate downward, thereby discouraging supply and inciting demand.

Under such a free-market regime, the discount rate might well be highly mobile, moving from 1% to 10% and back to 1%, for example, as markets cleared in response to changing short-term balances.

So what?

Likewise, the world is full of long-term savers like pension funds, insurance companies, bond funds and direct household investors on the supply side, and a long parade of sovereign, corporate and household borrowers on the demand side.

Through an endless process of auction, arbitrage and allocation, the yield curve would find its proper shape and levels. And as with the case of a free market in money, the yield curve of the debt market would undulate, twist, turn and otherwise morph in response to changing factors with respect to supply of savings and demands for debt capital.

It goes without saying that under such a regime, savers would be rewarded with high rates when demands for business investment, household borrowings and government debt issuance were large. At the same time, financial punters, business speculators, household high-livers and deficit-spending politicians alike would find their enthusiasm severely dented by high and rising yields when the supply of savings was short.

What would be the harm, it must be asked, in letting economic agents in their tens of millions bid for savings in order to find the right price of debt capital at any given time?

Why concentrate the task among 12 people who, as Janet Yellen's endless babbling so thoroughly demonstrates, can't possibly figure it out, anyway?

There are three reasons given as to why capitalism's monumental and crucial tasks of setting the price of money and debt cannot be trusted to the free market. But all of them are wrong; all of them are a variation of the giant Keynesian error that capitalism self-destructively tends toward entropy absent the ministrations of the state, and especially its central banking branch.

The first of these is the notion that debt is the keystone to prosperity and that a central bank fueled credit pick-me-up is warranted whenever economic growth begins to falter or business-cycle conditions weaken.

In fact, the truth is more nearly the opposite as we demonstrate at length in Chapter 6. The U.S. economy's leverage ratio today is triple its historic pre-1970 level, while the trend rate of real GDP growth has fallen by 80%.

Likewise, the second argument for activist central banking—the notion that the business cycle is inherently unstable and bleeds the economy of growth and wealth—is flat-out untrue. As we demonstrated above, every business-cycle downturn since the creation of the Fed in 1913 was the result of state action, not the inherent instabilities of the free market.

THE "FINANCIAL CONTAGION" MYTH AND THE FALSE CASE FOR ACTIVIST CENTRAL BANKING

At the end of the day, however, it is the fear of financial contagion and catastrophe of the type that allegedly arose in September 2008 that is the bogeyman ultimately undergirding the current cult of Keynesian central banking.

Yet the truth of the matter is that we didn't need Ben Bernanke and his self-proclaimed courage to print—and, as it happened, wildly and excessively so—to forestall an alleged Armageddon. As I documented in *The Great Deformation*, there was no run on the retail banks of America, and the post-Lehman meltdown in the financial markets would have burned out in the canyons of Wall Street had Washington not bailed out the gamblers.

So let's recall what actually happened, not the urban legends that arose at the time.

The Fed's balance sheet was about $900 billion before the Lehman meltdown, and it had taken 94 years to get there. The Bernanke Fed printed another $900 billion in just seven weeks after Lehman and $1.3 trillion more before Christmas Eve that year.

In the process, any crony capitalist within shouting distance of the canyons of Wall Street got bailed out with ultra-cheap credit from the Fed's alphabet soup of bailout lines.

Among these was the $600 billion AAA balance sheet at General Electric where CEO Jeff Imelt's bonus would have been jeopardized by spiking interest costs on his imprudently issued $90 billion in short-term commercial paper.

Ben had the courage to save Imelt's bonus by funding him at less than 4% for no good reason whatsoever. General Electric could have readily raised the funds through a dilutive issue of common stock or long-term debt.

He also had the courage to fund Morgan Stanley to the tune of $100 billion in cheap advances and guarantees. That gift kept this insolvent Wall Street gambling outfit alive long enough for CEO John Mack to jet down to Washington where he got short-sellers outlawed and collected a $10 billion TARP bailout—and all in less than two weeks!

Well, there is a better answer, and it requires no FOMC, Ben Bernanke or specious courage to rescue crony capitalist bandits like John Mack and Jeff Imelt.

It is called "mobilizing the discount rate." Implementation only takes green eyeshades.

That's right. Just a small number of competent accountants could do the job. Indeed, no Harvard, Princeton or even University of Chicago PhDs need apply.

For all the false jawing about Walter Bagehot's rules for stopping a financial crisis, a mobilized discount rate, not a hyperactive FOMC running around with hair afire and monetary fire hoses spraying randomly, is actually what the great English financial thinker had in mind.

To wit, Bagehot actually said that during a crisis central banks should supply funds freely at a penalty spread on top of a market rate of interest secured by sound collateral.

You don't need macroeconomic modelers with PhDs in econo-algebra to do that. You need accountants who can drill deep into business balance sheets and examine the collateral; and then clerks who can query the market rate of interest, add say 300–400 basis points of penalty spread, and hit the send bottom to eligible banks that have posted approved collateral.

Indeed, as we have seen, this was the sum and substance of the Fed's original design by Carter Glass, the great financial statesman who authored it. That's why he had 12 Reserve Banks domiciled in the different economic regions of the country and an essentially honorific but powerless board in Washington, DC.

As I indicated above, the 12 regional banks had no remit to target macroeconomic variables. They were not charged with managing, countering, flattening, or abolishing the business cycle. They could not even own government debt, and 91.7% (11/12) of their operations were to be conducted in the 11 regional banks away from Wall Street.

In short, the purpose of the Fed was actually to be a classic lender of last resort. The job of Carter Glass' "bankers' bank was liquefying the banking system on a decentralized basis, not monetary central planning or Keynesian macro-economic management.

Accordingly, the balance sheet of the Federal Reserve System was not intended to be a proactive instrument of national economic policy. It was to passively reflect the ebb and flow of industry and commerce. The expansion and contraction of banking system liquidity needs would follow from the free enterprise of business and labor throughout the nation, not the whims, guesstimates, confusions, and blather of a 12-person FOMC.

Needless to say, under the mobilized discount rate regime and bankers' bank that Carter Glass intended, the outcomes during the 2008 financial crisis would have been far different.

Bear Stearns was not a commercial bank, and would not have been eligible for the discount window. It would have been liquidated, as it should have been, with no harm done except to the speculators who had imprudently purchased its commercial paper, debt and equity securities.

Likewise, Morgan Stanley was insolvent and its doors would have been closed on September 25, 2008. That is, long before John Mack could have gotten the short-sellers of his worthless stock banned or collected his $10 billion gift from Hank Paulson.

Needless to say, the world would have little noted nor long remembered the chapter 11 filing of what was (and still is) a notorious gambling house. Likewise, GE would have paid higher rates for long term debt or new equity to refund its commercial paper, thereby dinging its earnings by a quarter or two and Jeff Imelt's' bonus that year.

Yet, exactly what does that matter to the Main Street economy?

In a word, what happened in the run-up to the great financial crisis and its aftermath never would have occurred under a mobilized discount rate regime conducted by a bankers' bank.

Funding costs in the money markets would have soared to 10% or even double digits. That would have caused speculators who had invested long and illiquid and borrowed cheap and overnight to be carried out on their shields, thereby accomplishing the exact historic function of interest rates—a crucial function that the Bernanke Fed destroyed when it essentially nationalized the federal-funds market in September 2008.

The magnitude of Bernanke's financial crime is best illustrated by its opposite. That is, what happened a century earlier during the great financial panic of 1907 when interest rates soared to 20% and even 60% on some days of extreme money-market stress.

As it happened, volatile and soaring money-market rates cleared out the speculators and the hopelessly insolvent, like the copper kings, real estate punters and trust-bank pyramid artists of the day.

At the same time, JP Morgan and his syndicate of bankers with their own capital on the line, re-liquefied the solvent supplicants who came to Morgan's library on Madison Avenue——but only after their green eye-shades had spent long nights proving up solid collateral for liquidity loans from the Morgan syndicate.

After all, it was their capital, which was one the line—not fiat credits issued by hitting the send button at the New York Fed.

In any event, by 1910 American capitalism was again booming. No Fed. No Bernanke. No harm done.

So in 2008, the money markets would have cleared, and any temporary expansion of the Fed's balance sheet would have immediately shrunk once the crisis was over, and the discount loans were repaid.

And, yes, at 10%, 15% or even 25% and a penalty spread to boot, they would have been paid off real fast.

That's what a real lender of last resort would look like. Janet Yellen's crony capitalist flophouse is the very opposite.

REAL BILLS AND THE TRUE EVIL OF KEYNESIAN CENTRAL BANKING: GOVERNMENT DEBT MONETIZATION

By the same token, a real central bank of the pre-Keynesian era would not now own $4.5 trillion of government debt and guaranteed paper. In fact, it would own none at all because monetization of the public debt was never the purpose of central banking.

The purpose was to liquefy business-loan books and the traded markets in real bills, which were essentially receivable-type claims on finished goods in the channels of distribution. Unlike government debt, the latter represented production already done and banking collateral that could be collected within a relatively short period of 30 to 90 days when the underlying goods were sold.

In this context, the classic central bank's discount window would generally do more volume when business and trade were flourishing and less when activity contracted. In that modality, it was the servant of market capitalism, not its taskmaster.

Even more importantly, this kind of commercial collateral is self-limiting and anchored in goods that real businesses have already produced in anticipation of market demand. In essence, businesses issuing receivables paper were the actual risk takers. In order to generate finished products and trade bills, they had already made the decision to go long on raw materials, work-in-process, labor and other overheads.

Needless to say, compared to government debt this kind of business-generated and working capital-based "credit" was a fish of an altogether different kettle. That is, real bills drawn on finished goods were not merely open-ended promises to pay on the unsecured credit of a business firm or on the account of future taxpayers; they were discounted streams of presently anticipated customer payments which could be readily assessed as to commercial quality, risk and collectability.

Stated differently, in discounting commercial bills, central banks performed a higher banking function, not a macroeconomic management and central-planning mission. That meant that the free market was the ultimate determinant of the level and price of short-term business credit.

Accordingly, if businessmen became too exuberant in the production of finished goods, the discount rate on commercial bills would rise sharply in order to draw additional funding into the market and in recognition that added risk inherent in an over-supplied goods market.

Since the business cycle is ultimately an inventory stocking and de-stocking cycle, the implications were straightforward. Namely, that a mobilized discount rate on trade paper was an automatic governor of the business cycle—the unseen hand of Adam Smith, as it were.

Contrary to the false Keynesian predicate, therefore, an honest free market does not have a recessionary death wish. An honest, variable price of money determined by supply and demand militates against the build-up of excesses, and causes a quick painful liquidation of losses when excesses do occur.

There was another even more crucial aspect of pre-Keynesian central banking. To wit, it was strictly verboten to discount term debt and other less-liquid capital securities. So not only was central bank purchase of government bonds unthinkable; it was also true for equipment loans and corporate bonds, as well.

What this meant in economic terms is that business-fixed capital had to be financed out of the private savings pool. The interest rate on time deposits or insurance company annuities, therefore, is what determined the cost of long-term loans and debentures; and the greater the demand for the latter, the higher the yield on the former, and vice-versa.

The laws of supply and demand thus cleared capital markets. There was no artificial central bank bid, no falsification of yields and no diversion of cheap, subsidized credit into financial engineering games rather than productive assets. The modus operandi of capital markets, in fact, was to fund productive investment with a prospective return greater than the market price of capital, not rank speculations that would end up as mal-investments and losses.

Moreover, if governments were to issue debt, such as for public works or war bonds, these had to be funded out of the same private savings pool. The two were in direct competition—so the price of debt or bond yields would reflect that effect.

And that gets us to the true evil of Keynesian-era central banking. To wit, the only effective brake on the propensity of politicians in today's social democracies to issue public debt is an honest capital market.

This used to be called the "crowding-out effect." It occurred when excessive government borrowing caused long-term interest rates to rise sharply, thereby leading to the cancellation of business investments that could no longer meet their rate-of-return hurdles.

In a word, the likes of industrialists, homebuilders, construction companies and capital-equipment suppliers (and their employees, suppliers and communities) are the natural political constituencies that countervail the tendency of democratic politicians to grease the pork barrel and indulge the demands of organized recipients of entitlements and other subventions.

Rising interest rates were an immediate signal that there is no fiscal free lunch. They gave efficacy to the historic fear of fiscal deficits among conservative politicians, and forced governments to make budgetary choices between curtailment of spending, increasing taxes or higher interest rates owing to greater borrowing.

Alas, Keynesian central banking destroyed these fundamental checks and balances of fiscal governance. If nothing else, the past three decades of soaring public debt has proven in spades that the historic fear of "debt monetization" among the financially literate classes was well grounded.

As I explained in *The Great Deformation* the resulting destruction of fiscal discipline did not happen overnight. On the one hand, the political system—especially among GOP rank-and-file politicians—was still populated with believers in the old-time religion of balanced budgets, and actually voted that way.

That's why in the early days of the Reagan administration, for example, Senate Leader Howard Baker labeled the huge supply-side tax cut as a "riverboat gamble." He and the Senate GOP elders were only willing to entertain it if they got spending cuts first, and could see some path in the fiscal arithmetic to a balanced budget at an early date.

Likewise, the Greenspan-era central bankers never explicitly acknowledged they were monetizing the public debt in increasingly greater proportions. All the bond buying was rationalized as simply a means to economic stimulus and coaxing more aggregate demand into the US economy in order to meet its Humphrey-Hawkins targets.

But after Bernanke's $1.3 trillion debt-buying blitz in 13 weeks after the Lehman event and then 93 straight months of ZIRP and an eventual 5X expansion of the Fed's balance, the cat was effectively out of the bag.

Notwithstanding the procedural niceties of monthly QE targets, federal-funds-rate targets and secondary market purchases of securities by the New York Fed from the primary dealers, the underlying truth is undeniable.

Namely, that a high proportion of the exploding public debt after the financial crisis was monetized.

The Fed and other central banks and their associated sovereign-wealth funds, in fact, now own upwards of 50% of the publicly traded Treasury and federally guaranteed GSE securities.

So like Earnest Hemingway's famous description of the route to bankruptcy, monetization of the public debt happened slowly at first, and then all at once. Ronald Reagan broke the taboo on giant fiscal deficits and, at length, Dick Cheney pronounced that they didn't matter anyway.

But it was the lapsed gold bug, Alan Greenspan, who opened the door to massive central bank bond purchases by expanding the Fed's balance sheet from $200 billion to $700 billion during his tenure at a time when it shouldn't have been expanded at all, as we will explain in the next chapter.

So doing, however, Greenspan fueled the epic $45 trillion financial bubble that crashed in 2008, thereby paving the way for his more doctrinaire Keynesian successors—Bernanke and Yellen—to go all in.

Needless to say, there is no cure for the nation's looming fiscal disaster under the current Keynesian central banking regime. It has turned the monetary and fiscal tables upside down.

The Fed no longer has anything to do with the remit given to it by Carter Glass—one that was grounded in the central banking model of the day—to function as a "bankers' bank" and to passively liquefy the market for real trade bills generated on the free market.

Instead, it has morphed into a statist monster that is engaged in the two most destructive games imaginable. To wit, monetary central planning and monetization of the public debt.

The former has already falsified the money and capital markets, destroyed honest price discovery, turned Wall Street into a gambling casino and the C-suites of corporate America into financial engineering and strip-mining operations which are sucking the financial lifeblood from the Main Street economy.

Likewise, the latter has eliminated any vestige of fiscal rectitude in the political system. That is evidenced by the fact that Washington has spent $2 trillion on unfunded wars and has legislated not a single material entitlement reform or tax increase during the entirety of this century—even as it was adding upwards of $15 trillion to the public debt.

The utter lack of prospect for change was well underscored during the presidential candidate acceptance speeches at the recent party conventions. Hillary Clinton embraced a laundry list of Bernie Sanders' free stuff and Donald Trump hardly mentioned the ticking fiscal time bomb that he will inherit if elected.

This simply proves, however, that as a practical matter it is too late for conventional fiscal-improvement plans and laundry lists of spending cuts, entitlement reforms and revenue-raising measures. That's because the natural constituencies for fiscal retrenchment have been destroyed by a central bank committed to open-ended monetization of the public debt.

Yet in that baleful reality there is also a hint of the way forward. When the coming recession and subsequent financial crash finally destroys the credibility of the current Keynesian central banking regime there will be an opportunity for a fundamental reset of the central banking function.

Needless to say, the very worst thing to do would be to opt for some "rules-based" version of what the Fed is doing today. I have in mind here a special place in monetary hell for Professor Taylor's crypto-Keynesian rule for pegging interest rates.

According to Taylor, it's all real simple. Just peg the money-market rate at its appropriate Humphrey-Hawkins level—calculated via some arithmetic hocus-pocus based on gaps between actual and targeted levels of unemployment and inflation. That is to say, he would have the Fed jump from the Keynesian frying pan into the Friedmanite fires while shackled in mathematical chains.

By contrast, the best thing to do would be to revive the great Carter Glass and his original central banking model. That is to say, abolish the FOMC and discretionary intervention in financial markets by the Fed, and also ban it from owning, borrowing or collateralizing in any other way treasury debt and other federally guaranteed paper.

In one fell swoop that would put an end to the twin evils—monetary central planning and monetization of the public debt—that today threaten capitalist prosperity and democratic government. So doing, it would revive honest price discovery in the money and capital markets, thereby purging them of the cheap carry-trade finance and drastically underpriced hedging insurance on which the entire regime of Bubble Finance is based.

At length, the immense stock- and bond-market bubbles of the present era would be deflated and capital markets would revive as a venue for real money savers to meet productive asset investors and borrowers and strike an honest, economically warranted price.

Likewise, the C-suites of corporate America would go back to investing in the future of their companies, not financial-engineering maneuvers designed to cause a pop in their stock prices and an early harvest from their stock options.

So, too, politicians tempted to pile more onto the nation's already-staggering public debts would have a clarifying experience that has been AWOL essentially since 1994 when Greenspan capitulated to the bond vigilantes.

To wit, they would see interest rates rise in the government bond market in response to more public-debt issuance and hear a crescendo of complaints about "crowding out" by businessmen and other capital users. "Price discovery" would supplant fiscal free lunches even in the halls of government.

At the end of the day, all that should remain of the monster that now inhabits the Eccles Building is the lender-of-last-resort function. But its remit would be the one designed by Carter Glass, not the massive mission creep embedded in the rolling financial coup d'état staged by Greenspan-Bernanke-Yellen since 1987.

Accordingly, eligible borrowers would be precluded from bringing treasury debt, Fannie/Freddie securities, corporate bonds, real estate loans, junk bonds, ETFs or any other capital-markets securities to the discount window. In other words, nothing of what the Keynesian central planners have piled on to the $21 trillion of central bank balance sheets around the world.

As a result, capital markets would be made honest again because every scrap of paper traded there would be fully at risk. There would be no repo-style daisy chains in which inflated bonds are treated as "assets" that become the collateral for still more debt, even more speculator bids and yet-higher prices and more collateral.

At the same time, eligible paper would consist entirely of claims on business receivables and finished inventory. That is, late-stage working capital that already reflects new value-added production and the ground-level risk assessments of the entire chain of supply.

Moreover, here is where the PhDs would take their leave and the green eye shades would take their seats. Unlike the insane growth of credit since 1987—from about $8 trillion to $64 trillion—there could be no artificial credit inflation under a Glassian central bank. That is, so long as under its foundation law eligible collateral was restricted to high quality, late-stage business working capital, and those standards were upheld by a rigorous credit review process.

Needless to say, this not only implies the repeal of Humphrey-Hawkins, but also a strong mandate in the new Fed charter that it is explicitly not in the business-cycle-management business. Nor is its job in anyway related to macroeconomic performance and the level or rate of growth in GDP, jobs, housing, car sales or anything else in the goods-and-services economy.

The fact is, gains in output, living standards and sustainable wealth are outcomes produced by workers, entrepreneurs, savers, investors, inventors and speculators on the free market. They are not a gift of the central bank or any other state action. A Main Street economy in Flyover America that has ground to a halt and is buried in unpayable debts is surely proof of that.

CHAPTER 5:

Trump Isn't All Wrong About Trade Deficits—How Washington's Money Printers Betrayed American Workers

N EEDLESS TO SAY, THE LACK OF GOOD JOBS LIES AT THE BOTTOM OF THE wealth and income drought on Main Street, and recent jobs reports provide still another reminder.

During the last seven months, goods-producing jobs have been shrinking again, even as the next recession knocks on the door. These manufacturing, construction and energy/mining jobs are the highest paying in the U.S. economy and average about $56,000 per year in cash wages. Yet it appears that the 30-year pattern shown in the graph below—lower lows and lower highs with each business cycle—is playing out once again.

So even as the broadest measure of the stock market—the Wilshire 5000—stands at 11X its 1989 level, there are actually 20% fewer goods-producing jobs in the United States than there were way back then.

This begs the question, therefore, as to the rationale for the "Jobs Deal" we referenced in Chapter 1 and why Donald Trump should embrace a massive swap of the existing corporate and payroll taxes for new levies on consumption and imports.

The short answer is that it's necessary to ameliorate the giant monetary-policy mistake initiated by Greenspan 29 years ago. The latter left Main Street households buried in debt and stranded with a simultaneous plague of stagnant real incomes and uncompetitively high nominal wages.

It happened because at the time that Mr. Deng launched China's great mercantilist export machine during the early 1990s, Alan Greenspan was more interested in being the toast of Washington than he was in adhering to his lifelong convictions about the requisites of sound money.

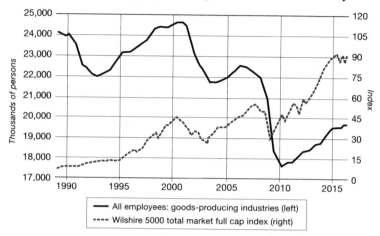

Indeed, he apparently checked his gold-standard monetary principles in the cloak room when he entered the Eccles Building in August 1987. Not only did he never reclaim the check; he embraced its opposite—the self-serving institutional anti-deflationism of the central bank.

This drastic betrayal and error resulted in a lethal cocktail of free trade and what amounted to free money. It resulted in the hollowing out of the American economy, because it prevented American capitalism from adjusting to the tsunami of cheap manufactures coming out of China and its East Asian supply chain.

The full extent of the Fed's betrayal of Flyover America can only be fathomed in relationship to the counterfactual To wit, what would have happened in response to the so-called "China price" under a regime of sound money in the United States?

The Fed's Keynesian economists and their Wall Street megaphones would never breath a word of it, of course, because they have a vested interest in perpetuating inflation. It gives inflation-targeting central bankers the pretext for massive intrusion in the financial markets and Wall Street speculators endless bubble-finance windfalls.

But the truth is, a sound-money policy would have led to falling consumer prices, high interest rates and an upsurge of household savings in response to strong rewards for deferring current consumption. From that enhanced flow of honest domestic savings the supply side of the American economy could have been rebuilt with capital and technology designed to shrink costs and catalyze productivity.

But instead of consumer price deflation and a savings-based era of supply-side reinvestment, the Greenspan Fed opted for a comprehensive inflation regime. That is, sustained inflation of consumer prices and nominal wages, massive inflation of household debt and stupendous inflation of financial assets.

To be sure, the double-talking Greenspan actually bragged about his prowess in generating something he called "disinflation." But that's a weasel word. What he meant, in fact, was that the purchasing power of increasingly higher (and therefore increasingly more uncompetitive) nominal American wages was being reduced slightly less rapidly than it had been in the 1980s.

Still, the consumer price level has more than doubled since 1987, meaning that prices of goods and services have risen at 2.5% per year on average even on the BLS's downwardly biased reckoning. Notwithstanding all the Fed's palaver about "low-flation" and undershooting its phony 2.00% target, American workers have had to push their nominal wages higher and higher just to keep up with the cost of living.

But in a free-trade economy the wage-price inflation treadmill of the Greenspan Fed was catastrophic. It drove a wider and wider wedge between nominal U.S. wage rates and the marginal source of goods and services in the global economy.

That is, U.S. production was originally off-shored owing to the China price with respect to manufactured goods. But with the passage of time and spread of the central bank driven global credit boom, goods and services were off-shored to places all over the EM.

The high nominal price of U.S. labor enabled the India price, for example, to capture massive amounts of call-center activity, engineering and architectural-support services, financial company back-office activity and much more.

At the end of the day, it was the Greenspan Fed that hollowed out the American economy. Without the massive and continuous inflation it injected into the U.S. economy represented by the 120% rise in domestic prices since 1987, nominal wages would have been far lower, and on the margin far more competitive with offshore wages.

That's because there is a significant cost-per-labor-hour premium for offshoring. The 12,000 mile supply pipeline gives rise to heavy transportation charges, logistics control and complexity, increased inventory carry in the supply chain, quality-control and reputation-protection expenses, lower average productivity per worker, product-delivery and interruption risk and much more.

In a sound-money economy of falling nominal wages and even more rapidly falling consumer prices, American workers would have had a fighting chance to remain competitive, given this significant offshoring premium.

But the demand-side Keynesians running policy at the Fed and U.S. treasury didn't even notice that their wage-and price-inflation policy functioned to override the offshoring premium and to thereby send American production and jobs fleeing abroad.

Indeed, they actually managed to twist this heavy outflow of goods and services production into what they claimed to be an economic-welfare gain in the form of higher corporate profits and lower consumer costs.

Needless to say, the basic law of economics—Say's law of supply— says societal welfare and wealth arise from production; spending and demand follow output and income.

By contrast, our Keynesian central bankers claim prosperity flows from spending. So they had a ready (but phony) solution for the gap in household consumer spending that initially resulted when jobs and incomes were sent off-shore.

The de facto solution of the Greenspan Fed was to supplant the organic spending power of lost production and wages with a simulacrum of demand issuing from an immense and continuous run-up of household debt. As we saw in Chapter 2, what had been a steady 75–80% ratio of household debt to wage and salary income before 1980 erupted to 220% by the time of Peak Debt in 2007.

The nexus between household-debt inflation and the explosion of Chinese imports is hard to miss. Today monthly Chinese imports are 75X larger than they were when Greenspan took office in August 1987.

At the same time, American households have buried themselves in debt, which has risen from $2.7 trillion in 1987 to $14.3 trillion at present. Even after the financial crisis and supposed resulting deleveraging, the household leverage ratio is still in the nosebleed section of history at 180% of wage and salary earnings.

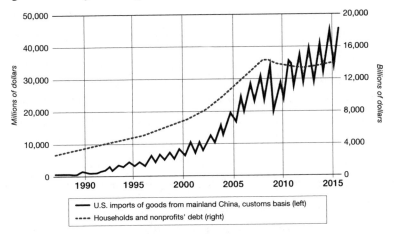

U.S. imports of goods from mainland China, customs basis (left)
Households and nonprofits' debt (right)

Stated differently, had the household-leverage ratio not been levitated in this nearly parabolic fashion, total household debt at the time of the financial crisis would have been $6 trillion, not $14 trillion.

In effect, the inflationary policies of the Greenspan Fed and its successors created a giant offshoring hole in the supply side of the U.S. economy, and then filled it with $8 trillion of incremental debt, which has now become a permanent albatross on the Main Street economy.

At the end of the day, the only policy compatible with Greenspan's inflationary monetary regime was reversion to completely managed trade and a shift to historically high tariffs on imported goods and services.

That would have dramatically slowed the off-shoring of production, and would also have remained faithful to the Great Thinker's economics. As we indicated earlier, in 1931 Keynes turned into a vociferous protectionist and even wrote an ode to the virtues of "homespun goods."

Alas, inflation in one country behind protective trade barriers doesn't work either, as was demonstrated during the inflationary spiral of the late 1960s and '70s. That's because in a closed economy surrounded by trade barriers, easy money does lead to a spiral of rising domestic wages and prices owing to too much credit-based spending; and this spiral eventually soars out of control in the absence of the discipline imposed by lower-priced foreign goods and services.

In perverse fashion, therefore, the Greenspan Fed operated a bread-and-circuses economy. Unlimited imports massively displaced domestic production and incomes—even as they imposed an upper boundary on the rate of CPI gains.

The China price for goods and India price for services, in effect, throttled domestic inflation and prevented a runaway inflationary spiral. The ever-increasing debt-funded U.S. household demand for goods and services, therefore, was channeled on the margin into import purchases that drew on virtually unlimited labor and production supply available from the rice paddies and agricultural villages of the emerging market (EM) economies.

In a word, the Fed's monetary inflation was exported.

Free trade also permitted many companies to fatten their profits by arbitraging the wedge between Greenspan's inflated wages in the U.S. and the rice paddy wages of the EM. Indeed, the alliance of the Business Roundtable, the Keynesian Fed and Wall Street speculators in behalf of free money and free trade is one of history's most destructive arrangements of convenience.

In any event, the graph below nails the story. During the 29 years since Greenspan took office, the nominal wages of domestic production workers have soared, rising from $9.22 per hour in August 1987 to $21.26 per hour at present. It was this 2.3X leap in nominal wages, of course, that sent jobs packing for China, India and the EM.

At the same time, the inflation-adjusted wages of domestic workers who did retain their jobs went nowhere at all. That's right. There were tens of millions of jobs off-shored, but in constant dollars of purchasing power, the average production-worker wage of $383 per week in mid-1987 has ended up at $380 per week 29 years later.

And that's based on the Fed's understated inflation. Based on the Fly-over CPI, real wages have declined substantially since 1987.

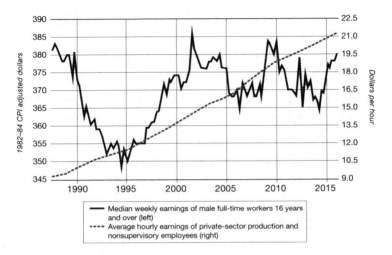

By contrast, during the span of that 29-year period the Fed's balance sheet grew from $200 billion to $4.5 trillion. That's a 23X gain during less than an average working lifetime.

Greenspan claimed he was the nation's savior for getting the CPI inflation rate down to around 2% during his tenure; and Bernanke and Yellen have postured as would-be saviors owing to their strenuous money-pumping efforts to keep it from failing the target from below.

But 2% inflation is a fundamental Keynesian fallacy, and the massive central bank balance-sheet explosion that fueled it is the greatest monetary travesty in history.

Dunderheads like Bernanke and Yellen say 2% inflation is just fine, because under their benign monetary management everything comes out in the wash at the end—wages, prices, rents, profits, living costs and indexed social benefits all march higher together with tolerable leads and lags.

No they don't. Jobs in their millions march away to the offshore world when nominal wages double—even though the purchasing power of the dollar is cut in half over 29 years.

These academic fools apparently believe they live in Keynes' imaginary homespun economy of 1931!

The evident economic distress in Flyover America and among the Trump voters now arising from it in their tens of millions are telling establishment policy makers that they are full of it; that they have had enough of free trade and free money.

But this is all a historical travesty. The immediate issue is, what can be done now to wind-back the clock?

The solution lies in the counterfactual to the Greenspan/Fed Inflation Regime. Under sound money, the balance sheet of the Fed would still be $200 billion, household debt would be a fraction of its current level, the CPI would have shrunk 1–2% per year rather than the opposite and nominal wages would have shrunk by slightly less.

Under those circumstances, there would have been no explosion of U.S. imports because U.S. suppliers would have remained far more competitive and domestic demand for imported goods and services far more subdued. To wit, what amounts to a statistical Trump Tower in our trade accounts—where total imports exploded by 6X—couldn't have happened under a regime of sound money.

For instance, if the CPI had shrunk by 1.5% annually since 1987 and nominal wages by 0.5%, the average nominal production wage today would be $8 per hour, meaning that American labor would be dramatically more competitive in the world economy versus the EM price than it currently is at $22 per hour.

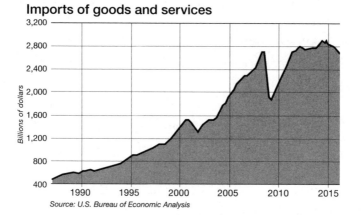

Imports of goods and services

Source: U.S. Bureau of Economic Analysis

But real wages would be nearly one-third higher at $500 per week compared to the actual of $380 per week shown above (1982 $). At the same time, solid breadwinner jobs in both goods and services would be far more plentiful than reported currently by the BLS.

Needless to say, the clock cannot be turned back, and a resort to Keynes' out-and-out protectionism in the context of an economy that suckles on nearly $3 trillion of annual goods and services imports is a non-starter. It would wreak havoc beyond imagination.

But it is not too late to attempt the second best in the face of the giant historical detour from sound money that has soured the practice of free trade. To wit, public policy can undo some of the damage by sharply lowering the nominal price of domestic wages and salaries in order to reduce the cost wedge versus the rest of the world.

A BETTER ALTERNATIVE THAN PROTECTIONISM— ELIMINATE THE PAYROLL TAX WEDGE ON THE COST OF AMERICAN LABOR

It is currently estimated that during 2016 federal social insurance levies on employers and employees will add a staggering $1.1 trillion to the U.S. wage bill. Most of that represents Social Security and Medicare payroll taxes.

The single greatest things that could be done to shrink the Greenspan/ Fed nominal-wage wedge, therefore, is to rapidly phase out all federal payroll taxes, and thereby dramatically improve the terms of U.S. labor trade with China and the rest of the EM world. Given that the nation's total wage bill (including benefit costs) is about $10 trillion, elimination of federal payroll taxes would amount to an 11% cut in the cost of U.S. labor.

On the one hand, such a bold move would dramatically elevate Main Street take-home pay, owing to the fact that half of the payroll tax levy is extracted from worker pay packets in advance. In the case of a Rust Belt industrial worker making $25 per hour, for example, it would amount to an additional $4,000 per year in take home pay.

Moreover, elimination of payroll taxes would be far more efficacious from a political point of view in Trump's Flyover America constituencies than traditional Reaganite income tax rate cuts. That's because nearly 160 million Americans pay social insurance taxes compared to fewer than 50 million who actually pay any net federal income taxes after deductions and credits.

At the same time, elimination of the employer share of federal payroll taxes would reduce the direct cost of labor to domestic business by upwards of $575 billion per year. And as we have proposed in the Jobs Deal, the simultaneous elimination of the corporate income tax would reduce the burden on business by another $350 billion annually.

By all fair accounts, the corporate income tax is the most irrational and unproductive element of the U.S. tax code. But as I learned working on its replacement as a young aide on Capitol Hill in the early 1970s, it gets demagogued by the political left and harvested for loopholes by the K-Street lobbies in a never-ending and pointless legislative joust.

Therefore, when you hear mainstream politicians talking about reforming or cutting the corporate tax rate because it is the highest in the world, yawn. The nominal rate is 35% but the effective rate averages under 20% and last quarter the likes of IBM posted a negative rate.

Indeed, during the eight years ending in 2014, nearly two-thirds of U.S. corporations paid no taxes at all. That's why the corporate income tax—which generates barely $350 billion in receipts per year—is better understood to be the lawyers, accountants, consultants and K-Street lobby full employment act

Needless to say, that is a mighty force of inertia, and in that sense is emblematic of why the status quo is failing. It is no secret that the corporate tax has always posed an insuperable challenge to match business income and expense during any arbitrary tax period, but that in a globalized economy in which capital is infinitely mobile on paper, as well as in fact, the attempt to collect corporate-profits taxes in one country has become pointless and impossible.

It simply gives rise to massive accounting and legal maneuvers such as the headline-grapping tax inversions of recent years. Yet notwithstanding 75,000 pages of IRS code and multiples more of that in tax rulings and litigation, corporate tax departments will always remain one step ahead of the IRS.

That is, the corporate tax generates immense deadweight economic costs and dislocation—including a huge boost to off-shoring of production to low-tax havens—while generating a meager harvest of actual revenues. Last year, for example, corporate tax collections amounted to just 1.8% of GDP compared to upwards of 9% during the heyday of the American industrial economy during the 1950s.

By pairing the elimination of the corporate tax with a giant increase in worker take-home pay, however, Donald Trump might actually make some progress where the GOP has tilted at windmills for decades.

Needless to say, you don't have to be a believer in supply-side miracles to agree that a nearly $1 trillion tax cut on American business from the elimination of payroll and corporate income taxes would amount to the mother of all jobs-stimulus programs!

Self-evidently, the approximate $1.5 trillion revenue loss at the federal level from eliminating these taxes would need to be replaced. We are not advocating any Laffer Curve miracles here—although over time the re-shoring of jobs that would result from this 11% labor tax cut would surely generate a higher rate of growth than the anemic 1.6% annual real GDP growth rate the nation has experienced since the turn of the century.

It is not my purpose to delve into the details of the giant tax swap proposed here. But suffice it to say that with $3 trillion of imported goods and services and $10 trillion of total household consumption, the thing to tax would be exactly what we have too much of and which is the invalid fruit of inflationary monetary policy in the first place.

To wit, the foregone payroll- and corporate-tax revenue should be extracted from imports, consumption and foreign oil. An approximate 15% value-added tax on roughly $9 trillion of final-consumption spending (assuming medical care and other necessities are exempted) would generate about $1.4 trillion per year and fall heavily on imported goods.

The balance of the $1.5 trillion revenue loss could be recouped via a variable levy designed to peg landed petroleum prices at $85 per barrel. That would generate about $100 billion, assuming world oil prices average $35 per barrel in the period immediately ahead.

At the same time, a variable levy on petroleum (and other energy) imports would establish an $85 per BOE price umbrella under which domestic shale, alternative energy and conservation could thrive in response to domestic prices that were guaranteed to remain in place, and not be whipsawed by short-run volatility in crude market prices.

Such a price-driven scheme would also permit the cancellation of the massive array of green- and black-energy subsidies, tax credits and guarantees that give rise to far more crony-capitalist waste and corruption than they do competitive energy.

CHAPTER 6:

America's Rolling LBO and Why There Have Been No Breadwinner Job Gains Since the Year 2000

I N EFFECT, AMERICA HAS UNDERGONE A ROLLING NATIONAL LEVERAGED buy-out (LBO) since the Gipper's time in office. It is the result of the Washington and Wall Street policy consensus in favor of permanent deficit finance, stock market–centered "trickle-down" stimulus by the Fed and massive borrowing by the household and business sectors of the private economy.

So the U.S. economy is now stuck in the ditch because it has lever-aged itself to the hilt over the past three decades. The vast majority of Americans are no longer living the dream because Wall Street speculators and Washington politicians alike have led them into a debt-fueled fantasy world that is coming to a dead end.

Indeed, this deformation has been long in the making and reaches back nearly a half-century. To wit, once the Federal Reserve was liberated from the yoke of Bretton Woods and the redeemability of dollars for gold by Nixon's folly at Camp David in August 1971, financial history broke into an altogether new channel.

As shown in the chart on the next page, since 1971 total public and private debt outstanding soared from $1.6 trillion to $64 trillion or by 40X. By contrast, nominal GDP expanded by only 16X. The very visage of the chart tells you that the former is crushing the latter.

Accordingly, the nation's leverage ratio soared from its historical groove around 1.5X GDP to 3.5X GDP. That's massive; it's two extra turns of debt on national income. At the old pre-1971 ratio, which had been proved by a century of prosperity, total debt outstanding today would be only $29 trillion.

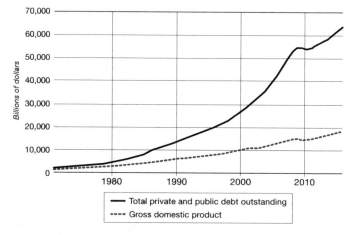

This means the American economy is now lugging around about $35 trillion of extra debt. Yet the consequences of this epic debt binge are unequivocal, and they refute entirely the reigning Keynesian presumption that debt is the magic tonic of prosperity.

To the contrary, as documented below the trend rate of real GDP growth has been heading steadily and dramatically lower since the 1960s. More debt ultimately means less growth, not more.

In this context, the period between 1953 and 1971 was the modern golden age. During that span the nation's leverage ratio hugged closed to the 1.5X historic constant and real GDP growth averaged 3.8% per annum.

Moreover, there was no acceleration of the leverage ratio in that interval, meaning there was no temporary boost to spending derived from higher credit extensions rather than current production and income. Accordingly, living standards rose strongly. Real median family income increased from $33,000 to $54,000 (2014 $) or by 2.8% annually.

On the eve of Nixon's Camp David follies in Q2 1971, and after this long interval of debt-free growth, total debt outstanding amounted to just $1.7 trillion. This compared to GDP of $1.16 trillion, meaning that the national leverage ratio stood at 1.47X—right in the heart of its historical channel.

During the next three decades there occurred the inflationary money-printing era of the 1970s and the rise of the Greenspan easy-money and wealth-effects policies after 1987. Consequently, debt grew explosively and the national leverage ratio climbed to unprecedented heights. By Q4 2000, total debt outstanding had soared to $28.6 trillion or to 2.73X the $10.5 trillion annual rate of GDP generated during that quarter.

Yet even as the nation's debt ratio was soaring, the rate of real GDP growth slowed only modestly to 3.2% per annum. That's because the sharp, one-time upward ratchet of the nation's leverage ratio—the first stage of its LBO—did goose the growth rate by fueling household consumption by means of a massive gain in mortgage debt.

Greenspan proudly called this MEW or "mortgage equity withdrawal." He argued that by extracting cash from their castles and using the proceeds for trips to the auto-dealer lots, home-improvement centers and Disneyworld, households were elevating their consumption levels and trigging a virtuous cycle of higher production, employment, output and wealth.

Not exactly. Having evolved from a gold bug to an ersatz Keynesian during his years in Washington, Greenspan was dead wrong about the allegedly virtuous cycle of debt. Some meaningful share of the 3.2% GDP growth during that three-decade period was simply stolen from the future, and it's not hard to see that the latter has already arrived.

The nation's self-LBO was completed during the next 7 years. Total debt outstanding rose by a staggering $25 trillion to $53.6 trillion during that brief interval, but the expansion of nominal GDP was far more subdued. The latter rose by just $4.4 trillion to $14.8 trillion.

That meant the Keynesian parlor trick was rapidly losing its potency. The national leverage ratio did get boosted from 2.73X to 3.61X during the final seven-year Greenspan/Bernanke credit party, but self-evidently it generated far less incremental GDP.

To wit, during the 1971 to 2000 period about $27 trillion of debt growth generated $9 trillion of nominal GDP growth, representing a 3:1 ratio. By contrast, during the final 7 years of the Fed's debt bubble, the ratio of new debt to GDP soared to just under 6:1.

But that wasn't all. Even as it was taking more and more debt to generate a dollar of nominal income, the growth rate of real GDP was slowing further.

On a peak-to-peak basis between Q4 2000 and Q4 2007, real GDP growth averaged only 2.4% per year. The inevitable distortions, inefficiencies, misallocations and malinvestments generated by credit-fueled growth were already catching up.

For all practical purposes, Peak Debt arrived during the final credit blowoff in 2007–2008. Since then, total debt outstanding has grown by another $10 trillion to $64 trillion, but the nation's leverage ratio has stabilized in the nosebleed section of history at 3.5X national income.

Here's the thing. The U.S. economy is now deep in the payback phase of the great central bank credit bubble. Nominal growth of household spending now depends on current production and income; the Keynesian parlor trick of goosing consumption today by borrowing from the future is over and done.

And since Keynesians believe that household consumption is the driving force of the economy, they are at an especially acute dead end. As we saw in Chapter 2, households not only reached Peak Debt in 2007–2008; they have been slowly ratcheting downward their leverage ratios of debt-to-wage and -salary income ever since.

What had been stolen from the future is now being given back. Consumers could not shop the nation to prosperity—even if they wanted to.

Accordingly, real GDP has grown at only a 1.2% rate per annum since Q4 2007. That's just 31% of the 3.8% annual growth rate generated during 1953–1971 by a U.S. economy that had adhered to the historic leverage mean of 1.5X.

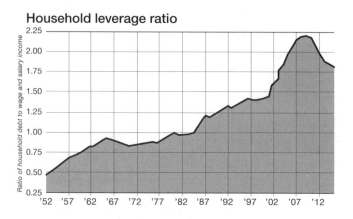

Household leverage ratio

THE GREENSPAN ERA DEBT BINGE—
WRONG ROAD TAKEN

Needless to say, policymakers of the golden era—most especially Fed Chairman William McChesney Martin, President Eisenhower, and even John Kennedy's Treasury Department——did not believe that rising debt was the keystone to prosperity. They feared it, and looked to the enterprise of business and labor on the free market to generate growth and prosperity.

As is clear from the above, the real debt surge began when Greenspan took office in August 1987, and that's also when Bubble Finance got stood up as national policy.

Indeed, in response to the infamous 25% stock market crash of October 1987, shortly after his arrival at the Eccles Building, the purported financial Maestro launched the nation's central bank down the road of chronic easy money and massive monetary intrusion in the financial markets.

The fruit of that wrong-headed monetary path is straightforward. There was just $11 trillion of total credit market debt—government, household, business and finance—outstanding at the time Greenspan discovered the printing presses in the basement of the Eccles Building. That small mountain of debt has grown by a staggering $53 trillion during the years since then.

That five-fold debt gain in less than a generation represents a radical discontinuity from the past history of American capitalism.

In fact, for more than a century after U.S. industrialization really took-off during the 1870s, in fact, the ratio of total public and private debt to national income held steady at about 150%. And that was true with only slight variations during periods of boom and bust, as well as war and peace.

That modest amount of economy-wide leverage might well be considered the golden mean. During the century ending in 1970, the US standard of living rose 20-fold and the nation's economy grew like nothing before it in the history of the planet.

No longer. As shown in the chart on the next page, the trend rate of real GDP growth has dropped by a stunning 70%.

During the rising phase of this debt eruption, of course, the U.S. economy had quite a party. During the 1990s and for a time prior to 2007 these massive borrowings goosed consumption spending in the household sector and fixed asset investment in business.

But then the due bill arrived at the time of the great financial crisis. Since the last peak in December 2007, real national output has crawled forward at just 1.2% per annum based on Washington's faulty inflation gauges, and hardly at all based on the true rate of inflation as measured by our Flyover CPI.

Needless to say, the mainstream narrative amounts to a studied attempt to obfuscate the dramatic seven-decade-long southward journey depicted in the gray bars of the chart below. That's because the political, financial and media elites who shape the news and public dialogue are essentially anti-historical incrementalists.

They operate from headlines and short-term deltas. They boast about the gains from last month and last quarter but never explain or take accountability for the periodic financial and economic collapses that have sharply lowered average or trend rates of economic growth and living-standard gains since 1987.

Worse still, the elite narrative bamboozles the public with recency bias. You would never know that the startling uphill climb depicted in the red line of the chart even happened.

The great inversion
GDP growth rate vs. national leverage ratio

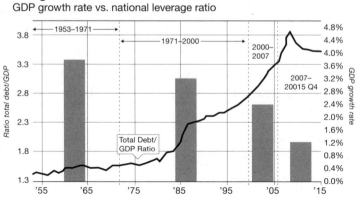

Nor do the talking heads of Wall Street or the spokesmen and apologists for the Fed ever acknowledge that the current 3.5X ratio of debt to income is an unprecedented and dangerous departure from the 1.5X historic norm. Yet the latter stalwart feature of the financial system was still firmly in place as recently as 1971.

Even as the chart captures the sweeping deterioration that has beset the nation's economic fundamentals, that outcome is not due to some inherent flaw of capitalism. The above baleful development is the modern state at work; it's the product of the elite consensus about money printing, financialization, perpetual Washington stimulus and bailouts and the cult of the stock market.

Not surprisingly, the same media and groupthink commentariat that was utterly surprised and shocked by the rise of Trump and Bernie has no clue either about the nation's debilitating LBO and the reverse Robin Hood redistribution that it has foisted upon the American economy.

Much of the elites actually think that Obama's ballyhooed 78 straight months of jobs growth and high stock markets is evidence that the U.S. economy has been fixed, and that the chilling financial crisis of 2008 was just some aberrational bump in the road.

No it wasn't. The meltdown of 2008 was just spring training for what comes next.

As we indicated previously, the purpose of this book is to debunk these establishment fairy-tales, and to thereby explain the deep economic predicate for the rise of Donald Trump in particular and the growing anti-establishment sentiments of the American public generally.

Equally importantly, it aims to document the extent and the causes of the financial and economic rot that has descended on the US economy, and to provide a fundamental roadmap for its amelioration.

Whether Donald Trump has any affinity for some or all of these measures remains to be seen, as he alternates between statist curveballs and capitalist pronunciations from one day to the next. But if he does reach the White House, at least the architects of America's ruinous policy-inflicted LBO will find themselves pounding the pavement in search of a new line of work.

NO REAL JOB GAINS SINCE THE TURN OF THE CENTURY

Exhibit number one in the indictment of Washington and Wall Street policy consensus is the fact that there has not been a single additional breadwinner job created in America since the turn of the century.

Not one!

In fact, one-and-one-half million of these jobs has been lost on a net basis. There were 71.2 million full-time, full-pay breadwinner jobs reported by the BLS for June 2016 compared to 72.7 million back when Bill Clinton was packing his bags to vacate the White House.

The jobs we are referring to here generate about $50,000 per year in cash compensation and for the most part are year-around 40-hour-per-week jobs. They extend from the manufacturing, construction, energy and mining sectors to a wide expanse of the so-called service economy. The latter encompasses finance, insurance and real estate, technology and communications, warehousing and distribution, transportation, the white-collar professions, business management and support services and the core government sector outside of education.

All that, and no net new job gains in 16 years.

And that's not the half of it. This wipeout also comes after a mind-boggling full-court press of "stimulus" by the nation's economic rulers. The nation's public debt soared from $5.5 trillion to nearly $20 trillion during that period, while the Federal Reserve's balance sheet exploded by 9X.

That's right. Every dollar of growth in the Fed's balance sheet is another dollar of fiat credit conjured from thin air and injected into the financial system. But not withstanding $4 trillion of such "stimulus" since the turn of the century, there is not one new breadwinner job.

The establishment's excuses for that stunning failure are intellectually bogus, even farcical. The hard-core Keynesian academics like Professor Paul Krugman say that these empty results are for want of not doing more.

Apparently, if Uncle Sam had increased the public debt to $40 trillion, and had the Fed printed $8 trillion of new money, America would be rolling in real breadwinner jobs. And if that didn't do the trick, why, just go for a tripling or quadrupling. After all, when you have the revealed truth from J.M. Keynes himself, you can never dispense enough of it.

The more pragmatic apologists for the Wall Street and Washington debt and money-printing extravaganza of the last 16 years are even more ludicrous. They claim it's all a matter of patience and more time. The "headwinds" are supposedly now finally abating and "escape velocity" is just around the corner.

Let's see. This is the third-longest business recovery in American history, and before the next president is sworn in, it will be 92 months old compared to a postwar average of 61 months. So the truth of the matter is that time is the enemy, not the excuse. The business cycle clock is about ready to run-out of gas again, and still no breadwinner job gains.

Actually, it's worse. In a healthy economy, breadwinner jobs would have been growing at 2% per year since the turn of the century. There would be 100 million of them today—a gain of 29 million relative to the flat line shown in the chart below.

Breadwinner economy

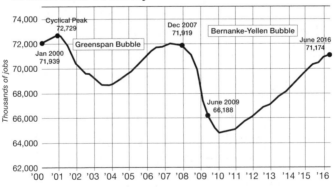

Needless to say, the policy elite's pettifoggery that suffices on the *New York Times* op-ed pages and bubblevision has fooled no one on Main Street. Working folks know that the establishment's debt-and-money-printing bacchanalia has been an absolute failure because there are no good jobs.

They also know that the triple-digit gains reported by the BLS nearly every month and celebrated in the financial media are essentially a propaganda hoax.

These "jobs" consist entirely of transient low-pay jobs in the part-time economy and low-productivity jobs in the HES Complex (health, education and social services). Main Street knows that these gigs are all that's available and that you can't earn a real living or support a family on most of the 72 million positions that comprise these categories.

Even then, there is less to the reported monthly gains than meets the eye. That's because the serial booms and busts triggered by the Federal Reserve have badly yo-yo'd the employment cycle and sharply diminished the level of permanent job growth.

To wit, since January 2000, the BLS has reported gross monthly job gains of 20.6 million, but 7.4 million or 36% of these were "born-again" jobs. That is, they were put on the BLS monthly scoreboard, lost during the two recessions since the turn of the century, and then counted again during the subsequent recoveries.

As we will demonstrate more fully later on, the quality of these born-again jobs has also deteriorated badly. But even giving full credit to busboy, bellhop, bartender and other limited-hours-per-week gigs, the net jobs gain amounts to just 13.2 million or 66,000 per month since the year 2000.

That's just 36% of the 180,000 per month growth of the nonretired adult population during the period. Tens of millions of potential workers have simply slipped into the shadows of welfare, dependency and hand-to-mouth subsistence.

So let it be said clearly. Even as the Wall Street and Washington elites were prospering mightily from soaring government borrowing and a radically inflated stock and bond market, this policy has been a jobs disaster for Main Street America.

In fact, the propagandistic excuses and obfuscations made for this patent failure are so analytically threadbare and mendacious as to make Donald Trump sound like an intellectual powerhouse by comparison.

THE "CARRIER" VOTE AND THE TRUTH ABOUT JOBS

Among the many surprising twists during the GOP primaries was the fact that Trump not only won the GOP nomination, but locked it up early and essentially did so in the Indiana primary.

That was supposed to be Senator Cruz's last stand. But in hindsight, the conventional rightwing senator from Texas ended up getting blown away by the "Carrier" vote. United Technology's plan to move its air conditioner factory to Mexico became Donald Trump's whipping boy, and the metaphor had deep resonance.

And for good reason. Since the year 2000, the United States has lost 5 million of its highest paying full-time jobs in the goods producing economy—that is, energy and mining, construction and manufacturing. Indiana was just Flyover America writ large.

At the turn of the century, there were 24.7 million goods-producing jobs, but then a devastating counter-cycle began. After the 2002–2007 Greenspan housing boom there were only 22 million such jobs, marking a 11% decline in the midst of what was claimed by the mainstream media to be an awesome "Goldilocks" business cycle expansion.

And then it got still worse. Notwithstanding endless crowing by the White House and Fed about a huge jobs recovery, there were only 19.6 million goods-producing jobs in June 2016. That amounted to another 11% decline in the midst of what the Washington and Wall Street elite claim to be a solid recovery.

In all, that's a 21% shrinkage since the turn of the century. Yet since the fount of productivity and efficiency gains in any economy is goods production, it is not surprising that U.S. productivity growth has nearly ground to a halt.

The mainstream pundits did not see this coming, of course, because they are beguiled by the false Keynesian consensus about the U.S. economy—whether they acknowledge it or not.

To wit, Greenspan-era monetary policy has not rescued the American economy from crisis, recession and underperformance. To the contrary, it has actually hollowed it out by facilitating the vast off-shoring of goods production and supplanting it with a phony, unsustainable debt-based simulacrum of prosperity and growth.

Indeed, the chart on the next page does not represent a miracle of capitalism owing to technology and automation, as the Cassandras of the establishment narrative contend. Instead, it reflects the betrayal of capitalism by the money printers, statists and gamblers who have hijacked national policy.

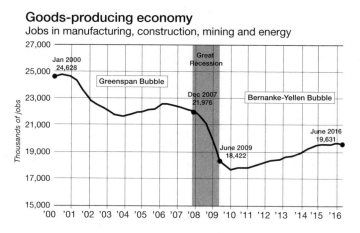

Goods-producing economy
Jobs in manufacturing, construction, mining and energy

Even then, the above dismal picture is rationalized by the Fed and its Wall Street megaphones as unimportant owing to mix change. These higher paying "old-economy" jobs have supposedly shifted to white-collar employment in finance, technology, entertainment and other domestic services.

No they haven't! As indicated earlier, there are still nearly 1.5 million fewer full-time, full-pay "breadwinner jobs" in the United States today than in January 2001.

In fact, the 71.2 million jobs currently in this category—which, as enumerated above, includes all of the full-time, full-pay sectors in the service economy—account for just half of the establishment payroll jobs reported in the BLS monthly survey.

As indicated, these are mostly year-around 40-hour-per-week jobs that pay an equivalent annual wage of $50,000 on average. More importantly, they account for upwards of two-thirds of the actual payroll dollar disbursements in the nonfarm economy.

To be sure, even the average "breadwinner job" at $50,000 per year is not evidence of galloping affluence. But these jobs are the best of what we have, and the total has been going nowhere for the last decade and a half, even as the adult population (over 16 years) has risen from 212 million to 252 million.

Yes, roughly 8 million of that adult-population gain represents baby boomers that have joined the Social Security rolls. But that leaves 32 million more potential workers and no net gain in breadwinner jobs at all.

Stated differently, the Trump voters don't watch CNBC. Or if they do, they are savvy enough to dismiss its specious celebration of America's phony bicoastal prosperity and especially the monotonously stupid and profoundly misleading ritual of "Jobs Friday."

The voters know from experience that those millions of "new jobs" are mainly part-time gigs that come and go between the financial crashes. The latter, in turn, arise every seven years or so out of the machinations of Wall Street, Washington and the Fed.

According to the Keynesian commentariat, of course, these low-quality, low-pay, bread-and-circuses jobs are no different than any others. Even if the generated only 10 or 20 hours per week of minimum-wage work, it's all part of the jobs "print."

So they appear on bubblevision each month to urge the rubes to buy stocks because the Fed is making everything all better. But it's a huge lie. The underlying reality is that the American jobs market continues to deteriorate at an alarming pace.

The Trump voters presumably are not sufficiently educated to understand all this—or to recognize that most of the employment slots that the BLS guesstimates from its deeply flawed surveys and models are not remotely comparable.

Whether the BLS headline is comprised of minimum-wage maids at the Plaza Hotel or $30-per-hour set-up men on the former Carrier air conditioner line in Indiana supposedly doesn't matter. It's all good, according to their Keynesian betters.

In fact, of the paltry net gain of just 5.8 million new payroll jobs since the December 2007 precrisis peak nine years ago, nearly 2 million (or fully one-third) of the jobs have been in bars, restaurants, hotels, sports stadiums and amusement parks.

These jobs average less than 27 hours per week and pay an average of less than $15 per hour. They would generate an annual wage of barely

$20,000 per year if they were year-around jobs, which they most definitely are not.

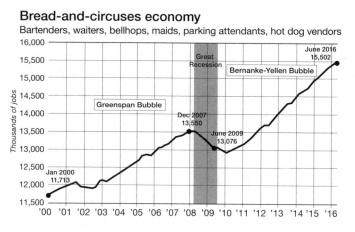

Bread-and-circuses economy
Bartenders, waiters, bellhops, maids, parking attendants, hot dog vendors

Nor is this just some temporary aberration from the Great Recession that is still being worked out. In fact, during this entire century to date, only 13.2 million net new payroll jobs have been created, but 5.4 million of them have been in the broader part-time economy. The latter includes the above leisure and hospitality jobs, as well as retail clerks, temp-agency workers and low-wage service labor.

So not only is there a severe and growing jobs deficit, but 41% of all the net payroll jobs created since the year 2000 are low-wage gigs that come and go with the season and the cycle, not "jobs" as they word was once understood.

The not-so-secret reality is that Trump voters have gotten stuck in these dead-end jobs or fear they will end up there or have friends and family who have no other options.

Needless to say, America's 40 million part-timers know they are not winning; they are barely staying above the water line of economic survival.

Given these realities, the phony charade of Jobs Friday is especially galling to the Flyover America. It is an excuse for the casino gamblers to inflate stock prices even further, and for White House politicians like the current incumbent to brag about the purported success of their economic stewardship.

But the Trump voters have not been fooled. They know the American economy is failing and that they have been left behind. And they also can clearly see that Washington's massive borrowing and spending programs and the Fed's monumental free-money gifts to Wall Street have done nothing at all to ameliorate their plight.

Part time economy

Bartenders, waiters, bellops, maids, shoe repair, retail clerks & temp help payrate=$20k/yr.

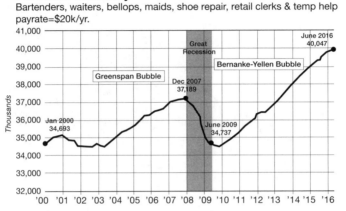

Indeed, the ultimate measure of labor-market health in a globally integrated economy and gig-based employment system is total hours worked. Even setting aside the fact that the quality of these hours has deteriorated and real pay rates have declined, the actual trend is dismal.

Since the turn of the century, labor hours in the nonfarm economy have advanced at an anemic rate of just 0.4% annually. That is only one-fourth of the 2.0% rate, which prevailed during the prior 16 years.

Needless to say, that radical downshift is not due to demographics. As we have seen, the adult working age population has actually grown by 32 million since the year 2000.

At the same time, it puts the lie to the alleged virtuous circle of Keynesian stimulus. There has been no effective pump priming of consumption, production, incomes and jobs.

Indeed, the Fed's balance sheet has grown by 900% during the last 16 years, while the cumulative rise in annual labor hours has been only 6.7%.

That contrast is stunning, and even if it doesn't fully grasp the technical facts, Flyover America has no doubt that the system is rigged in favor of the bicoastal elites. After all, when the production of money comes in at 135 times the amount of new work, you don't need a PhD from the Princeton economics department to see that the economics game in America is no longer on the level.

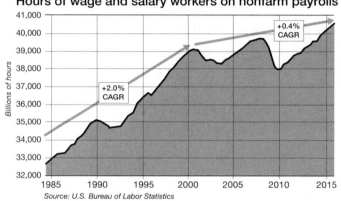

Hours of wage and salary workers on nonfarm payrolls

Source: U.S. Bureau of Labor Statistics

CHAPTER 7:

Falling Backwards in Flyover America— Why Real Household Income Is Down 21% Since 2000

GIVEN THESE DISMAL REALITIES OF THE JOB MARKET IT IS NOT SURPRISING that median household incomes have been heading south for several decades.

In fact, constant dollar median household income—based on an accurate measure of inflation—is down 21% since the turn of the century. Working Middle America has never before had such a deep and sustained setback—even during the Great Depression.

The drastic deterioration of middle class living standards depicted below, of course, is heatedly denied by the ruling elites. Yet their disavowal is based on the flagrant manipulation of the inflation data by the BLS based on a pseudo-science called "hedonics."

Supposedly, this adjustment to the actual sticker price of goods and services takes account of "quality" improvements like airbags on autos, and higher speeds and functionality on computers. Then again, candy bars get smaller, fast food gets less nutritious, retail purchases—including online commerce—require more unpaid self-service labor and Chinese-made toasters go to the junk heap far faster than such appliances did decades ago.

Never mind. Hedonics was never meant to be scientific or balanced. In fact, it was a back door ruse to trim the cost of Social Security and other entitlement COLA's concocted by Alan Greenspan and George H.W. Bush's chief economists back in the 1990s. They accomplished by statistical stealth the Social Security cuts that Ronald Reagan failed to obtain in the open arena of legislative action during the 1980s.

Consequently, the BLS' inflation measuring stick has become increasingly inaccurate. This hedonics distortion has been further compounded by the underweighting and mismeasurement of the four horsemen of inflation—food, energy, housing and medical—that absorb the preponderant share of Main Street paychecks.

As detailed below, those systemic errors have been remedied in what we call the Flyover CPI. When median household incomes are deflated by this more accurate cost-of-living index, the reason that Main Street feels it is being left behind becomes starkly evident.

In a word, the purchasing power of its wages and savings is being eviscerated. What had been $68,000 in today's purchasing power at the turn of the century is barely $55,000 today.

So when Donald Trump tells voters that the system is rigged, they have solid reason to concur. When he proclaims that America isn't winning anymore, they know he's talking about them.

And, yes, when he talks about the crooked establishment he strikes a chord, as well. Rigging the inflation rate with a sawed-off ruler may put lipstick on the official data, but it does not change the truth of steadily shrinking living standards on Main Street America.

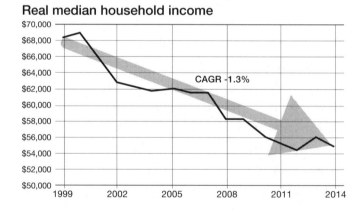

Real median household income

CAGR -1.3%

WHY INCOMES AND WAGES ARE FALLING IN FLY-OVER AMERICA

As we indicated, the persistent shrinkage of real wages and net worth in Flyover America is no accident or blemish of capitalism. It is a consequence of the Washington and Wall Street consensus in favor of printing press money, rock bottom interest rates and 2% inflation targeting. Together and at length, these misguided policies have buried Main Street households in inflation and debt.

Neither of these millstones is even acknowledged by the mainstream narrative because they have been essentially defined away. By the lights of the Fed and its Wall Street acolytes, in fact, debt has been christened a growth tonic while inflation is held to be a special form of monetary goodness that levitates economic output, incomes and jobs.

Alas, that's just plain old tommyrot. There is no case for siding with more inflation as a matter of policy and there is much history to warn us of the dangers of rampant debt.

With respect to the scourge of the ever escalating cost of living, the chart below tracks a modified CPI which includes the aforementioned heavier weights than the regular CPI for the four horsemen of inflation— food, energy, medical and housing. It also incorporates a more accurate measure of market-based medical costs and housing/shelter costs.

This "Flyover CPI" is a far more honest indicator of the actual cost of living pressures faced by Main Street households, therefore, than the sawed-off measuring rod used by the Fed called the PCE deflator less food and energy.

Needless to say, during the 29-year span since Alan Greenspan's arrival at the Fed in August 1987 most people have needed food, heating, transportation, shelter and medical care. The Flyover CPI based on an accurate measuring of those necessities has risen by 3.1% per year during that period.

That relentless rise in living costs has not slowed down since the turn of the century, as shown in the chart below. Yet compared to the 3.1% per annum gain in the actual cost of living in Flyover America since the year 2000, the Fed's favorite measure has risen by just 1.7% annual.

The wedge between these two inflation measures is not just a statistical curiosity; it's a big deal and a commentary on why the Washington Beltway and Flyover America are two ships passing in the dark.

In fact, just since the turn of the century the actual cost of living on Main Street has risen by 40% more than acknowledged by the nation's purported guardians of price stability at the Federal Reserve. That the political class in Washington and the speculators on Wall Street, therefore, are clueless about the deep economic distress afflicting Main Street America is not at all surprising.

Flyover CPI vs. Core PCE

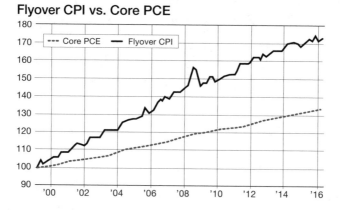

Indeed, this relentlessly increasingly cost of living explains the rise of Donald Trump more than anything else. The fact is, when the purchasing power of hourly wages is deflated by this honest measure of inflation, their buying power is 5% lower than it was 30 years ago. Wage earners are not winning anymore, not by a long shot.

This baleful condition is directly attributable to the Washington and Wall Street policy regime. That's because the Keynesian central banking model adopted at the Fed after 1987 had it exactly upside down.

At the time and ever since, the dominant new force in the world economy has been export mercantilism in Asia and elsewhere. As we demonstrated in Chapter 5, the eruption of vast new industrial capacity drained the Asian rice paddies of cheap labor, thereby emitting unprecedented deflationary pressures on global wage rates.

In the face of the "China price" on goods and labor, what was needed in America, therefore, was the very opposite of what Washington's Keynesian academics and policy apparatchiks delivered. As we explained in Chapter 5, under a regime of free markets and sound money there would have been high interest rates, domestic wage and price deflation, high savings rates and massive reinvestment in the nation's aging capital stock.

Especially after Mr. Deng opened China's export drive by radically devaluing the yuan in 1994, the only way that real labor incomes could have risen in the US, in fact, is via a reduction in nominal wage rates offset by an even faster rate of annual decline in the CPI and other costs of production in the domestic economy.

THE KEYNESIAN MYTH OF "STICKY" WAGE RATES

Needless to say, the Keynesian academics who dominate the Fed and the monetary policy narrative cannot even fathom that possibility because they are enthrall to the ancient texts of JM Keynes, which proclaimed that nominal wages are inherently "sticky" and can't adjust downward like other economic prices.

That was pure claptrap during the 1930s and ever more so today. "Sticky" wages only happen when there are state enforced union monopolies and employers are precluded upon penalty of jail from offering lower nominal rates to any willing takers.

Stated differently, the "sticky" wages hypothesis is a purely political proposition, not an economic truth. It was opportunistically embraced by statist redistributionists and the union movement alike.

For the latter, it was a rationale for pure protectionism. For the former, it was a justification for workplace-originated income redistribution—and then for Washington- based monetary intervention to counteract the loss of jobs and production that is the inherent result of artificially high labor prices.

In truth, there is endless evidence that wages aren't sticky—notwithstanding the rearguard action of unions and labor law protectionism. For instance, the North American auto industry cut fully loaded auto plant wages from $60 per hour to $30 per hour when Toyota and the rest of the transplants established production in Kentucky, Alabama and other right-to-work states in the south.

Indeed, in the absence of NLRB protectionism and labor practice harassment, and then the $85 billion taxpayer bailout of the UAW auto plants in 2008–9, the lion's share of the U.S. auto industry would have moved from the Rust Belt to the South. Nominal wages would have been sharply reduced in the process.

The same is true with high wage unionized grocery stores. A huge share of the grocery store business has now migrated to the far lower nonunion hourly rates at Wal-Mart. Ditto for the migration of construction work from building trades union dominated firms to nonunion competitors.

At the end of the day, "sticky wages" is a euphemism for labor protectionism and the "sticky" allocation of production and resources. So from Greenspan forward, the Fed was busy fueling U.S. inflation and thereby undermining the competitiveness of domestic production and jobs on a theory that belongs in the museum of academic crackpottery.

As we indicated, the Fed's deliberate accommodation of steadily rising nominal wages led to off-shoring of jobs, not an expansion of real worker incomes. That is the driven driving force behind Donald Trump's apparent crude protectionism. So suffice to say that he is correct in insisting that Washington policy caused the hollowing out of the U.S. economy over the last 25 years.

For the most part, however, that was not owing to bad trade deals made by Washington. Instead, it was the inherent result of inflationary monetary policies. Under the latter, the Fed enabled domestic households and businesses to borrow at deeply subsidized, uneconomic rates and spend the proceeds on imports that were not being earned by American exports.

So the workers of Flyover America got the worst of both worlds. Taking the average nominal wage rate from $7 per hour to $22 per hour over the last 30 years resulted in a drastic loss of competitiveness and U.S. based goods-and-services production. At the same time, when nominal wage rates are deflated by the Flyover CPI, it is evident that their purchasing power has ended up 5% lower after 30 years of money printing at the Fed and massive Bubble Finance windfalls on Wall Street.

Real average hourly earnings
Production and nonsupervisory employees

In this context, there is another reason why the elites who make and communicate national policy couldn't be more wrong. Their wrong-headed Keynesian model not only embodies a bogus theory about wage rates but actually postulates that domestic inflation is a good thing.

We refer here to the Fed's 2.00% inflation target and the spurious claim from the Eccles Building and its Wall Street megaphones that there is actually a deficiency of inflation. In a world of the China price that is just plain asinine.

Worse still, it's based on the myth propagated by Bernanke and other modern Keynesians that nominal incomes among economic agents all march higher in lockstep as the central bank pursues its spurious 2.00% annual inflation targets.

In fact, there is no lockstep march or equitable inflation at all. The incomes and wealth of the bicoastal elites gain far more from financialization and asset inflation than they lose to the CPI, while stagnant nominal wages in the flyover zones are relentlessly squeezed by too much inflation in the cost of daily living.

In a word, today's central banking policy inflates Wall Street and punishes Main Street. One point of evidence for the latter is that new firms and jobs are not being created at a pace to keep up with growth in the working age population. Accordingly, the labor force participation rate has been falling for two decades, even as the value of financial assets has soared.

So Wall Street is winning and Flyover America is losing. There is a reason Donald Trump is resonating with the latter—and it's not just red neck racism and xenophobia, either.

It's the handiwork of the Washington and Wall Street corridor. Capitalist growth, dynamism and prosperity is being extinguished in America because it is being betrayed by a rogue central bank and the Washington politicians, Wall Street gamblers and tech-sector bubble riders who prosper from it.

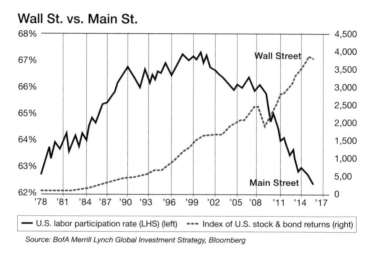

Wall St. vs. Main St.

Source: BofA Merrill Lynch Global Investment Strategy, Bloomberg

HOW FLYOVER AMERICA GOT BURIED IN DEBT

Worse still, the Fed's monetary central planners have no clue that high taxes, transfer payments and public debt undermine the economy's supply side incentives, productivity and capital efficiency. They assume, in effect, that consumption is the magic elixir of economic health and that any spending for that purpose will do.

In fact, the whole objective of interest rate repression is to induce households and businesses to leverage-up and spend at rates higher than warranted by current incomes and cash flows—even if it does encumber their future with ever increasing debt service obligations.

Accordingly, a big share of the household income/spending gap that resulted from Washington's off-shoring policies was backfilled with debt—especially prior to the financial crisis. During the two decades after 1987, household debt erupted by nearly 7X. Even after the year 2000, household debt grew by nearly $7.5 trillion—more than double the $3.4 trillion gain in nominal personal consumption expenditure (PCE).

In all, what had been just $2.7 trillion of household debt—credit cards, auto loans, mortgages and other loans—at the time of Greenspan's 1987 arrival in the Eccles Building soared to $14.2 trillion on the eve of the financial crisis. Bubble finance literally buried Main Street America in mortgages and other consumer debt.

Total household debt

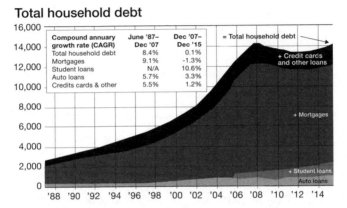

Compound annuary growth rate (CAGR)	June '87– Dec '07	Dec '07– Dec '15
Total household debt	8.4%	0.1%
Mortgages	9.1%	-1.3%
Student loans	N/A	10.6%
Auto loans	5.7%	3.3%
Credits cards & other	5.5%	1.2%

Nor was this $11.6 trillion gain in household debt simply a reflection of an expanding economy and rising nominal incomes. To the contrary, as we demonstrated in Chapter 2, the household leverage ratio went virtually parabolic, climbing from about 100% of wages and salaries in 1987 to nearly 220% by the early 2008 peak.

And that didn't happen because Main Street households suddenly became financial profligates and debt addicts. The explosion of household debt, in fact, was induced by the Wall Street/ Washington housing bubble.

Part of the latter was attributable to the feckless campaign for homeownership promoted by both ends of Pennsylvania Avenue via the massive mortgage subsidies conferred by Fannie Mae and Freddie Mac; the rest was owing to the Fed's unrelenting efforts to push interest rates far below their honest, market-clearing levels.

Needless to say, this massive, prolonged tampering with the price and risks of home mortgage debt deformed the entire residential housing market, causing prices to rise far above levels that would have occurred in an honest, unsubsidized market. In fact, between Greenspan's arrival at the Fed in August 1987 and the housing bubble peak in 2007, the nominal value of residential housing stock rose from $5.5 trillion to $22.5 trillion or by 4X.

Again, that eruption of the market value of residential housing wasn't at all a reflection of a booming economy and bigger GDP. The value of the housing stock had been 110% of GDP in 1987, but by the time that Greenspan and his merry band of money printers were finished it had reached 155%—a figure well beyond anything previously recorded or even imagined.

The greatest extent of that $17 trillion inflation of the housing stock, of course, occurred in the bicoastal precincts. But it did lift handsomely the value of 60 million owner-occupied homes in the flyover zone, as well. That is, until the whole Washington/Wall Street-inflated housing edifice came crashing down after 2007.

In the end, the entire housing/mortgage bubble amounted to a one-time parlor trick of monetary policy. So long as the household leverage ratio kept rising, it permitted families to supplement spending from their current wages and salaries with the proceeds of incremental borrowings.

This ratcheting-up of household debt and spending, in turn, caused currently reported consumption and GDP to be enlarged as well.

HOW FLYOVER AMERICA WAS DUPED BY MEW

For a time this artificial goosing of living standards by the central bank money printers did help insulate Flyover America from feeling the full brunt of its shrinking job opportunities and the deflating purchasing power of its pay checks. What it couldn't afford, it borrowed.

No more. As is evident in the chart below, the household LBO is over and done. After peaking at 220% of wage and salary income in 2007, the household leverage ratio has retracted to about 180%.

Yet that modest decline does not mean American households are out of the woods; the household leverage ratio is still more than double the

75%-85% level that pre-dated the Greenspan era and remains far above pre-1980 levels that had been consistent with healthy and sustainable household finances.

At the same time, the modest deleveraging so far is a leading indicator of the distress that has been felt in Flyover America since the Great Recession. Self-evidently, the preponderant majority of households have been forced to cut their consumption expenditures back to the levels of current earnings, which, in turn, are not rising nearly as fast as the 3.1% inflation rate afflicting Flyover America.

Accordingly, living standards are now shrinking. The sharp rise in the leverage ratio between 1987 and 2007 had induced households to live beyond their means. But the end of that faux prosperity has now brought them back to reality. Indeed, traversing the "payback" side of the leverage curve, they have become disillusioned, sullen and desperate.

There is also no secret or mystery as to how America's working households were led into this appalling debt trap. The fact is, the befuddled Greenspan actually bragged about it when he celebrated the higher consumption levels that were being funded by MEW (mortgage equity withdrawal).

That was just Fedspeak for the fact that under its interest rate repression policies, American families were being massively incentivized and encouraged day and night by cash-out mortgage financing ads ("Lost another one to Ditech!") to hock their homes to the mortgage man and splurge on the proceeds. This reached nearly a $1 trillion annual rate and 9% of disposable personal income at the peak just before 2008.

Yes, that did buy a lot of extra new cars, flat-screen TVs, vacations, trips to the mall, landscaping projects, kitchen remodels and man caves, among others. But even as Greenspan's vocabulary conceded at the time, this was spending financed by balance sheet "extractions", not current "earnings".

So what was happening behind the screen during Greenspan's spurious MEW campaign was deplorable. The faithless Washington and Wall Street elites were actually spurring American households to strip-mine the equity from their homes and bury themselves in mortgage debt.

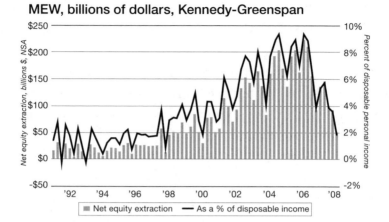

Total mortgage debt outstanding thus soared from $1.8 trillion to $10.7 trillion—or by nearly 6X—during the 21-year period ending in 2008. And even though housing prices more than doubled, the ratio of equity to owner-occupied housing asset value plunged from 67% to 37% over the period.

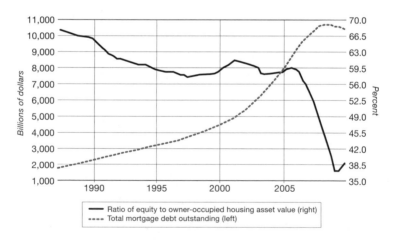

The depletion of homeowner equity during the Greenspan housing bubble era was a profoundly destructive turn of events. It not only resulted in the trauma of foreclosure for upwards of 15 million households in the years since 2007, but also left tens of millions of additional households— many of them rapidly aging baby boomers—far less financially secure than they had been prior to the Washington engineered housing boom.

Indeed, it is not hard to put a price tag on the enormity of the incremental debt burden now being lugged around by American households. To wit, had the historic debt-to-wage-and-salary ratio not been catapulted to its current debilitating level and, instead, remained at the historic 80%, household debt today would amount to about $6.5 trillion.

That means the $14.3 trillion of currently outstanding household debt represents an extra $8 trillion. And that is the financial albatross, which is spreading financial insecurity and deficiency across Flyover America.

So it is more than fair to say that Greenspan and his money printers are as responsible for the rise of the Trumpist insurrection as is any other single force. That's because for upward of 75% of all households their "castle" is their principal and only significant financial asset. Yet the nation's misguided financial rulers induced them to hock it to the rafters.

The MEW party ended nine years ago, of course, but virtually Greenspan's entire MEW is still there. Flyover America may not know exactly how it got buried in such massive debts, but it knows that the current Washington and Wall Street Bubble Finance regime has left it high and dry.

So even as they now suffer a relentless shrinkage of living standards, these contractual debt obligations are chasing the huge cohort of baby-boomers right into their retirement golden years.

Accordingly, and contrary to the elite media, it is not just racism and xenophobia that is bringing Flyover America to the Trump bandwagon. Actually, they are being herded there by $14.3 trillion of crushing debts.

WHEN MASSIVE DEBT IS NEVER ENOUGH

Nor is the once and former housing bubble the extent of the Main Street debt trap. The very essence of the Fed's lunatic ZIRP policy is to insure that no balance sheet space goes unleveraged. So, even as household mortgage debt has been reduced by about $1.3 trillion since the 2008 peak, the difference has been back-filled by a huge surge in auto loans and student debt.

And this is where the Keynesian foolishness of our ruling elites becomes downright perverse. If the 2008–9 financial crisis signaled anything to the nation's central bank, it was that the household sector urgently needed to dramatically reduce debt levels and roll-back the huge upward ratchet in leverage ratios that had materialized over the previous two decades.

But the Keynesian model is essentially a doomsday machine because it presumes that no amount of leverage is too much if it results in enhanced spending flows during the current period. So instead of encouraging debt reduction and a sharp rebound in the savings rate, the Fed did exactly the opposite of what the doctor ordered.

That is, it took the interest rate to the zero bound and kept it pinned there for 93 straight months in a desperate effort to coax any borrower who could fog a rearview mirror or sign a student enrollment form to take out a loan and spend it forthwith.

LAST RODEO FOR THE SUBPRIMES

In effect, this was the last rodeo of the sub-primes. There is no other way to describe 120% loan-to-value ratios for autos that rapidly depreciate, or $40,000 worth of "loans" to undergraduate students who have no income and no way to demonstrate that they can or will repay.

This means, of course, that there will be another round of defaults just around the corner— and even before. For example, the default rate for student loans in actual repayment mode—rather than in permanent kick-the-can "student" status—is already in excess of 20%.

But that's not the half of it. The real crime is that our vaunted central bankers and other policy makers have been reduced to drafting the most marginal credits left in the U.S. economy to carry-out their delusionary belief that America can "borrow and spend" its way to prosperity.

In the auto sector, in fact, we have the ultimate example of that kind of debt-fueled perpetual-motion machine. To wit, literally 100% of the gain in auto sales since the 2010 cyclical bottom has been funded with new borrowings.

As a result, the booming auto sales sector is not nearly what it has been cracked up to be. Sales have already peaked for this cycle, but given the growth in households and driving age population since 2007, an annualized sales rate of 18 million units or higher should be the permanent norm, not a fleeting peak.

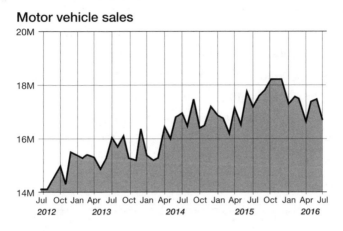

Motor vehicle sales

This unsustainable debt-fueled auto-sales recovery is dramatically evident in the chart below. Since the auto cycle bottom in mid 2010, retail motor vehicle sales have rebounded at a $360 billion annual rate, whereas auto loans outstanding have risen by $355 billion.

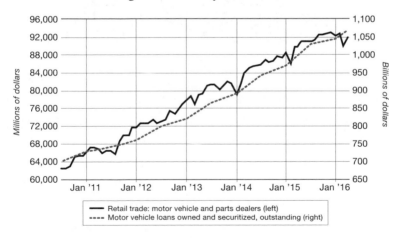

But here is a data point that completely belies the illusory debt-fueled prosperity of the auto sector, and, instead, underscores how Flyover America is being led even deeper into the Fed's colossal debt trap.

To wit, nearly one-third of vehicle trade-ins are now carrying negative equity.

That means that prospective new-car buyers are having to stump-up increasing amounts of cash to pay off old loans, which, in turn, is pressuring volume-hungry lenders and dealers to extend loan-to-value ratios to even more absurd heights than the 120% level now prevalent.

That's kicking the metal down the road with a vengeance!

In fact, outstanding subprime auto debt is nearly 3X higher than it was on the eve of the financial crisis, and average loan terms at nearly 70 months are a ticking time bomb. That's because cars depreciate faster than loan balances can be paid down over that extended duration, meaning more and more of outstanding auto credit will be under water in the future.

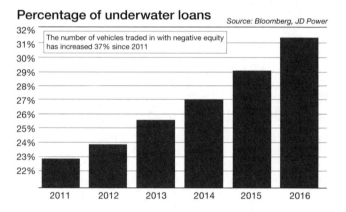

Percentage of underwater loans *Source: Bloomberg, JD Power*

The number of vehicles traded in with negative equity has increased 37% since 2011

And that's the skunk in the woodpile. With today's technology auto loans are supposed to be inherently low risk. If push-comes-to-shove the repo man can find cars anywhere in America and tow them back to the lender for re-sale.

But this assumes that used-car prices will remain at current levels, and that's the catch. The coming tidal wave of vehicles coming off lease is fixing to send the used-car market and the whole trillion dollar auto-financing system into a tailspin during the next four years.

Needless to say, ground zero for the great auto repo rampage ahead will be Flyover America.

Indeed, payback time is already peeking just around the corner. The virtuous cycle of declining used-car volumes and rising used-car prices has exhausted itself. Yet that was crucial to the debt financed car-buying spree since early 2010 because it meant rising trade-in prices and there-fore enhanced capacity to make down payments and loan terms.

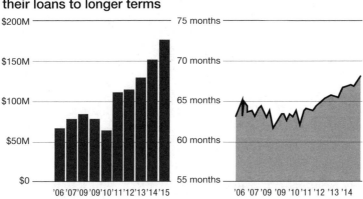

Subprime car loans outstanding and people extending their loans to longer terms

Stated differently, Main Street households were again being lured into cheap loans that do not provide a stable foundation for the eventual rollover of their vehicles and the loans encumbering them.

Indeed, that's exactly what happened last time around. In the run-up to the new auto sales crash in 2008–9, used-car prices plunged by 20% and new light-vehicle sales fell from an 18 million annual rate to barely 10 million at the bottom of the cycle.

By contrast, during the first three years of the post-June 2009 recovery, used-car prices soared by 24%, enabling the credit fueled recovery of new-vehicle sales shown in the graph.

The worm is now fixing to turn because the used-car market is facing an unprecedented tsunami of used-vehicles coming off loans, leases, rental fleets and repossessions. As shown above, used-vehicle prices have been weakening for the last several years, but between 2016 and 2018 upwards of 21 million vehicles will hit the used-car market compared to just 15 million during the last three years.

This means used-car prices are likely to enter another swoon like 2006–8, causing trade-in values to plummet and thereby draining the pool of qualified new-car borrowers.

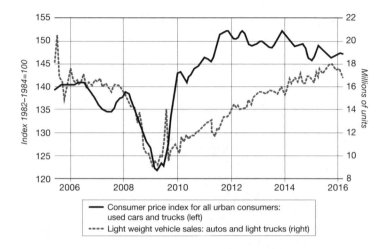

Likewise, new-car loan and lease finance will be shrinking because the estimated "residuals" on leases and collateral value on loans will be lower. That means loan-to-car price ratios will come down—just as trade-in values on existing vehicles are also dropping. The resulting financing gap means lower sales and production rates in the auto sector.

In short, there has not been a healthy recovery of the auto industry owing to 93 months of ZIRP and the Fed's massive money printing escapades. This misbegotten monetary stimulus has only generated a deformed auto financing cycle that is now reversing and that will soon be extracting its pound of payback.

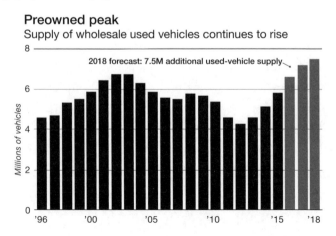

Indeed, when the cycle turns down, fogging a rearview mirror is never enough.

To be sure, there is nothing very profound about the certainty that an auto credit boom always creates a morning after hangover, and that the amplitudes of these cycles is getting increasingly violent owing to the underlying deterioration of auto credit. Currently, credit scores are dropping rapidly and upwards of 80% of new retail auto sales are loan or lease financed.

Moreover, the race to the bottom is happening once again in the lease market. That is, monthly lease rates have gotten so ridiculously cheap that the implied residual values are at all-time highs. This means that when the used-car-pricing down cycle sets in during the flood of vehicles ahead, massive losses will be generated, causing a sharp contraction of the leasing market, as well.

Stated differently, the auto sales piece of retail sales has virtually nothing to do with a rebounding consumer. It's a reflection of an artificially bloated and unstable credit cycle that is about ready to take the plunge, and thereby deliver another blow to the faltering economics of Flyover America.

THE STUDENT LOAN BINGE—A GENERATION OF DEBT SLAVES

The only thing worse than the MEW legacy plaguing seniors is what's happening on the other end of the demographic curve. Among student age Americans, the degree of debt enslavement has become even more draconian.

In the last decade alone, total student loans outstanding have nearly tripled, rising from $500 billion in 2006 to $1.34 trillion at present. And for reasons laid out below, a disproportionate brunt of this massive student loan burden is being shouldered by Flyover America

That's mainly because the preponderant share of the nation's 25 million higher education students comes from the flyover zones. Those precincts still had a semblance of a birth rate 25 years ago, unlike the culturally advanced households of the bicoastal meccas.

Stated differently, these staggering debt obligations were not incurred by Wellesley College art history majors or even needs-based diversity students at Harvard Law School. They are owed by the inhabitants of mom and pop's basements scattered over the less advantaged expanse of the land.

After all, the Ivy League schools including all of their graduate departments account for only 140,000 students or 0.5% of the nation's total. Even if you add in the likes of MIT, Stanford, Caltech, Northwestern, Duke, Vanderbilt and the rest of the top 20 universities you get less than 250,000 or 1% of the student population.

The other 24 million are victims of the feckless Washington and Wall Street ideology of debt and finance. To wit, tuition, fees, room and board and other living expenses have erupted skyward over the last two decades because Washington has poured in loans and grants with reckless abandon and Wall Street has fueled the madcap expansion of for-profit tuition mills.

Even setting aside the minimum $50,000 annual price tag at private institutions, the tab has soared to $20,000 annually at public 4-year schools and nearly $30,000 per year at the tuition mills.

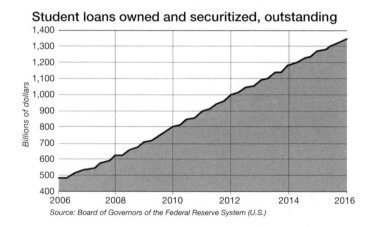

Student loans owned and securitized, outstanding

Source: Board of Governors of the Federal Reserve System (U.S.)

These figures represent semi-criminal rip-offs. They were enabled by the preternaturally bloated levels of debt and finance showered upon the student population by the denizens of the Acela Corridor.

So the former now tread water in an economic doom loop. Average earnings for 35 year-olds with a bachelor's degree or higher are $50,000 annually, compared to $30,000 for high school graduates and $24,000 for dropouts.

Thus, the sons and daughters of the flyover zones feel compelled to strap-on a heavy vest of debt in order to finance the insanely bloated costs of higher education. But once "educated," the overwhelming majority end up with $30,000 to $100,000 of debt or more.

In this regard, the so-called for-profit colleges like Phoenix University, Strayer Education and dozens of imitators deserve a special place in the halls of higher-education infamy. At their peak a few years ago, enrollments at these schools totaled 3.5 million.

But overwhelmingly, these "students" were recruited by tuition harvesting machines that make the all-volunteer U.S. Army look like a piker in comparison. To wit, typically 90% of the revenues of these colleges are derived from student grants and especially loans—hundreds of billions of them—but less than one-third of that money went to the cost of education, including teachers, classrooms, books and other instructional costs.

At the same time, well over 33% went to SG&A and the overwhelming share of that was in the "S" part. That is, prodigious expenditures for salesmen, recruiters, commissions and giant bonuses and other incentives and perks.

Needless to say, this made for good growth and margin metrics that could be hyped in the stock market. In fact, after the cost of education and all of the massive selling expense to turbocharge enrollment growth was absorbed, there was still upwards of 35–40% of revenue left for operating profits.

That's right. For a decade until the Obama administration finally lowered the boom after 2011, the fastest growing and most profitable companies in America were the for-profit colleges.

In short order they became a hedge fund hotel, meaning that the fast money piled into the for-profit college space like there was no tomorrow. So doing, they often drove PE ratios to 60X or higher, bringing instant riches to start-up entrepreneurs and top company executives, who, in turn, were motivated to drive their growth and profit "metrics" even harder.

At length, they became tuition mills and Wall Street speculations that were incidentally in the higher education business—or not. The combined market cap of the six largest public companies went from less than $2 billion to upwards of $30 billion in a decade.

The poster boy for this scam is surely Strayer Education. Between 2002 and the 2011 peak, its sales and net income grew at 25% per year and operating profit margins clocked in at nearly 40%.

Not surprisingly, Strayer was peddled as the second coming of "growth" among the hedge funds. The momo chasers thus pushed its PE ratio into the 60–70X range in its initial growth phase, and it remained in the 30–40X range thereafter.

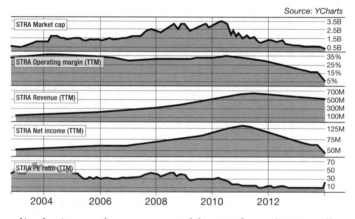

Source: YCharts

Accordingly, its market cap soared by 7X from $500 million to $3.5 billion at the peak. The hedge funds made a killing.

Then the Federal regulators threw on the brakes, and it was all over except the shouting. Total market cap of more than $27 billion disappeared from the segment within three years after 2011 and the hedge fund hotel experienced a mass stampede for the exits.

What was left were millions of thirty-something's in Flyover America stuck with crushing unpaid loans, educations of dubious value and a lot more years in mom and pop's basement.

Should any of these tuition mills have even existed, let alone been valued at 60X earnings—earnings that did not derive from real economic value added and that were totally at the whims of the U.S. Department of Education?

Of course not.

But then again, after 20 years of radical financial repression, Wall Street has been turned into a casino that scalps Flyover America whenever it gets half the chance.

PART 2

BUBBLE FINANCE
AND ITS RUINS

CHAPTER 8:

Government Entitlements: The World's Sixth-Biggest Economy and the Coming Insolvency of Social Security

B ECAUSE THE MAIN STREET ECONOMY IS FAILING, THE NATION'S entitlement rolls have exploded. About 110 million citizens now live in households that receive some form of means tested benefits. When Social Security is included, more than 160 million citizens get checks from Washington.

The total cost is nearly $3 trillion per year and rising rapidly. America's entitlements sector, in fact, is the sixth biggest economy in the world.

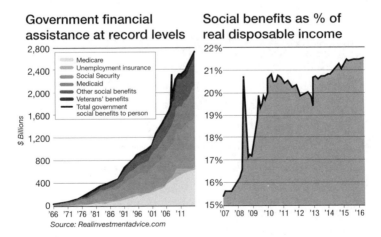

Source: Realinvestmentadvice.com

Yet in a society that is rapidly aging to the tune of 10,000 baby boom retirees per day, this 50% dependency ratio is not even remotely sustainable. As we show later in this chapter, Social Security itself will be bankrupt within 10 years.

Still, there is another even more important aspect of the mainstream narrative's absolute radio silence about the monumental entitlements problem. Like in the case of the nation's 30-year LBO, the transfer payments crisis is obfuscated by the economic blind spots of our Keynesian central banking regime.

Greenspan, Bernanke, Yellen and their posse of paint-by-the-numbers economic plumbers have deified the great aggregates of consumer, business and government spending as the motor force of economic life. As we have repeatedly insisted, however, this derives from their primitive notion of bathtub economics.

In the present instance, this bogus model assumes that the supply-side of the economy is always fully endowed or even over-provided. By contrast, the perennial problem is purportedly a shortfall of that theoretical ether called "aggregate demand".

So the job of the central bank is to pump reserves and credit into the macroeconomy until the resulting incremental spending—including by government—has caused "full employment GDP" to be filled to the brim.

That's especially true when government borrowing is used to fund transfer payments. Almost without exception transfer payment recipients live hand-to-mouth. Consequently, virtually 100% of the proceeds go into the spending stream (PCE) with little leakage or lag.

It's an altogether different matter, of course, when transfer payments are funded out of current taxation. That's purely a zero-sum game in which income producers have less to spend or save and recipients have more. So borrowing to fund the nations massive flow of transfer payments is actually some kind of Keynesian nirvana.

At the same time, the ruling elite's vestigial Keynesian fetish about "aggregate demand" means that ideas of quality, sustainability, efficiency, discipline, and prudence or, for that matter, even economic justice and equity, never enter the narrative. Likewise, the possibility that current spending bloated by debt and transfer payments isn't sustainable has simply been defined out of existence.

It matters not a whit to the Keynesian policymakers, for example, whether the considerable expansion of household consumption spending (PCE) depicted below originated in disability checks, second mortgages or car loans at 120% loan-to-value. All spending is good, apparently, even if it was deposited by a passing comet.

What counts is the incremental gains in GDP compared to last quarter and in proxies for demand such as job counts and housing starts versus prior month. That's what fuels bullish spasms in the Wall Street casino. And when the business cycle eventually ends, there is always a scapegoat to blame, such as an oil price shock or a financial market meltdown.

HOW THE ESTABLISHMENT'S 'GROWTH' SWINDLE WORKS

The following graph depicts how the establishment's "growth" swindle actually works. There are currently 126 million prime working age persons in the US between 25 and 54 years of age. That's up from 121 million at the beginning of 2000.

Yet even as the current business cycle is rolling over, the 77.1 million persons employed full-time from that pool is still 1.2 million below its turn of the century level!

That's right. Only 61% of the prime working age population has full-time jobs. That compares to 65% as recently as the year 2000.

So it might be wondered: How is it possible that real consumption expenditures rose by a whopping $3.1 trillion or 38% during the same 16-year period that the number of full-time prime age workers was actually dropping?

Yes, the employment shown in the chart below is supplemented by part time workers, where the ranks have grown modestly, and also by the steadily rising participation rate of Wal-Mart greeters among the over 65 cohort. But the fact remains that on the margin the 38% real gain in consumer spending since the year 2000 was funded from sources other than pay envelopes.

Among the alternative sources, which played a major role in funding the nation's shopping cart, of course, was the explosion of government transfer payment. In fact, during the last 16 years government transfer payments have grown at 6.2% annually or by nearly 2X the 3.3% growth of nominal wage and salary disbursements.

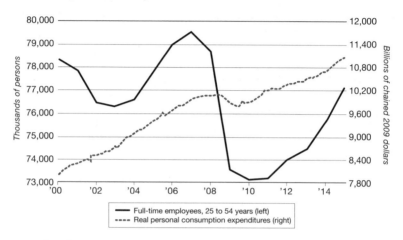

Accordingly, as shown in the next chart, transfer payments soared by $1.7 trillion during the period. This means the gain in transfer payments amounted to nearly 50% of the entire gain in wage and salary disbursements to the nation 150 million employed persons.

Needless to say, that astonishing and unsustainable trend has been completely ignored by the Wall Street and Washington peddlers of consumption based economics.

The Fed has never once mentioned the rapidly deteriorating quality of household income and spending during the last 15 years. And in crowing about all the part-time and "born again" jobs it has purportedly created, the Obama White House has never remotely acknowledged that its vaunted "recovery" has been largely built on transfer payments and debt.

TRANSFER PAYMENTS NOW EQUAL 40% OF PRIVATE WAGE AND SALARY DISBURSEMENTS

So "deterioration" is not an inappropriate word. As a matter of public policy, nearly $3 trillion per year of transfer payments may represent a bargain that society has chosen to make for reasons of equity and social welfare. But that doesn't gainsay the fact that the underlying economics are an altogether different matter.

To wit, in May 2016 total transfer payments amounted to fully one-third of all the wage and salaries disbursed to the entire work force of the United States. And if you grant the old-fashioned assumption the government salaries are funded by taxation rather than production, then transfers amount to nearly 40% of wage and salary disbursements to private sectors employees.

So let's put the chart below in plain English. Sixteen years is not a blip; it's an embedded trend. When the transfer payment flows to "takers" over that span have fast approached the earnings of "producers", you have a system that will, at length, go tilt.

The practical point, of course, is that continued full funding of this huge fiscal burden—and giant prop under household consumption—will require higher taxes today or increased public debt, which amounts to higher taxes tomorrow.

As we will see later, in fact, either course would only aggravate the coming crisis. Yet the Washington and Wall Street consensus in behalf of consumption based GDP growth—no matter how it is funded—is deafening. Even self-proclaimed fiscal conservatives like Paul Ryan are in complete denial.

Speaker Ryan's budgets in the House have always given the core of the entitlement-spending monster—Social Security and Medicare—a ten-year free pass. In the politics of American governance, of course, that's the same thing as forever because Congress never gets to the so-called "long-run" fiscal equation.

So at its recent convention, the GOP's present-day version of Mr. Conservative told the voters an absolute lie when he assured them that no one within a decade of retirement, plus the 55 million already on the rolls, will face even a dime of cutbacks. Donald Trump's know-nothing posture on entitlements was made to look only slightly more implausible by comparison.

In fact, there is no alternative to subjecting affluent retirees to a severe means-tested cutback of their Social Security and Medicare benefits. And it must start right now, not two decades down the road.

That much is patently clear and statistically baked into the cake. But the mainstream narrative blithely ignores the coming transfer payments crisis because of a wholly misplaced confidence in central banking.

Notwithstanding the blatant failure of 93-months of ZIRP and $3.5 trillion of bond buying to produce anything except a tepid, deeply subpar recovery, and one that is now running out of steam, establishment policy-makers—and scorekeepers like the CBO— assume that the Fed will keep the GDP expanding to the brim of full employment for the indefinite future, world without end.

That's convenient, of course, because it essentially defines the crisis away. If you project high economic growth long enough, the modeled GDP will always outrun the projected expansion of the transfer payment burden.

Except it won't happen. The ticking time bomb shown in the chart below, in fact, is anchored in the giant social insurance programs. But as we show in the next section, even those vaunted "trust funds" will be empty within the next decade after you set aside of utterly implausible rosy scenario economic assumptions on which both the Federal budget and trust fund projections are based.

Government transfer payments have grown twice as fast as wages & salaries since 2000

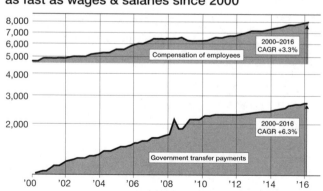

SOCIAL SECURITY—TRUST FUND CONFETTI AND THE COMING INSOLVENCY

Here follows a deconstruction of rosy scenario. It underscores why the nation's entitlement based consumption spending will hit the shoals in the decade ahead.

In their most recent report, the so-called "trustees" of the Social Security system said that the funds near-term outlook had improved. So the stenographers of the financial press dutifully reported that the day of reckoning when the trust funds run dry has been put off another year—until 2034.

The message was essentially: "Take a breath and kick the can."—"That's five Presidential elections away!"

Except that is not what the report really says. On a cash basis, the OASDI (retirement and disability) funds spent $859 billion during 2014 but took in only $786 billion in tax revenues, thereby generating $73 billion in red ink.

By the trustees' own reckoning, in fact, the OASDI funds will spew a cumulative cash deficit of $1.6 trillion during the 12-years covering 2015–2026.

So measured by the only thing that matters—hard cash income and outgo—the social security system has already gone bust. What's more, even under the White House's rosy scenario budget forecasts, general fund outlays will exceed general revenues (excluding payroll taxes) by $8 trillion over the next twelve years.

Needless to say, this means there will be no general fund surplus to pay the OASDI shortfall.

Uncle Sam will finance the entire $1.6 trillion cash deficit by adding to the public debt. That is, Washington plans to make Social Security ends meet by burying unborn taxpayers even deeper in public debt in order to fund unaffordable entitlements for the current generation of retirees.

The question thus recurs. How did the "untrustworthies" led by Treasury Secretary Jacob Lew, who signed the 2015 report, manage to turn today's river of red ink into another 20 years of respite for our cowardly beltway politicians?

They did it, in a word, by redeeming phony assets; booking phony interest income on those non-existent assets; and projecting implausible GDP growth and phantom payroll tax revenues.

And that's only the half of it!

The fact is, the whole rigmarole of trust fund accounting enables these phony assumptions to compound one another, thereby obfuscating the fast approaching bankruptcy of the system. And, as we will demonstrate later on, that's what's really happening—even if you give credit to the $2.79 trillion of so-called "assets" which were in the OASDI funds at the end of 2014.

Stated differently, the OASDI trust funds could be empty as soon as 2026, thereby triggering a devastating 33% across the board cut in benefits to affluent duffers living on Florida golf courses and destitute widows alike.

Needless to say, the army of beneficiaries projected for the middle of the next decade—what will amount to the 8th largest nation on the planet—would not take that lying down.

There would be blood in the streets in Washington and eventually staggering tax increases to fund the shortfall. Such desperate measures, of course, would sink once and for all whatever faint impulse of economic growth and job creation that remained alive in the US economy at the time.

In short, the latest untrustworthies' report amounts to an accounting and forecasting house of cards that is camouflaging an impending social, political and economic crisis of a magnitude not seen since the Great Depression or even the Civil War. So here follows an unpacking of the phony accounting edifice that obscures the imminent danger.

The place to start is with the one data series in the report that is rock solid. Namely, the projected cost of $15.5 trillion over the next 12 years to pay for retirement and disability benefits and the related (minor) administrative costs.

This staggering figure is derived from the fact that the number of beneficiaries will grow from 59 million to 79 million over the next twelve years. And each and every one of these citizens has a payroll record that entitles them to an exact monthly benefit as a matter of law.

Even the assumed COLA adjustment between 2-3% each year is pretty hard to argue with—since it is nearly dead-on the actual CPI increase average since the year 2000.

FUNNY MONEY ACCOUNTING—TRUST FUND "ASSETS" ARE PURE CONFETTI

By contrast, the funny money aspect comes in on the funding side. The latter starts with the $2.79 trillion of "assets" sitting in the OASDI trust funds at the end of 2014.

In truth, there is nothing there except government accounting confetti. This figure allegedly represents the accumulated excess of trust fund income over outgo historically, but every dime of that was spent long ago on aircraft carriers, cotton subsidies, green energy boondoggles, prison facilities for pot smokers, education grants, NSA's cellphone snoops, space launches and the rest of Washington's general government spending machine.

So when the untrustworthies claim that that Social Security is "solvent" until 2034 the only thing they are really saying is that this $2.79 trillion accounting artifact has not yet been liquidated according to the rules of trust fund arithmetic. And under those "rules" it's pretty hard to actually accomplish that—not the least due to the compounding of phantom interest on these phantom assets.

To wit, the 2015 report says that the OASDI funds will earn $1.2 trillion of interest income during the next twelve years. To be sure, the nation's retirees and savers might well ask how Washington's bookkeepers could manage to get the assumed 3.5% interest rate on the government's assets compared to the 0.3% ordinary citizens earn on a bank account or even 1.4% on a 10-year treasury bond.

But that's not the real scam. The skunk in the woodpile is actually an utterly arbitrary and unjustifiable assumption about the rate of nominal GDP growth and therefore the associated gain in projected payroll tax revenues coming into the trust fund.

What the untrustworthies have done here is indulge in the perfidious game of goal-seeked forecasting. That is, they have backed into a GDP growth rate sufficient to keep payroll tax revenues close to the level of benefit payouts, thereby minimizing the annual cash deficit.

This, in turn, ensures that the trust fund asset balance stays close to its current $2.7 trillion level in the years just ahead, and, mirabile dictu, permits it to earn upwards of $100 billion of "interest" each year.

Too be sure, beneficiaries could not actually pay for their groceries and rent with this sort of trust fund "income", but it does keep the asset balance high and the solvency can bouncing down the road a few more years.

But here's the thing. Plug in a realistic figure for GDP growth and payroll tax revenue increases and the whole trust fund accounting scheme collapses; the bouncing can runs smack dab into a wall of trust fund insolvency.

To wit, the untrustworthies who wrote the report assumed that nominal GDP would grow at a 5.1% annual rate for the next 12 years. Yet the actual growth rate has never come close to that during the entire 21st century to date. At best these people are dreaming, but the truth is they are either lying or stupid.

Given the self-evident headwinds everywhere in the world, and year after year of failed "escape velocity" at home, no one paying a modicum of attention would expect US GDP to suddenly get up on its hind legs and race forward as far as the eye can see.

Yet that's exactly what the Social Security untrustworthies have done by assuming nominal GDP growth 35% higher than the actual 3.8% compound growth rate since the year 2000.

But it's actually worse. Since reaching peak debt just prior to the financial crisis, the US rate of GDP growth has decelerated even more.

And going forward, there is no meaningful prospect of recovery in the face of the growing deflationary tide in the global economy and the unavoidable necessity for the Fed and other central banks to normalize interest rates in the decade ahead. Failing that they will literally blow-up the world's monetary system in a devastating currency race to the bottom.

Thus, during Q1 2008, which marked the end of the domestic credit binge, nominal GDP posted at $14.67 trillion, and during the most recent quarter it came in at $18.44 trillion. That amounts to a seven-year gain of just $3 trillion and an annual growth rate of 2.8%.

Now surely there will be another recession before 2026. If not, we will end up with 200 straight quarters of business cycle expansion—a preposterous prospect never remotely experienced previously.

Indeed, in our modern central bank driven world, where both recessions this century have resulted from the bursting of financial bubbles, the proposition is even starker. Namely, the Washington untrustworthies are assuming no bursting bubbles or market crashes for 18 years!

Not a chance!

The historical business cycle expansions depicted below make clear that there will be another business cycle downturn. After all, contrary to the untrustworthies assumption that the current business cycle will last forever, and, in the analysis at hand for 200 months through the end of 2026, the average expansion since 1950 has lasted just 61 months and the longest ever was only 119 months.

During the last business cycle contraction, in fact, nominal GDP declined by 3.4% between Q3 2008 and Q2 2009. And when you average that in with the 3.3% nominal GDP growth rate which we have had during the so-called recovery of the last four years, you not only get the aforementioned 2.8% trend rate of nominal GDP growth, but you are also hard-pressed to say how it can be bested in the years ahead.

Business cycle recovery length
CBO fantasy vs. history

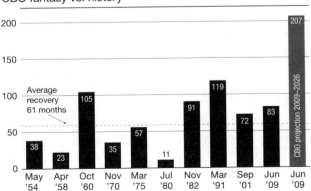

Indeed, as we will demonstrate more fully later, there is a now an unprecedented deflationary tide rolling through the world economy owing to the last 15 years of rampant money printing and financial repression by the central banks. By collectively monetizing upwards of $20 trillion of public debt and other existing securities and driving interest rates toward the zero bound in nominal terms and deep into negative territory in real terms, they have generated two massive, deflationary distortions that have now sunk deep roots in the world economy.

First, as we demonstrated earlier worldwide credit market debt outstanding has soared from $40 trillion to $220 trillion during the last two decades. This means future economic growth practically everywhere on the planet will be freighted-down by unprecedented, debilitating debt-service costs.

At the same time, massive overinvestment in mining, energy, shipping and manufacturing spurred by central bank enabled cheap capital has generated a huge overhang of excess capacity. This is already fueling a downward spiral of commodity and industrial prices and profit margins, and there is no end in sight.

Iron-ore prices, which peaked at $200 per ton a few years back, for example, are now under $50 and heading for $30. Likewise, coal prices, which peaked at $400 per ton, are heading under $100, while crude oil is heading for a retest of the $35 level hit during the financial crisis, and copper is on track to plunge from its recent peak of $4 per pound toward $1.

These deflationary currents will suppress nominal-income growth for a decade or longer owing to a now-commencing counter-trend of low capital investment, shrinking industrial profits, tepid wage growth and falling prices for tradable goods and services.

Accordingly, even maintaining the average nominal GDP growth rate of 2.8% realized over the last seven years will be a tall order for the U.S. economy.

Needless to say, the law of compound arithmetic can be a brutal thing if you start with a delusional hockey stick and seek to bend it back to earth.

PHANTOM GDP GROWTH: WHY OASDI WILL GO BUST BY 2026

In this case, the trustees' report's 5.1% GDP growth rate assumption results in $31 trillion of GDP by 2026. Stated differently, compared to only $3 trillion of nominal GDP growth in the last 7 years, we are purportedly going to get $14 trillion in the next 12 years.

But let's see. If we stay on the current 2.8% growth track, then GDP will come in at $24 trillion in 2026. Since OASDI payroll taxes amount to about 4.5% of GDP, it doesn't take a lot of figuring to see that trust fund income would be dramatically lower in a $7 trillion smaller economy.

To be exact, the untrustworthies have goal-seeked their report to generate $1.425 trillion annually of payroll-tax revenue 12-years from now. Yet based on a simple continuation of the deeply embedded GDP growth trend of the last seven years, payroll-tax revenue would come in at only $1.1 trillion in 2026 or $325 billion lower in that year alone.

And here's where the self-feeding illusion of trust fund accounting rears its ugly head. What counts is not simply the end-year delta, but the entire area of difference under the curve. That's because every cumulative dollar of payroll tax shortfall not only reduces the reserve asset balance, but also the phantom interest income earned on it.

So what happens under a scenario of lower payroll tax revenues is that the $2.7 trillion of current trust fund "assets" begins circling the accounting drain with increasing velocity as time passes. In effect, the permission granted to Washington to kick the can by this year's untrustworthies report gets revoked, and right fast.

To wit, instead of a cumulative total of $13.2 trillion of payroll tax revenue over the next 12 years, the actual, demonstrated GDP growth path of the present era would generate only $11.2 trillion during that period. That $2 trillion revenue difference not only ionizes most of the so-called trust fund assets, but also reduces the ending balance so rapidly that by the final year interest income computes to only $25 billion, not $100 billion as under the current report.

In short, by 2026 trust fund revenue would be $400 billion per year lower owing to lower taxes and less phantom interest. Accordingly, the current modest projected trust fund deficit of $150 billion would explode to upwards of $600 billion after the last of the phony interest income was booked.

Needless to say, that massive shortfall would amount to nearly 33% of the projected OASDI outgo of $1.8 trillion for 2026. More importantly, instead of a healthy cushion of $2.4 trillion of assets (or two years' outgo) as the untrustworthies projected last year, the fund balance would be down to just $80 billion at year-end 2026.

Now that's about 15 days of the next year's OASDI outlays. The system would go tilt. Benefits would be automatically cut back to the level of tax revenue or by 33%. The greatest social crisis of the century would be storming out of every hill and dale in the land.

Yes, Jacob Lew is a Washington-Wall Street apparatchik who wouldn't grasp the self-destructing flaws of trust fund accounting if they smacked him in the forehead. And the same is apparently true for the other trustees.

But here's where the venality comes in. In order to goal-seek to 5% nominal GDP growth, the trustees report assumes that real GDP will average 3.1% per year through the year 2020.

Now, c'mon. Since the pre-crisis peak in late 2007, real GDP growth has averaged only 1.2% annually, and only 1.8% per year during the entire 16 years of this century.

Anybody who signed up for 3.1% real growth through 2020—that is, for scorching growth during month 67 through month 140 of a tepid business cycle expansion that is already long-in-the-tooth by historical standards—is flat-out irresponsible and dishonest.

Calling their mendacious handiwork the "untrustworthies' report" is actually more flattering than they deserve.

CHAPTER 9:

"Morning in America" Never Was— How the Federal Debt Went From $1 Trillion to $35 Trillion in Four Decades

ONE OF THE GREAT VIRTUES OF THE TRUMP CANDIDACY IS THE Donald's propensity to lob wild pitches—knowingly or not—at the sacred cows of Imperial Washington, thereby exposing the tissue of hypocrisy and cant, which surrounds them.

But within the herd of revered ruminants none is slathered in more hypocrisy than the federal budget and official Washington's unctuous professions of devotion to safeguarding the "full faith and credit of the United States."

The truth of the matter, of course, is that our rulers have been marching the nation's fiscal accounts straight toward national bankruptcy for the last 35 years, at least. And since the arrival of Ben Bernanke at the Fed, Washington's actual policy with respect to the nation's "credit" has been to debauch it.

So Donald Trump's recent rumination about negotiating a "discount" on the federal debt was priceless. It caused a Beltway chorus of fiscal house wreckers to loudly harrumph and admonish the GOP candidate about the sanctity of Uncle Sam's credit promises.

DEFAULT IS ACTUALLY OFFICIAL WASHINGTON POLICY

In fact, however, the unschooled Trump had merely mentioned out loud what is already the official policy of the U.S. government. He called them out, and they screamed like banshees.

Here's why. For 93 months now the Federal Reserve has pegged interest rates to the zero bound. It believes that come hell or high water, the U.S. economy must have 2.00% inflation in order to grow and prosper, and that shoveling free money into the canyons of Wall Street is just the ticket to make this happen.

Other than a handful of rubes from the congressional hinterlands, there is nary a Washington operative from either party who has questioned the appropriateness or effectiveness, let alone the sanity, of the Bernanke-Yellen 2.00% inflation totem.

But what hitting this sacred inflation target really means, of course, is that exactly 30 years from today investors would get back 54.5 cents in inflation-adjusted money per dollar of principal on the U.S. Treasury long bond.

If that's not default, it is surely a far deeper "discount" than even The Donald had in mind while jabbering to CNBC about his years as the King of Debt.

As we noted earlier, of course, the monetary geniuses who peddle the 2% inflation gospel claim we are all in it together. That is, prices, wages, profits, rents and even indexed social benefits allegedly all march upwards at 2% per year.

Save for minor leads and lags in timing, therefore, no one is financially worse for the wear; there is no inflationary default.

Actually, not on your life. That's an official whopper that offends facts and logic on a scale that even Donald Trump rarely attains.

The truth is, savers get whacked and borrowers get windfalls. The wages of upper-end workers keep-up while the purchasing power of paychecks lower down the ladder shrinks continuously. Social Security recipients get recompense but private pensioners get shafted.

Likewise, under the Fed's deliberate debt default policy traditional fixed income portfolios wither, even as the leveraged gamblers of Wall Street scalp monumental profits from zero-cost carry trades.

Indeed, the 2% inflation campaign in the real world is the very opposite of the Keynesian lockstep claim. Its incidence among economic agents and classes is actually capricious and inequitable in the extreme.

The debt-addicted politicians of Washington, of course, have no clue that the Fed is an engine of default and random redistribution. Nor do they have inkling that it is destroying the savings function, which is the ultimate key to capitalist prosperity.

Too be sure, they spend a goodly amount of time waxing about their endless affection for America's working people. The often-sensible Governor Kasich, for example, never finished a single GOP primary debate without the sappy claim that he understood how to improve the U.S. economy because his father was a mailman!

Needless to say, mainstream politicians like Kasich, who also pound the table in behalf of the Fed's vaunted "independence," have never looked at the graph below. It shows real wages since the Fed went full tilt with printing press money in 2007. This is not a picture of 2% lockstep.

Less educated and lower wage workers have experienced shrinking real wages and for a self-evident reason. On the margin, they are more exposed to the lower nominal wages of foreign goods and services competitors than are workers on the upper end of the jobs and income ladder.

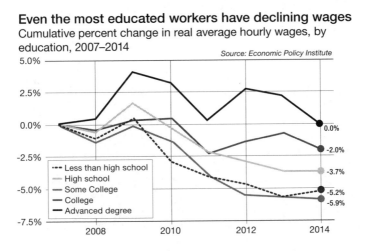

Even the most educated workers have declining wages
Cumulative percent change in real average hourly wages, by education, 2007–2014

Source: Economic Policy Institute

In fact, the chart's three categories of workers with less than college degrees have experienced a 4% to 6% decline in real hourly wages since 2007, even based on the BLS' understated inflation. Why in the world, then, does the Fed incessantly strive for more inflation and even more random punishment to the less privileged?

At the end of the day, Fed policy amounts to a grand scheme of random monetary default. But after Trump had the temerity to broach the topic—whether by inadvertence or by purpose—the spendthrifts of the Imperial City scrambled to smother us in a verbal blanket of phony fiscal rectitude.

FISCAL HYPOCRISY OF THE BELTWAY BLOVIATORS

In that regard, there are few more noxious precincts of statist fiscal hypocrisy than that occupied by the ranks of scribblers at "Politico." And among these scolds and bloviators, there are few Washington apparatchiks more culpable than Gene Sperling, who headed Obama's economic policy council.

According to Sperling's snarky rebuke of Trump's purely hypothetical suggestion, everything that has been done in the Imperial City these last several decades should have been done. Certainly, there is no fiscal crisis that might warrant radical ideas like those proffered by Donald Trump.

Let's see. Between December 2008 and the present, the public debt exploded from $10.7 trillion to $19.4 trillion.

That means that on Obama's watch, and with Sperling's presumptive advice, new public debt was issued equal to 80% of the total debt created during the entire prior 220 years of the republic and the tenure of 43 presidents.

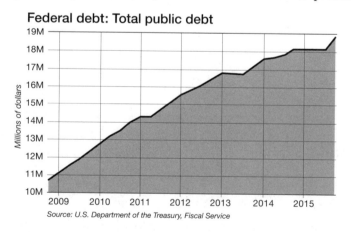

Federal debt: Total public debt

Source: U.S. Department of the Treasury, Fiscal Service

Well now. In light of the above debt eruption, has Sperling and his ilk ever considered how high interest rates might actually be, save for the massive bond market fraud carried out by the Fed and the rest of the world's central banks?

Even the economically benighted types among us, apparently Donald Trump included, know that neither Washington, the IMF or the G-20 has repealed the law of supply and demand. Nor has the CIA yet classified as a state secret the amount of sovereign debt and other financial assets that the central banks of the world have vacuumed-up in the name of monetary "stimulus" over the past two decades.

PHONY DEFENSE OF UNCLE SAM'S FULL FAITH AND CREDIT

As we have demonstrated, in fact, about $19 trillion of sovereign debt and related securities—including more than half of the publicly traded U.S. Treasury securities—has been sequestered in central bank vaults since the mid-1990s.

All of that debt would have otherwise massively burdened the world's limited supply of real savings—from income—thereby causing interest rates to soar. Instead, it was made to disappear from market circulation by monetary authorities hitting the "buy" key on their digital printing presses.

And the Bushbama enablement of this giant backdoor form of default on honest debt via the appointment of avowed Keynesian money printers to the Fed isn't the half of it.

Whenever a corporal's guard of Capitol Hill fiscal antediluvians has tried to stop the government-spending machine by refusing to raise the federal debt ceiling, their Beltway betters have cried "full faith and credit."

So time and again the so-called debt ceiling has been raised to validate deficits already incurred. So doing, our Washington rulers did not even bother to reform entitlements, raise revenue or sharply curtail discretionary spending because they knew that the Fed and its front-running Wall Street punters would buy-up the continuing flood of new Treasury paper.

In fact, after so many years of being house trained by the Fed, Washington's ruling class has turned wild fiscal irresponsibility into a self-conferred virtue. For example, Sperling sniffed that Trump should get himself educated by attending "Hamilton" next time he visits Broadway: "generations of Americans have benefited from a historical commitment started by Alexander Hamilton to ensure the full faith and credit of the U.S. is rock solid."

Obama's former chief fiscal strategists then pedantically averred that Trump is utterly bereft of the wisdom and courage displayed by the Obama White House when it starred down the 2011 debt ceiling challenge of GOP backbenchers: "does anyone doubt that such Trumpisms could lead to a global panic with unknown economic harm to the global economy and the long-term economic reputation of the United States?"

Well, here's a newsflash for Gene Sperling and the rest of his "full faith and credit" choir of fiscal saboteurs. Roughly 80% of federal spending consists of transfer payments, debt service and other essentially locked-in commitments under law.

Accordingly, the debt ceiling is the only frail reed by which the inexorable expansion of this fiscal doomsday machine can be arrested. That's because the tiny band of fiscal patriots left in Washington has no power whatsoever to directly stop the entitlement and automatic spending machine.

Indeed, under the extant Democrat White House you would have needed a two-thirds vote to override the veto of any entitlement reform that could not possibly have slipped through Capitol Hill in the first place. So stopping the borrowing authority is the only way to get leverage to stop the spending.

Thus, when the "full faith and credit" chest-thumpers on both ends of Pennsylvania Avenue quashed the backbench uprising in August 2011, they insured that Washington's actual march toward default would continue unabated.

So doing they carried out the Big Lie. Namely, loudly and publicly denying that the U.S. Treasury secretary has the constitutional power to allocate and prioritize spending in the absence of new borrowing authority.

He does—even by the lights of liberal constitutional scholars like Professor Laurence Tribe of Harvard Law School. In fact, not paying military suppliers, highway contractors, Pell Grant recipients, cotton farmers and local public transit authorities their scheduled reimbursements and grants would concentrate the mind of Washington like nothing else.

Alas, that's why they never make choices and rarely say no. The preposterous lie that their hands are tied absent a debt-ceiling increase is far more politically convenient.

Yet these people have the audacity to chastise Donald Trump for toying out loud with the possibility of default? In fact, it is the Beltway ruling class that has been marching resolutely in that direction year in and year out for the better part of three decades.

As we documented in Chapter 8, for example, government transfer benefits have soared from $1 trillion per year at the turn of the century to $2.7 trillion at present.

Even then, the baby boom bulge driving this budget breakout is just getting up its demographic head of steam. During the next 15 years the entitlement tsunami will truly become a fiscal doomsday machine.

Thus, while Beltway hacks like Sperling have been harrumphing about full faith and credit and the sanctity of the humongous debts that they are piling on to generations born and unborn, the nation's fiscal doomsday equation has been permitted to run its course unmolested by Washington's supposed fiscal watchmen.

Even by the lights of the CBOs Keynesian scorekeepers, the budget deficit will hit $1.4 trillion and 5% of GDP by 2026 under current policy, meaning that another $10 trillion would be added to the public debt during the next decade as a whole.

And that assumes, as we have seen, no recession for 17 years and a rate of nominal GDP and wage growth that is 45% higher than that over the last decade.

Imagine what will happen in the real world when the Red Ponzi finally crumbles in China and the global economy plunges into a prolonged deflationary recession

What will occur, in fact, is that the public debt will rise by at least $15 trillion in the decade ahead under even a halfway-decent economic scenario. Add that to the $20 trillion which the next president will inherit and you have, as we documented earlier, a $24 trillion GDP lugging around a $35 trillion national debt.

Needless to say, Sperling has left the White House and is now out humping for Hillary, who promises to lower the Medicare age to 50 years and distribute a goodly amount of other free stuff from Bernie's playbook.

And that would be on top of the 150% of GDP public debt that is already baked into the cake.

ONLY YESTERDAY, THE PUBLIC DEBT WAS LESS THAN $1 TRILLION

Alas, the fiscal menace at loose in the land long predated Donald Trump.

In fact, it has been gathering momentum for the last 35 years. Astonishingly, a public debt which is practically *$20 trillion* today and heading for *$35 trillion* soon was less than $1 trillion in 1981.

Indeed, in the great fiscal scheme of things, Oct. 22, 1981 seems like only yesterday. That's the day the U.S. public debt crossed the $1 trillion mark for the first time. It had taken the nation 74,984 days to get there (205 years).

Your author remembers October 1981 perhaps better than most because as the nation's budget director at the time, I had some splainin' to do. Ronald Reagan had waged the most stridently anti-deficit campaign since 1932, when, ironically, FDR promised a balanced budget while denouncing Herbert Hoover as a "spendthrift.

Likewise, Governor Reagan had denounced Jimmy Carter's red ink and promised a balanced budget by 1983.

But as 1981 unfolded and the U.S. Treasury borrowed large sums each day to fund what we were pleased to call Jimmy Carter's "inherited deficits," the trillion dollar national debt threshold rushed upon us. And, in truth, it came far more rapidly than had been anticipated because by the fall of 1981, the Reagan White House had enacted the largest tax reduction in American history.

On top of that, it had also green-lighted a huge defense buildup, yet, as we liked to rationalize at the time, had made little more than a "down payment" on sweeping reforms of domestic spending and entitlements.

The latter were supposed to happen in subsequent years and had been designated by a placeholder in the out-year budgets infamously labeled the "magic asterisk." In fact, there was nothing magic or devious about it.

Washington well recognized that it represented large and painful reforms of Social Security and other middle class entitlements that were to happen in 1982 and beyond.

Needless to say, we never got there. What happened, instead, is that the GOP embraced a revisionist fiscal policy, which at first was called "grow your way out"; and, eventually, was articulated by the nefarious Dick Cheney as simply "deficits don't matter."

Additionally, a new regime came to the Fed in August 1987 when lapsed gold bug, Alan Greenspan, discovered that he could run the Fed's printing press with gusto, yet falsely claim credit for the disinflation of the 1990s.

As we showed in Chapter 5, however, it was the tens of millions of Chinese peasants streaming from the rice paddies into Mr. Deng's export factories that was actually responsible for Greenspan's tepid "disinflation." That history-changing development, in fact, inaugurated two decades of goods and labor deflation on a worldwide basis, allowing the Fed to monetize a growing portion of the ballooning national debt with seeming impunity.

LAST DAYS OF THE OLD-TIME FISCAL RELIGION

Yet none of that was anticipated in October 1981. Most of Washington was still in thrall to the old-time religion, fearing the untoward effects of chronic budget deficits and unbridled rise of the public debt. That is, that massive Treasury borrowing would "crowd" out private investment and eventually grind economic growth to a halt.

Even the Gipper, ever the optimist, did not want to trifle with this core precept of fiscal rectitude. With no inconsiderable reluctance, therefore, he embraced legislation to vault the national debt over the $1 trillion mark, while at the same time chiseling back his cherished tax cuts and defense build-up.

Back then, there was really no choice. You couldn't have found a single dyed-in-the-wool Keynesian or even Marxist economist who would have embraced the path of massive, permanent government borrowing and debt monetization by the central bank which actually ensued over the next three decades.

So Washington stumbled forward at the $1 trillion mark. By October 1981, with the U.S. economy sliding back into a double-dip recession, the fiscal math of Reaganomics was already beginning to burst at all the budgetary seams.

The Reagan tax cut had triggered a monumental bidding war on Capitol Hill among special interest lobbies, and had ended up reducing the permanent out-year revenue base by about 6.2% of GDP—compared to the original pure supply-side rate cut of less than 3.5% of GDP.

Likewise, the defense budget was supposed to have grown at about 5% in real terms for a few years, but the Pentagon had spooked the new president into authorizing a decade-long spending spree that would have tripled defense outlays by the mid-1980s (the neocons told him the Evil Empire was flexing for military victory when it was actually tumbling into economic collapse).

Needless to say, the modest domestic-spending cuts enacted during the Reagan administration's initial honeymoon did not even make a dent in these monumental excesses on the tax and defense fronts.

So in the fall of 1981, it was not merely the symbolic ignominy of crossing the trillion-dollar national-debt threshold for the first time that weighed on the White House. It was actually driven by fear that acquiescence in giant, permanent deficits would lead to economic ruin.

And by the standards of the past, where even Lyndon Johnson's infamous "guns and butter" deficit of 1968 had only amounted to 2.5% of GDP, the outlook was indeed dire. As I put it at the time, the nation faced 6% of GDP deficits "as far as the eye can see."

And there's one more salient point. The nation's central bank was then being run by the great Paul Volcker, who was determined to break the back of the double digit inflation that his predecessors, William Miller and Arthur Burns, had foisted on the nation during the 1970s.

It goes without saying, therefore, that no one thought Volcker was about to monetize the federal debt in order to let spendthrift politicians at either end of Pennsylvania Avenue off the hook.

So for nearly the last time in history, Washington reluctantly repaired to the "takeaway" mode. During the next three years by hook and crook about 40% of the giant Reagan tax cut was recouped.

Likewise, the bountiful flow of the defense pork barrel was stretched out and tamped down. And, crucially for all that was to follow, they payroll tax was jacked-up by about 20% in the guise of rescuing the Social Security trust fund from insolvency in 1983.

Taken together, these measures of fiscal restraint did a not inconsiderable amount of good. They put a cap on the runaway deficits that would have otherwise occurred owing to the frenzy of tax cutting and defense spending in 1981 and the drastic recessionary shock to the economy that had resulted from Volcker's unavoidable monetary medicine.

Still, for the period 1982–86, the federal deficit averaged 5% of GDP. Nothing like that had every been imagined before outside of world war— not even by Professors Samuelson, Heller, Tobin and the other leading Keynesian lights of the day.

During the peacetime period from 1954 to 1964, for example, the federal deficit had averaged less than 1% of GDP and Eisenhower had actually achieved several modest surpluses during the period.

Indeed, the deficit breakout that ensued notwithstanding the fiscal retrenchment efforts of 1982–84 was even embraced by assistant professor Paul Krugman.

Back then he was on economics staff of the Reagan White House. Never once did he aver that the national debt at only 33% of GDP was way too small, and that open-ended "stimulus" was in order.

But then came Volcker's victory over inflation, a strong economic rebound and the "morning in America" campaign of 1984. For all practical purposes, the job of fully restoring fiscal rectitude was left unfinished— and permanently so, as it turned out.

What happened was that the structural deficit begin to shrink modestly. This was in part owing to the strong economic recovery of 1983–85 when GDP growth averaged 5% per year, and also due to the delayed revenues gains from three tax increase bills signed by Reagan during 1982–84 and the massive payroll tax increase that was buried in the so-called bipartisan Social Security rescue (1983).

MORNING IN AMERICA—
THE HISTORICAL INFLECTION POINT

And that was the historical inflection point. Thereafter, Social Security and Medicare entitlement reform was off the table due to the trick of the front-loaded payroll-tax increase.

This caused cash surpluses in the trust funds and the accumulation of intra-governmental accounting IOUs for the next two decades. At the same time, these front-end surpluses functioned to bury the long range fiscal disaster these intergenerational "social insurance" entitlements embody in 75-year projections that are always way too optimistic.

Likewise, the White House took any further tax increases or defense cuts off the table in January 1985. The spending-cut-weary politicians of both parties, in turn, were more than happy to oblige by shelving any further meaningful domestic spending reforms, as well.

So in 1985, fiscal policy went on automatic pilot—where it has more or less languished ever since. Even well before the fiscal madness of George W. Bush broke out in 2001, the handwriting was on the wall.

By the time the 12 years of the Reagan-Bush administrations had elapsed, the public debt had reached $4.3 trillion, and was then 4X the size of national debt that Jimmy Carter had left behind.

Ironically, Ronald Reagan, the scourge of deficit spending, and his 1980 primary opponent, George HW Bush, who had noisily campaigned against "voodoo economics," had teamed up to generate deficits that averaged 4.1% of GDP.

That initial 12-year plunge into permanent deficit finance was not owing to a weak economy or insufficiently robust real GDP growth, as Reagan revisionists have argued ever since. In fact, between 1982 and 1993, GDP growth averaged 3.6% annually and was at the top of the historic range.

No, it was a political choice that changed the policy landscape forever. The Reagan-Bush deficits amounted to 3X the average deficit that had been accrued during peacetime by FDR, Truman, Kennedy-Johnson and Jimmy Carter combined.

Accordingly, once the GOP had thrown in the fiscal towel, the Democrats would never again face Tip O'Neill's great fear. Namely, that they would be someday flushed out of their congressional majority owing to a 1946 style GOP attack on the Democrats' proclivity for deficit spending.

But there was something more. The economic ruin that was supposed to flow from large chronic fiscal deficits did not immediately happen—at least in the time frame that had been traditionally imagined.

Accordingly, the GOP gradually embraced a militant antitax doctrine that simply ignored the ballooning levels of national debt.

So in the blink of an historical eye, U.S. fiscal governance tumbled into the ditch. Both parties became advocates of free lunch economics, and the race toward national bankruptcy was on.

To be sure, Bourbon Democrats and the fading ranks of orthodox Republicans made one last run at restoring fiscal rectitude during the early Clinton days. And on paper, they made considerable progress.

Indeed, the federal budget registered surpluses during the last three years of the 1990s—albeit unsustainable ones owing to the massive one-time tax windfalls from Greenspan's dot-com bubble.

But the structural fiscal problem was not solved; it was merely temporarily buried beneath three delusions.

THE THREE GREAT FISCAL DELUSIONS

The first was that the giant Reagan defense build-up—which was actually a vast armada of conventional land, sea and air forces ideally suited to wars of invasion and occupation—would go quietly in the night when the cold war ended and the Evil Empire was no more. It didn't.

Instead, the military-industrial complex and its neocon propagandists panicked the nation into a pointless "war on terrorism" after the fluke tragedy of 9/11. Soon the defense budget had doubled, rising from under 3.0% of GDP during the early post–Cold War period to nearly 6.0% of GDP after Bush's war campaigns reached full intensity by 2007.

Likewise, the front-loaded payroll-tax hike eventually exhausted its capacity to deceive. Accordingly, by fiscal 2013 the OASI fund (retirement) ran a $95 billion cash deficit and the DI fund (disability) generated an additional $45 billion cash deficit. This means that on a combined basis, the cash deficit was nearly $140 billion annually and growing rapidly into the future.

In effect, the so-called Social Security surplus, which had financed the general fund deficit for more than two decades, had not simply disappeared. As we detailed at length in Chapter 8, they had now entered the liquidation phase of Washington's phony trust fund accounting scheme.

What this means is that the $19.4 trillion of public debt outstanding today is the real debt—not the convenient illusion peddled by Washington and Keynesian economists that the "publicly held" debt is only $13.5 trillion and therefore a "manageable" 75% of GDP.

Nope, the nation's true public debt ratio today is 106% of GDP. Thirty-five years on from the first trillion dollar crossing, the public debt burden on national income has tripled. And when you add the $3 trillion of state and local debt, the total public sector debt ratio is nearly 120% of GDP.

And that gets to the final question. How did Washington get away with this vast fiscal debauch? How did we get to the point where an unschooled outlaw candidate for president would utter the impertinence of default?

The short answer is that Trump is here because Washington's fiscal kick-the-can-game depended upon a central bank monetary parlor trick that left Flyover America behind, and that, in any event, is now over and done.

To wit, "crowding out" and high consumer price inflation never occurred because the Greenspan Fed launched the entire world economy down a path of massive credit expansion and financialization—an insidious process engineered by the concerted action of all the major central banks. That convoy of money printers generated large but dangerous central bank "vaults" where Uncle Sam's debt has been temporarily sequestered.

THE GLOBAL MONETARY ROACH MOTEL

It was the equivalent of a monetary roach motel: the bonds went in, but they never came out. What happened in practical economic terms is that central bank fiat credit was substituted for real savings from privately earned incomes in the financing of public debt.

Indeed, owing to currency pegging by the mercantilist export economies of Asia and the oil exporters nearly $5 trillion of the U.S. public debt has been absorbed by foreign central banks and sovereign wealth funds. Another $3 trillion is owned by the Fed. And still another $5 trillion, as indicated above, had been temporarily funded by intragovernmental trust funds that are now about to plunge into an irreversible liquidation mode.

Two thing are therefore evident. The first is that massive monetization of the public debt cannot go on much longer, or else the monetary system will be destroyed. That's what being stuck on the so-called zero-bound really means. And that's why the lunatic money printing in Japan is a sign that the end of the monetization era is at hand.

In the case of Japan, the largest debtor government in the world has already destroyed its own bond market—the BOJ is the only bid left at negative 0.2% on the 10-year JGB.

Secondly, as we also documented in Chapter 8, the U.S. nominal GDP has been growing at barely 3% annually for the last decade, and, in a deflationary world, it has no chance of breaking away from that constraint.

Accordingly, the ridiculously optimistic rosy scenario currently projected by CBO does not have a snowball's chance of materializing over the next decade.

In fact, the $10 trillion of cumulative baseline deficits over the next ten years projected by CBO is drastically underestimated. As we indicated above, Washington will generate at least $15 trillion of new public debt in the decade ahead under a realistic economic forecast that essentially assumes the next 10 years will perform as well as the past decade.

So the nation's current mountain of public debt will inexorably rise to $35 trillion by 2026 or so. Likewise, the giant financial bubble and vast malinvestments generated by the world's central banks over the last two decades now guarantee a long spell of global deflation.

That's why we believe that the U.S. nominal GDP will be lucky to reach $24 trillion by that same year (3% annual growth). The math computes out to a public debt equal to nearly 150% of GDP.

THE GLOBAL SOVEREIGN-DEBT MARKET— THE MOTHER OF ALL FINANCIAL BUBBLES

For all practical purposes, these budgetary realities mean an endless fiscal crisis lurks in the nation's future.

That's the real end game of a lamentable path of unprecedented fiscal profligacy embarked upon 35 years ago.

Needless to say, it was not Donald Trump who trashed the "full faith and credit of the United States" along the way.

Nor is it Donald Trump who offers the prospect of a solution. As we demonstrated in Chapter 1, his stated plans would make the nation's fiscal accounts even worse.

You don't need a lot of wonky budgetary detail to know that if you increase defense spending, massively cut taxes and exempt Social Security, you end up with even more red ink. That's what Ronald Reagan proved for all time.

No, the only thing which will arrest Washington's headlong toward fiscal ruin is the upcoming crash of the global bond market. It is the mother of all financial bubbles thanks to the $20 trillion of bond buying by the world's central banks over the past two decades.

This lunacy and financial fraud inserted the central banks' big fat thumb on the supply and demand scales in the world fixed-income markets, thereby causing the price of bonds to soar and their yields to virtually shrink to the vanishing point.

Indeed, within the proximate $40 trillion worldwide sovereign debt market, upward of $13 trillion of government debt trades at sub-zero yields and the weighted average yield of the total outstanding is less than 1%.

When QE finally ends in Europe and Japan, and it will end soon in order to avert monetary catastrophe, there will be a massive rush for the exists when the punters who now own trillions of sovereign debt on 95% repo realize the jig is up.

That is, without the massive artificial bid of central banks, the price of government debt is going to fall hard. That will threaten, in turn, to wipeout the accumulated capital gains of these bond market front-runners and crush the carry-trade spreads on which their speculative positioning is based.

Needless to say, when the fast money starts selling in order to lock-in what remains of their unspeakable windfall profits, there will be no bid for a falling knife.

Trillions will be lost. Government's that can't roll their massive but suddenly far more expensive debts will default. The Donald's expertise in that department, at least, should be given its due.

CHAPTER 10:

How the GOP Got Trumped— the Fiscal Follies of Johnny Lawn Chair and Faker Ryan

I N THE IMPROBABLE CANDIDACY OF DONALD TRUMP, THE REPUBLICAN PARTY got what it deserved. After all, its job in the context of American political democracy is to function as the nation's fiscal guardian. Yet that role hardly fits the GOP's new presidential nominee and erstwhile constructor of hotels and casinos, who now promises to build the greatest ever walls, roads, bridges, military and other accouterments of national greatness.

But then again, the GOP has been derelict on the fiscal front for most of the last for 35 years . Instead, it has become a gang of neocons, social cons, tax cons and just cons. Perhaps that's why Trump makes the latter so uneasy.

The first two of these contemporary GOP factions—the neocons and the "social cons" aggrandize the size and role of the state. This extends from the uninvited policing of the world's neighborhoods and nations to the unjust intrusion into domestic family, religious and social life.

The "tax cons" correctly recognize that private enterprise, not the state, generates prosperity and wealth and that tax barriers and disincentives to production, investment and work should be lowered whenever possible. But they fail to heed the great Dwight D. Eisenhower's fundamental rule for fiscal governance now that the cat of Big Government is out of the bag.

Namely, that tax cuts must be earned with off-setting retrenchment of the spending and entitlement accounts. That's how Ike balanced the budget several times during his eight year tenure, even as he struggled to reduce the military budget by 33% in real terms and chisel away at the economically stifling edifice of the Roosevelt/Truman war taxes.

The GOP's latter-day supply siders, unfortunately, did the opposite—especially during the era of Republican rule under George "Dubya" Bush. The "tax cons" joined hands with the neocons to protect and enlarge the Reagan warfare-state budget, expanding its present-day purchasing power to more than twice what General Eisenhower thought was adequate at the very peak of the Cold War. At the same time, they slashed the revenue base by nearly 4% of GDP with two giant unearned tax cuts.

So doing, they replicated the fiscal betrayal of the Reagan years with even less justification. Indeed, rather than pretending as did the Gipper that deficits would eventually go away owing to "growth," the tax cons of the Dick Cheney schism militantly proclaimed they didn't even matter.

In this context, the balance of rank-and-file congressional Republicans morphed into "just cons."

That is, they settled into the business of harvesting campaign loot from the K Street lobbies and the endless racketeering enterprises of the Imperial City. And especially after Citizens United opened the floodgates, the congressional GOP became a pure fund-raising machine that happened to dispense talking points favored by the neocons, social cons and tax cons—when, as and if convenient.

GOOD RIDDANCE TO JOHNNY LAWNCHAIR

And that gets us to the startling midterm upheaval in the House GOP leadership last fall. Except that leadership is hardly the word for the speakership of the feckless John Boehner or his replacement, by the equally spineless Congressman Paul Ryan.

As I will document below, under the faithless leadership of Boehner and Ryan the large GOP House majority has been turned into a dysfunctional, squabbling gang. Notwithstanding the 2010 election's Tea Party sweep, the House GOP has accomplished nothing on behalf of free enterprise, sound money and small government.

But worse still, it has utterly betrayed its core historical responsibility to defend the nation's fiscal solvency. On that score, its record is so abysmal that it might as well embrace the budgetary follies that Trump has so far managed to enumerate—for all the difference it would make.

As we showed in Chapter 9, the hoary excuse that a divided Senate and hostile Obama White House prevented the GOP House of Representatives from taking meaningful action on the fiscal front doesn't wash. The House GOP had a huge lever called the "debt ceiling" that time and again it surrendered with hardly a fight.

The fact is, had the House GOP leadership held fast and refused to raise the debt ceiling at $14.3 trillion way back in August 2011, and especially on the heels of its Tea Party election sweep, it would have forced the unthinkable on the Imperial City. And that would have made all the difference.

To wit, the Obama White House would have been required to prioritize and allocate spending down to the level of incoming revenue. Such an unheard of exercise of Uncle Sam temporarily living within his means would have broken the deadly shibboleth that every dime of Uncle Sam's bills must be paid once they are incurred.

Instead, payments to military vendors, local governments, student loan recipients, highway contractors and checks to federal employees and beneficiaries would have been deferred or cutback. The resulting wailing and gnashing of teeth among the legions at the federal trough would have been a wonder of political history.

In that fraught context, a determined speaker postured in behalf of the taxpayers and producers of Flyover America could have written his own ticket in terms of the entitlement reforms and spending cutbacks that would be necessary for him to lift the fiscal siege. The back of the federal doomsday machine—a budget in which upwards of 80% of outlays stem from entitlements, debt service and other automatic or contractual spending—would have been broken.

Needless to say, Boehner and then Paul Ryan after him took the route of accommodation and surrender in the name of "bipartisan governance." But the latter is no virtue of high-minded statesmanship; it's a pernicious invention of the Beltway's permanent ruling class designed to keep the pork and entitlements flowing, the national debt growing and the Fed's printing presses glowing red hot.

So here's the truth. The existing GOP leadership is far worse than even the false caricatures that the elite commentariat and ruling class has thrown up against Donald Trump.

In fact, there are few political hacks in Washington more deserving of everlasting ignominy than the retiring House speaker because he represented in one package all four gangs that have hijacked the Republican Party.

So we now offer a vehement good riddance to the man who has single-handedly destroyed whatever pathetic semblance of fiscal responsibility that remained in Washington prior to his baleful tenure.

The so-called bipartisan budget deal of 2015 that he confected as a parting gesture doesn't even deserve to be called a farce. It's actually just an extension of Washington's pathological lying to the American public about the monumental fiscal calamity now brewing.

More importantly, it's a case in point of why a confused and desperate Flyover America is turning to a strong man like Donald Trump to fix a system that it can plainly see is completely broken.

The chart below shows Washington's patented "kick-the-can" formula—employed for the second time since the phony sequester mechanism was put in place during the debt-ceiling crisis of 2011.

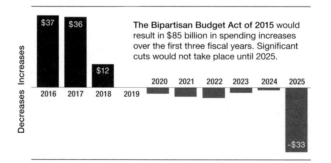

The Boehner/Obama deal will increase spending by $85 billion in the here and now by busting the FY 2016 and 2017 caps. This new red ink will then, purportedly, be off-set way down the road with gimmicks, imaginary IRS audit revenues and hazy disability benefit reforms which will never materialize. Never.

Indeed, these people are beyond shame. The big bulge of $33 billion of savings shown for the Neverland of 2025 is due to a sharp increase in assumed discretionary spending cuts and Medicare benefit reductions. That is, the very same programs that are being pumped up during the next three years!

And that's the same thing the Ryan-Murray bipartisan comprise did two years ago with respect to FY2014–15. In combination these 11th hour bipartisan shams have thus added $143 billion of real money to the national debt for the years through 2021, "paying" for them with imaginary savings to be realized after 2021. That is, until we get there—at which time anything which bites into the gravy train will be predictably deferred.

Nor is that the extent of Johnny Lawnchair's odious record of fiscal betrayal since 2011. In the first instance, he broke the will of fiscal conservatives just when they had Washington over the debt ceiling barrel in August 2011 with the promise of $1.5 trillion of entitlement savings via the super committee.

What an unrelieved farce that was. After yielding on the debt-ceiling increase and then being subjected to endless establishment media hounding about what a political mistake it had been, the rubes from Tea Party and soon discovered that "bipartisan compromise" is no such thing at all—it's a cover for political surrender.

The so-called super committee didn't even try to reform entitlements and hardly even meet. Instead, the Capitol Hill establishment simply faded into another Big Lie.

Not to be troubled, they said, when the super committee turned in an empty exam sheet at its due date in late 2011. Why, the very same $1.5 trillion of "savings" will now be achieved from discretionary defense and domestic appropriations accounts via the automatic sequester mechanism.

At length, those sequester caps started to bite in 2013. So Boehner sent out his budget lapdog—pedigreed fiscal faker and now his successor, Paul Ryan—to negotiate relief for the military-industrial complex and to ensure plentiful pork for GOP candidates in the 2014 election.

That particular task the fiscal faker from Wisconsin accomplished with alacrity—just as he did back in 2008–9 when the GM plant located in his district needed a bailout from the taxpayers.

THE 2015 BIPARTISAN DEAL—BOEHNER'S FASTEST FOLD EVER

Soon still-another election season was pending and yet-another debt-ceiling increase had been all used up. So, predictably, as the debt ceiling expiration approached in October 2015, Boehner folded so fast that the mainstream media barely knew he had gone to the White House.

On a lickety-split basis Johnny Lawnchair not only jettisoned two more years of the discretionary spending sequester, but also blew any other inconvenient fiscal restraint lurking between then and 2017. That included a perfectly reasonable and long scheduled increase in Medicare Part B premiums for the better off elderly and the impending action-forcing exhaustion of the Social Security disability trust fund.

In the best kick-the-can style, as we mentioned earlier, the latter will be funded by raiding $150 billion from the retirement trust fund, while pretending that Washington bureaucrats at the Social Security Administration will write new rules to prevent abuse of a program that is totally out of control.

And that word hardly describes the scandal of it. The program's budget cost has tripled in real terms just since 1990, mainly due to an explosion of "back pain" and "mental illness" cases. Those dubious diagnoses now account for fully 55% of recipients compared to less than 15% in 1961.

So here is an entitlement crying out for sweeping statutory reform and faced with a complete cessation of benefits before the 2016 election due to the impending exhaustion of the DI trust fund. But that kind of rare fiscal leverage is never used when you have the likes of Johnny Lawnchair and Faker Ryan negotiating a "responsible" bipartisan deal.

In any event, sooner or later workers will get socked with another round of payroll-tax increases to bailout the entirety of the OASDI trust fund complex, which we demonstrated in Chapter 8 will be insolvent by

2026. But in the interim, the military-industrial complex has surely been tickled pink by Boehner's parting betrayal of U.S. taxpayers.

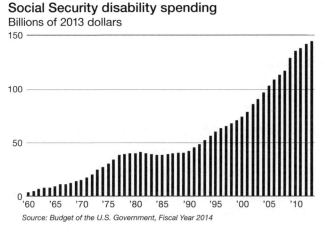

Social Security disability spending
Billions of 2013 dollars

Source: Budget of the U.S. Government, Fiscal Year 2014

In fact, the Boehner/Obama deal of 2015 will increase discretionary-spending authority by $112 billion over the next two years. This includes the $80 billion increase in the discretionary-spending caps plus another $32 billion increase for war contingencies and other national-security programs not subject to the sequester.

Not surprisingly, $72 billion, or nearly two-thirds of that budget-busting add-on, goes to the Pentagon, Washington's vast intelligence and spy networks and the State Department's security programs. Apparently all those extra billions were needed to contain the Russian bugaboo.

Yes, that seemed especially the case after Putin showed how you actually fight terrorists in Syria, and not by spending $500 million on 50 trainees—all of who were captured, shot or deserted within weeks of being placed in the field—as did the CIA.

But the military-industrial complex always needs more. With this further largesse, total U.S. national-security spending will touch nearly $800 billion next year, including the military, foreign and security aid, and veterans and related spending. That's two-thirds of Russia's entire 2015 GDP of $1.3 trillion!

Of course, we don't have a real industrial-state enemy in the world that could actually threaten the security and safety of citizens in Lincoln, Neb., and Boston, Mass. But that has not stopped Johnny Lawnchair from folding on the fiscal issue time after time in order to make a deal with liberal big spenders to get more funding for the military-industrial complex.

Can you say postretirement lobbying, consulting and speaking gigs? Don't bother. Boehner had been working on that for years.

HOW THE GOP LEADERSHIP RAN OUT THE FISCAL CLOCK

At the end of the day, however, the Speaker's most egregious sin has been to run out the clock on the possibility of fiscal retrenchment. After his parting shot which froze policy for another two years, there was no possibility of a true budget deal until the summer of 2017. That means no real impact on the budget numbers until CY 2019—since its takes several quarters to crank-up any meaningful revenue measures or entitlement reforms.

At that point in time (October 2019), of course, it would be exactly 123 months since the so-called Great Recession ended. Have we ever had an economic expansion that long—even during the years when the American economy was riding high and when the Fed had not yet exhausted its ability to goose credit and spending with easy money?

No we haven't. The longest expansion in history is 119 months and the average since 1950 is on 61 months.

So, effectively, Johnny Lawnchair and his sidekick Ryan compromised the nation's fiscal plight right into the next recession and the renewed outbreak of trillion dollar annual deficits. That is, to a point when Washington will once again be paralyzed with fear that actually paying our bills would drive the stumbling U.S. economy further into the drink.

And what possible excuse did Johnny Lawnchair have for delivering the nation into this absolutely certain fiscal catastrophe?

He didn't wish to demand that the president employ his constitutional powers to allocate and prioritize spending in the event Uncle Sam had exhausted his legal authority to borrow.

That's why Johnny Lawnchair deserves everlasting infamy—or at least until Paul Ryan comes up with new excuses for burying future generations in terminal debt.

SPEAKER PAUL RYAN: NEW OCCUPANT, SAME FAST-FOLDING LAWNCHAIR

Supposedly a new era was to dawn under Boehner's successor Paul Ryan. But not so. The lawn chair never left—it just got a new occupant.

After just 51 days in office, Ryan has forced the GOP to walk the plank on what under any honest form of fiscal accounting is a $2.5 trillion addition to the national debt.

Well, make that any form of accounting at all. This whole stinking pile of backroom deals was pushed through so fast that even CBO did not have a chance to fully analyze and score the bill.

In that regard, for the first time in his life, Harry Reid told the truth after this Ryan-Obama midnight special was whisked through the House and Senate at year-end 2015.

Said the man of legendary forked tongue, "Sometime in the darkness, the bill was finalized . . . [N]o legislation is perfect, but this is good legislation."

It should come as no surprise that Paul Ryan is a complete fiscal fake. After all, he has spent years braying about the national debt, but never saw a defense program he didn't want to fund or a bailout that would help his Wisconsin district that he couldn't rationalize.

Fiscal conservative? The man voted for the TARP bailout of Wall Street and the bailout of the GM/UAW thieves, too.

And year after year he had proposed a "Ryan budget- reform plan that was a complete fraud. He did not remove one dime from Social Security spending, ever.

Not even for the wealthy retired duffers who live on golf courses in Florida and Arizona.

Nor did his fiscal plans do anything about the $700 billion in annual cost of Medicare for at least a decade into the future. And he didn't even bother to balance the federal budget until 2037!

But what was so obnoxious about this latest pork-festooned betrayal of the taxpayers is that it was totally unnecessary.

Ryan could have simply announced that there is a new sheriff in the House and that no one would leave town until New Year's Eve if need be—unless the pork was excised first and the bills $680 billion worth of tax benefits, gimmicks and loopholes were either removed or off-set with honest "payfors."

Needless to say, Speaker Ryan had a totally different take. While this year-end fiscal abomination was just water over the damn, there will always another chance: "Congress can now move into 2016 with a fresh start . . ."

No it won't and most assuredly it hasn't. The Ryan/Obama FY2016 omnibus appropriations bill was just another ruse in a moveable fiscal scam that, as I outlined above, has been underway since the debt-ceiling crisis of August 2011.

Back then, Congress claimed to cut the 10-year deficit by $2 trillion, mainly through $1.2 trillion via the so-called appropriations sequester after the super committee failed to come up with equivalent entitlement and other permanent reforms.

But here's the skunk in the woodpile. Congress claimed $1.2 trillion in savings from discretionary-spending caps over a 10-year period through FY 2021, yet appropriations bills are good for only one year. So what it really did was establish a mechanism to have its cake and eat it too.

Because the future year caps are statutory, CBO must dutifully score them as a reduction in the budget baseline every time it does a ten-year projection. At the same time, during each annual appropriations cycle, Congress can modify or bust the caps entirely for the current year, and then either take a "one-time" hit to the deficit or find gimmicks to off-set some or all of the cost.

In fact, every year since 2011, Congress has lifted the discretionary-spending caps for the current fiscal year in order to make room for bloated domestic and DOD appropriations. Ryan's omnibus bill did exactly the same.

To wit, discretionary appropriations for DOD and domestic agencies during FY 2016 and FY 2017 will be $100 billion per year higher than the annual caps adopted with so much fanfare back in 2011.

Thus, we are now halfway through the ten-year cycle initiated in the August 2011 crisis—so savings from the sequester caps on the annual appropriations bills should have totaled at least $500 billion by now. In fact, when you cut through all the gimmicks, ruses, re-estimates and program reconfigurations that have been deployed in the interim the actual savings would amount to a rounding error around zero.

FAKER RYAN AT WORK—CHIMPS AND OCO

There are two features of the current bill which expose the manner in which this moveable scam operates. The first is something called CHIMPs or changes in mandatory programs. These gems are claimed to be budget authority cuts that offset appropriations which exceed the caps.

In the current bill these CHIMPs savings for FY 2016 total $18.6 billion, and they permitted literally hundreds of add-ons to be stuffed back into the 12 appropriations bills.

But only $0.6 billion or 3% of these CHIMPs savings will actually reduce cash outlays. By contrast, $13 billion represents savings in FY 2016 that get added back in FY 2017. And the remaining $5 billion are technical cuts to budget authority that will never results in a dime of cash savings during any year.

Likewise, Congress has stuffed $73.7 billion into the OCO (overseas contingency operations) bucket, which in theory was set up to cover the one-time and unusual cost of military operations in Iraq and Afghanistan.

Apart from the fact that Imperial Washington does nothing abroad on a one-time basis and that wars of intervention are not a contingency but a permanent policy, there was never any justification for exempting these expenditures from the caps in the first place,

After all, spending is fungible. When it comes to allocating the multi-billion annual operating cost of a carrier battle group stationed in the Persian Gulf between it "peacetime baseline" and its "war contingency" elements, for instance, you can get any answer which is convenient.

The point is that the OCO has provided a huge cookie jar for spending increases that nullify even the modified appropriations ceilings that Congress has enacted each year since 2011.

This year (FY 2016) roughly $15 billion of the OCO will go to the State Department for foreign aid and other international-security programs, and this figure is up roughly $6 billion from a similar OCO allocation last year.

At the same time, the omnibus bill cuts the State Department's "regular" appropriation by about $5 billion, and re-allocates these funds to a huge smattering of pork and add-ons to the other domestic appropriations bills.

On a net basis, therefore, everybody wins . . . except the taxpayers.

That is, the State Department's available funding will be up by $1 billion as between the regular and OCO buckets, while appropriations for the domestic agencies will be higher by $5 billion. Yet none of this will show up in the $1.066 trillion ceiling on discretionary spending.

It's all backdoored through the OCO!

THE MOVEABLE BUDGET SCAM— PHONY 10-YEAR "BASELINE" PROJECTIONS

The larger point is that the Fed's massive repression of interest rates has spawned a fiscal culture of unspeakable deception, duplicity, lies and dysfunctionality on Capitol Hill.

On the one hand, it means that the $19 trillion of national debt can be serviced on the cheap—currently at a weighted average yield of about 1.8%. Accordingly, debt service costs which would be upwards of $1 trillion under normalized interest rates (5%) are currently only about $350 billion. So the politicians—even self-proclaimed fiscal hawks like Ryan—feel no financial pressure, and become accustomed to blithely kicking the can.

At the same time, the moveable fiscal scam described above has resulted in an utterly deceptive 10-year deficit forecasts—even after funding the national debt on the cheap.

The CBO's so-called baseline projections show out-year spending far lower than what is actually built into the system, and not merely due to the deceptive rosy-scenario economic forecasts I exposed in Chapter 9.

The long-term deficit outlook is further understated owing to the phony out-year caps and entitlement reforms that CBO is required by Congress to credit.

That's right. Congress has no intention of allowing these future-year fiscal curtailments to become effective, but still insists on counting them when summing up completely phony 10-year savings totals. Yet when the "out-years" become the current year, they are simply suspended, deferred or covered up with new offsetting out-year savings gimmicks like those in last year's omnibus bill.

By the same token, baseline revenues are projected to be far higher than will actually materialize under current policy. That's due to the operation of the same kind of moveable scam on the income side of the budget ledger.

In this case, there are literally hundreds of billions per year of tax incentives, subsidies and loopholes that have been in the IRS code for years or even decades that are made to artificially and abruptly expire a year or two down the road. Accordingly, CBO scores a commensurate increase in the out-year revenue base, thereby contributing to the appearance that the long-term deficit is shrinking.

But when we get to the statutory expiration dates, these provisions never happen and the huge revenue drains continue. The culprit is something called that annual "tax extender" bill, which mostly just rolls forward the expiration dates by a year or two so that the CBO can keep projecting sunny fiscal skies ahead.

This is evident in spades in the $680 billion worth of so-called tax-extenders also contained in last year's omnibus bill. One of them is the corporate tax credit for research and experimentation, which costs about $12 billion per year in foregone revenue.

Now that particular item has been "extended" about 16 times over the past decades, meaning that out-year budget projections have always included higher revenue from the expiration of a major tax loophole that the bipartisan majority and their K-Street paymasters never, ever intended to happen.

In fact, the proof is now in the pudding. In a token gesture of honesty, the current bill actually makes the research credit permanent, and thereby reduces 10-year revenues by $113 billion. So, finally, that particular chunk of phantom revenue will be no more.

Unfortunately, that can't be said for much else in the tax components of the package. For instance, the completely unjustifiable and wasteful tax credits for solar and wind energy have been "expiring" almost annually since they were enacted years ago. This time they were extended effectively for three and one-half years at a cost of $26 billion, according to the Joint Tax Committee.

In truth, the giant lobby behind these boondoggles has demonstrated its insurmountable power so many times over the last few years that there is no chance these "expirations" will ever happen. So the actual 10-year cost of these renewable-energy provisions is more like $75 billion.

THANKS, SPEAKER RYAN—YOU DIDN'T REPEAL OBAMACARE, YOU DOUBLE SHUFFLED IT

One of the most egregious cases of this kind of double shuffle pertains to the three Obamacare taxes, which are deferred by several years at an alleged cost of $28 billion. In truth it's more like $260 billion.

Here's why. Recall that the true cost of Obamacare was in the trillions, but it was outrageously disguised as a deficit reducer through a series of huge gimmicks, such as changing the student loan program from an entitlement to a direct loan; and also through a series of stiff taxes on insurers, medical devices and so-called Cadillac medical plans.

However, these so-called "pay fors" were back-loaded into the middle of this decade in order to pacify the intense political opposition to them and to assemble the razor-thin partisan majority by which the program was enacted in 2010.

In particular, core Democrat constituencies like the labor unions were violently opposed to the so-called "Cadillac tax" on expensive, gold-plated employer health plans. That was even after the threshold plan value was raised to $27,000 per year for family coverage before the 40% tax kicks in. So the inception date was deferred into the distance future—to 2018.

Well, the distant future is now getting closer, and like with almost everything else in Obamacare that created intensive political opposition, such as the employer mandate, the time had come time to kick the can.

So the Cadillac tax was deferred two years until 2020. Likewise, the tax on medical devices was "paused" for 2016 and 2017—an action consistent with previous pauses and deferrals.

That's right. They had the audacity to say they paused the thing that they never intend to become effective. In that same vein, in fact, the health-insurers tax that pays for part of the Obamacare subsidies to families up to 3X the median income was also paused for a year.

The plain fact of life is that none of these out-year Obamacare taxes will ever be collected. Accordingly, the real hit to future deficits is in the order of one quarter trillion dollars over the next 10 years.

The above matters do not even begin to itemize the fiscal largesse embedded in the omnibus bill. But they do crystalize the underlying moveable fiscal scam at work—a systematic process by which future spending growth is disguised and future revenue collections vastly exaggerated.

In last year's omnibus bill alone, the true impact on revenues over 10 years was about $1.2 trillion, not the $523 billion scored by the CBO. After the interest-carry cost even at the low rates assumed by the CBO, the add-on to future deficits is on the order of $1.5 trillion.

Likewise, the CBO scores the spending increases at $158 billion over the next decade, but for all practical purposes this bill marks the de facto end of the sequester caps that were enacted in 2011. Accordingly, if you eliminate the phony out-year reductions that are still embedded in the CBO baseline, spending would be about $1 trillion higher after interest carry.

In short, Speaker Ryan's first turn at bat produced a $2.5 trillion budget buster!

And that's not the half of it.

As we indicated previously, given the lags in the legislative process and implementation schedules, meaningful cash savings and deficit reductions could not be effectuated until FY 2019 or FY 2020 at the earliest.

Still, no one has outlawed the business cycle, and by then this so-called recovery would be 125 months old.

So for the next president to escape a recessionary downturn in the U.S. economy and Uncle Sam's fiscal footings is not even a remote possibility in a world that is plunging into a deflationary recession even now.

So here's the truth. When you add back the trillions of phony spending cuts and revenue increase that are built into the current budget baseline and throw-in the next recession, we have estimated that the real world addition to the national debt will be at least $15 trillion during the next ten years.

And that will be piled on top of the $20 trillion of public debt that will be in place by the time of the 2017 inauguration.

Can this nation manage a $35 trillion public debt at the very time that the baby boom is retiring at a rate of 10,000 per day?

That's not likely under any circumstances—but most certainly never under the watch of fiscal fakes like Speaker Paul Ryan.

So maybe Donald Trump's reluctance to support the speaker's reelection bid was based on more than what meets the eye.

Yes, The Donald has no plan at all to fix the nation's fiscal crisis, as we have demonstrated previously. But perhaps he does realize that if elected his job will be to clean up the crushing fiscal folly bequeathed by those swell bipartisan regulars—Johnny Lawnchair and Faker Ryan.

CHAPTER 11:

America's Bridges Are Not Falling Down: The Perennial Myth of Crumbling Infrastructure

THERE IS A GOOD REASON WHY DONALD TRUMP'S CAMPAIGN HAS BEEN light on policy details. To wit, it seems that every time he gets specific he manages to serve up a steaming pile of hogwash.

So when he told Fox News that he would double-down on Hillary's $275 billion infrastructure boondoggle, The Donald was right on cue. And in pulling his new $500 billion infrastructure program straight out from under his comb-over, he also demonstrated he has no idea what he is talking about on this topic, among many.

> "Donald Trump on Tuesday proposed a plan to rebuild U.S. infrastructure that costs "at least double" the amount that Hillary Clinton has floated, in what would amount to a massive new government program . . . Well, I would say at least double her numbers, and you're going to really need more than that. We have bridges that are falling down. I don't know if you've seen the warning charts, but we have many, many bridges that are in danger of falling."

No, Donald, the bridges of America are not falling down, and the nation's infrastructure—to the extent that it is any business of Imperial Washington at all—is not "crumbling." Actually, Washington's primary job is maintenance of the Interstate Highway System, and that's in pretty good shape, including its heavily trafficked bridges.

More importantly, if additional investment is needed in the interstate highway grid, then the users should pay for it with a modest increase in the gasoline tax.

Or better still, Washington merely needs to rescind the earmarks that divert upwards of 67 percent of the existing $45 billion per year of gas tax revenues to state and local roads, mass transit, bike trails, walking paths, weed removal, transportation museums and countless other diversions. In short order the system would be in tip-top shape.

But that's not the half of Trump's wild pitch on this one. Having swallowed the infrastructure myth hook, line and sinker, the GOP candidate went a horrid step further and talked up an "infrastructure bank"—the Democrats' favorite backdoor route to further ballooning the nation's already-crushing public debt.

Despite insisting that "I'm doing the biggest tax decrease," Trump saw no sweat at all in coming up with the half trillion dollar price tag for his latest brainstorm:

> "We'll get a fund. We'll make a phenomenal deal with the low interest rates," he said. Who would provide the money? "People, investors. People would put money into the fund. The citizens would put money into the fund," he said, adding that he'd use "infrastructure bonds from the country, from the United States."

95% OF INFRASTRUCTURE IS NOT A FEDERAL RESPONSIBILITY

Upward of 95 percent of what passes for infrastructure investment—highways, roads, streets, bridges, airports, seaports, mass transit, water and sewer, the power grid, parks and recreation etc.—are the responsibility of the private sector and should be paid for by users or, arguably, constitute local public goods and amenities. The latter should be managed by state and local governments and be funded by local users and taxpayers.

But give the Beltway lobbies and racketeers an inch and they will take a mile. After decades of federal mission creep, there is virtually no aspect of "infrastructure" spending that has not wormed its way into the federal budget.

That's why the nation has $19.4 trillion of public debt already. But there is also a larger issue. Namely, what's the point of federalism and some 89,000 units of state, county and local government if these taxpayer funded agencies can't even provide for fare box revenues on local bus routes, maintenance of secondary highways and streets or water and sewer services to local residents?

When all of this gets federalized on an ad hoc basis, of course, you end up with the worst of all possible worlds. That is, random redistribution of resources among localities; waste and inefficient pork barrel allocation of funding and a centralization of politics where the permanent governing class always wins and working taxpayers are left out in the cold.

Even in the case of just highways, the extent of mission creep and pork barrel politics is stunning. The 47,000 miles of interstate highways constitute only 1.1 percent of the 4 million miles of streets, roads and highways in the entire nation.

Indeed, the reason we have state, county, municipal and township government in the United States is precisely to take care of the 99 percent of road surfaces that the great Dwight D. Eisenhower said should remain a nonfederal responsibility—even as he pioneered the Interstate highway system and trust fund.

Yet less than $15 billion, or one-third of the trust fund's receipts, goes to the Interstate Highway System Ike fathered. The rest gets auctioned off by the congressional politicians to state, county and local roads and to the far-flung array of non-highway purposes mentioned above.

Worst still, at the center of this abuse and corruption-ridden Washington infrastructure spending complex is a tissue of myths, exaggerations and lies which provide a veneer of justification for its inherent plunder, waste and unfairness.

That is to say, when the Beltway bandits run low on excuses to run-up the national debt they trot out florid tales of crumbling infrastructure, including dilapidated roads, collapsing bridges, failing water and sewer systems, inadequate rail and public transit and the rest.

This is variously alleged to represent a national disgrace, an impediment to economic growth and a sensible opportunity for fiscal "stimulus." But most especially it presents a swell opportunity for Washington to create millions of "jobs."

Moreover, according to the Obama Administration's latest budgetary gimmick—and one now apparently embraced by The Donald—this can all be done in a fiscally responsible manner. Yes, that would be via the issuance of "green ink" bonds by a national infrastructure bank, as opposed to the conventional "red ink" bonds by the U.S. Treasury.

The implication, of course, is that borrowings incurred to repair the nation's allegedly "collapsing" infrastructure would be a form of "self-liquidating" debt. That is, these "infrastructure" projects would eventually pay for themselves in the form of enhanced national economic growth and efficiency.

Needless to say, that's what the government of Japan has been saying for the last 25 years. With debt at 235 percent of GDP, in fact, what is being liquidated is the nation's taxpayers, not its "construction" bonds.

DILAPIDATED INFRASTRUCTURE: BOGUS BELTWAY PROPAGANDA

Besides that, the evidence for dilapidated infrastructure is just bogus Beltway propaganda. It is cynically peddled by the construction and builder lobbies and by state and local officials looking to fob the bill onto any taxpayers except their own.

A recent jeremiad about the phony infrastructure crisis by one Philip K. Howard is par for the course. Howard is a lawyer and founder of a lobby group sporting a name—"Common Good"—which is reason in itself to be wary:

> But almost every category of U.S. infrastructure is in a dangerous
> or obsolete state—roads and bridges, power generation and trans-
> mission, water treatment and delivery, ports and air traffic control.
> There is no partisan divide on what is needed: a national initiative
> to modernize our 50- to 100-year-old infrastructure. The upside is

as rosy as the status quo is dire. The United States can enhance its competitiveness, achieve a greener footprint and create upward of 2 million jobs.

That entire paragraph is pure hogwash. The overwhelming share of the nation's infrastructure is not obsolete or dangerous, is not being starved for dollars; and has virtually nothing to do with the dramatic trend-line of decline in Main Street growth, investment, good jobs and real living standards.

Moreover, the infrastructure that actually does qualify for self-liquidating investment is overwhelmingly local in nature—urban highways, metropolitan water and sewer systems and airports. These should be funded by users fees and levies on local taxpayers—not financed by Washington issued bonds and pork-barreled through its wasteful labyrinth of earmarks and plunder.

In the above quoted passage, Howard attempts to throw in everything but the kitchen sink in his list of purportedly crumbling infrastructure. But as we have seen, the Interstate Highway System is at the center of the federal- government role, but it's not crumbling at all. Indeed, since it could be maintained in high style for 0.17% of GDP, where's the beef?

It's certainly not in what Howard identified as the "power generation and transmission" sector. In fact, national investment spending for this purpose, as shown below, has been running in the $90–$100 billion range annually for the last half-decade—or more than triple the level of the early 2000s.

Even after accounting for a 25 percent rise in the GDP deflator over the last 15 years, current investment in the utility sector is more than double its 2004 level.

The self-evident point is that there have been no blackouts, brownouts or power shortages of any kind that could plausibly have interfered with economic production and growth during that period. In fact, if there is not an electric power availability problem—and there clearly has not been—then most of the claim that an infrastructure binge will boost economic growth washes out.

Stated differently, growth is based on efficient use of economic re-sources, not gross investment spending. You build utility plants when you need more megawatts to power Main Streetproduction, not because some Washington lobbies want taxpayers to buy concrete, steel, electrical com-ponents and labor in order to build redundant capacity.

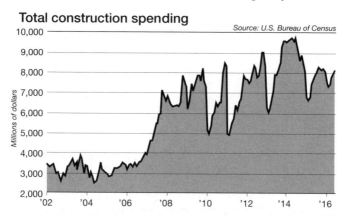

Total construction spending

But that's because it is not economically competitive, not because capi-tal investment is being starved. After all, the overwhelming share of utility investment is accounted for by the private sector and is debt financed.

In fact, what the infrastructure lobbyists are really complaining about is economic outcomes they don't like. That is, only a tiny fraction of the ample utility power available to U.S. businesses and households is generated by green fuel such as wind and solar.

But that's because it is not economically competitive, not because capi-tal investment is being starved. After all, the overwhelming share of utility investment is accounted for by the private sector and is debt financed.

To borrow a phrase, propagandists like Philip Howard are actually bringing coals to Newcastle. That is to say, thanks to the Fed's misguided financial repression policies, long-term utility financing has never been cheaper in real terms. The idea that there is a financing shortage for util-ities and power is just plain ridiculous.

Indeed, the typical double-shuffle or hidden agenda of the infrastructure cheerleaders is revealed by Howard's curious claim that $30 billion is "wasted" each year due to inefficient power transmission. Now, how in the world does he know that?

Of course, there is inherent frictional power loss in the process by which central-station bulk power is distributed through high voltage power lines and then across the local distribution grid. But it's a matter of physics and economic trade-offs. If you invest a lot more in high performance transmission systems, you will absolutely get less power loss, but the investment may never pay for itself, either.

In any event, that's a pricing issue and could readily be alleviated—to the extent that it exists—by intelligent rate reform.

Dig deep enough, however, and it becomes obvious that a whole phalanx of the infrastructure lobby is really composed of radical environmentalists. The infrastructure they want to replace is not crumbling and an impediment to economic growth; it's actually a low-cost contributor to growth and jobs which happens to emit carbons.

In fact, this completely ulterior—and false— agenda against carbon emissions is actually admitted to—even if inadvertently—by Howard:

> "The wasted electricity from the obsolete power grid is the same as the output of 200 average coal-burning power plants—causing an extra 280 million tons of carbon to spew into the air each year."

Right. Replace perfectly good conventional transmission capacity with ultra-high cost advanced transmission technology. That way you can add even more debt to the nation's balance sheet and force the shutdown of perfectly serviceable coal-fired power plants, too!

NO SEWER SHORTAGE, EITHER

Another category of alleged infrastructure starvation is waste water and sewage treatment, and here the story is even worse.

Ever since the EPA started making multibillion-dollar grants for sewer plants during the early 1970s, municipalities have been wasting massive amounts of resources building over-sized plants, and then under-charging their business and residential customers for their use.

So the truth in this category is not starvation but economic obesity!

Accordingly, under a regime of full economic pricing for waste treatment services the nation's infrastructure budget could be sharply reduced. That's because higher, unsubsidized prices at the municipal system intake pipe would cause an outpouring of technological innovation and practice changes among users and waste generators. Such innovation and user conservation investments, in turn, would dramatically reduce the capacity requirements and cost of end-system treatment plants.

Moreover, even under the current system of waste treatment socialism, there are no facts whatsoever that support the starvation argument. Current annual spending for waste treatment has ranged between $22 and $26 billion per year. That's 20 percent higher than a 15 year ago— even after adjustment for the 25 percent gain in the GDP deflator during the interim.

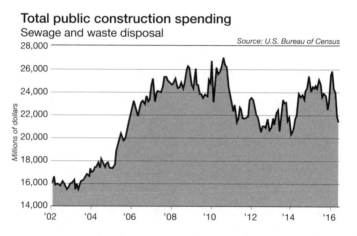

LOCAL ROADS AND STREETS: THE PROBLEM IS MUNICIPAL CORRUPTION AND UNION MONOPOLIES, NOT FISCAL STARVATION

Now, it is absolutely true that in selective localities in the U.S. there are obsolete sewage-treatment plants, just as in the case of roads and streets. But you can't blame that on inadequate spending. The real problem is local government corruption, inefficiency, pork barrel politics and the excessive power of the municipal unions and the construction trades.

That's true in spades for the local transportation sector. The disgraceful condition of roads and streets in places like New York City and Philadelphia, for example, is owing to the fact that billions have been siphoned off by drastically overpaid union labor and deeply corrupted contract award processes.

Needless to say, waste and corruption are the very opposite of a funding shortfall. In fact, nationwide highway spending has averaged between $80 and $95 billion since 2009 or about 30% higher in real terms than a decade earlier.

Moreover, if the voters really want better roads and streets throughout the localities of the nation there is one simple solution: raise state and local gas taxes and other user fees and tolls.

Stated differently, the proof is ultimately in the pudding. There is apparently nothing that Americans treasure more than their autos and the freedom to motor far and wide. If they can't be persuaded to pay higher road taxes and tolls, then by definition there is not a "shortage" of highway investment.

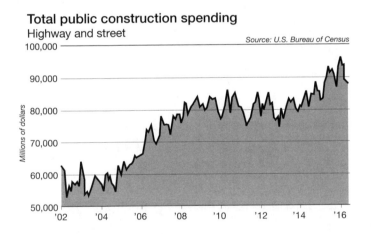

Total public construction spending
Highway and street

WHAT'S REALLY CRUMBLING IS THE KEYNESIAN CASE FOR ENDLESS DEBT

At the end of the day, what is "crumbling" is not the nation's infrastructure, but the case for deficit spending; that's what the infrastructure brouhaha is all about.

It's just another variation of the misbegotten Keynesian notion that the state can command economic growth via borrowing or printing money in order to fuel "aggregate demand." Accordingly, there is ultimately no difference in the economic waste represented by federal borrowing to build over-sized sewage plants or unused local roads and that which would result from building debt-funded pyramids.

In fact, however, true economic growth and wealth generation stems from the supply side of the economy. That is, from the exertions and productivity of labor and the efficiencies, innovations and investments generated by entrepreneurs.

And that leads to the real reason for our present stall speed economy. Over the last 16 years, there has been a 20% decline in real net business investment (after depreciation of the existing capital stock), while labor hours utilized by the business economy have inched forward by less than 6 percent over the entire period.

Moreover, there has been a stunning decline in net business formation and entrepreneurial activity. If Washington really wants to deal with faltering economic growth it should work on removing the regulatory, tax and welfare state barriers to these ominous supply side trends, not boosting the already more than adequate level of infrastructure investment.

Net business formations

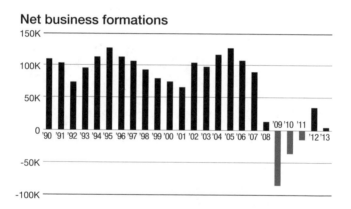

Indeed, we do not need any more federal subsidies for any category of infrastructure—especially transportation. For instance, airport capacity and modernization is already being funded at $36 billion per year mainly from ticket taxes, general aviation user fees and the like.

If that isn't enough, as indicated by air-traffic congestion and crowded airports, there is a simple solution. The 10 percent of the population that accounts for 90 percent of air travel should pay for higher investment spending via increased user charges on their tickets or landing fees on their G-5s.

Likewise, if the $65 billion currently being spent to subsidize the capital and operating costs of local mass transit systems is not enough, then let local taxpayers absorb the burden, not unborn generations that will inherent the nation's $19.4 trillion public debt.

And when it comes to enhancing real economic productivity and growth, nothing could be more inimical than to pour tens of billions into hopeless white elephants like Amtrak and the Obama Administration's high-speed rail boondoggle.

In short, the infrastructure bleaters have it exactly upside-down. The economic crisis confronting the nation is owing to the state getting way too big, not because public spending on infrastructure or anything else has been shortchanged.

THE HOARY MYTH OF CRUMBLING BRIDGES FALLING DOWN

As I indicated earlier, the mythology about crumbling bridges is especially egregious and is based on the occasional bridge failure that becomes a momentary cable news sensation. But these stories are not representative of the actual facts and deserve a special debunking because the "crumbling bridges falling down" story has become a symbol of the entire phony campaign for massive infrastructure spending and borrowing.

And that gets us to The Donald's crumbling bridges. Nowhere is the stark distinction between myth and reality more evident than in the case of the so-called deficient and obsolete bridges.

To hear the K Street lobbies tell it, motorists all across America are at risk of plunging into the drink at any time, owing to defective bridges. Even Ronald Reagan fell for that one.

During the long trauma of the 1981–82 recession, the Reagan Administration had stoutly resisted the temptation to implement a Keynesian-style fiscal-stimulus and jobs program—notwithstanding an unemployment rate that peaked in double digits.

But within just a few months of the bottom, along came a Republican secretary of transportation, Drew Lewis, with a presidential briefing on the alleged disrepair of the nation's highways and bridges. The briefing was accompanied by a Cabinet Room full of easels bearing pictures of dilapidated bridges and roads and a plan to dramatically increase highway spending and the gas tax.

Not surprisingly, DOT Secretary Drew Lewis was a former governor and the top GOP fundraiser of the era. So the Cabinet Room was soon figuratively surrounded by a muscular coalition of road builders, construction machinery suppliers, asphalt and concrete vendors, governors, mayors and legislators and the AFL-CIO building-trades department.

And if that wasn't enough, Lewis had also made deals to line up the highway safety and beautification lobby, bicycle enthusiasts and all the motley array of mass transit interest groups.

They were all singing from the same crumbling infrastructure playbook. As Lewis summarized and Donald Trump is apparently now channeling, "We have highways and bridges that are falling down around our ears—that's really the thrust of the program."

EVEN THE GIPPER FELL FOR FALLING BRIDGES

President Reagan soon joined the chorus:

> "No, we are opposed to wasteful borrow and spend," he recalled.
> "That's how we got into this mess. But these projects are different.
> Roads and bridges are a proper responsibility of government, and
> they have already been paid for by the gas tax."

By the time a pork-laden highway bill was rammed through a lame duck session of Congress in December 1982, the president's speechwriters had gone all-in for the crumbling- infrastructure gambit.

Explaining why he signed the bill, the scourge of Big Government noted, "We have 23,000 bridges in need of replacement or rehabilitation; 40 percent of our bridges are over 40 years old."

So here we are 34 years later, and those very same bridges are purportedly still falling down!

THE "DEFICIENT" BRIDGES OF MADISON COUNTY

But they aren't. What we are dealing with can best be described as "The Tale of Madison County Bridges to Nowhere."

In fact, there could not be a more striking example of why Donald Trump is way off the deep-end with his half-trillion-dollar infrastructure boondoggle, and also why the principle that local users and taxpayers should fund local infrastructure is such a crucial tenet of both fiscal solvency and honest government.

In this context, the crumbling-bridges myth starts with the claim by DOT and the industry lobbies that there are 63,000 bridges across the nation that are "structurally deficient." This suggests that millions of motorists are at risk of a perilous dive into the cold waters below.

But here's the thing. Roughly one-third, or 20,000, of these purportedly hazardous bridges are located in six rural states in America's midsection: Iowa, Oklahoma, Missouri, Kansas, Nebraska and South Dakota.

The fact that these states account for only 5.9% of the nation's population seems more than a little incongruous but that isn't even half the puzzle. It seems that these thinly populated town and-country states have a grand total of 118,000 bridges.

That is, one bridge for every 160 citizens. Men, women and children included.

And the biggest bridge state among them is, yes, Iowa. The state has 3 million souls and nearly 25,000 bridges—one for every 125 people.

So suddenly the picture is crystal clear. These are not the kind of bridges that thousands of cars and heavy-duty trucks pass over each day. No, they are mainly the kind Clint Eastwood needed a local farmwife to locate—so he could take pictures for a National Geographic spread on "covered bridges."

Stated differently, the overwhelming bulk of the 600,000 so-called "bridges" in America are so little used that they are more often crossed by dogs, cows, cats and tractors than they are by passenger motorists.

These country bridges are essentially no different than local playgrounds and municipal parks. They have nothing to do with interstate commerce, GDP growth or national public infrastructure.

If they are structurally deficient as measured by DOT engineering standards, that is not exactly startling news to the host village, township and county governments that choose not to upgrade them.

So if Iowa is content to live with 5,000 bridges—1 in 5 of its 25,000 bridges—that are deemed structurally deficient by the DOT, why is this a national crisis?

Self-evidently, the electorate and officialdom of Iowa do not consider these bridges to be a public-safety hazard or something would have been done long ago.

The evidence for that is in another startling "fun fact" about the nation's bridges. Compared to the 19,000 so-called "structurally deficient" bridges in the six rural states reviewed here, there are also 19,000 such deficient bridges in another group of 35 states—including Texas, Maryland, Massachusetts, Virginia, Washington, Oregon, Michigan, Arizona, Colorado, Florida, New Jersey and Wisconsin, among others.

But these states have a combined population of 175 million, not 19 million as in the six rural states; and more than 600 citizens per bridge, not 125 as in Iowa. Moreover, only 7 percent of the bridges in these 35 states are considered to be structurally deficient rather than 21 percent as in Iowa.

So the long and short of it is self-evident: Iowa still has a lot of one-horse bridges, and Massachusetts—with 1,300 citizens per bridge—does not. None of this is remotely relevant to a purported national-infrastructure crisis today—any more than it was in 1982 when even Ronald Reagan fell for "23,000 bridges in need of replacement or rehabilitation."

CALIFORNIA CAN PAY FOR REPAIRING ITS OWN BRIDGES

Yes, the few thousand bridges actually used heavily in commerce and passenger transportation in America do fall into disrepair and need periodic reinvestment. But the proof that even this is an overwhelmingly state and local problem is evident in another list maintained by the DOT.

That list is a rank ordering called "The Most Travelled Structurally Deficient Bridges." These are the opposite of the covered bridges of Madison County, but even here there is a cautionary tale.

It seems that of the 100 most heavily traveled bridges in the U.S. by rank order, and which were in need of serious repair in 2013, 80 percent of them are in California!

Moreover, they were overwhelmingly state highway and municipal road and street bridges located in Los Angeles, Orange County and the Inland Empire. Stated differently, Governor Moonbeam has not miraculously solved California's endemic fiscal crisis; he'd just neglected the local infrastructure.

There is no obvious reason why taxpayers in Indiana or North Carolina need to be fixing California's bridges so that the latter can continue to finance its outrageously costly public-employee pension system.

And so it goes with the rest of the so-called infrastructure slate. There is almost nothing there that is truly national in scope, and little that is in a state of crumbling and crisis.

Indeed, the one national asset—the Interstate Highway System—is generally in such good shape that most of the "shovel ready" projects on it back during the Obama stimulus turned out to be resurfacing projects and over-passes to nowhere.

Most of the resurfacing jobs, for example, were not yet needed and would have been done in the ordinary course anyway. Likewise, the construction of new overpasses mostly occurred on lightly traveled country roads that had happily been dead-ends for decades.

One thing is clear. There is no case for adding to our staggering $19.4 trillion national debt in order to replace the bridges of Madison County; or to fix state and local highways or build white elephant high speed rail systems; or to relieve air travelers of paying user fees to upgrade local airports or local taxpayers of their obligation to pay fees and taxes to maintain their water and sewer systems.

At the end of the day, the ballyhooed national infrastructure crisis is a Beltway racket of the first order. It has been for decades.

And now even The Donald has taken the bait.

AMTRAK—A NATIONAL HAZARD AT ANY SPEED

Amtrak's May 2015 tragic accident in Philadelphia was yet another occasion for the crumbling infrastructure lobbies to beat the tom-toms for more spending.

But the real hazard here is Amtrak itself. For more than 40 years it has been a colossal waste of taxpayer money and the very embodiment of what is wrong with state intervention in the free market economy.

Worse still, the pork barrel politics that drive its handouts from Uncle Sam virtually guarantee that as time goes on, Amtrak will become an increasing hazard to public safety, as well.

It seems like only yesterday, but one of my first assignments as a junior staffer on Capitol Hill was to analyze the enabling legislation that created Amtrak in the early 1970s. I was working for an old-fashioned conservative congressman, and his first question was, "How will it ever make a profit when we are running the trains from a congressional hearing room in the Rayburn Building?"

He couldn't have been more clairvoyant. While its sponsors claimed Amtrak would be spewing black ink by 1974, the answer to my boss's question was simple: never!

But you didn't need to wait 42 years to prove it. There is not even a remote case that subsidizing intercity rail travel is a proper or necessary function of the state.

Amtrak accounts for well less than 1 percent of intercity passenger miles. On every one of its 44 routes, there are bus- and air-travel alternatives. And that is to say nothing of automobile travel—in cars with drivers today or in the driverless kind tomorrow.

Moreover, the evidence overwhelmingly shows that passenger trains will never be economically competitive outside of a handful of densely populated corridors. By contrast, what was absolutely guaranteed from day one back in 1970 is that a government-controlled passenger rail system crisscrossing the United States would become a monumental congressional pork barrel—an endless rebuke to rational economics.

And that it has. The cumulative taxpayer subsidy since 1972 totals more than $75 billion in dollars of today's purchasing power. During the span of nearly a half century, Amtrak has operated upwards of 40 routes that have never, ever made even an operating profit.

WHY AMTRAK IS AN ECONOMIC LOSER

Yet the operating-profit test is itself a red herring. Like its aviation competitors, Amtrak is massively capital intensive.

It maintains 21,000 miles of track, 100 rail stations, operates around 2,500 locomotives and passenger cars, and requires an extensive, costly infrastructure of communications and signaling systems, electric traction networks and a huge array of bridges, tunnels, switching yards, repair facilities, fencing and other right-of-way improvements and ancillary buildings.

On a replacement basis, its entire capital asset base would easily amount to $50 billion (about $40 billion of track and infrastructure and $10 billion of rolling stock).

And that giant figure underscores the economic part of the Amtrak hazard. Even with a generous assumption that the useful lives of its equipment, rolling stock and infrastructure would average 25 years, Amtrak's economic depreciation would amount to $2 billion per year.

Since it generates roughly 8 billion passenger miles annually, this means that its capital- consumption expense amounts to about 25 cents per passenger mile.

So here's the thing. The average airline fare in the U.S. is about 15 cents per passenger mile, and the average inter-city bus fare is about 11 cents per mile.

Now how in the world does it make sense to operate a lumbering passenger rail system in which the true economic cost of its capital assets alone is 65 percent to 130 percent higher than the profitable fares charged by the perfectly adequate and available alternative modes of transportation?

Stated differently, you are deep in the hole before you start even one Acela train on its route between Washington and Boston or one long-distance train on its 1,750-mile route between Chicago and Los Angeles.

But in the operations department, it goes without saying that Amtrak—burdened as it is with its endless array of congressional mandates and directives—is not exactly a model of efficiency or financial discipline.

Thus, Amtrak's fully loaded wage-and-benefits tab is about $2 billion per year and is spread over 20,000 employees. Needless to say, at $100,000 per employee Amtrak's costs are not even in the same zip code as its far more efficient for-profit competitors in the airline and bus transit industries.

On top of its massively bloated and featherbedded payroll, Amtrak also generates another $1.3 billion of expense for fuel, power, utilities, supplies, repair parts and operational and management overheads. Accordingly, its total operating budget at $3.3 billion amounts to about 40 cents of expense per passenger mile.

That is, its operating costs are 3–4X the ticket price of its air and bus competitors!

The economic arithmetic is thus insuperable. On a system-wide basis, Amtrak's combined capital and operating expense would amount to about 65 cents per passenger mile if it were honestly reckoned.

That is, in the absence of federal and state subsidies and the implicit subsidies that private railroad companies transfer to Amtrak via deeply below-market fees for utilization of their tracks and facilities. Indeed, 95 percent of Amtrak's route-miles and 70 percent of its passenger-miles are generated on lines leased from freight railroads, which—owing to regulatory mandates—Amtrak pays only a trivial 2 cents per passenger mile. This figure is not remotely reflective of the real economic costs.

By contrast, Amtrak's ticket revenues amount to hardly 30 cents per passenger mile. So, contrary to Amtrak's claim that it has nearly reached break-even, its true economics reflect the very opposite. Namely, a giant political pork barrel in which system revenues cover less than 45 percent of its all-in economic costs to society.

Nor can this disability be remedied by reforming the system and paring back its routes to just the profitable corridors. Even the Northeast corridor generates only 10 cents of "operating profits" per passenger mile. Throw in the capital costs and even Amtrak's so-called profitable lines are still deeply underwater.

To wit, a recent inspector general report estimated that the replacement cost of the Northeast-corridor infrastructure alone was about $15 billion, which would amount to $400 million per year on an amortized basis or 20 cents per passenger-mile. Add in another 5 cents per passenger-mile for locomotives and rail cars and you have 25 cents of capital costs.

So there is a reason why even the Northeast corridor has never been privatized. It would lose at least 15 cents on each of the 2 billion passenger miles that Amtrak's Northeast corridor generates annually in the absence of much higher fares.

These baleful facts regarding the Acela and regional routes in the Washington-Boston corridor are damming enough. Yet the rest of the system embodies just plain insensible economic waste.

The aforementioned Chicago-Los Angeles route, for example, has operating costs of 35 cents per passenger mile; and total costs with capital consumption would be at least 50 cents per mile—even giving allowance for the lower capital intensity of long-distance routes.

The problem is that you can get an airline coach fare today between the Chicago and Los Angeles pair for $200, or 11 cents per mile. And you don't need to spend 22 hours on the train, either.

As it is, Amtrak's current fare on this route is about 15 cents per passenger mile and apparently it cannot go much higher if it wishes to remain competitive with air.

Yet why in the world should bus drivers in Minneapolis pay federal taxes in order to provide what amounts to a $600 subsidy per ticket on the 180,000 tickets that are sold annually on the Chicago-Los Angeles route? And the latter is only typical of most of the other routes outside the Northeast corridor.

Obviously, there is no means test to get a $600 subsidy from Amtrak, or any other plausible criterion of public need. Like so much else which emanates from Washington, these Amtrak subsidies are distributed willy-nilly—in this case to retirees with enough time and money to see the country at leisure or to people with fear of flying who don't wish to drive.

SECRETARY DREW LEWIS AGAIN— A WOUNDED WHITE ELEPHANT, TOO

So Amtrak is a white elephant as a matter of economics, but when it comes to public safety, it is actually a wounded one. That's because when push comes to shove and Congress is faced with limited budget headroom, it always elects to short change the capital budget rather than reduce the scope of Amtrak's far-flung operations and eliminate any of the 44 routes that crisscross the nation's congressional districts.

I actually learned that lesson during the so-called Reagan Revolution. My original plan was to eliminate Amtrak entirely, and it would have saved upward of $60 billion in the decades to come. At the get-go, the Gipper was all for it. Not a proper function of government, he nodded.

Then his secretary of transportation and previously chief GOP fundraiser and governor of Pennsylvania explained that the Gipper was right— but not quite. The Northeast corridor (NEC) routes were an exception.

They provided a valuable economic function—so by paring the system back to these high density routes the Amtrak budget could be cut in half. Moreover, after some up-front capital spending, the NEC could be transformed into a profitable business and eventually sold to the private sector in an IPO.

That's just the thing, said President Reagan.

Then it got to Capitol Hill and the Republican politicians said we are all for cutting the Amtrak budget by 50 percent, but to get the votes we need to do it "our way." Upon which the Gipper replied, yes, we are here first and foremost to shrink the runaway federal budget—so do what you must to get those savings.

They did. They drastically pared back the capital budget and kept virtually all of the routes and operating subsidy costs in place. When Uncle Sam came up short, capital investment could be deferred, but the pork barrel had to be fed.

In the bye and bye, of course, Amtrak's budget was restored all the way back to Jimmy Carter's "wasteful" levels and actually hit record amounts during the Republican governments of 2001–2008. But even then there was never enough appropriations to keep this giant white elephant properly fed—so capital investment was perennially short-changed and the system's fixed assets steadily deteriorated.

Whether last year's disaster was caused by human error or not, the larger certainty is that the system has been chronically starved of capital. But the solution is not for a bankrupt government in Washington to pour more money down the Amtrak rat hole in the name of "infrastructure investment," as the big spenders are now braying.

Instead, Amtrak should be put out of its misery once and for all. Otherwise its longstanding hazard to the taxpayers is likely to be compounded by even more public safety disasters, too.

THE INFRASTRUCTURE-BAILOUT DANGER AHEAD

There is overwhelming evidence that private investment, productivity and enterprise is failing badly in Flyover America owing to three decades of Bubble Finance. The nation's large corporations, in particular, are not growing because they are being strip-mined by their top executives in pursuit of a stifling spree of financial engineering and stock options harvesting.

So the key to restoring Main Street prosperity is not launching an infrastructure financing bank as the Beltway bandits keep insisting and even Donald Trump has now advocated. That will result in waste of capital, malinvestments, reduced economic efficiency and an even more bloated public sector than we already have.

The bank that needs addressing, in fact, is the nation's central bank. Until the Fed's massive intrusion in financial markets is eliminated via abolishing the Federal Open Market Committee and government-debt purchases as described in Chapter 4, there is virtually no prospect of reigniting capitalist vigor and growth in the United States

What that means, therefore, is that a half-trillion-dollar infrastructure spree like the one The Donald pulled out from under his comb-over represents a very dangerous idea.

To wit, it would add measurably to the $35 trillion of public debt that is already baked into the cake, and put the politicians of the Imperial City knee-deep in the distribution of prodigious amounts of pork barrel. In fact, they desperately need to get on with the opposite—a painful process of fiscal retrenchment that is unavoidable if national bankruptcy is to be prevented.

Worse still, adding to the nation's monumental debt pile in the face of nominal GDP growth that is stuck under the 3 percent barrier, as documented earlier, would be nearly suicidal. It would raise the ratio of public debt to national income—which is already on a path toward 150 percent—to even more crushing levels.

At the end of the day, Donald Trump knows a lot about debt, and its dangers when it gets out of hand, and almost nothing about the economics of growth and public infrastructure.

Would that he sound the alarm about the former. The public infrastructure crusade, by contrast, is just another Beltway boondoggle of the kind that he has loudly condemned and which have already brought Flyover America to the brink of ruin.

CHAPTER 12:

On the Impossibility of "Helicopter Money" and Why the Casino Will Crash

As the stock market reached its lunatic peak near 2,200 in August, the certainty that the Fed is out of dry powder and that the so-called economic recovery is out of runway gave rise to one more desperate pulse of hopium on Wall Street.

Namely, that the central banks of the world were about to embark on outright "helicopter money", thereby jolting back to life domestic economies that are sliding into deflation and recession virtually everywhere—from Japan to South Korea, China, Italy, France, England, Brazil, Canada and most places in-between.

That latter area especially includes the United States. Despite Wall Street's hoary tale that the domestic economy has "decoupled" from the rest of the world, the evidence that the so-called recovery is grinding to a halt is overwhelming.

After all, the real GDP growth rate during the year ending in June was a miniscule 1.2%. It reflected the weakest four-quarter rate since the Great Recession.

And even that was made possible only by an unsustainable build-up in business inventories and the shortchanging of inflation by the Washington statistical mills. Had even a semi-honest GDP deflator been used, the U.S. economy would have posted zero real GDP growth over the past year, at best.

So the stock market's 19% melt-up from the February 11 interim low of 1829 on the S&P 500 was positively surreal. There was not an iota of sustainability to it. In fact, "interim" is exactly the right word for a low that is going a lot lower, and soon.

Indeed, the spring-summer rebound was the work of eyes-wide-shut day traders and robo-machines surfing on a thinner and thinner cushion of momentum. What must come next, in fact, is exactly what happens when you stop pedaling your bicycle. To wit, momentum gets exhausted, gravity takes over and the illusion of stability is painfully shattered.

But these revelers are going to need something stronger than the hope for "helicopter money" to avoid annihilation when the long-running central bank con job finally collapses. Indeed, that denouement lies directly ahead because helicopter money is a bridge too far, while valuations are literally teetering in the nosebleed section of history.

As to the latter point, the S&P 500 companies posted Q2 2016 earnings for the latest 12 month period at $86.94 per share. So at the August bubble high, the market was being valued at a lunatic 25.2X reported earnings.

Even in a healthy, growing economy that valuation level is on the extreme end of sanity. But actual circumstances are currently more nearly the opposite. That is, earnings have now been falling for six straight quarters in line with GDP growth that has slumped to what amounts to stall speed.

In fact, reported earnings for the S&P 500 peaked at $106 per share in the 12 months ended in September 2014. That means that earnings had fallen by 19% since then, even as the stock market moved from 1950 to nearly 2,200, or 13% higher.

This is called multiple expansion in the parlance of Wall Street, but it's hard to find a more bubblicious example. Two years ago the market was trading at just 18.4X meaning that on the back of sharply falling earnings the PE multiple had risen by 37%!

Valuation multiples are supposed to go up only when the economic and profits outlook is improving, not when it's unmistakably deteriorating as at present. But during the 2016 spring-summer melt-up these faltering fundamentals were blithely ignored on the hopes of a second half growth spurt and, failing the latter, that the Fed would again pull the market's chestnuts out of the fire.

The growth spurt absolutely has not happened, and the recent sharp decline in the level of in-bound containers at the West Coast ports means that the U.S. retail sector is not provisioning for any rebound in sales during the coming fall and holiday seasons.

That's why the Wall Street gamblers are so desperately hoping for helicopter money. And that desperation is intensified by the fact that the Fed is out of dry powder via its current tool kit of "extraordinary" measures employed since the financial crisis.

To wit, in the event the economy visibly drifts into recession, the Fed cannot go to sub-zero interest rates without triggering a Donald Trump–led domestic political conflagration. The long-abused savers and retirees of Flyover America would finally grab their torches and pitchforks.

Nor can it abruptly shift to a huge new round of QE without confessing that $3.5 trillion of the same has been for naught.

Yet "helicopter money" isn't some kind of new wrinkle in monetary policy, at all. It's an old-as-the-hills rationalization for monetization of the public debt—that is, purchase of government bonds with central bank credit conjured from thin air.

It's the ultimate in "something for nothing" economics. That's because most assuredly those government bonds originally funded the purchase of real economic resources such as labor hours, contract services or dams and aircraft carriers.

As a technical matter, helicopter money is exactly the same thing as QE. Nor does the journalistic confusion that it involves "direct" central bank purchases of public debt from the U.S. Treasury make a bit of difference.

Instead of direct purchases, suppose Washington issues government debt to the 23 primary dealers on Wall Street in the regular manner. Further, assume that some or all of these dealers stick the bonds in inventory for three days, three months or even three years, and then sell them back to the Fed under QE (and most likely at a higher price).

So what!

The only thing different technically about "helicopter money" policy is that it would just circumvent the dwell time in dealer (or "investor") inventories but result in exactly the same end state. In that event, of course, Wall Street wouldn't get the skim.

WHY HELICOPTER MONEY IS A MORTAL THREAT TO FISCAL DEMOCRACY

But that's not the real reason why helicopter money policy is so loathsome. The unstated essence of it is that our monetary politburo would overtly conspire and coordinate with the White House and Capitol Hill to bury future generations in crushing public debts.

They would do this by agreeing to generate incremental fiscal deficits—as if Uncle Sam's current $19 trillion isn't enough debt—which would be matched dollar for dollar by an increase in the Fed's bond-buying, or monetization rate. That amounts not only to teaching children how to play with matches; it's tantamount to setting fiscal forest fires across the land.

There are a few additional meaningless bells and whistles to the theory, but its essential crime against democracy and economic rationality should be made very explicit. To wit, it would amount to a central bank power grab like no other because it insinuates our unelected central bankers into the very heart of the fiscal process.

Needless to say, the framers delegated the powers of the purse—spending, taxing and borrowing—to the elected branch of government, and not because they were wild-eyed idealists smitten by a naïve faith in the prudence of the demos.

To the contrary, they did so because the decision to spend, tax and borrow is the very essence of state power. There is no possibility of democracy—for better or worse—if these fundamental powers are removed from popular control.

Yet that's exactly what helicopter money policy would do. Based on the Keynesian gobbledygook I debunked in Chapter 4 about the purported gap between full-employment or "potential GDP" and actual output and employment, the FOMC would essentially set a target for the federal deficit.

In practice, it would also likely throw in some gratuitous advice about deficit composition between tax cuts, infrastructure spending and social betterment. The recommended mix would arise from an FOMC whim as to whether in their wisdom its 12 members thought household consumption or fixed-asset investment needed to be goosed more.

At one level, of course, it is to be expected that the people's elected representatives would relish this "expert" cover for ever-bigger deficits and the opportunity to wallow in the pork barrel allocation of the targeted tax cuts and spending increases.

There is surely not a single hard-core New Dealer turning in his grave who could have imagined a better scheme for priming the pump.

Yet helicopter money turns the inherently dangerous idea of fiscal borrowing in a democracy into an outright monetary fraud, and that prospect is sure to kindle vestigial fears of the public debt even among today's politicians.

Indeed, there is a long history on exactly that point. For example, even New Dealer FDR worried about the rising public debt, and "Fair Dealer" Harry Truman positively loathed it.

Likewise, the power-mad Lyndon Johnson essentially voluntarily vacated the Oval Office when he finally agreed to a substantial tax hike in early 1968 order to stem the deficit hemorrhage from his guns and butter policies.

Even the greatest deficit spender of his time—Ronald Reagan— thought the resulting explosion of the public debt was half Jimmy Carter's fault and half due to defense spending increases, which didn't count in his unique way of reckoning the national debt.

Likewise, the clueless George W. Bush thought the Greenspan housing boom would last forever and thereby cause the nation's fiscal accounts to come back into balance on their own. Similarly, Barack Obama has insisted that the $9 trillion of new public debt on his watch to date was owing to the Great Recession—a one-time impact that his policies have purportedly remedied.

By contrast, the deliberate, wanton addition of trillions to the public debt just so that the Fed can print an equivalent amount of new credit out of thin air is a fish of an altogether different kettle. When push comes to shove, even today's Beltway politicians are likely to find the underlying theory of helicopter money to be beyond the pale.

And that's especially true owing to the Bernanke fillip.

It goes without saying, of course, that the Bernank is no hero whatsoever—notwithstanding his self-conferred glorification for the courage to print. In fact, he is a demented paint-by-the-numbers Keynesian who has a worse grasp on the real world than the typical astrologer.

That's why the crucial element in his helicopter-money scheme, as he explained in a recent Washington Post op-ed, will leave them scratching their heads even in the always credulous corridors of Capitol Hill.

According to Bernanke, the secret sauce of helicopter money is an explicit and loud announcement by the Fed that the gobs of incremental public debt will be permanent. It will never, ever be repaid—not even in the fictional by-and-by of the distant future.

But the reason for it is downright lunatic.

To wit, unless current taxpayers are assured that future taxes will not rise owing to Washington's helicopter-money handouts and tax breaks, says the Bernank, they won't spend the government gifts they find strewn along the path of flight!

That's right. When a road-building boom from helicopter-money appropriations results in surging demand at the sand and gravel pits, the small-time businessman involved won't buy any additional trucks or hire any additional drivers until Washington assures them that they won't pay higher taxes 25 years hence!

Only in the Eccles Building puzzle palace does such drivel not elicit uncontainable guffaws. Only in Sweden do they give Nobel Prizes for the academic obscurantism called "rational expectations theory" that is the basis for Bernanke's whacky theories.

WHY HELICOPTER MONEY WILL BE A GIANT DUD IF TRIED IN THE U.S.

So at the end of the day, "helicopter money" is just a desperate scam emanating from the world's tiny fraternity of central bankers who have walked the financial system to the brink, and are now trying to con the casino into believing they have one more magic rabbit to pull out of the hat.

They don't. That's because helicopter money will not pass the laugh test even in the Imperial City, and, more importantly, because it takes two branches of the state to tango in the process of implementation.

Unlike ZIRP and QE, helicopter money requires the peoples' elected representatives to play, and to do so on an expedited basis. As described above, the Congress and White House must generate large incremental expansions of the fiscal deficit—so that the central bankers can buy it directly from the U.S. Treasury's shelf, and then credit the government's accounts at the Federal Reserve with funds conjured from thin air.

But this assumes there is still a functioning government in Washington and that politicians have been 100% cured of their atavistic fears of the public debt.

Alas, what is going to cause helicopter money to be a giant dud—at least in the U.S.—is that neither of these conditions are extant.

Regardless of whether the November winner is Hillary or The Donald, there is one thing certain. There will be no functioning government come 2017. Washington will be the site of a political brawl of deafening and paralyzing aspect—like none in U.S. history, or ever.

At the same time, the existing budget deficit is already reversing, and will end the current year at more than $600 billion. That's baked into the cake already based on the recent sharp slowdown in revenue collections, and means that the FY 2016 deficit will be one-third higher than last year's $450 billion.

Moreover, when the new Congress convenes next February the forward budget projections will make a scary truth suddenly undeniable. As we showed in Chapter 9, the nation is swiftly heading back toward trillion-dollar annual deficits under existing policy and even before the impact of a serious recessionary decline.

The reality of rapidly swelling deficits even before enactment of a massive helicopter money fiscal stimulus program will scare the wits out of conservative politicians, and much of the electorate, too. And the prospect that the resulting huge issuance of Treasury bonds will be purchased directly by the Fed will only compound the fright.

What fools like Bernanke haven't reckoned with is that sheer common sense has not yet been extirpated from the land. In fact, outside of the groupthink of a few dozen Keynesian academics and central bankers, the very idea of helicopter money strikes most sensible people as preposterous, offensive and scary.

Even if Wall Street talks it up, there will be massive, heated, extended and paralyzing debate in Congress and the White House about it for months on end. There is virtually no chance that anything that even remotely resembles the Bernanke version of helicopter money could be enacted into law and become effective before CY 2018.

SO NEXT COMES THE CRASH

Will the boys and girls and robo machines still in the casino after the current election gong show is over patiently wait for their next fix from a Beltway governance process that is likely to be in sheer pandemonium and stalemate?

We think the odds are between slim and none. As we indicated previously, if Trump is elected the fiscal process will lapse into confrontation and paralysis for an indefinite spell.

And if Hillary is elected, the Republican House will become a killing field for almost anything she proposes, and most especially the rank Keynesian apostasy of outright and massive debt monetization.

Yet absent a massive new round of monetary juice like helicopter money, the stock market will not be able to avoid its Wile E. Coyote moment. That's because the "priced-in" forward earnings on which the casino gamblers are counting are pure fantasy.

In fact, there is an air pocket below the market even if the U.S. economy stumbles sideways temporarily, and a high speed down-elevator shaft when and as the economy finally rolls over.

As incredible as it may seem, Wall Street's sell-side hockey sticks are actually pointing to an out-of-this-world 41% earnings gain for calendar 2017 to $122 per share compared to the $86.94 posted for the 12 months ending in June 2016.

Obviously, that can't happen without a massive surge in sales growth or a huge further expansion of profit margins. Neither of these happy outcomes, however, is even remotely on the horizon.

After hitting a cyclical peak of 10.1% of sales in Q2 2014, the profit margins of the S&P 500 companies have already embarked upon the inexorable process of mean reversion, sliding to 9.3% in Q2 last year and 9.1% in the June 2016 quarter.

Moreover, that slide is just the beginning. In the event of an actual lapse into recession, current near-peak profit rates would really get slammed. Compared to the peak of 9.4% in Q2 2007, for instance, the S&P 500 operating margin plunged to just 6.2% by the bottom in Q2 2009.

At the same time, the chance that corporate earnings will be rescued by a surge of sales growth is virtually nonexistent. Indeed, the so-called "incoming" economic data are flashing warnings of a slumping economy, not one that is exhibiting the perennial Wall Street delusion of "escape velocity."

Exhibit number one is total business sales, including manufacturing, wholesale and retail trade. Unlike the virtually useless monthly jobs data which is based on a tiny sample and is egregiously manipulated and modeled by BLS bureaucrats, business sales are the big enchilada. They capture a reasonably accurate picture of the current pace of economic activity.

Indicative of the comprehensive reach of this series is that during the most recent month (June), the annualized run rate of sales was about $15.7 trillion, representing a huge slice of the GDP. But that figure was down by $550 billion or 3.4% from its peak level two years ago—a sharp deterioration from the 5%-10% annual rates of gain during the initial years of the recovery.

The chart on the next page provides powerful historical context. Rather than the will-o'-the-wisp of "escape velocity" what it actually indicates is the onset of clear recessionary conditions.

Moreover, what militates strongly against an imminent reversal of this slumping sales trend is the fact that inventories are piled high throughout all three sectors of the business economy.

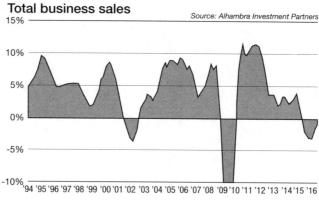

Total business sales

Source: Alhambra Investment Partners

That's not only a sure sign that end sales have weakened and businesses have over-produced and overstocked; it's also a classic trigger for cutbacks in production and employment to bring inventories back into alignment with sales. In other words, a recession.

The chart below is dispositive. After a 15-year march lower owing to new technology and just-in-time management, the inventory to sales ratio exploded during the Great Recession. Business over-produced until the very last minute when confidence in the Fed's Goldilocks economy was finally shattered by the Lehman bankruptcy on Sept. 15, 2008.

We are now deep into Goldilocks 2.0, and businesses are again over-producing and overstocking. It will simply take another catalyst—such as a market crash, currency crisis or Trump election victory—to drive the current 1.39X ratio of inventories-to-sales to the 1.45–1.50X zone where the U.S. economy plunged into recession during the fall of 2008.

In fact, an inventory liquidation driven recession is virtually guaranteed. And that means that retrenchment in production will cause the excess labor being hoarded by businesses at present to be abruptly chucked overboard just as it was after May 2008.

Even though the Great Recession commenced in the fall of 2007, it was in the 12 month period ending in May 2009 that 6.5 million, or 75% of the recession period jobs losses actually happened.

In short, the inventory-sales ratio speaks to what happens next. By contrast, the BLS' monthly headline jobs number is not only a lagging indicator, but its trend-cycle model adjustments make it even worse by significantly overstating the actual excess labor being inventoried at present.

Yet our Keynesian school marm at the Fed thinks the U.S. economy is expanding nicely because of these useless figures. No wonder the casino gamblers are still at the tables.

Total business: inventories to sales ratio

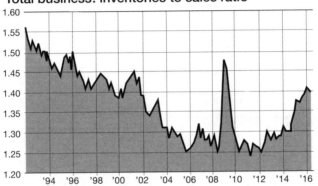

There is plenty of additional evidence for weakening sales, but the 5.9% Y/Y plunge in inbound containers during July at the Port of Long Beach was especially timely and telling. The latter is the nation's busiest port and point of entry for the vast flow of imports from China and the Far East, and a barometer of the outlook for fall and Christmas sales among U.S. retailer.

A drop of this magnitude hardly suggests a sales rebound anytime soon—a prospect that is reinforced by the most recent data on freight volumes. For example, intermodal shipments on North American railroads during the second quarter were down by 6.1% versus prior year. This marked the first such decline in the past 25 quarters, and another clear sign of flagging domestic economic momentum.

Even more significantly, the Cass Freight Index is now back to its 2013 levels. This index measures freight volumes for all modes of domestic transit and is based on $2 billion per month of actual transactions processed by Cass for hundreds of customers in the packaged-goods, food, automotive, chemical, OEM and heavy-equipment businesses.

Weakening throughput in these sectors is another sign that the present so-called recovery is getting long in the tooth after 86 months, and especially so in the face of some of the growing headwinds mentioned below.

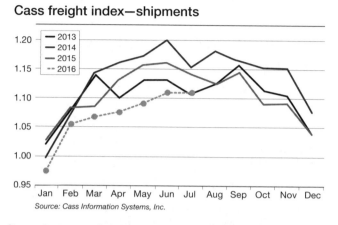

Cass freight index—shipments

Source: Cass Information Systems, Inc.

We believe these weak business-sales and freight-volume trends are an especial threat to the market's current lofty valuations. That's because on a market-cap-to-sales basis, the S&P 500 is now in wholly uncharted waters. In fact at nearly 2.5 standard deviations higher than its historical median, it now towers far above even the peaks reached in 2000 and 2008.

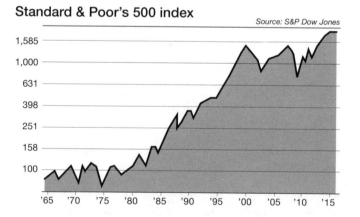

Standard & Poor's 500 index

Source: S&P Dow Jones

Consequently, if business sales continue to falter and margins continue to compress, the stock market is vulnerable to a drastic downward re-rating of valuation multiple.

As indicated by the market's stunning complacency during the spring-summer melt-up, hope apparently always springs eternal in the

Wall Street casino. But we believe that time, trends and events are all finally closing in.

On the economic front, there is simply no catalyst for a sales-and-growth rebound left, including an exhausted consumer sector that has once again run up record debts to a staggering $14.3 trillion. Even auto sales have rolled over, and understandably so.

As we indicated earlier, since the rebound began in early 2010, automotive sales have risen by $360 billion and auto debt by $355 billion. That is, anyone who could fog a rearview mirror got a loan and has a car or SUV—even if only on a temporary basis until the repo man arrives.

Likewise, there are no signs of help coming from business investment or exports. Orders for the former are now down by 12% from their September 2014 peak. Similarly, exports have dropped by 13%—with no signs of a rebound in orders from faltering East Asian, European and EM customers.

Finally, even the housing rebound is grinding to a halt. Permits for new single-family dwellings during July—a leading indicator of future housing construction—were down 6.1% from 2015, and this compares to 10% to 20% gains during the last several years.

Moreover, the fact that even the housing "recovery" is reaching exhaustion is especially telling. That's because it never really recovered from the thundering crash of 2008–10 in the first place. As shown in the chart on the previous page, last month's single-family permits were lower than they were in 1960!

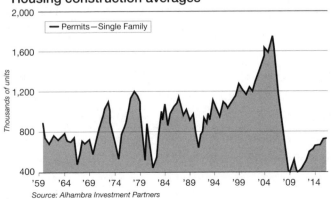

Housing construction averages

Source: Alhambra Investment Partners

That's right. The housing sector has time traveled backward by half a century. And that's hardly a confirmation of a stock market trading at 25.2X.

THE WALL STREET EXCLUDING-ITEMS HOCKEY STICK—2008 REDUX

So, barring some virtually inconceivable earnings miracle, the market's nosebleed valuation at 25.2X is an accident waiting to happen. The last time it was near that level outside of outright recession was on May 16, 2008, and the parallels are uncanny.

At that point, March 2008 LTM (latest 12 months) earnings on a GAAP basis had posted at $60.39 per share. So when the market hit an intraday high of 1,430, the implied multiple was nearly 24X.

Needless to say, it was a long way down from there. In fact, ten months later the market was 53% lower, and S&P reported earnings actually bottomed that quarter at $6.86 per share, or 90% lower.

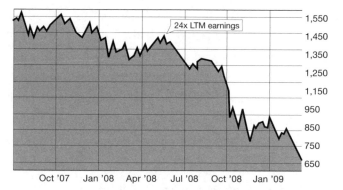

Needless to say, all of this is airily dismissed by Wall Street on the grounds that the earnings figures cited above are based on GAAP. And who would credit GAAP?

That is, besides the several thousand white-collar "criminals" domiciled in federal hospitality facilities who undoubtedly rue the day they violated it; or the tens of thousands of bureaucrats at the SEC, DOJ and state attorneys general offices who make a living enforcing it; or the far greater numbers of white-collar defense attorneys who make an even better living parsing its fine points.

Then again, you don't have to make a fetish of GAAP, even if several billion dollars annually of law enforcement and regulatory intrusion insist upon it. In fact, back in May 2008—at a time that even the White House's Council of Economic Advisers said there was no recession in sight and Bernanke was preaching mainly blue skies ahead—LTM "operating earnings" had posted at $77 per share.

So even using Wall Street's preferred "ex-items" rendition of earnings, the market was trading at a pretty sporty 18.6X.

Alas, a recession had already been underway for six months, but no one had bothered to tell the Eccles Building and their Wall Street acolytes. The latter mainly peddle stocks, but are otherwise known as "street economists" and "equity strategists."

Here's the thing. Even the LTM "operating earnings" number at the time was down by 16% from its cyclical high of $91.50 per share that had been posted three quarters earlier (June 2007 LTM).

But like now, the Street insisted that the "earnings bottom" was in, and that 2008 profits would come in at over $100 per share or 30% higher than the March 2008 LTM actual.

At it happens, the certified operating earnings number for the June 2016 LTM period was $98.36 per share.

That means that the market was trading at 21.8X Wall Street's preferred earnings measure at the peak of the August 2016 melt-up. That's 17% higher than the 18.6X delusion back in May 2008, and also something more.

Like eight years ago, the March operating earnings number is down 14% from its peak of $114.50 posted for September 2014. And also like back in 2008, expected forward year earnings of $133 per share are 35% above current levels.

WALL STREET'S QUARTER-TRILLION-DOLLAR ACCOUNTING FIB

In truth, all of this is worse than déjà vu. That's because the casino's financial narrative has been so corrupted by recency bias and accounting promiscuity that it has no idea what the profits picture really is or where it is going.

So it is worth documenting just how far the "earnings" narrative has departed from GAAP. Near the end of a cycle, in fact, this "GAAP gap" becomes egregiously wide.

As the Wall Street Journal recently documented, Wall Street's ex-items or pro forma version of S&P 500 earnings came in at *$1.040 trillion* in CY 2015 compared to GAAP earnings of *$787 billion*. It would appear that CEOs and CFO's who filed their SEC statements on penalty of prison time, averred that their actual profits were exactly *$256 billion* smaller than what they told their investors.

As it happens, that quarter-trillion-dollar fib is exactly the size of the ex-items charade back in 2007. It seems as if companies actually need a periodic recession so that they can toss into the kitchen sink the write-offs for all the dumb deals and investment mistakes they made while the bubble was still inflating.

And despite Wall Street protestations that these "ex-items" charges against profits are "nonrecurring" the truth of the matter is that they do consume cash or capital, and they do permanently weaken the balance sheet of companies that take these charges.

To wit, goodwill write-offs for failed M&A deals result in losses on the cash or stock originally paid to the seller. Likewise, equipment and property write-offs for closed plants and stores dissipate corporate resources, as do massive severance expenses for fired employees. And surely the tens of billions of stock options issued to executives are a real charge to income, not an "ex-items" expense to be ignored.

There is a reason why all of these so-called nonrecurring or ex-items expenses are strictly included in GAAP income statements, and the fact that they can be lumpy on a quarterly basis at the individual company level is hardly a reason to disappear them.

The rather obvious solution would be to smooth or amortize them into income at the company level. But for the S&P 500 as a whole there is not excuse at all. Operating charges and so-called nonrecurring charges are all averaged into one giant pot representing upward of $10 trillion in annual sales, anyway.

In short, the one and only purpose of the "GAAP gap" is to make the market seem far less expensive than it actually is. And on that score, Wall Street has been corrupted beyond repair.

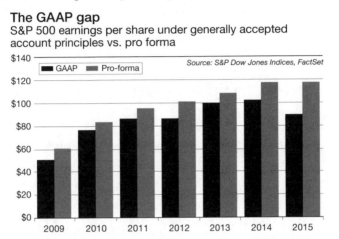

The GAAP gap
S&P 500 earnings per share under generally accepted account principles vs. pro forma

WALL STREET'S GREAT SHRINKING HOCKEY STICK

In any event, not only are Wall Street's hockey sticks extremely crooked from an accounting point of view, but they are also egregiously predictable in the magnitude by which they deflate as one-year forward estimates are eventually overtaken by reality.

To wit, in March 2014, the one-year forward estimate for CY 2015 came in at $135 per share of "operating earnings" for the S&P 500. At length, CY 2015 unfolded—bringing with it a collapse of oil and materials prices and a sharp slowdown of global growth that came as a big surprise to Wall Street.

Accordingly, the S&P scorekeepers now certify that actual operating earnings for CY 2015 came in at $100.45 per share. Apparently, in a world where "one-timers" don't count, that gigantic 26% miss doesn't count, either.

That's because in March 2015, the Street "bottoms up" consensus for 2016 was pegged at, yes, $135 per share, again.

The problem is that the 2016 hockey stick had already been rolled-down to just $111 per share as of June. Yet even if there is no further earnings decline in Q3 and Q4, earnings will total just $100 per share for 2016. That would be another 25% miss.

Never fear. The Street consensus estimate for 2017 as of this past March was $136 per share for the third year in a row.

But that has already been walked down to $130 per share and there are still six more quarters of downgrades to go. Yet this is not the least bit surprising. Walking the hockey stick back is what Wall Street equity analysts do.

WHY THE NEXT STOCK MARKET CRASH IS NEAR

Notwithstanding all of Wall Street's crooked accounting and shrinking hockey sticks, one salient truth remains. Namely, that the Fed has not outlawed the business cycle, and this one is fast approaching its sell-by date.

Stated differently, a PE multiple of 25.2X reported earnings is wholly unreasonable under any circumstance, but most especially at the tail end of a business cycle when profits will inexorably take a heavy hit.

Consider what happened last time. Even based on Wall Street's preferred "ex-items" accounting, profits peaked at $91.50 in Q2 2007 and kept falling until Q3 2009.

They bottomed there at $39.60 per share, or 57% lower. And on a GAAP basis earnings actually dropped to $6.86 per share, representing a 90% plunge from the peak.

But never mind. The sell-side's projected 41% gain in GAAP earnings from current levels through the year ending in December 2017 does surely suggest that history is irrelevant. By the lights of Wall Street, the Keynesian nirvana of permanent full employment and ceaseless business expansion, world without end, has apparently arrived.

That's because by that point in time the current business expansion will be 102 months old. And even that unlikely outcome would surely end in recession and a cyclical collapse in earnings not long thereafter.

Moreover, as shown below, there are only three business expansions since 1950 that are even in the 102-month ballpark.

The first of these was the Kennedy-Johnson expansion of the 1960s, which started with Ike's balanced budgets and William McChesney Martin's prudent monetary policies and ended with LBJ's guns and butter blow-off. The extended period of payback and the stagflationary 1970's thereafter more than offset the 106 months of expansion.

Likewise, the Reagan expansion lasted for 92 months, but as we have seen only because Volcker was fired in 1987 and replaced by the printing press policies of Alan Greenspan.

Finally, the 120 month expansion recorded during the 1990s is no real record at all. It was fueled by Greenspan's adoption of full frontal Bubble Finance in 1994 and was achieved by a massive build-up of household debt and the launch of the great housing and real estate bubbles that came crashing down a decade later.

And it also came at the expense of a destructive domestic inflation that caused the off-shoring of a huge chunk of the nation's breadwinner jobs, as we documented in Chapter 5.

By contrast, these is virtually no prospect of either monetary or fiscal "stimulus" in the years ahead, while the headwinds from the end of the 20-year global credit and CapEx bubble will only intensify as time goes on.

In short, what's coming is not a 102-month or even 120-month scenario for a record business cycle expansion.

The recovery/expansion is already fairly strong

Recessions	Duration (months)	Expansions	Duration (months)
1945	8	1945–48	37
1948–49	11	1949–53	45
1953–54	10	1954–57	39
1957–58	8	1958–60	24
1960–61	10	1961–69	106
1970	11	1970–73	36
1973–75	16	1975–80	58
1980	6	1980–91	12
1981–82	16	1982–90	92
1990–91	8	1991–2001	120
2001	8	2001–07	73
2008–2009	18	2009–?	84 so far
Averages:		Averages:	
1854–1919	21.6	1854–1919	26.6
1919–45	18.2	1919–45	35.0
1945–2009	11.1	1945–2009	58.4

Source: 2016 High Frequency Economics, Ltd.

Instead, what's coming is a flat-out rebuke to the casino gamblers who were still drinking the Fed's poisonous monetary Cool-Aid and valuing the S&P 500 at 18X a two-year forward earnings fantasy.

Indeed, if charts could do a Jim Cramer imitation, this one would say, "Sell, sell, sell!"

CHAPTER 13:

Busting the Banksters— The Case for a Super Glass-Steagall

THE MAINSTREAM NARRATIVE ABOUT "RECOVERY" FROM THE FINANCIAL crisis is a giant con job. And nowhere does the mendacity run deeper than in the "banks are fixed" meme—an insidious cover story that has been concocted by the crony capitalist cabals that thrive at the intersection of Wall Street and Washington.

That's not to say that the Wall Street cover story is hiding anything. In recent months even the mainstream media has published stunning evidence of malefactions and abuse at the great megabanks—especially Bank of America (BAC) and Citigroup (C).

Indeed, a recent Wall Street Journal exposé about the depredations of Bank of America shows that the latter is in a class all by itself when it comes to bankster abuse and criminality.

Not surprisingly, at the center of this latest malefaction is still-another set of schemes to grossly abuse the deposit-insurance safety net and enlist the American taxpayer in the risky business of financing high-rolling London hedge funds.

In this case, the abuse consisted of BAC funded and enabled tax-avoidance schemes with respect to stock dividends—arrangements that happen to be illegal in the United States.

No matter. BAC simply arranged for them to be executed for clients in London where they apparently are kosher, but with funds from BAC's

U.S.-insured banking entity called BANA, which most definitely was not kosher at all.

As to the narrow offense involved—that is, the use of insured deposits to cheat the tax man—the one honest official to come out of Washington's 2008–09 bank bailout spree, former FDIC head Sheila Bair, had this to say:

> I don't think it's an appropriate use . . . Activities with a substantial reputational risk . . . should not be done inside a bank. You have explicit government backing inside a bank. There is taxpayer risk there.

She is right, and apparently in response to prodding by its regulator, BAC has now ended the practice, albeit after booking billions in what amounted to pure profits from these illicit trades.

But that doesn't end the matter. This latest abuse by BAC's London operation is, in fact, just the tip of the iceberg; it's a symptom of an unreformed banking regime that is rotten to the core and that remains a clear and present danger to financial stability and true economic recovery.

And it's not by coincidence that at the very epicenter of that untoward regime stands a $2 trillion financial conglomerate that is a virtual cesspool of malfeasance, customer abuse, operational incompetence, legal and regulatory failure, downright criminality and complete and total lack of accountability at the board and top-executive level.

In short, BAC's seven-year CEO, Brian Moynihan, is guilty of such chronic malfeasance and serial management failures that outside the cushy cocoon of "too big to fail" (TBTF) he would have been fired long ago. Indeed, it is hard to believe that he would have survived very long even running a small chain of car washes in east Nebraska.

BANK OF AMERICA— THE $100 BILLION FINANCIAL MISCREANT

Since 2009, in fact, BAC has been the number-one employer of criminal and regulatory defense attorneys in the USA and the armies of accountants, consultants, forensic specialists, etc. which support them. So vast is the dragnet of lawsuits and legal actions that have been brought against it that

BAC's defense team amounts to an entire industry that should have its very own SIC code at the Commerce Department's data mills!

Already BAC has agreed to a stupendous disgorgement of fines, settlements and penalties that totals upward of $100 billion.

These stem not only from the mortgage abuses, where its Countrywide subsidiary was a lead perpetrator, but nearly every other aspect of its banking operations as well. The pejorative term "bankster" does well and truly apply perfectly to the BAC house of malfeasance and corruption.

So the question at hand is not simply BAC's dodgy dividend-tax-trading strategies or why Brian Moynihan still has a job. The real question is why a monumentally reckless, abusive and predatory behemoth like BAC even exists in the first place.

In addressing those questions we get to the meat of the matter. That is, the urgent need to repudiate the "banks are fixed" meme and to replace it with a sweeping new regime based on a Super Glass-Steagall operational and regulatory framework.

Moreover, this new deal must start with a macro-economic truth that is completely ignored and denied by the Beltway-lobby-driven narrative about the banking crisis.

To wit, the U.S. banking sector is vastly bloated, inefficient, unstable and destructive owing to a government policy regime that subsidizes and privileges banks in a massive and plenary manner. Accordingly, there is monumental overinvestment and malinvestments in the banking system. BAC is only a leading poster boy.

This truth is the very opposite of the erroneous mainstream predicate that ever more debt is the lynch-pin of capitalist growth and prosperity. By the lights of the Wall Street and Washington racketeers who dominate the debate, America's $18 trillion economy can't do without cheap and easy debt. Indeed, Main Street jobs and prosperity purportedly require more and more of it each and every quarter

In fact, the only reason that—eight years after what is claimed to have been a near Armageddon event—we are still plagued with TBTF, the regulatory monstrosity known as Dodd-Frank and the continuing tenure

of the likes of BAC and Brian Moynihan is the tyranny of this wholly misbegotten "moar debt" predicate.

In that context, it needs be further recognized that root-and-branch
reform won't hurt the Main Street economy in the slightest—notwithstanding the self-serving protestations of Wall Street princes like Jamie Dimon.
To the contrary, it will liberate inefficiently deployed people, capital and
technology for use in more productive parts of the economy.

At the end of the day, it is the false belief in the debt elixir of endless
debt that undergirds the inexhaustible pettifoggery and cowardice displayed
by Washington politicians and regulators alike when it comes to fixing the
banks. The latter simply threaten a lenders' strike, and any resolve to get to
the root of the problem promptly dissolves.

Nevertheless, direct evidence of the degree to which banking abuse and
corruption flows from the current government policy regime can be found
in the whistleblower's BAC narrative pieced together by the WSJ. The of-
fending activities took place at Merrill Lynch's "prime broker" offices in
London—and that kind of brokers' office, of course, deals not with dentists
and barristers but the billionaire titans of the global financial casino.

The essence of the scheme was to scalp huge profits from BAC's cheap
insured deposits by transporting them across the Atlantic so they could be
deployed in risky trades by the high-roller clients of its London prime broker.

Moreover, the transport of these insured deposit based funds to London from an entity called BANA did not involve an innocent mix-up way
down in the bowels of the bank. The funds were transferred on orders
from BAC's top executives at the holding company level. As the WSJ
succinctly explained:

> One afternoon in February 2011, bankers, traders and others
> crowded into a Bank of America auditorium in London for a
> "town hall" meeting . . . [about] changing the way they loaned
> money to certain clients . . . The money for the loans now would
> come through BANA rather than Merrill Lynch International.
>
> [Executives] told attendees that increasing the use of lower-cost
> cash (i.e. insured deposits) would give Bank of America a new

edge over competitors . . . [T]he funding would allow the bank to extend more loans to more hedge funds, including those with hard-to-sell investments, in turn generating more profits for the bank, according to internal documents and people involved in the discussions.

> " . . . can we make sure all new clients, where possible, are loaded right on to BANA? Where we can't I'd like to understand why," a senior investment-banking executive, Sylvan Chackman, wrote in an email to employees in January 2012.

Here's the thing. Never, ever should an insured deposit bank be operating a prime brokerage subsidiary in the Wild West arena of the London financial markets. Stated differently, it is absolutely nuts that BAC even owns Merrill Lynch, and it is even more preposterous that it does so because its former executives were forced to acquire Merrill Lynch at the point of a gun in December 2008.

The gunslingers, of course, were the two highest economic officials in the land, Ben Bernanke and Hank Paulson.

And the latter were commanding this action in pursuit of a crony-capitalist scheme to rescue Wall Street and prevent economic justice and efficiency from happening. That is, the shotgun marriage of BAC and Merrill was designed to prevent Mr. Market's determination to liquidate the utterly bankrupt and corrupt gambling house that Merrill Lynch had become in the run-up to the so-called financial crisis.

Self-evidently, this latest BAC scheme to abuse and arbitrage the deposit insurance safety net would not have happened had Glass-Steagall not been repealed in the first place.

Indeed, as we elaborate further on, the great financial statesman Senator Carter Glass had been totally opposed to deposit insurance owing to its potential for exactly this kind of abuse.

Unlike the debt-enthralled statists of the present era—such as Bernanke, Paulson, Geithner and all the rest of the Obama entourage—Senator Glass knew that gambling and banking do not mix; and that an endless stream of

Sylvan Chackmans would arise and order that "we make sure all new clients, where possible, are loaded right on to BANA [aka the U.S. taxpayer]."

Actually, however, mere restoration of the old Glass-Steagall is not nearly enough. A banking regime that can produce $100 billion worth of sanctions against a single institutions needs to be replaced root and branch.

If not, it is only a matter of time before the next contagion of London Whales and tidal wave of toxic products and trades arising from Wall Street's financial meth labs triggers another financial panic and meltdown.

CITIGROUP AND THE CROMNIBUS CAPER

That's because Bank of America is no outlier. The egregious gambling dens that have metastasized on Wall Street over the past three decades remain almost wholly intact, and Citigroup is another poster boy.

At the time of the 2008 crisis, it was completely and hopelessly insolvent. Its giant web of holding company gambling and money-churning operations should have been put in Chapter 11, and the underlying insured bank should have been put into FDIC receivership. No insured mom-and-pop depositor would have lost a dime.

Yes, the depositor payoffs would have been " costly" to Uncle Sam, but that cost was created long before September 2008. It was a product of the whole federal deposit-insurance scheme and its abuse by giant banking supermarkets that should never have been permitted in the first place.

Unfortunately, insult has been added to injury by subsequent developments. To wit, the Washington and Wall Street policy elite has actually doubled down. They flooded the banking system with even cheaper money via ZIRP and QE, while establishing a regulatory counter-point under Dodd-Frank that is worse than useless.

Needless to say, the hard-pressed taxpayers of America should never again be forced to bailout the crony capitalist plunder that was enabled by the Fed's free money machine in the run-up to the 2008 financial crisis. Yet for eight straight years the madmen (and women) of the Eccles Building have pegged the cost of bank deposit money at essentially zero, thereby enabling the banks to earn spread profits on the backs of Main Street savers and retirees.

At the same time, Washington has pretended to be fixing the banks via an opaque regulatory shitstorm called Dodd-Frank. The latter ignores all the underlying causes of the too-big-to-fail banks, and, instead, has blanketed the financial system in the kind of regulatory spaghetti that causes vast deadweight compliance costs, but does absolutely nothing to stop the Wall Street banksters from perpetrating their toxic schemes.

Indeed, the reason that structural reform, including breaking up the giant financial conglomerates, is so imperative was crystalized two years ago by a naked Wall Street power grab in the congressional backrooms. It involved a Citigroup-drafted sneak attack on Washington's tepid effort to curtail one of the more egregious gambling habits of some of the big banks.

These incorrigible larcenists had been trying to gut the "push out" provisions of Dodd-Frank for more than three years prior to what became the Cromnibus appropriations bill in the lame duck congressional session after the 2014 election.

The provision under attack boiled down to a simple and urgently necessary injunction to the banks. Namely, that you can't roll the dice in the "derivatives" gambling halls with taxpayer guaranteed deposits.

In light of the inherent dangers of what even Warren Buffet once called "financial weapons of mass destruction," it is self-evident that no bank—not even the mighty Citigroup—should be allowed to bring these incendiary devices within a country-mile of the taxpayer-enabled FDIC guarantee program.

So what Dodd-Frank proposed was actually quite sensible. It said to the giant Wall Street banks—go ahead and swing for the fences, but do it in a holding company subsidiary. If something subsequently goes boom in the night, it's on your earnings and bonuses—not the taxpayers' hard-earned bucks.

If there was anyone left on Wall Street with a sense of decency and a modest comprehension of what free-market capitalism is about, they would not have been looking a gift horse in the mouth.

The Dodd-Frank provision that came under its furious attack, in fact, was hardly a slap on the wrist. If Congress had really meant to fix the system that supposedly brought us to the cusp of Armageddon in September 2008, it would not have bothered with Dodd-Frank at all.

THE ORIGINAL GLASS-STEAGALL AND ITS DEMISE

Instead, Washington should have gone to the root of the problem and passed a Super Glass-Steagall that would have dismembered the giant banks by statutory edict, and kicked the Wall Street–based gambling houses like Citigroup out of the FDIC entirely.

The fact is, deposit insurance has been coopted and abused by the Wall Street megabanks for decades. It now stands as a vast perversion of what had actually been intended—misguided or not—way back in the dark hours of 1933–34.

Back then there were three people in Washington who counted when push came to shove—President Roosevelt, Senator Glass and Congressman Steagall. FDR was against deposit insurance because he thought it would be abused by Wall Street, and for once he was right.

Senator Glass was against it, too. As one of the true financial statesmen of modern times he did well and truly understand the dangers of moral hazard and fractional reserve banking propped up by the state.

Alas, Congressman Steagall was a demagogic foe of Wall Street. But he also wanted deposit insurance to protect the red-neck depositors of Alabama, who had been taken to the cleaners by banksters of local origin.

So we got deposit insurance for the proverbial "little guy" and a sharp separation of banking and commerce at the insistence of Senator Glass. FDR went along for the ride after actually threatening to veto the bill on account of his belief that someday, in fact, it would be egregiously abused by the banks.

For at least a generation, as it happened, Wall Street kept its distance and its lobbyists at home. After all, for the next several decades it was still run by the chastened survivors of the 1920s' gambling orgies and the Crash of 1929

By contrast, today we have almost the opposite history. Wall Street is run by a generation that has been bailed-out too many times to count and that has been blatantly and egregiously coddled by perverse central bank theories and practices that have turned the nation's capital and money markets into veritable gambling casinos.

As I have previously explained, this includes such practices as the stock market puts, the wealth-effects doctrine and years and years of ZIRP.

The latter is nothing more than free gambling money that can be used to fund the carry trades. That is, it's free overnight money to buy anything with a yield or prospect of short-term gain—and that can be rolled over day after day with the assurance from the Eccles Building that the cost of carry is fixed and subject to change only upon ample notice.

MICHAEL CORBAT—CRONY-CAPITALIST POSTER BOY

In fact, the spoiled rotten generation now running Wall Street is personified by the current Citigroup CEO. The unconscionable raid on the taxpayers described above did not occur because the banks hirelings were sitting around K Street looking for an issue for which to bill their client.

No, the command to mount this deplorable attempt to take the entire budget of the United States hostage in the middle of the night came straight from the C-suite at Citigroup. So just consider the monumental hutzpah of Michael Corbat and his Wall Street confederates.

In point of fact, these unvarnished crony capitalists had been trying to gut Dodd-Frank and especially the Volcker rule and the "push out" standard for years.

But their case was so threadbare and self-serving that they could not even buy the necessary votes through the normal legislative process. And that's notwithstanding millions of PAC contributions and every accouterment of the lobbying trade at their disposal. Their attempt to gut the push-out provision was, in fact, a dead letter on Capitol Hill.

So during the lame duck session in December 2014, they resorted to the low road. Owing to its usual dysfunction, Congress had once again failed to pass the appropriations bills for the current fiscal year which had been underway for 80 days.

Therefore it had again resorted to an 11th hour punt via a giant omnibus appropriations bill. The latter authorized $1.1 trillion of spending in 1600 pages of fine print bedecked with prodigious helpings of pork. No one could have possibly read or comprehended it in the several days between the vote and when it had been fashioned in the backrooms during the wee hours of the night.

In short, the so-called Cromnibus caper was appalling enough in its own right. But the fact that the CEO of Citigroup had ordered his henchmen to pile on is stark testimony to the insuperable arrogance of the generation that now runs Wall Street and to their sheer sense of "entitlement."

That is to say, Wall Street's movers and shakers have come to believe that Washington is there to do "whatever it takes" to ensure that Wall Street profits are fattened one more quarter. After all, the share prices of the gambling halls which operate there, and the executive options and bonuses of the executives who run them, must never fail to advance.

Yes, Michael Corbat is a Citigroup "lifer" and is just doing his corporate duty in behalf of shareholders. But that's precisely the problem.

There should be no Citigroup "lifers" whatsoever—because there should have been no Citigroup left standing. In fact, "C" is testimony to the financial folly of the last three decades.

Indeed, Michael Corbat is a "lifer" from this whole misbegotten chapter, going back to his days at Salomon Brothers and his rise through the Sandy Weill machine and all the departments and far-flung operations of Citigroup after it finally came together.

We have no clue about what he learned about banking along the way. But there is absolutely no doubt that what he did learn over that journey is that Washington exists to do Wall Street's bidding.

The truth is, the generation represented by Michael Corbat knows nothing about the idea of the "public interest" as opposed to private advantage. It is steeped in the practice of crony capitalism, but it knows nothing of free markets.

After all these years of Washington's rank servility, in fact, Wall Street leaders like Corbat now think taking the people of America hostage in the middle of the night is all in a corporate day's work.

That's also why Dodd-Frank is a crony capitalist regulatory puzzle palace that will not do one bit of good. Instead, its incomprehensible 1,700 pages of legislative pettifoggery has become a Beltway lawyers, accountants and lobbyists full employment act.

Rather than market based financial discipline and efficiency, what it has given rise to is 10,000 pages of obscurantist rule-makings that are suffocating mid-sized and community banks with compliance trivia while anesthetizing Washington's sleepwalking politicians—until the next crisis.

THE KEY TO BANKING REFORM: HOG TIE THE FED

By contrast, a Super-Glass/Steagall would entail a legislated breakup of the multi-trillion behemoths like Bank of America, Citigroup, Wells Fargo and JPMorgan. It would also encompass a sharp rollback of FDIC insurance to only "narrow" banks which take deposits and make loans, and it would eliminate the Fed's discount window privileges for any financial institution involved in trading, underwriting and proprietary risk-taking.

Most importantly, Super Glass-Steagall would also hog-tie the Fed by ending discretionary interest rate pegging and the entire gamut of FOMC market interventions and securities price falsification.

The latter point, in fact, is the sine qua non of true banking reform. As we demonstrated in Chapter 4, our debt saturated economy—with $64 trillion of credit market debt outstanding representing an unsustainable leverage ratio of 3.5X national income—does not require artificially priced credit to rejuvenate growth and prosperity.

Nor is there any point whatsoever in perpetuating ZIRP and the Fed's long-standing and destructive regime of financial repression. The major consequence of 93 months on the zero bound has been a massive transfer of income—upward of $250 billion per year—to the banking system from the hides of savers and depositors.

The relevance here is that BAC and most of the other giant financial conglomerates would be insolvent without these arbitrary transfers.

Given BAC's $1.2 trillion deposit base, in fact, the Fed's financial repression probably reduced its funding costs by at least $30 billion last year compared to a free market pricing environment.

Needless to say, that wholly unwarranted and economically wasteful subsidy amounts to more than double the $14.6 billion of net income BAC posted in the most recent 12 months, and is more than 8X the size of its dividend distributions.

And, no, in the face of free-market interest rates, BAC and other banks would not have automatically made up the difference via higher yields on its loans and assets.

The fact is, BAC's loan book today is smaller than it was on the eve of the crisis because as we demonstrated in Chapter 6, U.S. households and businesses have reached a condition of Peak Debt."

Accordingly, in a free market the current central bank–driven deformation of pricing would be unwound. Interest rates on savings would rise more than yields on borrowings because demand for market rate debt—as opposed to Fed subsidized rates—would fall sharply.

Stated differently, BAC and most other giant banks are solvent only because the lion's share of their earnings have been indirectly manufactured by the monetary central planners in the Eccles Building.

Yet no matter how interest rates and profit spreads might ultimately shake out on the free market, one thing is certain. To wit, there is not a snowball's chance in the hot place that BAC could have earned the $75 billion in dividends and share repurchases it made over the last decade. Not even close.

So what real banking reform would do is strip the giant banks like BAC, Citi, JPM, Wells Fargo—and the next tier as well—of the deposit cost subsidies which accrue from Fed financial repression, as well as their access to the discount window and FDIC insurance.

By the same token, once the mega banks were stripped of these state-conferred privileges and subventions, they would be free to operate any financial business they wished. And they would be free to employ whatever balance sheet arrangements their at-risk depositors, bond investors and equity holders would permit.

The banking behemoths keep demanding less government interference and regulation. Well, Super Glass-Steagall would provide the free market they claim to desire.

Getting from here to there requires one more Super Glass-Steagall feature. The nation's handful of mega- banks have operated so long in the corrupt world of bailouts and state conferred moral hazard that they are inherently unstable and prone to the errors and abuses for which BAC and C are the poster boys.

Moreover, none of them would have gotten to their current size without the serial M&A campaigns and roll-ups that were enabled by the current rotten banking regime. Giant, multi-trillion banking conglomerates would not arise in a free market because there are simply no demonstrated economies of scale in banking beyond a few hundred billion in balance sheet footings, at most.

So cap their size at 1% of GDP, or about $200 billion, during the transition period when they are being weaned from their state crutches, subsidies and privileges and finding their sea-legs on the free market.

At the end of the day, cesspools like BAC and Citi need to be completely drained. And the only way to get them out on the free market where this could actually be accomplished is through the enactment of the kind of Super Glass-Steagall described below.

SUPER GLASS-STEAGALL— A MODEL FOR SWEEPING CHANGE

As indicated, Super Glass-Steagall would consign today's handful of giant financial services conglomerates to the arena of pure free enterprise, where they would live or die at the hands of competition and their value to customers. There would be no bailouts of alleged too-big-to-fail institutions because this proposed enactment would strip the statute books of every vestige of authority to rescue banks with assets greater than $200 billion (<1% of GDP).

To remove any doubt, it would also impose multi-million fines and jail time for top officers of the Federal Reserve and U.S. Treasury if they tried to circumvent any of the new Super Glass-Steagall restrictions. So doing, it would reassure the American public that the larcenous crony capitalism of the last two decades has been abolished and that the ability of the racketeers of K-Street to corrupt the halls of government has been drastically curtailed.

In order to further purge the hoary myth of "systemic importance" and "financial contagion" from the Washington excuse bag, banks with more than $200 billion in assets would be denied access to the Fed's discount window. Likewise, they would be ineligible to have their deposits backed by FDIC insurance.

Accordingly, the failure of a behemoth like Citigroup would not threaten to bankrupt FDIC as it did during the 2008 crisis. Even more crucially, the giant banking conglomerates would not become a pretext for the power-hungry bureaucrats at the Fed to yell "contagion!" during a time of financial dislocation, thereby giving themselves an excuse to bailout their Wall Street wards.

That's because under a new Super Glass-Steagall type regime most banks below the $200 billion threshold would drastically limit their counter-party risk exposure to the dozen or so too-big-to-insure banks in the United States.

Today, giants like JPMorgan, Bank of America, Citi, Well Fargo and the other usual suspects including the charted banks of Goldman and Morgan Stanley are viewed as privileged wards of the state. But without the implicit backing of Uncle Sam, smaller banks would be forced to put a market based risk discount on their exposures to such free market behemoths.

This would leave approximately 6,000 commercial banks and thrifts below the size threshold to offer FDIC insurance to all currently covered depositors. There could be no demagogic claim that ordinary citizens were being consigned to potential financial ruin.

So the argument that blue-haired widows and financially uninformed wage workers need the protection of universal deposit insurance just doesn't cut it. They could still obtain FDIC coverage on their deposits and savings, but only at what would be thousands of narrow banks engaged solely in the business of deposit taking and lending.

At the same time, the public could be assured that taxpayers were not unwittingly underwriting Citigroup's $53 trillion of derivative exposures or the $51 trillion at Goldman and JPM. Likewise, the risky multi-trillion trading books of the big banks would be sequestered in a pure free-market arena.

Finally, to ensure that the Fed's discount window and deposit insurance was not abused even by smaller banks, the 6,000 remaining federally privileged institutions would also be prohibited from engaging in trading, underwriting, investment banking, private equity, hedge funds, derivatives and other activities outside of deposit taking and lending.

The overwhelming share of midsize and community banks do not participate in these activities today, anyway. But if their customers demanded such services in the future, and they wished to remain in competition with the big free market banks under Super Glass-Steagall, they would have to spin-off such activities to separate, independent companies—just as did the big Wall street banks after the original Glass-Steagall was passed in 1934.

In short, these latter inherently risky economic functions would be performed on the free market by at-risk banks and financial-services companies. The latter could never get too big to fail or too big to manage because the market would stop them first; or, after the fact, they would be disciplined by the fail-safe institution of bankruptcy.

No taxpayer would ever be put in harm's way by trades like those of the London Whale.

TODAY'S BANKS ARE WARDS OF THE STATE, NOT FREE-MARKET ENTERPRISES

Besides, severing the big banks' pipeline to the federal bailout trough and putting the big Wall Street banks back on a free-market-based level playing field is the right thing to do. Today's multi-trillion banks are simply not free enterprise institutions entitled to be left alone.

Instead, as we have shown, they are wards of the state dependent upon its subsidies, safety nets, regulatory protections and legal privileges. Consequently, they have gotten far larger, more risky and dangerous to society than could ever happen in an honest, disciplined market.

Foremost among these artificial props is the Fed's discount window. The latter provides cheap, unlimited funding at a moment's notice with no questions asked. The purpose is to ensure banking-system liquidity and stability and to thwart contagion, but it also nullifies the essential bank management discipline and prudence that comes from fear of depositor flight.

Likewise, FDIC insurance essentially shields banks' balance sheets and asset-management practices from depositor scrutiny. Whatever its merits in behalf of the little guy, there is no doubt that deposit insurance is a font of moral hazard and excess risk-taking in the bonus-driven executive suits.

Indeed, the function of maturity transformation (borrowing short and lending long)—which is the essence of fractional-reserve banking—is inherently risky and unstable. Once upon a time the state attempted to limit banks' propensity for excesses by permitting injured depositors to bring suit against stockholders for double their original investment. That tended to concentrate the minds of bank boards and stock-owning executives.

The opposite incentives prevail in today's bailout regime. Under current legal and regulatory arrangements shareholders and boards face no liability at all—let alone double liability—for mismanagement and imprudent risk taking.

Instead, insolvent or failing institutions are apt to be bailed out; and even if share prices are permitted to plunge, boards and executives are likely to be given new stock options struck at the post-collapse price. That happened in every big bank in America after the 2008 meltdown.

Likewise, prior to the establishment of the Fed and its bailout windows, the big New York money center banks were required to remain super liquid by holding cash reserves equal to 20% or more of deposits. In that regard, the post-Keynesian history books have been stripped of the fact that even at the peak of the infamous banking crisis on the eve of FDRs inauguration in March 1933, none of the big New York City banks had lines at their teller windows or were in any way illiquid or insolvent.

By contrast, one of Greenspan's most deleterious actions was to essentially reduce cash reserve requirements to zero. Owing to the release of such immobilized assets and the costs of carrying them, of course, banks became more profitable.

Yet the ultimate cost of keeping the banking system liquid was not eliminated; it was just transferred to public institutions including the Fed, FDIC and eventually the U.S. Treasury via TARP.

TWO DECADES OF BANK-MERGER MANIA MADE IT WORSE

All of these violations of free market discipline have had a cumulative historical effect that's no longer tolerable. And these distortions, disincentives and moral hazards were immensely compounded by two decades of monstrous bank merger roll-ups that resulted in incomprehensible and unmanageable financial services conglomerates like Citigroup and BAC.

Indeed, the worst excrescence of that trend—the merger of Travelers and Citibank—happened only after the old Glass-Steagall was repealed in 1999.

Once these unnatural and inherently unstable multi-trillion-dollar financial services conglomerates came into existence after the turn of the century, the subsequent regulatory acquiescence in the 30-to-1 leverage ratios achieved by the Wall Street brokers, including the vast investment-banking operations inside Citigroup, Bank of America and JPMorgan, only added insult to injury. So did the regulatory lapse that enabled Citigroup and others to establish trillion-dollar off-balance-sheet SIVs during the run-up to the financial crisis.

Indeed, as we indicated earlier, the Citigroup style of rogue financial behemoths should have been put out of their misery by the FDIC when they failed in 2008. But their screaming insolvency—including that of Goldman, Morgan Stanley, Bank of America and others—was covered up by multitrillion-dollar bailouts from the Fed's alphabet soup of liquidity infusions and TARP.

Indeed, Washington's desperate thrashing around in the bailout arena resulted in the worst of all worlds. The problem caused by too-big-to-manage government-enabled financial conglomerates was made far bigger by Washington-sanctioned and directed megamergers. These included the shotgun marriage of Bank of America and Merrill Lynch, the federally subsidized takeovers of Bear Stearns and Washington Mutual by JPMorgan and the rescue of Wachovia by Wells Fargo.

These mergers were outright madness. As shown in the chart below, we now have five federally subsidized and underwritten behemoths that control $7 trillion of assets and nearly 50% of the banking market. And these figures do not include Goldman Sachs and Morgan Stanley, which also have bank charters, and would add another $1.7 trillion of assets and bring the concentration level to upward of 60%.

By contrast, before the age of Bubble Finance really got underway in 1990, the combined balance sheet footings of the five largest U.S. banks were only $400 billion or barely 5% of today's level; and their collective market share was just 10%.

Assets concentration for the 5 largest U.S. banks and thrifts since 1990

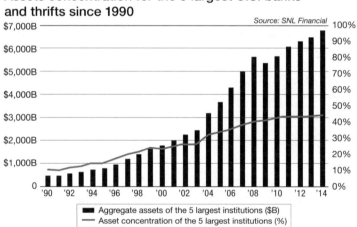

Again, this is not about bigness per se or anti-trust populism, but about dangerous financial conglomerates that would not even exist without the dispensations of government, and would not persist if they did not hire half of the K Street lobby complex to protect their privileges.

At the end of the day, the destructive form of central banking carried out by the Fed, ECB, BOJ and other major central banks needs to be eliminated entirely. But in the interim, bringing the worst excesses of Wall Street to heel under a Super Glass-Steagall regime would go a long way toward preventing another financial meltdown like that of September 2008.

And that gets us to the 2016 campaign. By embracing this kind of Super Glass-Steagall, Donald Trump would consolidate his base in Flyover America and reel in some of the Bernie Sanders throng too.

The latter will never forgive Clinton for her Goldman Sachs speech whoring. And that's to say nothing of her full-throated support for the 2008 bank bailouts and the Fed's subsequent giant gifts of QE and ZIRP to the Wall Street gamblers.

To be sure, the big Wall Street banks will whine that they face unfair competition from giant foreign banks that are protected, subsidized and privileged by their governments. But there is a simple answer to that straw man.

If the free market does not reward giant financial conglomerates for the risk-reward equations buried in their derivatives books or opaque holdings of junk bonds, OTC bilateral trades or the maturity mismatches in their funding accounts, then they do not add to efficient economic production or wealth creation.

So let foreign banks pursue this wasteful folly until the cows come home. And foreign socialist governments are more than welcome to bear the losses, even as their crony capitalist banksters scalp the windfall profits.

CHAPTER 14:

Bubbles in Bond Land—
It's a Central Bank-Made Mania

SOMETIMES AN APT JUXTAPOSITION IS WORTH A THOUSAND WORDS, and here's one that surely fits the bill.

Last year Japan lost another 272,000 of its population as it marched resolutely toward its destiny as the world's first bankrupt old-age colony. At the same time, the return on Japan's 40-year bond during the first six months of 2016 has been an astonishing 48%.

That's right!

We aren't talking Tesla, the biotech index or Facebook. To the contrary, like the rest of the Japanese yield curve, this bond has no yield and no prospect of repayment.

But that doesn't matter because it's not really a sovereign bond anymore. These Japanese government bonds (JGBs) have actually morphed into risk-free gambling chips.

Front-running speculators are scooping up whatever odds and sots of JGBs remain on the market and are selling them to the Bank of Japan (BOJ) at higher and higher and higher prices

At the same time, these punters face virtually no risk. The BOJ already owns 426 trillion yen of JGBs, which is nearly half of the outstandings. And that's saying something, given that Japan has more than one quadrillion yen of government debt, which amounts to 230% of GDP.

Moreover, it is scarfing up the rest at a rate of 80 trillion yen per year under current policy, while giving every indication of sharply stepping up its purchase rate as it segues to outright helicopter money.

It can therefore be well and truly said that the BOJ is the ultimate roach motel. At length, virtually every scrap of Japan's gargantuan public debt will go marching into its vaults never to return, and at "whatever it takes" in terms of bond prices to meet the BOJ's lunatic quotas.

THE BIG FAT BID OF THE WORLD'S CENTRAL BANKS

Surely, BOJ Governor Kuroda will go down in history as the most foolish central banker of all time. But in the interim the man is contributing— along with Draghi, Yellen and the rest of the central bankers' guild—to absolute mayhem in the global fixed-income market.

The effect of their massive bond purchases, or so-called QE policies, has been to radically inflate sovereign-bond prices. The big fat bid of central bankers in the benchmark government-securities sector, in turn, has caused drastic mispricing to migrate into the balance of the fixed-income spectrum via spread pricing off the benchmarks, and from there into markets for converts, equities and everything else.

Above all else, the QE-driven falsification of bond prices means that central banks have supplanted real money savers as the marginal source of demand in the government bond markets. But by their very ideology and function, central bankers are rigidly and even fiercely price inelastic.

For example, the madman Draghi will pay any price—absolutely any price—to acquire his $90 billion per month QE quota. He sets the price on the margin, and at present that happens to be a yield no lower than negative 0.4% for a Eurozone government security of any maturity. Presumably that would include a 500-year bond if the Portuguese were alert enough to issue one.

Needless to say, no rational saver anywhere on the planet would "invest" in the German 10-year bund at its recent negative 20 bps of yield. The operational word here is "saver" as distinguished from the hordes of leveraged speculators (on repo) who are more than happy to buy radically overpriced German bunds today.

After all, they know the madmen at the ECB stand ready to buy them back at an even-higher price tomorrow.

Yet when you replace savers with central bankers at the very heart of the financial price-discovery process in the benchmark bond markets, the system eventually goes tilt. You go upside-down.

THE FISCAL EQUIVALENT OF A UNICORN— "SCARCITY" IN SOVEREIGN-DEBT MARKETS

That condition was aptly described in a recent Wall Street Journal piece about a new development in sovereign-debt markets that absolutely defies human nature and the fundamental dynamics of modern welfare-state democracies.

To wit, modern governments can seemingly never issue enough debt. This is due to the cost of their massive entitlement constituencies, special-interest racketeers of every stripe and the prevalence of Keynesian-style rationalizations for not extracting from taxpayers the full measure of what politicians are inclined to spend.

Notwithstanding that endemic condition, however, there is now a rapidly growing "scarcity" of government debt—the equivalent of a fiscal unicorn. As the WSJ noted:

A buying spree by central banks is reducing the availability of government debt for other buyers and intensifying the bidding wars that break out when investors get jittery, driving prices higher and yields lower. The yield on the benchmark 10-year Treasury note hit a record low Wednesday.

"The scarcity factor is there but it really becomes palpable during periods of stress when yields immediately collapse," he said. "You may be shut out of the bond market just when you need it the most."

Owing to this utterly insensible "scarcity," central banks and speculators together have driven the yield on nearly $13 trillion of government debt—or nearly 30% of total outstandings on the planet—into the subzero zone. This includes more than $1 trillion each of German and French government debt and nearly $8 trillion of Japanese government debt.

Nor is that the extent of the subzero lunacy. The Swiss yield curve is negative all the way out to 48 years, where recently the bond actually traded at -0.0082%.

So we do mean that the systematic falsification of financial prices is the sum and substance of what contemporary central banks do.

Forty years from now, for example, Japan's retirement colony will be bigger than its labor force, and its fiscal and monetary system will have crashed long before. Yet the 10-year JCB traded at negative 27 bps recently while the 40-year bond yielded a scant 6 basis points!

When it comes to government debt, therefore, it can be well and truly said that "price discovery" is dead and gone. Japan is only the leading edge, but the trend is absolutely clear. The price of sovereign debt is where central banks peg it, not even remotely where real money savers and investors would buy it.

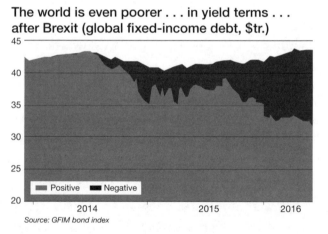

The world is even poorer . . . in yield terms . . . after Brexit (global fixed-income debt, $tr.)

Source: GFIM bond index

Still, that's only half the story, and not even the most destructive part. The truth of the matter is that the overwhelming share of government debt is no longer owned by real money savers at all. It is owned by central banks, sovereign wealth funds and leveraged speculators.

As to the speculators, do not mistake the repo-style funding deployed by speculators with genuine savings. To the contrary, their purchasing power comes purely from credit (repo) extracted from the value of bond collateral, which, in turn, is being driven ever higher by the big fat bid of central banks.

What this means is that real money savings—which must have a positive nominal yield—are being driven to the far end of the sovereign yield curve in search of returns, but most especially ever deeper into the corporate-credit risk zone in quest of the same.

THE PURE LUNACY OF MARIO DRAGHI

Nowhere is the irrational stampede for yield more evident than in the European bond markets. After $90 billion per month of QE purchases by the ECB, European bond markets have been reduced to a heap of raging financial-market lunacy.

It seems that Ireland has now broken into the negative-interest-rate club, investment-grade multinationals are flocking to issue 1% debt on the euro-bond markets and, if yield is your thing, you can get all of 3.50% on the Merrill Lynch euro junk-bond index.

That's right. You can stick your head into a veritable financial meat grinder and what you get for the hazard is essentially pocket change after inflation and taxes.

Remember, the average maturity for junk bonds is in the range of seven to eight years. During the last 10 years Europe's CPI averaged 2.0%, and even during the last three, deflationary years the CPI excluding energy averaged 1.2%.

So unless you think oil prices will be going down forever or that the money printers of the world have abolished inflation once and for all, the real after-tax return on euro junk has now been reduced to something less than a whole number. It might be wondered, therefore, whether the reckless stretch for "yield" has come down to return-free risk.

Well, not exactly. Yield is apparently for desperate bond managers and other suckers.

In fact, among the speculators who wear big-boy pants, the bond markets are all about capital gains and playing momo games. It's why euro junk debt—along with every other kind of sovereign- and investment-grade debt—is soaring. In a word, bond prices are going up because bond prices are going up. It's an utterly irrational speculative mania that would make the Dutch tulip-bulb punters proud.

In the days shortly before Draghi issued his "whatever it takes" ukase, for instance, the Merrill Lynch euro high-yield index was trading at 11.5%. So speculators who bought the index then have made a cool 230% gain if they were old-fashioned enough to actually buy the bonds with cash.

And they have been laughing all the way to their estates in the South of France if their friendly prime broker arranged to hock the bonds in the repo market even before payment was due. In that case, they're in the 1,000% club and just plain giddy.

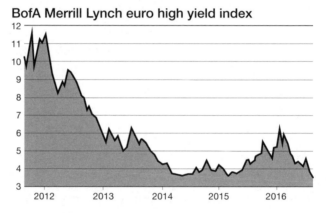

BofA Merrill Lynch euro high yield index

Does Mario Draghi have a clue that he is destroying price discovery completely? Do the purported adults who run the ECB not see that the entire $20 trillion European bond market is flying blind without any heed to honest price signals and risk considerations at all?

Worse still, do they have an inkling that the soaring price of debt securities has absolutely nothing to do with their macroeconomic mumbo jumbo about "deflation" and "low-flation"? Or that they are in the midst of a financial mania, not a " weak rate environment" due to the allegedly "slack" demand for credit in the business and household sectors?

In fact, European financial markets are being stampeded by a herd of front-runners who listen to Draghi reassure them on a regular basis that come hell or high water, the ECB will buy every qualifying bond in sight at a rate of $90 billion per month until March 2017. Full stop.

Never before has an agency of the state so baldly promised speculators literally trillions in windfall gains by the simple act of buying today what Draghi promises he will be buying tomorrow.

And that will be some tomorrow. As more and more sovereign debt sinks into the netherworld of negative yield and falls below the ECB's floor (-0.4%), there will be less supply eligible for purchase from the outstanding debt of each nation in the ECB's capital key.

This is price fixing with a vengeance. It is no wonder that repo rates recently have plunged into negative territory.

But here's the thing. The geniuses at the ECB are not cornering the market; they are being cornered by the speculators who are recklessly front-running the central bank with their trigger finger on the sell button.

Everything in the European fixed-income market—sovereign and corporate—is now so wildly overpriced and disconnected from reality that the clueless fools in Frankfurt dare not stop. They dare not even evince a nuance of a doubt.

So this is a house of cards like no other. Greece remains a hair from the ejection seat, yet everything is priced as if there is no "redenomination" risk.

Likewise, with the European economies still dead in the water, and notwithstanding some short-term data squiggles in the sub-basement of historic trends, the debt of Europe's mostly bankrupt states is priced as if there is no credit risk anywhere on the Continent outside of Greece.

Well, then, just consider three fundamentals that scream out danger ahead. Namely, public-debt ratios continue to rise, GDP continues to flatline, and the Eurozone superstate in Brussels continues to kick the can and bury its member states in bailout commitments that would instantly result in political insurrection in Germany, France and every other major European polity were they ever to be called.

WHY THE EUROZONE IS A FINANCIAL POWDER KEG

In short, Europe is a financial and political powder keg. The ECB is bluffing a $40 trillion debt market (including bank loans), and the Brussels apparatchiks are bluffing 300 million voters.

The only problem is that the true facts of life are so blindly obvious that it's only a matter of time before these bluffs are called. And then the furies will break loose.

In the first place, the EU-19 is marching toward the fiscal wall, and even Germany's surpluses cannot hide the obvious. During the last six years, the collective debt-to-GDP ratio among the Eurozone nations has gone from 66% to 91% of GDP. The sheer drift of current policy momentum will take the ratio over the 100% mark long before the end of the decade.

EU government debt to GDP

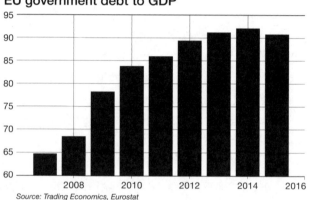

Source: Trading Economics, Eurostat

Secondly, notwithstanding the ebb and flow of short-term indicators, there is no evidence whatsoever that Europe is escaping its no-growth rut. Indeed, euro-area industrial output has continued to flat-line, and remains 10% below the precrisis peak, and even below the level achieved way back in 2002.

You can't grow your way out of debt on the basis of a profile like that shown in the next graph. Even then, the underlying truth is more daunting because the picture is flattered by Germany's exports to China and the emerging markets that are fast coming to a halt.

Thirdly, the state sector in Europe has gotten so big that politics are paralyzed. Accordingly, it is virtually impossible that the true barrier to growth—crushing taxes and interventionist dirigisme—can be eliminated.

Check out recent promarket policy actions in Italy, France or Spain. There have been none that amount to anything—unless you consider the newly conferred right of French shopkeepers to be open 12 Sundays per year rather than 5 to be anything other than symbolism.

In fact, since the financial crisis the state sector in the Eurozone has continued to envelop more and more of the GDP, rising from 45% of output in the EU-19 in 2007 to nearly 50% today.

Industrial production

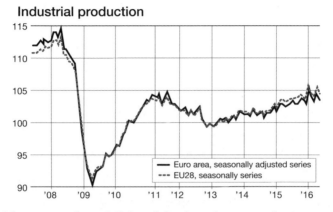

So with no growth and rising debt, how long can the Brussels bureaucrats continue to bluff? Yet here is a breakdown of the 331 billion euros that each of the Eurozone nations owe on Greece alone.

Importantly, the next table includes each country's so-called Target2 liabilities at the ECB, which has actually loaned 110 billion euros to Greece against "collateral" provided by the Greek national bank. That collateral, of course, is the massive unpayable debt of the Greek government!

Is it possible that France could absorb its $70 billion share and see its 10-year bond remain at today's 20 bps? Is it likely that Italy's paralyzed government would last even a day if its $60 billion of Greek guarantees were called or that its 10-year bond would trade for even a nanosecond longer at today's 1.20%?

Would not the bombastic crooks that run the Spanish government send a few legions of crusaders into Greece before they made good on the $42 billion they are on the hook for? Would the bond speculators basking in the Riviera not hit the sell button at the sound of the Spanish hoofs?

So, yes, the euro and the Eurozone do not have a prayer of surviving. It is only a question of when the bluff of the German leadership and a handful of bureaucrats in Brussels and Frankfurt is called.

They have fed their electorates the delusion that Greece is fixed, financial markets have been stabilized and the rest of the Eurozone has benefited from the survival of the single currency.

In fact, worldwide bond managers and speculators are tickled pink because nearly all of Greece's $350 billion of unpayable debt—on which they would have suffered grievous losses—has been transferred to the taxpayers of the EU-18. Whatever the precise scenario and timing, therefore, this big lie will be exposed when the Greek economy and democracy finally buckles under the weight of the absurd obligations that have been imposed upon them by Merkel and the Brussels apparatchiks.

In a word, Greece is finished, the bailout commitments will be called, and all hell will break loose in a $20 trillion bond market that is in thrall to a raging central bank–induced mania.

Official exposure to Greece in EMU by country and type
April 2015

	Member states			Eurosystem	Total		Nominal GDP
	Bilateral loans	EFSF	SMP	Intra Eurosystem liabilities	bn	% of GDP	(2014, bn)
Austria	1.6	4.3	0.8	3.1	9.8	3.0	329
Belgium	1.9	5.2	1.0	3.9	12.0	3.0	4.2
Cyprus	0.1	0.0	0.1	0.2	0.4	2.4	18
Estonia	0.0	0.4	0.1	0.3	0.8	4.0	20
Finland	1.0	2.7	0.5	2.0	6.2	3.0	204
France	11.4	30.9	5.6	22.4	70.3	3.3	2,143
Germany	15.2	41.2	7.1	28.5	92.0	3.2	2,908
Greece	0.0	0.0	0.8	3.2	4.0	2.2	179
Ireland	0.3	0.0	0.5	1.8	2.6	1.4	185
Italy	10.0	27.2	4.8	19.5	61.5	3.8	1,617
Malta	0.1	0.2	0.0	0.1	0.4	5.0	8
Netherlands	3.2	8.7	1.6	6.3	19.8	3.0	656
Portugal	1.1	0.0	0.7	2.8	4.6	2.6	173
Slovakia	0.0	1.6	0.3	1.2	3.1	4.2	75
Slovenia	0.2	0.6	0.1	0.5	1.4	3.9	37
Spain	6.7	18.1	3.5	14.0	42.3	4.0	1,058
Total	52.9	141.9	27.7	110.0	331.4	3.3	10,012

THE LUNATIC CHASE FOR YIELD IS GLOBAL

The destruction of honest pricing in the European bond market is only the tip of the iceberg. Our lunatic central bankers have unleashed a worldwide pincer movement among market participants that is flat-out suicidal. To wit, the leveraged fast-money gamblers everywhere on the planet are chasing prices ever higher as the sovereign bonds of "open to buy" central banks become increasingly scarce.

At the same time, desperate bond-fund managers, who will lose their jobs for just sitting on cash, are chasing yields rapidly lower on any bond issued anywhere that still has a positive current return.

This is the reason, for example, that they are chasing yield out the duration curve to 30-year and even 50-year paper. Accordingly, the 30-year U.S. Treasury bond has produced a 22% return during the last six months. To say the least, that's not shabby at all considering that its current yield is just 2.25%.

All the rest, of course, is capital gains—meaning that the whole scenario is nuts. A recent Wall Street Journal piece entitled "35-Year-Old Bond Bull on Its Last Legs" quotes a European fund manager who explains why everything is going haywire:

> Neil Dwayne, global strategist at Allianz Global Investors, is still buying. "Every piece of analysis we do on the bond market tells us they are structurally overvalued," he said. But he is buying US Treasurys anyway. "That's what you have to do when you have the ludicrous valuations in Europe and Japan."

Exactly. The poor man is buying a bond he hates because Draghi and Kuroda have driven him out of what amounts to a $15 trillion corner of the sovereign-debt market.

So in addition to front-runners on repo, we now have institutional fund managers from all over the world piling into the U.S. bond market in a frantic chase after the last positive yield standing. Thus, when the 10-year U.S. Treasury note hit a low yield of 1.34% in July, it literally made history. There has never been a lower yield since 1790.

Needless to say, this planetary scramble for yield puts Janet Yellen right in the financial dunce chair where she belongs.

She and the rest of her posse keep insisting that 93 months of ZIRP and $3.5 trillion of bond buying (QE) have so far produced no serious signs of overvaluation or bubbles. But, pray tell, what does she think is happening in the U.S. Treasury market at this very moment?

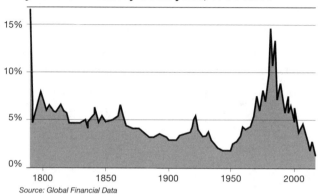

10-year U.S. Treasury bond yield, 1790-2016

Source: Global Financial Data

Over the last seven years, the Fed has done its level best to drive U.S. Treasury yields into the sub-basement of economic plausibility. Now the other major central banks are helping it to finish the job.

Needless to say, with the other major 10-year government bonds actually in sub-zero land, this can't go on much longer. The weighted average yield in the entire developed world government-bond market skidded to just 40 bps in early July. At the current rate of decline, the entire global market could be in the subzero zone by the end of the year.

You could call this central bank–driven yield stripping. And the latter would be bad enough if its effects were limited to just the vast moral hazard it poses to governments and politicians all over the world.

After all, we are now entering the zone in which government debt is tantamount to free money. In fact, Germany issued new 10-year bunds recently that actually bear a negative coupon.

But as we suggested above, it is not just politicians who are being lulled into the delusion of free money. The central bank–driven stampede for yield has spilled over into every nook and cranny of the fixed-income and equity markets around the world.

Anything that prices on a spread basis against sovereign debt, or that is impacted by the endless destructive arbitrages that falsification of bond prices inherently generate, has been drastically overvalued.

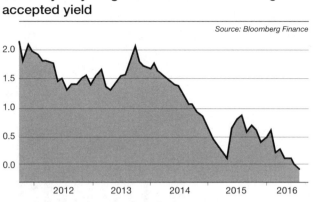

Germany 10-year government auction average accepted yield

Source: Bloomberg Finance

THE DESTRUCTIVE FRENZY IN THE U.S. CORPORATE-BOND MARKET

It now appears that U.S. corporate-bond issuance will hit a record $1.7 trillion this year—or 55% more than the last blow-off in 2007. And that is due to one reason alone—bond managers are desperate for yield and are moving out the risk spectrum exactly as our monetary central planners have ordained.

And that's not the half of it. The other side of the coin is that the massive proceeds from this orgy of bond issuance are not going into productive investments in plant, equipment, technology and other forms of business-efficiency and capacity enhancement. As we demonstrated in earlier chapters, real net business investment in the United States is still 20% below its turn-of-the-century level.

Instead, this corporate fundraising spree is being cycled right back into the stock market in the form of share buybacks, M&A deals and other financial-engineering maneuvers. Since the financial crisis, in fact, upward of $7 trillion has gone into stock buybacks and M&A deals.

This massive purchasing power, in turn, has driven the stock market to the perilous heights described in Chapter 12. It has effectively turned America's C-suites into stock-trading rooms. Our stock-option-crazed CEOs and boards are doing nothing less than de-equitizing their balance sheets and eating their seed corn.

Someday the due bill will arrive. But in the interim, corporate finances are being ransacked owing to the scramble for yield set in motion by central banks and the $13 trillion of subzero sovereign debt that has been generated during the last two years.

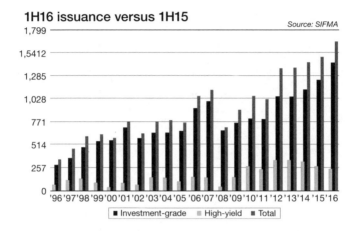

1H16 issuance versus 1H15

Source: SIFMA

■ Investment-grade   ■ High-yield   ■ Total

But this monumental deformation is so recent that there is very little negative-coupon debt that has yet been issued in the marketplace. Subzero land is overwhelmingly a phenomenon of the secondary market, meaning $13 trillion of bonds are trading at significant premiums to par—and, in some Japanese and German issues, massively so.

THE GIANT VOLCANO OF UNCOLLECTIBLE CAPITAL GAINS IN GLOBAL BOND MARKETS

In short, the global bond market has become a giant volcano of uncollectible capital gains. For example, long-term German bunds issued four years ago are now trading at 200% of par.

Yet even if the financial system of the world somehow survives the current mayhem, the German government will never pay back more than 100 cents on the dollar.

What that means is there will eventually be a multi-trillion-dollar bond implosion as speculators and bond-fund managers alike scramble to cash in their capital gains at the first sign that the global bond markets are breaking and heading back to par or below. And it is not just the "winners" who will be stampeding for the exits.

There will also be an even larger and sorrier band of "losers" in an even greater state of panicked flight. We refer here to all the Johnny-come-lately bond managers on the planet who are today buying trillions of bonds at a premium to par. For example, the price of the 4% coupon Italian bonds that have traded up to a 1.2% yield owing to Mario Draghi's $90-billion-per-month buying spree will get absolutely monkey hammered when the ECB's big fat bid finally ends.

To be sure, these befuddled money managers claim to have no choice or that these premium bonds still have a slightly better yield than sub-zero. Yet what they are actually doing is strapping on a financial suicide vest. These premiums absolutely must disappear before maturity, and most probably suddenly, violently and all at once when the great global bond bubble finally implodes.

Likewise, there are nearly $3 trillion of junk bonds and loans out-standing in the United States alone, and that is double the level extant on the eve of the great financial crisis. But double the money embodies far more than double the risk.

That's partially because the drastic, central bank–induced compression of benchmark bond yields has been transmitted into ultralow absolute levels of junk-bond yields via spread pricing. Compared to all of modern history, current junk-bond yields in the 5–6% range are just plain ridiculous.

After all, long-term junk-bond losses have been in the 3–4% range, inflation is still running close to 2% on a trend basis and taxes have not yet been abolished. So the sheer math of it is that the average single-B junk bond today has negative value—and that's before the next default cycle really kicks into gear.

And junk-bond defaults like never before in history are coming with a vengeance. That's because a very substantial portion of current junk-credit outstandings went into speculations that even leveraged-buyout shops wouldn't have entertained 15 years ago.

To wit, it was used to fund radical commodity-price speculations in the shale-patch, mining and other commodity plays, subprime auto-lending schemes and financing for stock buybacks and dividend recaps by highly leveraged companies. Accordingly, the embedded business and credit risk in the $3 trillion of outstanding U.S. junk bonds and loans is off the charts.

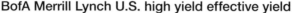

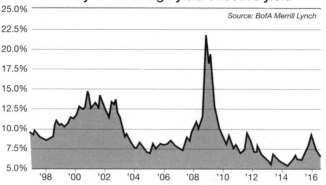

BofA Merrill Lynch U.S. high yield effective yield

Source: BofA Merrill Lynch

Already by midyear 2016, defaults in the shale patch had taken down 40% of outstandings. Even cautious rating agencies like Fitch now project high-yield bond defaults will hit nearly $100 billion in 2016, or double last year's already-elevated levels.

But as usual the rating agencies are far behind the curve. Standard and Poor's, for example, projects that by June 2017 today's rapidly rising defaults will only hit the 4–7% range. But they are smoking the same thing they were in 1989, 1999, and 2007!

In fact, the junk-bond sector will soon be hit by a double whammy that will push loss rates to unprecedented levels. That's because there is already a deeply embedded loss due to the distortions of ZIRP/NIRP on benchmark bond pricing. When the central banks of the world are eventually forced to shut down their printing presses and permit rates to normalize, these losses will be transmitted across the entire credit spectrum.

On top of that, the massive global deflation/recession currently unfolding means defaults will easily soar far above the prior 11–12% peaks shown below. And the next peak default cycle will last far longer than the historic results shown in the chart because this time the central banks will not be in a position to reflate the bond and other financial markets.

The prior default peaks shown below are part of the two-decade-long supercycle of global credit and investment growth. Each junk-bond market break was quickly reversed by successive rounds of central bank money printing.

But the world economy is now stranded at Peak Debt, and the central banks are out of dry powder. The latter have reached the limits of subzero rates, the credibility of QE is fading fast and Bernanke's fleet of helicopter-money drops will never get off the ground in the United States or Germany, and that's mainly what matters.

So this time recessionary conditions will persist, and the implied revenue growth in most junk-bond deals will never happen. The resulting cumulative buildup of cash-flow shortfalls, therefore, will be immense. This means that a far larger share of issuers will eventually default—especially given the elevated credit risk already embedded among commodity-oriented issuers.

Moreover, as the junk-bond default rate continues to rise, the "extend and pretend" market, which has forestalled defaults in the last few cycles, will also dry up. Consequently, hidden defaults will finally come to the surface, and issuers will resolve their inability to pay in the bankruptcy courts, not in the junk-refinancing markets.

U.S. speculative-grade default rate

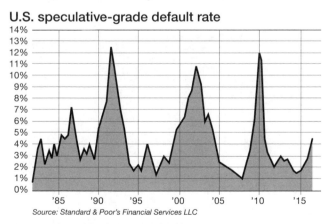

Source: Standard & Poor's Financial Services LLC

FINANCIAL EXPLOSIVE DEVICES (FEDS) AND THE COMING FINANCIAL CARNAGE

Yet the junk-bond sector is only a small section of the coming bond-market carnage. The scramble for yield generated by central bank financial repression, in fact, has systematically impregnated the global markets with FEDs (financial explosive devices).

Even as approximately 200 principal central bankers and senior staff have spent the last seven years pushing interest rates toward the zero bound or below, there have been millions of financial operators and capital users scouring the earth for ways to escape it.

Recently, one of these zero-bound escape routes blew sky high when the 9.5% contingent convertible bond of 2049 issued by an obscure German bank, Bremen Landesbank, plunged by 40% from 120 to 73 in just minutes—a move that has, in turn, spooked broader global markets.

It turns out that Bremen LB is a $29 billion German state-owned bank heavily invested in shipping loans that is now facing massive write-downs and the need to raise capital from its principal owners—German Landesbank NordLB, the city of Bremen and the savings-banks association in North Rhine-Westphalia.

Here's the thing. All the parties involved had stumbled into risk that extended way over the end of their financial skis. Indeed, the cliff-diving bonds were at the very end of a long chain of mispricings emanating from today's central banking regime.

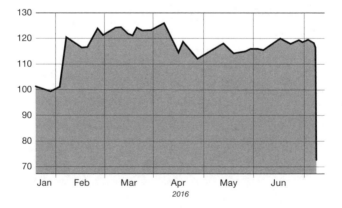

It originated a while back when central banks made cheap debt available to households in the United States and Europe. That caused a consumption boom there and an oversized export boom in China and the Far East.

Next, more cheap capital enabled by the Asian central banks funded an artificially large investment boom in China and in its emerging-markets supply chain, which, in turn, caused demand for bulk, crude oil and container-ship capacity to surge.

Needless to say, still-more cheap capital generated a massive excess of highly leveraged ship-building capacity that needs cash flow to service its debt. So the huge state-enabled ship-building industries of China and South Korea built new ships like there was no tomorrow and, to move the iron, priced them near marginal cost.

Then, even-more-yield-hungry capital hooked up with the growing surplus of these "new builds," funding on high leverage what is ultimately a day rate commodity (that is, shipping capacity).

Even then, the daisy chain was not done. The bank arrangers and other intermediaries who bought and financed the surplus ships that the central bankers indirectly built needed to enhance their own returns. So they funded their newly acquired "assets" with yield bait like the Bremen LB contingent bonds that blew sky high on a moment's notice.

The one thing that is absolutely true in a $300 trillion global financial market is that Bremen LB is not a one-off. After a $20 trillion central bank printing spree and 93 months on the zero bound, these kinds of FEDs exist in the tens of thousands.

Soon we will know their names.

After all, creating this kind of fiery demise is what central banks ultimately do.

CHAPTER 15:

Revolt of the Rubes—Bravo, Brexit!

AT LONG LAST THE TYRANNY OF THE GLOBAL FINANCIAL ELITES HAS BEEN slammed good and hard. You can count on them to attempt another central bank–based shock-and-awe campaign, but it won't be credible, sustainable or maybe even possible.

The central bankers and their compatriots at the EU, IMF, White House, U.S. Treasury, OECD, G-7 and the rest of the Bubble Finance apparatus have well and truly overplayed their hand. They have created a tissue of financial lies—an affront to the very laws of markets, sound money and capitalist prosperity.

After all, what predicate of sober economics could possibly justify $13 trillion of sovereign debt trading at negative yields?

Or a stock market trading at 25X reported earnings in the face of a faltering global economy and a tepid domestic U.S. business cycle expansion that at 87 months is already long in the tooth and showing signs of recession everywhere?

And that's to say nothing of the endless ranks of insanely overvalued "story" stocks like Valeant was and the megalomaniacal visions of Elon Musk still are. Or the coming proof that Facebook's digital billboard is subject to cyclical slump and that its ballyhooed 1.7 billion monthly users are today's equivalent of dot-com-era "eyeballs."

So there will be payback, claw back and traumatic deflation of the bubbles—plenty of it, as far as the eye can see.

On the immediate matter of Brexit, the British people have rejected the arrogant rule of the EU superstate and the tyranny of its unelected courts, commissions and bureaucratic overlords.

As Donald Trump was quick to point out, they have taken back their country. He urges that Americans do the same, and he might just persuade them.

But whether Trumpism captures the White House or not, it is virtually certain that Brexit is a contagious political disease. In response to June's history-shaking event, determined campaigns for Frexit, Spexit, Nexit, Grexit, Italxit, Hungexit and more centrifugal political emissions will next surely follow.

And if Trump loses, there may even be a small uproar from the Lone Star state on behalf of Texit!

Smaller government—at least in geography—is being given another chance. And that's a very good thing because more localized democracy everywhere and always is inimical to the rule of centralized financial elites.

REVOLT OF THE RUBES—WHY THE FINANCIAL ELITE'S DAYS ARE NUMBERED

To be sure, our financial rulers are not about to take the rise of Trump or the verdict of the British voters lying down. They are already unleashing a wave of propaganda and fear mongering about the dangers of even minor departures from the policies and arrangements of the status quo.

In Britain, for example, they did not even wait for the body to get cold. Within days of the vote, the establishment oracles were out in force proclaiming that Brexit would be effectively cancelled on a de facto basis because separation from the Eurozone was too complicated for the mind of man to accomplish.

Apparently, like in the case of the first negative vote on TARP, a few days of currency and stock market turmoil were supposed to have taught the rubes who voted for it the errors of their ways. And if that wasn't sufficient, a coming wave of economic setbacks would be sure to do the job of repudiating the referendum.

The argument is that the unwashed masses outside of Greater Lon-don—who overwhelmingly voted for Brexit—have shot themselves in the foot economically based on some atavistic fears of immigrants and cultural globalization and racism, even.

But those impulses are dismissed by the masses' establishment betters as just momentary emotional outbursts. Right soon the rubes will remember where their bread is buttered, and demand a second referendum in order to reboard the EU's purported economic gravy train.

On the heels of the Brexit shock, for example, Gideon Rachman, one of the *Financial Times'* numerous globalist scolds, professed that his depression about the Brexit vote had already given way to a worldly vision of relief:

> But then, belatedly, I realized that I have seen this film before. I know how it ends. And it does not end with the UK leaving Europe.
>
> Any long-term observer of the EU should be familiar with the shock referendum result. In 1992 the Danes voted to reject the Maastricht treaty. The Irish voted to reject both the Nice treaty in 2001 and the Lisbon treaty in 2008.
>
> And what happened in each case? The EU rolled ever onwards. The Danes and the Irish were granted some concessions by their EU partners. They staged a second referendum. And the second time around they voted to accept the treaty. So why, knowing this history, should anyone believe that Britain's referendum decision is definitive?

But of course Rachman's dismissive meme is exactly why Brexit happened. The international financial elites, who have been controlling the levers of power at the central banks, finance ministries and supranational official institutions for several decades now, have become so accustomed to not taking no for an answer that they can't see the handwriting on the wall.

To wit, the rubes are fed up and are not going to take it anymore. In voting to flee the domineering EU superstate domiciled in Brussels, they saw right through and properly dismissed the establishment's scary bedtime stories about the alleged economic costs.

REFUTATION OF THE ESTABLISHMENT'S SCARY BEDTIME STORIES—THE UK ECONOMY DOESN'T NEED HELP FROM BRUSSELS

After all, the UK is a net payer of $10 billion per year in taxes into the EU budget and gets an economically wasteful dose of Continental-style regulatory dirigisme in return. And that is to say nothing of the loss of control at its borders and the de facto devolution of its lawmaking powers and judicial functions to unelected EU bureaucracies.

At the same time, increased trade is generally a benefit, but it is not one that requires putting up with the statist tyranny of the EU. That's because the EU-27, and especially Germany, needs the UK market for its exports far more than the other way around.

So after Brexit is triggered, the EU will come to the table for a new trade arrangement with the UK because these faltering socialist economies desperately need the exports. At the same time, the British negotiators will be free for the first time to seek more advantageous trade arrangements with the United States, Canada, Australia and others.

It doesn't take too much investigation to see that the UK has come out on the short end of the trade stick. And contrary to globalist propaganda, persistent and deepening trade deficits are a big problem. If coupled with a weakening domestic savings rate, they mean that a country is getting ever deeper into international debt.

The UK economy exhibits that dual disability to a fare-thee-well. Its international accounts have been plunging further into the red for 20 years. At 5% of GDP its current-account deficit—which includes the favorable benefits of service exports from the City of London and earnings on foreign investments—is among the highest in the developed-market world.

To put it bluntly, the UK is slowly going bankrupt.

Moreover, the source of the abysmal overall current-account deterioration shown above is absolutely attributable to its one-sided trade imbalance with the EU-27. As shown in the following graph, Britain's EU deficit has been widening ever since 2000, while its trade surplus with the rest of the world has actually been steadily growing.

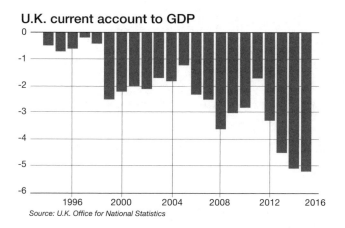

U.K. current account to GDP

Source: U.K. Office for National Statistics

This point here is not about mercantilism. The bilateral balance with any particular country or trading bloc does not ultimately matter if the overall current-account trend is healthy. That's just comparative advantage at work.

Instead, the point is that the EU-27 needs British markets to the tune of a net 65-billion-euro surplus annually. And more than half of that surplus is attributable to Germany, which earns upward of 40% of its trade surplus with the rest of the EU from the UK.

Continuation of an open trade arrangement, therefore, does not require the sacrifice of British democracy and home rule to the statist overlords of Brussels; it only requires a trade deal that provides mutual economic benefits and no entangling engagements with the socialist infrastructure of the Continent.

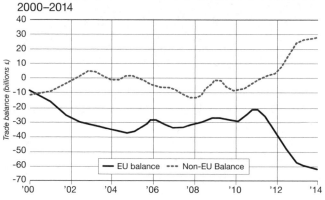

U.K. trade balance with EU and non-EU countries
2000–2014

Moreover, these negative trade trends have not been ameliorated by a domestic savings frenzy that could finance the outflow in a healthy manner. To the contrary, the British household savings rate has been heading dangerously south for the last several decades.

In a manner similar to the Greenspan-era debt spree in the United States that we described in Chapter 5, the Bank of England has induced British households to live high on the hog by leveraging up their balance sheets.

From a pre-1980 ratio at 50% debt to income, the leverage ratio of British households rose to 100% by the turn of the century and peaked at 140% on the eve of the financial crisis. Like in the United States, it has come down slightly since then, but at 130% it is still 2.5x its historic level.

So the UK's giant current-account deficits, in fact, are being financed by foreign lenders and central banks and the Bank of England.

The UK's huge current-account deficits so beloved by the Keynesian and Goldman Sachs apparatchiks who run its policies are not a gift of EU membership at all. They are the curse of the horrid money-printing excesses of the Bank of England and the European Central Bank that have left the UK economy leveraged to the hilt.

U.K. household saving ratio

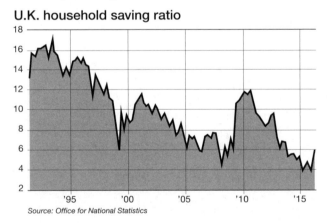

Source: Office for National Statistics

WHY STAYING IN THE EU WILL NOT CURE THE UK'S REAL PROBLEMS

The same is true of the public sector. The UK has run chronic, deep budget deficits since the early 1990s. Since then, its public-debt-to-GDP ratio has soared from 35% to nearly 85%.

These data make crystal clear, of course, that the UK has a giant problem of living far beyond its means, and that all of the leftist kvetching about the conservative government's so-called "austerity" policies is a lot of political balderdash.

In fact, the Cameron government has buried British taxpayers in debt, even as it proclaimed its adherence to fiscal rectitude. As is evident from the chart, the only reduction in the spending share of GDP on its watch is due to the end of the global recession. At nearly 44%, state outlays still take a larger share of the economic production than they did under the previous Labour governments.

Here's the point. Staying in the EU cannot help ameliorate the UK's real economic and fiscal problems in the slightest. What it needs is lower taxes, less welfare and a dramatic reduction of government regulatory intervention. These are not policy directions that stir the juices in Brussels.

So the noisy meme that the Brexit voters have done themselves irreparable economic harm is patent nonsense. By contrast, whether they fully understood it or not, they have liberated the UK from what will be the economic disaster of "more Europe."

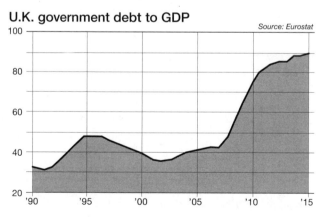

U.K. government debt to GDP

Source: Eurostat

ESCAPE FROM THE EUROZONE TRAIN WRECK JUST IN THE NICK OF TIME

Indeed, if there ever was a phrase that encapsulated the idea of an incendiary contradiction, "more Europe" is surely it. What it means to the French and Mediterranean left is debt mutualization and a common treasury from which to expropriate German prosperity.

By contrast, to the Germans it means the imposition of ever-more-onerous EU fiscal controls so that it can continue to kick the can of its giant liabilities for the EU bailouts and the European Central Bank's "Target2" balances down the road.

These German exposures are enormous—with upward of $75 billion already drawn on the European Stability Mechanism and European Financial Stability Facility bailout funds and Target2 balances of $700 billion at the present time. These Target2 balances represent the credits and debits among the national central banks of the EU-19 that execute day-to-day policy for the European Central Bank.

Needless to say, were the Eurozone and euro to go down in flames, the German Bundesbank would end up with enormous claims against other central banks, especially those of Spain, Greece, Portugal and Italy, and little ability to collect.

Indeed, short of reviving the Panzer divisions, Germany has no options at all. It has effectively taken itself hostage to the tune of the $700 billion it has "loaned" to its central bank partners that cannot possible pay. Thus, those monumental Target2 balances are a ticking financial bomb and the real reason that Germany's historic monetary orthodoxy has given way to Draghi's money-printing madness.

In a word, Germany has acquiesced in an insane fiscal transfer system conducted by the European Central Bank in the guise of monetary policy because it dare not allow the euro and European Central Bank system to collapse.

Likewise, Draghi's $90 billion monthly rate of QE purchases is really not about "low-flation," private-sector credit stimulation, job growth or any of the other macroeconomic variables, anyway.

To the contrary, its not-so-hidden purpose is to flat-out monetize the debt of Italy, Spain, Greece, Portugal, France and the rest of the Eurozone bankrupts at negligible interest rates, thereby gifting them with deeply subsidized cost of carry on their crushing public debts.

Self-evidently, these Draghi-confected bond rates could never be remotely attained in an honest bond market. Yet they are absolutely necessary to maintain the charade of fiscal solvency among these woebegone practitioners of welfare-state socialism.

So the doomsday machine rolls on. Recently, Greece's Target2 balance was negative $100 billion, while Spain's was negative $325 billion and Italy's was negative $300 billion. In short, the "EU-18" owes Germany so much that permitting any country to leave is unthinkable in Berlin.

The call for "more Europe," therefore, does not arise from cosmopolitan enlightenment, as the elite media avers; it is a desperate gambit to keep alive an utterly flawed and contradiction-ridden monetary, fiscal and political union that never should have been concocted in the first place and that is now several decades past its "sell by" date.

By the same token, the forces of Brexit and their populist counterparts throughout the Continent are not simply an instance of the rubes venting nationalistic, xenophobic, racist and other dark impulses. To the contrary, the rubes simply want their governments back, and in that impulse they are on the right side of history.

The truth is, it is the "European project" that represents the darker impulses. The Brussels/Frankfurt rule of the financial elite has little to do with free trade or the maintenance of peaceful relationships among the states of Europe, and nothing at all to do with furthering capitalist prosperity.

Instead, it is a tyranny based on a muddled brew of globalism, statism, financialization and the cult of central banking. Its days are numbered because even the rubes can see that it doesn't work and that its massive internal contradictions are heading for a spectacular implosion.

The British voters have decided to get out of harm's way. Hopefully, there will soon be many other cases of the rubes in revolt.

THE BANKING-SYSTEM ROT AT THE HEART OF THE EUROZONE

So the shocking Brexit vote was about a lot more than the unwashed British masses rebuking their ruling-class betters. It actually marked the beginning of the end for the EU superstate and the incendiary regime of Bubble Finance that lies at the heart of it.

In fact, the rot is well advanced in the two large Eurozone economies outside of Germany. That is, France and Italy are especially vulnerable to a banking-system breakdown, and the associated spillover impact on debt-burdened fiscal accounts and already-fragile national economies.

As we have insisted, financial prices cannot be falsified indefinitely. At length, they become the subject of a pure confidence game and the risk of shocks and black swans that even the central banks are unable to offset. Then the day of reckoning arrives in traumatic and violent aspect.

Exactly that kind of Lehman-scale crisis is now descending on Europe and its massive, bad-debt-ridden banking system.

The latter carries $35 trillion of assets, which represents twice the combined GDP of the EU-28 (including the UK), and also reflects a ratio to GDP that is twice that of the U.S. banking system.

The problem is that Europe's monster banking system has $1.5 trillion of bad debt according to official institutions like the IMF—and in reality probably will have much more when the next global recession sweeps through its welfare-state-encumbered economies.

Worse still, it is highly leveraged with assets equal to 25x equity capital at the big French banks, for example. In fact, leverage risk is actually much worse when the true measure of capital—tangible net worth—is compared to total asset footings.

In that regard, even Deutsche Bank is imperiled. Its current asset footings of $1.8 trillion compare to only $57 billion of tangible net worth, meaning it is leveraged at 31X. Likewise, Italy's largest bank, Unicredit, has $16 billion of tangible net worth against $940 billion of assets. That gives it a leverage ratio of 59X.

At the same time, the European Central Bank's massive interest-rate-repression policies since Draghi's "whatever it takes" edict of August 2012 have crushed earnings on corporate and sovereign bonds, even as banks have incurred huge charges against soured loan books.

Accordingly, during the most recent year the largest European banks earned a miniscule 0.18% return on assets compared to just under 1.0% for the largest U.S. banks.

These baleful conditions have been no secret, but until last summer speculators in European bank stocks were willing to believe Mario Draghi could do no wrong and that Europe could print its way back to prosperity.

No more. Bank stocks were already down by 30% prior to the UK referendum, and subsequently plunged by as much as 50% from the highs of 2015. And what changed, above all else, was confidence.

It has now become evident that Draghi's $90 billion per month of bond buying has not shocked the Eurozone economies out of their torpor, meaning that bad debts continue to rise. At the same time, the European Central Bank's desperate lurch into subzero rates has essentially eliminated bond yields entirely, as we documented in Chapter 14.

In short, Draghi has impaled Europe's loss-ridden banking system on a profitless yield curve, even as loan demand among Europe debt-ridden businesses and households hugs to the flat line of a struggling economy.

This means there is no solution except for the European banking system to raise massive amounts of new capital. Not surprisingly, this potential dilution shock has sent even the bank-stock gamblers heading for the exit ramps.

Indeed, the STOXX 600 bank index is now back to its mid-2012 level. Draghi's bluff has been called.

EU bank stocks

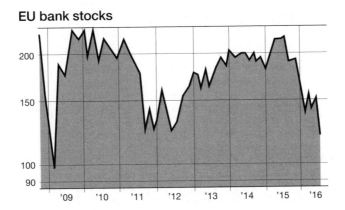

In a word, we think Brexit was the match that lit a European banking crisis, and that the implosion of Europe's banking system will take down the EU and the European economies, as well.

The enormity of that threat, in fact, could not be more aptly symbolized than by the virtual meltdown of Deutsche Bank (DB). Until a few years ago it was Europe's most prestigious and profitable bank, but now its very survival outside of a German/EU bailout is in question.

More importantly, the collapse of its earnings and market cap since the eve of Draghi's "whatever it takes" ukase is a powerful tell.

Despite the fact that the European Central Bank's printing presses were running white hot, DB's market cap has now imploded by $50 billion, or 75%. Likewise, its bottom line has shifted from a $7.5 billion annual profit to an $8 billion loss in the most recent year.

Indeed, this collapse of Europe's most important bank occurred in an economic backdrop of crab-like real GDP growth that amounted to just a cumulative 2.2% in the EU-19 during the entire seven-year period since 2008. Even much of that was attributable to the German export machine and booming markets for high-end capital and consumer goods in China and its supply chain.

Those markets are now drying up. The gathering global deflation, in fact, leaves European economies fully exposed to its rapidly unfolding banking crisis, the failure of the European Central Bank's money-printing campaign, and the rise of anti-EU populist movements throughout the Continent.

WHY THE EU SUPERSTATE WILL FAIL— THE FRENCH DISCONNECTION

As indicated above, we believe the impending breakdown of the EU amidst a global recession will hit France and Italy especially hard. That's because they have the most oversized and undercapitalized banking systems in Europe, along with horrid economic and fiscal fundamentals.

As to the former, France's banking system is the granddaddy of corpulence. Total assets in the system amount to $9.5 trillion—a figure that is nearly 4X its $2.4 trillion GDP. Likewise, Italy's banking assets total $4.3 trillion, or 2.4X its $1.8 trillion GDP.

In both cases these banking-to-GDP ratios are off the charts. They reflect not only highly leveraged domestic economies, but also massive external lending to sectors like global shipping and energy that are now being hammered by vast excess capacity, plunging cash flows and rising defaults.

That's their Achilles heel. In the case of Italy, for example, there are now about $2.6 trillion of loans in its banking system, and upward of 17% are nonperforming. In relative terms, that is nearly 4X the bad-debt ratio that prevailed in the U.S. banking system at the peak of the subprime crisis.

Needless to say, these $440 billion of nonperforming loans are growing rapidly, but are not even close to being fully reserved. In fact, Monte Paschi, Unicredit and three other big Italian banks have $130 billion of nonperforming loans that are unprovisioned. That compares to total book equity of just $138 billion in Italy's entire banking system at the end of Q1 2016, meaning that Italian banks are essentially insolvent.

The French banks are only slightly less impaired. But given the combined $14 trillion balance sheet of the French and Italian banks, one thing is quite certain. To wit, when their banking systems go into an accelerating meltdown, France and Italy will end up in a bruising conflict with Berlin and a fractured EU governance process in Brussels.

This potential fracture has already erupted over the EU's brand-new rules requiring a "bail-in" of depositors and bondholders. The latter requires that the depositors and bondholders would take huge losses before tax funds could be injected into domestic banking systems. Italian Prime Minister Renzi has already noisily demanded that these rules be suspended, as has the CEO of France's second-largest bank.

The plain fact is that the imposition of bail-ins in either country would cause a massive depositor run and a crushing sell-off among bondholders. In addition to trillions of deposits, the three largest French banks—BNP Paribas, Société Générale and Crédit Agricole Group—also have issued $1.1 trillion of bonds and other long-term liabilities, while the Italian banks have upward of $300 billion of bonds outstanding.

Furthermore, in yield-starved Europe these bank bonds are widely held by retail investors. This means that a bail-in would generate massive losses and voter insurrections, and cause the near-instantaneous fall of their left-of-center and socialist governments.

On the other hand, absent a bail-in the EU doesn't remotely have the resources to recapitalize these monster banks. Nor does Germany have the political will or financial capacity to any longer foot the lion's share of the bill.

That gets to the true problem. In the absence of EU intervention, neither France nor Italy have the fiscal capacity to prop up their own banking systems because they are essentially tapped out.

Thus, France's public debt has been relentlessly rising, and is up by nearly 50% just in the last nine years. It now amounts to 85% of GDP, and would rapidly cross the 100% threshold in the context of a recession and a major bank-bailout program.

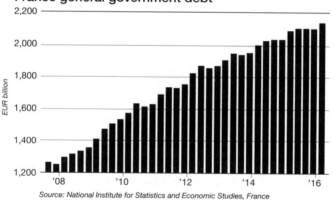

France general government debt

Source: National Institute for Statistics and Economic Studies, France

And that's not the half of it. Nearly 50% of France's $2.4 trillion of public debt was recently trading at subzero yields.

That's right. The bond markets have been so deformed by the European Central Bank, the Fed and other central banks that a socialist dead-ender government like that of French President Hollande is being presently paid to borrow money!

There is a word for that: lunacy.

But the operative word for our purposes is "presently." In truth, subzero rates are an unsustainable momentary aberration. Were the EU to splinter and France be required to prop up its own banks, yields on its debt would soar, widening its fiscal gap even further.

The fact is, France is a socialist basket case. The state has been steadily and surely devouring the entire private economy.

Consequently, the government sector is now pushing 57% of GDP, and it has not stopped climbing toward the upper right of the graph for nearly four decades. Indeed, it is virtually inconceivable that the relentless expansion of the French state shown below can ever be stopped by democratic means—or any other, for that matter.

The baleful implication is that France's oppressive level of taxation on virtually everything—incomes, labor, consumption, luxuries, capital—has virtually no chance of being eased without triggering an immediate eruption of deficits and public debt.

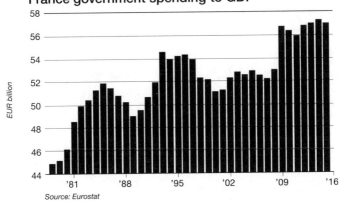

France government spending to GDP

Source: Eurostat

At the same time, France's massive tax burden—which now amounts to 52% of GDP—has kept its economy pinned close to a flat line ever since its modest postcrisis rebound. Total real GDP today is only 4% higher than it was in 2008, and as often as not quarterly GDP has been negative.

Likewise, notwithstanding a 1.4% average inflation rate since 2008, the nominal value of gross capital formation still has not recovered to 2008 levels, nor has manufacturing production.

This means that in real terms the industrial core of the French economy has been shrinking. GDP has crawled forward at 0.4% per year since the precrisis peak only because prodigious government borrowing allowed the state to fund sufficient transfer-payment spending and direct public-sector purchases to make up for the industrial shortfall.

In fact, as shown in the graph below, French industrial production in physical or real terms is actually 17% below its precrisis peak, and below turn-of-the-century levels by nearly that much.

Accordingly, we believe the French economy is going down for the count. In the face of a shrinking industrial core owing to oppressive taxation, monopolistic union wages and huge welfare-state inducements for idleness, there is no reason why that it can continue to borrow its way to even the tepid growth of the recent past.

This means, in turn, the growth of its public debt will continue to outpace a stagnant or even shrinking nominal GDP, thereby pushing its public-debt ratio ever higher. Under those circumstances, therefore, there is not a chance in the world that it can bail out its monumental $9.5 trillion banking sector, or that its $1.2 trillion of subzero public debt can avoid a thundering collapse.

Nor is the eventual collapse of France's sovereign-bond and banking bubbles necessarily a matter for the distant by-and-by.

The populist candidate Marine Le Pen is already well in the lead for France's 2017 presidential election. Brexit has now given dramatic new impetus and credibility to her anti-EU platform.

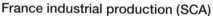

France industrial production (SCA)

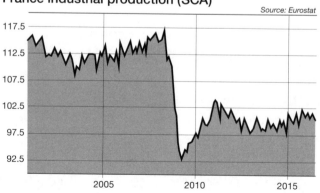

Source: Eurostat

Even the possibility of a Frexit win next year would trigger a relentless wave of selling by the Draghi front-runners who are now buying the 10-year bonds of this terminally ill state at a mere 20-basis-point yield.

In theory, of course, the clueless Draghi is pegging French bond rates in the subzero zone in order to jump-start inflation. In practice, he is setting up a monumental financial explosive device that could erupt at any moment owing to Frexit risk, European recession, EU break-up, a German revolt at the European Central Bank or numerous other potential catalysts.

WHY THE EU SUPERSTATE WILL FAIL—THE ITALIAN JOB

Needless to say, the banking collapse and fiscal breakdown in Italy is even more severe than that of France. That's in part because the capital deficit in Italy's banking system is bigger, but also because Italy's towering public debt is far greater in proportionate terms at 133% of GDP.

So the notion that recent yields of 1.20% on the Italian 10-year bond even remotely compensate for the risk embedded in Italy's fiscal and economic chamber of horrors is just plain laughable. And that's to say nothing of the risk that the EU itself will ultimately succumb to a wave of populist insurgency, including a Five Star Movement–led move to take Italy out of the euro.

There is probably no better gauge of Mario Draghi's "whatever it takes" folly than the massive rally that subsequently occurred in the 10-year bond of his home country. The Italian economy improved not one whit after 2012, and its fiscal ratios continued to worsen.

So the 500% gain in the value of its benchmark bond was entirely due to traders front-running the European Central Bank's announced bond-market interventions and purchases. Never before has an arm of government showered such insensible windfalls on speculators—who, more often than not, funded their positions with repo loans, which, also thanks to the European Central Bank, were essentially costless and risk free.

Indeed, Italy is truly a case of the blind leading the blind. As indicated above, its giant, bloated banking system is essentially insolvent with $440 billion in nonperforming loans, but on top of that it also holds $300 billion of Italian sovereign debt.

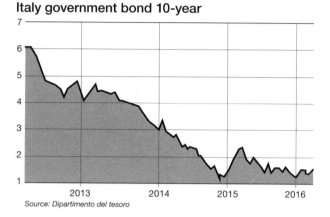

Italy government bond 10-year

Source: Dipartimento del tesoro

Italy's languishing economy would be toast, in fact, if its banks were not propped up by the state. Real GDP is still 8% below its 2008 level— and that's with loans from Italy's massive *$4.3 trillion* banking system embedded in every nook and cranny of its state-managed economy, and with a further boost from state transfer payments and direct spending financed, on the margin, by government borrowing.

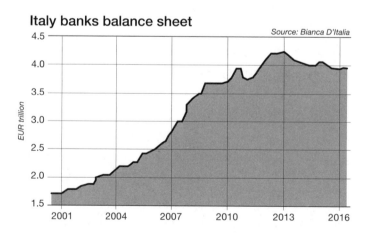

Italy banks balance sheet

Source: Bianca D'Italia

EUR trillion

Yet an Italian state bailout of its own banking system is a circular proposition; it has been the banking system that has brought a growing share of new government-debt issues.

Needless to say, these government-debt securities are vastly overvalued owing to the Draghi bond-buying spree. They would instantly plummet in price were the speculators who have been front-running Draghi's QE campaign ever to lose confidence in the European Central Bank or the ability and willingness of an Italian government to continue the giant fiscal charade now in place.

In short, a normalization of rates would cause the interest carry cost on Italy's giant government debt to soar by 3X or even more. Indeed, the combination of Italy's massive public debt, state-strangled economy and shrinking labor force amount to a doomsday machine in every sense of the word.

As it happens, this implicit existential challenge is materializing right now. The Renzi government has been desperately attempting to organize a bank bailout, but has run smack into the trauma-inducing bail-in rules described above.

That EU banking framework, of course, would not only would mean massive losses for depositors and bank debt-holders, but also the instant collapse of the Renzi government.

Accordingly, Renzi has ceaselessly attempted to get a waiver of the new rules on the grounds that the Italian banking crisis has been dramatically intensified by the Brexit shock.

Yet German resistance is rooted in a powerfully self-evident reason— namely, that the bail-in rules are designed to prevent new fiscal crises in member states and the need for more German-funded bailouts.

So now Italy faces the real possibility of a depositor run on its banks, and a devastating liquidity crisis in its $4.3 trillion banking sector.

Accordingly, either the EU must open up the floodgates to a renewed round of bailouts, which would likely result in the collapse of Merkel's government, or it must authorize Italy to spend upward of $50 billion to recapitalize its banks and keep the $300 billion of government debt they hold safely in their vaults.

Then again, with public debt already at 133% of GDP, why would anyone except Mario Draghi, with his printing press, be buying 10-year Italian bonds at a 1.20% yield?

Stated differently, once the European Central Bank stops monetizing its debt, it's curtain time for the Italian debt market, banking system and economy. But if it doesn't stop, the perpetuation of negative interest rates will take down the entire European financial system.

Italy government debt to GDP

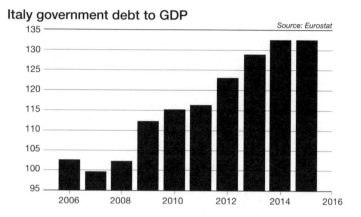

There is really no way out of the Italian Job. The industrial core of Italy's economy is a far-worse basket case than even that of France. As shown in the next chart, industrial production is now 25% smaller than it was at the precrisis peak and also the year 2000.

Stated differently, so far during the 21st century Italy's industrial economy has shrunk by one-quarter, and each modest attempt at recovery has rolled over. The gains after 2005 were lost to the Great Recession. The rebound from the latter was lost to the Eurozone financial crisis of 2011–12, and all of Mario Draghi's bond-buying madness has not been able to generate any lift at all during the last three years.

So the question recurs. How does a deteriorating economy support enough government borrowing to keep a giant insolvent banking system going, pay the interest on an already-monumental public debt and then borrow even more to inject Keynesian-style "stimulus" into a moribund private sector?

It can't. That's why the Italian Job will sooner or later take down the EU superstate.

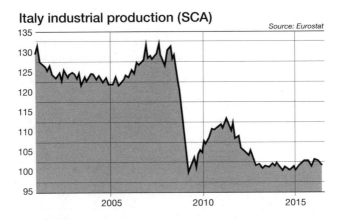

Italy industrial production (SCA)

Source: Eurostat

WHY THE BREXIT REVOLT WILL SPREAD

The combustible material for more referenda and defections from the EU is certainly available in surging populist parties of both the left and the right throughout the Continent.

In fact, another hammer blow to the Brussels/German dictatorship will surely happen in Spain, and probably before the end of 2016. That's because the corrupt, hypocritical, lapdog government of Prime Minister Rajoy is surely on its last legs, and properly so.

Rajoy is just another statist in conservative garb who reformed nothing, left the Spanish economy buried in debt and gave false witness to the notion that the Brussels bureaucrats are the saviors of Europe.

So despite still another election this year after the December 2015 elections resulted in paralysis, Spain still has no government, and Catalonia is still on a determined path to secession.

The anti-Brussels parties of both the left (Podemos) and the right (Ciudadanos) represent aroused constituencies that simply have had enough of the status quo and rule from Brussels. So not withstanding short-term parliamentary maneuvering, Spanish politics will remain splintered and paralyzed.

And that's the problem when the inexorable Eurozone financial crisis intensifies. There will emerge no government in Madrid strong enough or willing enough to execute Brussels' inevitable dictates in the event that the drastically overvalued Spanish bond market goes into a tailspin and requires another EU intervention.

So the next leg of the Brexit storm is foreordained. To wit, sovereign-bond prices throughout Europe have been lifted artificially skyward by the financial snake charmers of Brussels and the European Central Bank.

The massive rally in Spain's 10-year bond after Draghi's "whatever it takes" ukase was not due to Spain becoming more creditworthy or because its economy has come roaring back to life. In fact, industrial production in mid-2016 was 7% below the level it attained prior to Draghi's 2012 ukase, and 25% below its 2007 peak.

Indeed, Spain's industrial economy actually remains 19% smaller than it was at the turn of the century, before its euro-based domestic-borrowing and construction spree got underway. Likewise, its unemployment rate has dropped from 26% to 20%, but that's still more than double pre-boom levels.

The whole plunge of yields from 7% to a low of 1% in mid-2016 was due to the front-runners' stampede we described earlier. That is, the fast-money crowd was buying on repo what the European Central Bank promised to take off their hands at ever-higher prices in due course. They were shooting the proverbial ducks in a barrel.

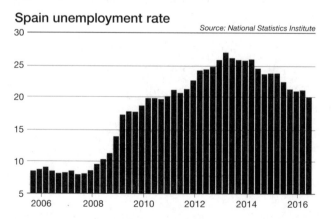

Spain unemployment rate

Source: National Statistics Institute

But as global "risk-off" gathers worldwide momentum, look out below. There will be no incremental bid from Frankfurt for a flood of carry-trade unwinds that will hit the sovereign-debt market. That's because the

European Central Bank will soon be embroiled in an existential crisis as the centrifugal forces unleashed by Brexit tear apart the fragile consensus on which Draghi's lunatic monetary experiments have depended.

In particular, the populist political insurgencies throughout Europe are as much anti-German as they are anti-immigrant. It is only a matter of time before Germany's acquiescence in the European Central Bank's massive bond-buying campaign—which essentially bails out the rest of Europe—will be abruptly ended by an internal political revolt against Merkel's accommodationist policies.

Moreover, the ongoing anti-EU upheaval in Spain is by no means unique. Italy's Five Star Movement, which just came from winning 9 out of 10 mayoral contests including Rome, will surely now be energized mightily. Its Northern League ally has already called for a referendum on exiting the euro.

Indeed, the prospect of anti-establishment revolts throughout the EU—including growing demands for a Dutch referendum—have drastically turned the tables. That is, during the great financial crisis our elite rulers cried financial "contagion."

That scary story generated panic among the politicians and acquiescence in the financial elites' crooked regime of massive bailouts and relentless money pumping. The effect of it was to bail out the gamblers from the Greenspan/Bernanke housing and credit bubble, and then to shower unspeakable windfalls on the 1% as the central banks reflated an even-more-monumental bubble during the regime of QE, ZIRP and NIRP.

But now the world's financial rulers are going to be on the receiving end of an even-more-virulent and far-reaching political "contagion"—that is, a tidal wave of voter demands to emulate the British people and take back their countries and their governments from the financial elites and politicians like David Cameron, Mariano Rajoy and Matteo Renzi who are their bagmen.

This time populist and insurgent politicians are not going to roll over for the rule of unelected central bankers and the international financial apparatchiks of the IMF and related institutions.

In that context, it can be confidently said that the Eurozone and European Central Bank are finished. That's because the monstrously inflated euro-bond market that Draghi created will implode if the front-running speculators lose confidence in the scheme or the European Central Bank emits even a smidgeon of doubt about its ability to run the printing press at $90 billion per month indefinitely, world without end.

At length, it will become evident that Draghi's "whatever it takes" gambit was the single most foolish act in the history of central banking. It assumed that the rule of the financial elite was limitless and endless.

Brexit proves that both assumptions are wrong. Now every nook and cranny of the world's bloated and radically mispriced financial casinos will face the same shock to confidence.

Central bankers everywhere will be on the run. And just in the nick of time.

CHAPTER 16:

The War on Savers and the 200 Rulers of Global Finance

THERE HAS BEEN AN ECONOMIC COUP D'ÉTAT IN AMERICA AND MOST OF the world. We are now ruled by about 200 unelected central bankers, monetary apparatchiks and their minions and megaphones on Wall Street and other financial centers.

Unlike Senator Joseph McCarthy, however, we actually do have a list of their names. They need to be exposed, denounced, ridiculed, rebuked and removed.

The first 30 include Janet Yellen, William Dudley, the other governors of the Fed and its senior staff. The next 10 include Jan Hatzius, chief economist of Goldman Sachs, and his counterparts at the other major Wall Street banking houses.

Then there is the demented Mario Draghi and the 25-member governing council of the European Central Bank and still-more senior staff. Ditto for the madman Kuroda-san and his minions at the Bank of Japan, as well as Goldman's plenipotentiary and governor of the Bank of England, Mark Carney; and also the Bank of Canada, the Reserve Bank of Australia and, not least, the People's Printing Press of China.

Also, throw in Christine Lagarde and the principals of the IMF and some scribblers at think tanks like Brookings and its latest monetary "scholar," Ben Bernanke. The names are all on Google!

That gets us to Lael Brainard. She's a Fed governor, one of the 200 and very typical. That is, she's never held an honest capitalist job in her life. She's been a policy apparatchik at the Treasury, Brookings and the Fed ever since moving out of her college dorm room.

Now Brainard is doing her bit to prosecute the war on savers. She wants to keep them lashed to the zero bound—that is, in penury and humiliation—because of the madness happening far away in the Red Ponzi of China. Its potential negative repercussions, apparently, don't sit so well with her—so she wants the Fed to continue sitting on interest rates at the zero bound, perhaps indefinitely:

> Brainard expressed concern that stresses in emerging markets including China and slow growth in developed economies could spill over to the U.S.

> "This translates into weaker exports, business investment, and manufacturing in the United States, slower progress on hitting the inflation target, and financial tightening through the exchange rate and rising risk spreads on financial assets."

THE CENTRAL BANKERS' CHEAP-DEBT MODEL—ONE CAPPUCCINO A DAY FOR A LIFETIME OF SAVINGS

In the name of a crude Keynesian economic model that is an insult to even the slow-witted, Brainard and her ilk are conducting a rogue regime of financial repression, manipulation and unspeakable injustice that will destroy both political democracy and capitalist prosperity as we have known it. They are driving the economic lot of the planet into a dark region of deflation, maldistribution and financial entropy.

The evil of it is vivified by a hypothetical old man standing at any one of Starbucks' 24,000 barista counters on any given morning. He can afford one cappuccino. He pays for it with the entire daily return from his bank account, where he prudently stores the savings of his lifetime.

But here's the thing. We refer not to just an ordinary working lifetime, but to one of extreme thrift and frugality. The result of an average wage and a far-above-average lifetime savings rate (>20%) would be certificates of deposit now totaling $250,000.

Yes, the interest earned at 30 basis points on a quarter-million-dollar nest egg buys a daily double shot of espresso in a cup of foamed milk!

What kind of crank economics contends that brutally punishing two of the great, historically proven economic virtues—thrift and prudence—is the key to economic growth and true wealth creation?

Nor is our one-cappuccino-per-day retiree an aberrant example. The household sector currently holds just under $11 trillion of bank deposits and money market funds. Yet the Fed's interest rate–repression policy easily lowers the money market interest rate by 275 basis points—say, from 3.25% to 0.5% or under.

Indeed, 3.25% is a modest estimate because with core inflation running at 2% it implies a normalized real yield of barely 1%. It also implies that Fed policies currently result in a giant fiscal transfer of upward of $250 billion annually from household depositors and savers to the financial system and ultimately to Wall Street speculators.

Apparently, this is Main Street's condign punishment for not spending that $11 trillion on trinkets at the mall and junkets to Disney World, and thereby validating that our monetary politburo calls the tune and can make the economy go boom by banging the interest rate lever until it hits the zero bound or lower.

Yet in this age of relentless consumption and 140-character tweets, what kind of insult to common sense argues that human nature is prone to save too much, defer gratification too long, shop too sparingly and consume too little?

This purported lack of profligacy, in fact, is the fundamental predicate of today's Keynesian central bankers. Forget all of their mathematical economics, dynamic-stochastic-general-equilibrium (DSGE) model regressions and rhetorical mumbo-jumbo about the zero bound, r-star, labor slack, inflation targets and the rest.

Our 200 unelected rulers are enthralled to a dogma of debt that is so primitive that it's just plain dumb. It boils down to the proposition that more debt always and everywhere is the magic elixir of economic growth and prosperity.

Nor does it matter a wit that savings rates are now in the sub-basement of historical trends, not too high, and that leverage ratios are at all-time highs, not too low.

Accordingly, by purchasing existing debt with digital credit conjured from the send key on their computers, our 200 central bank rulers make room for more and more of it. And they do so without the inconvenience of deferred consumption or an upward climb of interest rates owing to an imbalance of borrowings versus savings.

Likewise, by pegging the money market rate at zero or subzero, they enable even more debt creation via daisy chains of rehypothecation. That's the hocking by speculators of any and all tradable financial assets at virtually zero cost of carry in order to buy more of the same and then to hock more of them, still.

A WORLD UP TO ITS EYEBALLS IN DEBT

Contrary to this central banker dogma, therefore, the world has long since been up to its eyeballs in debt.

After the mid-1990s, the 200 rulers ignited a veritable tsunami of credit expansion. As I indicated earlier, worldwide public and private debt combined is up from $40 trillion to $225 trillion, or 5.5X during that two-decade span; it has grown four times more than global GDP.

So whatever has caused the growth curve of the global economy to bend toward the flat line in recent years, it surely is not the want of cheap debt. Likewise, the recurring financial crises of this century didn't betray an outbreak of unprecedented human greed or even deregulation; they were rooted in heretofore-unimagined excesses of leveraged speculation.

That's where massive financial bubbles come from. For example, that's how margined credit-default-swap wraps on the supersenior tranches of portfolios of CDOs (collateralized debt obligations) squared came into being before the last crisis, and how they eventually splattered in a manner that rattled the very financial foundations of the world.

That's also how it happened that upward of 10% of disposable personal income in 2007 consisted of mortgage equity withdrawal—that is, the cash obtained by Main Street Americans by hocking their homes.

It's also how the U.S. shale patch flushed $200 billion of junk debt down drill boreholes that required $75 per barrel of oil to break even on the return trip.

Likewise, you don't need any fancy econometrics to read the next chart, either. Since 1994, U.S. debt outstanding is up by $45 trillion compared to an $11 trillion gain in GDP. That's nearly $4.25 of debt for each dollar of incremental GDP.

If debt were the elixir, why has real final sales growth averaged just 1.2% per annum since Q4 2007? That's barely one-third of the 3.1% peak-to-peak rates of growth historically.

If the $12 trillion of U.S. debt growth since the eve of the Great Recession was not enough to trigger "escape velocity," just exactly how much more would have done the job?

Our 200 financial rulers have no answer to these questions for an absolutely obvious reason. To wit, they are monetary carpenters armed with only a hammer.

Their continued rule depends upon pounding more and more debt into the economy because that's all a central bank can do; it can only monetize existing financial claims and falsify the price of financial assets by driving interest rates to the zero bound or now, outrageously, through it.

But debt is done. We are long past the peak of it. After 93 months of ZIRP, Ms. Brainard's recent call for "watchful waiting" at 38 bps is downright sadistic.

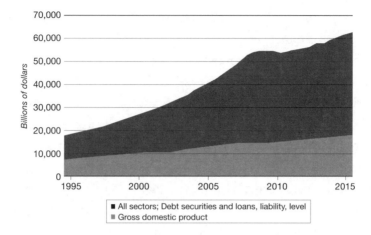

Where do she, Janet Yellen and the rest of their posse get the right to confiscate the wealth of savers in there tens of millions? From the Humphrey-Hawkins Act and its dual mandate?

No, they don't. As we showed in Chapter 4, it is a content-free enabling act etched on rubber bands; it memorializes Congress' fond hope that the people enjoy an environment of price stability, full employment and kindness to pets.

This elastic language hasn't changed since 1978, meaning that it mandates nothing specific on interest rates or any other economic targets. In fact, it enabled both Paul Volcker's 21% prime rate and the Bernanke/Yellen campaign of 93 months of free money to the Wall Street casino—with nary a legal quibble either way.

So what is at loose in the land is not public servants carrying out the law; it's a posse of Keynesian ideologues carrying out a vendetta against savers. And they are doing so on the preposterous paint-by-the-numbers theory that people are saving too much, borrowing too little and therefore not doing their central bank–ordained job of shopping until they drop, thereby putting points on the scoreboard of GDP and jobs.

That's complete rubbish, of course. In the first place, jobs are a supply-side thing. They are a function of the price and supply of labor and the real level of business investment, productivity and output—not the amount of nominal expenditure or GDP.

And most certainly they are not mechanically derived from the level of GDP clustered inside the United States' economically open borders. As we explained in Chapter 5, in the context of an economy inflated with debt and high costs and that is crisscrossed by monumental flows of global trade, capital and finance, more domestic borrowing, on the margin, leads to more jobs in China, not Youngtown, Ohio.

Likewise, "savings" are not an economic evil. To the contrary, on a healthy free market they finance the investment component of GDP today and tomorrow's capacity for growth and productivity, not a hoarder's knapsack of bullion.

Besides, the claim that a nation experiencing 10,000 baby boom retirements per day has too little savings is not only ludicrous; it's empirically wrong.

Household savings at the recession bottom in Q2 2009 amounted to $780 billion at an annualized rate, according to the GDP accounts. In Q2 2016, it was $763 billion, or 2% lower.

During that same 28-quarter "recovery" period, by contrast, personal consumption expenditures rose from $9.8 trillion to $12.7 trillion, meaning they were 30% higher.

So "savers" were actually saving less during the last seven years. They didn't get in the way of "spenders" spending nearly $3 trillion more.

PEAK DEBT AND THE SAVINGS DROUGHT

The truth is, central bank financial repression is at a dead end. Since balance sheets are saturated at Peak Debt and savings rates have been driven to all-time lows, the only thing that ZIRP and NIRP can accomplish is to brutalize savers and reward Wall Street speculators.

Indeed, banging the interest rate lever hard on the zero bound for so long has now taken our 200 financial rulers into truly Orwellian precincts. Governor Brainard's quote reproduced above, which echoes the fatuous propaganda of B-Dud (William Dudley), Goldman's viceroy at the New York Fed, claims that widening "credit spreads" are a reason to keep the policy rate pegged near the zero bound.

That is, widening credit spreads allegedly mean the market is doing the Fed's job voluntarily and preemptively!

No, it isn't. Credit spreads have been wantonly, dangerously and artificially compressed by massive central bank intrusion in the financial markets. Yet every time that markets begin to twitch with the ethers of normalization, the likes of B-Dud and Brainard take that as a sign to keep their boot on the savers' neck.

But by now the lunatic extent of their misfeasance should be evident to all. As we have indicated, from a cold start in 2015 the assembled central banks of the world have driven nearly $13 trillion of sovereign debt into the netherworld of negative yields, and with each passing day it gets more absurd.

Now, even well-rated corporate debt like that of Nestle is passing through the zero bound. Yet these dangerous fools have the nerve to claim that this mutant collapse of interest rates is caused by the state of the global economy, not their own massive financial repression, and that central banks that have not yet joined the Looney Tunes brigade of the European Central Bank, Sweden, Denmark, Switzerland and Japan in the outright subzero realm should consider doing so.

As we have demonstrated, the truth is the opposite. The amount of debt pouring into the negative-yield arena is not owing to weak growth; it's the handiwork of speculators buying bonds on NIRP-enabled repo. Their cost of carry is nothing, and the prices of NIRP bonds keep on rising.

So yields are plunging into the financial netherworld because speculators are front-running the financial death wish of the central banks.

Until they stop. At that point, look out below. The mother of all bubbles—that of the $100 billion global bond market—will blow sky-high.

At length, savers will get their relief and our 200 financial rulers will perhaps be lucky to merely end up in the stockades at a monetary version of The Hague.

Meanwhile, the war on savers continues to transfer hundreds of billions from savers to the casino in the United States alone—even as the global economy careens toward a deflationary collapse.

ZIRP AND NIRP ARE FUTILE AT PEAK DEBT

Needless to say, B-Dud is a moniker implying extreme disrespect, and Bill Dudley deserves every bit of it. He is a crony-capitalist tool and one of the Fed ringleaders prosecuting the current relentless, savage war on savers. Its only purpose is to keep carry-trade speculators gorged with free funding in the money markets and to bloat the profits of Wall Street strip-mining operations, like that of his former employer, Goldman Sachs.

The fact is, anyone who doesn't imbibe the Keynesian Kool-Aid dispensed by the central banking cartel can see in an instant that 93 months of ZIRP has done exactly nothing for the Main Street economy. Notwithstanding the Fed's gussied-up theories about monetary "accommodation" and closing the "output gap," the litmus test is really simple.

To wit, artificial suppression of free market interest rates by the central bank is designed to cause households to borrow more money than they otherwise would in order to spend more than they earn, pure and simple.

It's nothing more than a modernized version of the original, crude Keynesian pump-priming theory—except it dispenses with the inconvenience of getting politicians to approve spending increases and tax cuts in favor of the writ of a small posse of unelected monetary mandarins who run the Federal Open Market Committee and peg money-market interest rates at will.

But the whole enterprise is a crock. The consumer-spending pump can't be primed anymore because, as we demonstrated in earlier chapters, households reached a condition of Peak Debt at the time of the financial crisis.

On the eve of the financial crisis in Q1 2008, total household debt outstanding—including mortgages, credit cards, auto loans, student loans and the rest—was $14.313 trillion. That compare to $14.316 trillion outstanding at the end of Q1 2016.

That's right. After 93 months of ZIRP and an unprecedented incentive to borrow and spend, households have increased their total borrowings over the last seven years by the tiny sum of $3 billion, or by 0.02%!

That's Peak Debt in operation. To be sure, there has been a change in the mix—with mortgages and credit card balances down and auto- and student-loan balances significantly higher. But debt is fungible—so the truth about the aggregate of all household debt is stunning. Namely, not a single dime of the Fed's $3.5 trillion QE bond-buying spree left the canyons of Wall Street.

Stated differently, the entirety of private nonfinancial debt growth since the financial crisis and the inception of "extraordinary" monetary measures in the fall of 2008 has occurred in the business sector. Moreover, on a net basis even the modest growth of business debt during the last seven years has been recycled back into the speculative pools of Wall Street via stock buybacks, mergers and acquisitions, and leveraged buyouts.

So here in summary detail is what B-Dud and the small claque of Wall Street shills surrounding the Fed are actually hiding.

First, it is blindingly obvious that the household-credit channel of Keynesian monetary stimulus is over and done. During the 20 years after Greenspan took the helm at the Fed, household debt rose like a rocket.

From a level of $2.7 trillion in Q3 1987 it exploded to $14.3 trillion by Q1 2008. That represented an 8.5% rate of growth for two decades running, thereby dramatically outpacing the 5.5% rate of nominal GDP growth during the same period. Accordingly, household debt was ratcheted up on a one-time basis from 55% of GDP to 95% by the eve of the crisis.

So, yes, Greenspan's activation of the Fed's printing press during that period did goose the GDP by mortgaging household balance sheets. But that was a one-time parlor trick that is over and done, and will now tax household incomes for the indefinite future.

In fact, the demise of the household-credit channel of monetary transmission is far more drastic than implied by the usual Wall Street propaganda suggesting that the ratio of household debt service to disposable personal income (DPI) has come down sharply, and that U.S. consumers are once again in a position to borrow and spend like there is no tomorrow.

But that's a risible distortion. Both the numerator and denominator are drastically misleading. The numerator of debt-service costs is artificially low owing to ZIRP, meaning that sooner or later normalization of interest rates will cause debt-service costs to soar. More importantly, households do not pay interest and principal on their massive debt burdens out of DPI, either.

That's the wrong denominator. Nearly one-quarter of the household sector's disposable income, in fact, consists of transfer payments to old people and poor people—most of whom can't borrow at all or carry only minimal debt.

Instead, most of the current $14.3 trillion of household debt is owed by middle class wage and salary earners. It is their pool of earned income—amounting to $8.08 trillion at the end of Q1 2016—that services most of the household sector's debt. And it is here that the household debt ratio went skyward during the era of Bubble Finance, and still remains impaled on Peak Debt.

To wit, the $2.7 trillion of household outstanding debt when Greenspan took office in Q3 1987 amounted to 1.2X wage and salary disbursements, and was already significantly elevated from the pre-1980 trend of 0.8X income shown in the chart in Chapter 2.

As of Q1 2008, by contrast, the $14.3 trillion of household debt then outstanding amounted to 2.2X wage and salary income. And it was at that off-the-charts leverage ratio that the household-borrowing spree in America was stopped dead in the water.

Indeed, that ratio has now fallen partway back to earth at 1.8X income at the end of Q1 2016, but the true implications of that token level of deleveraging are the very opposite of what Wall Street claims. The Fed has been massively pushing on a string—as represented by the tiny 0.02% gain in household debt since Q1 2008—because households still have too much debt.

So the exhaustion of the Greenspan-Bernanke-Yellen parlor trick is plain as day. Debt soared from historic leverage ratios where it had traditionally been associated with healthy household finance, to 220% of wage and salary incomes by the eve of the financial crisis. But that was not an engine of permanent growth; it was a one-time leverage ratchet that has now reversed direction and entered its "payback" cycle.

Likewise, the modest growth of business debt since 2008 did not fuel added output, either. As we have demonstrated, instead of spending for plant and equipment, thereby spurring measured GDP growth today and economic productivity and efficiency over the longer run, it went into financial engineering. In so doing, it caused the massive inflation of existing financial assets in the secondary markets and thereby delivered untold windfalls to the 1% who speculate there.

Thus, at the end of Q1 2008 nonfinancial business debt stood at $10.3 trillion and since then has grown to $12.4 trillion. But about $500 billion of that went into increased balance sheet cash, leaving a net debt gain of $1.6 trillion.

While this gain is modest compared to the 4X increase in net business debt between 1987 and 2008, the more important point is that the business channel of monetary-policy transmission is broken too.

The Fed's drastic falsification of financial-asset prices has turned the C-suites of corporate America into gambling parlors. As we have previously demonstrated, all of the gains in business debt since 2008 have been flushed right back into Wall Street in the form of stock buybacks and debt-financed takeovers.

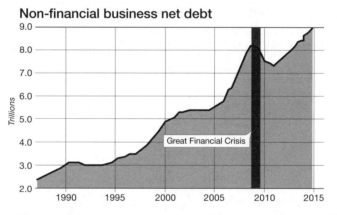

Non-financial business net debt

The evidence that zero interest rates have not promoted business borrowing for productive investment is also plain to see. During the most recent year (2015), U.S. business spent $429 billion on plant, equipment and software after depreciation. That was 9% less in constant dollars than during 2007 and more than 20% lower than net real business investment of $526 billion in the year 2000.

So the proof is in the pudding. You don't need fancy econometric regression analysis or DSGE models to see that ZIRP is a macroeconomic dud. Simple empirical data trends show that it hasn't goosed household borrowing and consumption spending, nor has it stimulated business investment.

And that's what makes Dudley, Yellen and the rest of the posse so detestable. They have deployed formulaic Keynesian incantations about an allegedly incomplete and fragile recovery to pleasure Wall Street speculators with free carry-trade funding for 93 months now, and by every indication are intending several more years of money market rates that are tantamount to zero.

At the end of the day, this is all about the Fed's deathly fear that Wall Street will stage a hissy fit if it is not guaranteed free or quasi-free gambling stakes for the indefinite future. That's why the monetary politburo dispatches B-Dud, Brainard and Yellen herself to periodically calm the robo-machines and hedge fund gamblers when the markets even hint at a smidgeon of decline.

Yet what about the tens of millions of Main Street savers and retirees who are being financially ruined by the writ of the FOMC? In a word, they are being sacrificed to the harebrained theory that the central bank can create lasting gains in output and societal wealth by rigging the price of debt and inflating the value of risky assets by subsidizing ceaseless gambling in the casino.

And do not think "harebrained" is an excessive term. The in-grown circle of a few hundred monetary apparatchiks in the world that run the whole central banking horror show have now persuaded themselves, in fact, that the nightmare of NIRP could be made even more efficacious by abolishing cash entirely.

Indeed, among these are the blatantly Keynesian editorial writers and commentators of the Financial Times. In a recent editorial that is so outrageously daffy that it could have been posted in The Onion, the FT let the cat out of the bag.

What these unspeakably dangerous monetary cranks argued was that cash should be abolished so that the central banks could get on with their job of stimulating "depressed" economies by setting interest at negative nominal rates.

In other words, it is apparently not enough that our hypothetical retiree, who saved $250,000 over a lifetime of work and forgone consumption, should earn just one cappuccino per day of interest on liquid savings deposits or Treasury bills.

No, the central bankers' posse now wants to actually expropriate these savings by extracting a monthly levy, and by throwing anyone in jail who attempts to hide their wealth outside the controlled banking system by keeping it in private script or unconfiscated greenbacks.

Since this very idea amounts to a frontal assault on civil liberties and economic justice, the FT should be left to condemn itself with its own words:

> But even as individuals have taken recent crises as reasons to stock up on banknotes, authorities would do well to consider the arguments for phasing out their use as another "barbarous relic," the moniker Keynes gave to gold . . . But even a little physical currency can cause a lot of distortion to the economic system.
>
> The existence of cash—a bearer instrument with a zero interest rate—limits central banks' ability to stimulate a depressed economy. The worry is that people will change their deposits for cash if a central bank moves rates into negative territory. The Swiss, Danish and Swedish central banks have pushed rates lower than many thought possible; but most policymakers still believe in an "effective" lower band not far below zero.
>
> The dominant argument for beginning the tightening cycle is to have enough "ammunition" for a new stimulus when the next downturn comes. Removing the lower band would leave central banks well equipped to deal with a slowdown even from near-zero starting points.

There you have it. The private economy and its millions of savers exist for the convenience of the apparatchiks who run the central bank.

And this view is not limited to the editorial scribblers at the FT. Their reasoning was identical to that offered by Harvard Professor Kenneth Rogoff, the former chief economist of the International Monetary Fund, who recently advocated abolishing high-denomination banknotes such as 100 and 500 notes.

So in their palpable fear of a Wall Street hissy fit and unrelieved arrogance, would they now throw millions of already-ruined retirees and savers completely under the bus by confiscating their cash?

Yes, they would.

THE CENTRAL BANKERS' BIG LIE— THE RISIBLE MYTH OF THE "SAVINGS GLUT"

The central bank war on savers is also rooted in a monumental case of the Big Lie. To wit, they claim that one Starbucks cappuccino per day on a $250,000 nest egg is owing to a global "savings glut" and low economic growth, not their deliberate pegging of interest rates on the zero bound and flattening of the yield curve through massive QE. Thus, Mario Draghi insisted recently that ultra easy monetary policy and NIRP

> "[are] not the problem, but a symptom of an underlying problem" caused by a "global excess of savings" and a lack of appetite for investment . . . This excess—dubbed as the "global savings glut" by Ben Bernanke, former US Federal Reserve chairman—lay behind a historical decline in interest rates in recent decades, the ECB president said.

Nor did Draghi even bother to blame it solely on the allegedly savings-obsessed Chinese girls working for 12 hours per day in the Foxconn factories assembling iPhones. Said Europe's mad money printer, the single currency area was "also a protagonist."

Actually, that's a bald-faced lie. Europeans are not saving too much. The household savings rate, in fact, has been declining ever since the inception of the single currency. And, as shown below, that long-term erosion has not slowed one wit since Draghi issued his "whatever it takes" ukase in August 2012.

Yes, double-talking central bankers like Draghi slip in some statistical subterfuge, claiming current-account surpluses are the same thing as a savings glut.

Actually, they are nothing of the kind. Current-account surpluses and deficits are an accounting identity within the world's Keynesian

GDP accounting schemes, and for all nations combined they add to zero except for statistical discrepancies.

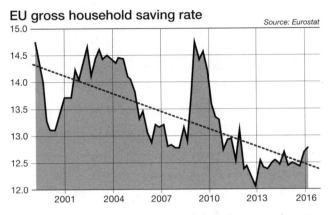

In fact, current-account surpluses and deficits are a function of central bank credit and foreign-exchange policies and their impact on domestic wages, prices and costs. Chronic current-account surpluses result from pegging exchange rates below economic levels and thereby the deflation of domestic wages, prices and production costs. By contrast, chronic current-account deficits, as demonstrated in Chapter 4, stem from central bank inflation of domestic debt, consumption, wages and costs.

Stated differently, what central bankers claim to be "excess savings" generated by households and businesses, which need to be punished for their sins, are actually deformations of world trade and capital flows that are rooted in the machinations of central bankers themselves.

During the 14 years before Draghi's mid-2012 "whatever it takes" ukase, which meant that he was fixing to trash the then-prevailing exchange rate of $1.30–$1.40 per euro, the Eurozone did not have a current-account surplus.

What Draghi cites as the "savings glut" problem is mainly his own creation.

That is, the Eurozone's recent current-account surpluses are the short-term result of the 20% currency depreciation the European Central Bank effected under his leadership, and also the temporary improvement in Europe's terms of trade owing to the global oil and commodities glut.

And even in the latter case, as we will demonstrate in Chapter 18, it is central bank action that originally led to the cheap-credit boom of the last two decades and the resulting overinvestment in global-energy and mining production capacity. It was that malinvestment-rooted deflation that the Eurozone imported, not a glut of internal savings.

In any event, the Eurozone surpluses since 2011 shown below do not represent consumers and businesses failing to spend enough and hoarding their cash. To the contrary, these accounting surpluses are just another phase of the world's massively deformed system of global trade and capital flows. The latter, in turn, is the fruit of a rotten regime of central bank falsification of money and capital markets.

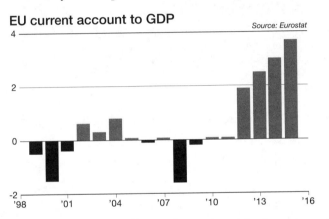

EU current account to GDP

Source: Eurostat

In fact, when savings are honestly measured, there is not a single major developed-market economy in the world that has not experienced a severe decline in its household savings rate over the last several decades. The U.S. household savings rate, for example, has not only dropped by more than half, but in so doing it was going in exactly the wrong direction.

That is, the giant 78-million-plus baby boom generation was demographically ambling toward the inflection point of massive retirement waves beginning in 2010. The savings rate should have been rising toward a generational peak, not sliding into the sub-basement of history.

In this regard, Japan is the poster child for the truth of the matter, which is that we have actually had the opposite—an antisavings famine in most of the developed world.

Thus, Japan's much-vaunted high-saving households back in its pre-1990 boom times have literally disappeared from the face of the earth.

Yet this baleful development occurred just when Japan needed to be building a considerable savings nest egg for the decades ahead when it will essentially morph into a giant retirement colony.

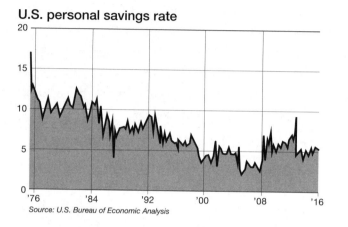

U.S. personal savings rate

Source: U.S. Bureau of Economic Analysis

The deep secular decline of household savings rates throughout the developed-market world is in itself the tip-off that central banks have drastically deformed the financial system. They are now telling the proverbial Big Lie about a phony "savings glut" in order to justify their continued savage assault on depositors.

In fact, under any historical rule of sound money, the kind of investment boom experienced by the emerging-market world during the last two decades would have been financed by the upsurge of a large savings surplus in the developed-market economies. So the world's monetary central planners have turned the laws of economics upside-down.

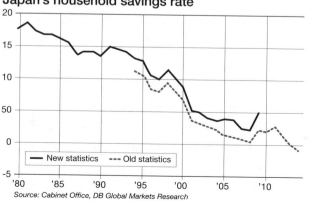

Japan's household savings rate

— New statistics   --- Old statistics

Source: Cabinet Office, DB Global Markets Research

THE UPSIDE DOWN OF KEYNESIAN CENTRAL BANKING

During the great global growth and industrialization boom between 1870 and 1914, for example, Great Britain, France, Holland and, to a lesser degree, Germany were huge exporters of capital. By contrast, the emerging markets of the day—the United States, Argentina, Russia, India, Australia and so on—were major capital importers.

That made tremendous economic sense. The advanced economies earned trade surpluses exporting machinery, rolling stock, steel, chemicals and consumer manufactures, and then reinvested these surpluses in loans and investments in ships, mines, railroads, factories, ports and public infrastructure in the developing economies.

The lynchpin of this virtuous circle, of course, was common global money—that is, currencies that had a constant weight in gold and which, accordingly, were convertible at fixed rates over long stretches of time.

English investors and insurance companies, for example, held sterling-denominated bonds issued by foreign borrowers because they knew the bonds were good as gold, and that their only real risk was borrower defaults on interest or principal.

Today's world of printing press money has turned the logic of gold standard capitalism upside-down. Accordingly, during the last several decades the East Asian export manufacturers have purportedly become voracious savers and capital exporters, while the most advanced economy on the planet has become a giant capital importer.

Indeed, Keynesian economists and so-called conservative monetarists alike have proclaimed these huge, chronic U.S. current-account surpluses to be a wonderful thing.

No, they aren't. Donald Trump is right—even if for the wrong reason.

The United States has borrowed approximately $8 trillion from the rest of the world since the 1970s, and not pursuant to the laws of economics, as the Keynesian/monetarist consensus proclaims. Instead, the unbroken string of giant current-account deficits shown next—the basic measure of annual borrowing from abroad—were accumulated in violation of the laws of sound money and were, in fact, enabled by Richard Nixon's abandonment of the dollar's convertibility to a fixed weight of gold in August 1971.

At length, the unshackled Fed found one excuse after another to flood the world with dollar liabilities. In fact, the Fed's balance sheet liabilities (that is, dollars) totaled just $65 billion before August 1971, meaning that it has exploded by 70X to $4.5 trillion in the years since.

This vast inflation of the monetary system, in turn, enabled total credit outstanding in the U.S. economy to soar from $1.7 trillion at the time of Camp David to nearly $64 trillion at present. As we documented in Chapter 6, that means the U.S. economy's ratio of total public and private debt to national income surged from its historic level of 1.5X in 1971 to 3.5X today.

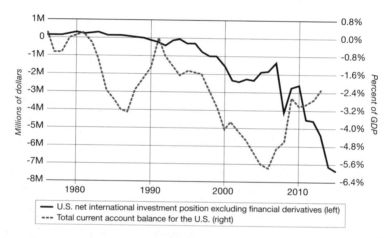

— U.S. net international investment position excluding financial derivatives (left)
--- Total current account balance for the U.S. (right)

Needless to say, the evil of this kind of massive money and credit inflation is that it is contagious. The last 45 years have proven in spades that there is no such thing as printing press money in one country.

In fact, the borrowing binge in America, Japan and Europe played right into the hands of the mercantilist policy makers in East Asia and the petro-states.

By pegging their currencies not to a fixed standard like gold, but to the massive emission of floating dollars, they appeared to become prodigious capital exporters and "savers." That's because in order to keep their currencies from soaring against depreciating dollars and euros, their central banks accumulated huge amounts of U.S. Treasuries and euro debt in the process of chronic, heavy-handed intervention in the foreign-exchange markets.

Folks, that's not a savings glut; it's the consequence of massive money printing and credit expansion on a worldwide basis. Had China not depreciated its currency by 60% in 1994 and kept it more or less linked to the Fed's flood of dollars ever since, its vaunted $4 trillion of FX reserves and the 60X expansion of its domestic credit—from $500 billion in the mid-1990s to $30 trillion at present—would not have happened in a million years.

China central bank balance sheet

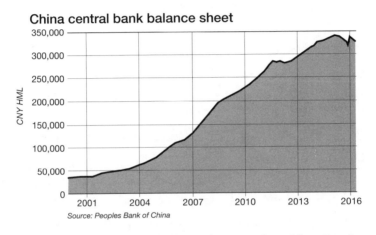

Source: Peoples Bank of China

The next graph, therefore, has nothing to do with a "savings glut." Had China's currency been linked to gold in 1994, the dollar's exchange rate against the renminbi would have collapsed long ago. America's ability to live beyond its means for decades by swapping Treasury debt for Chinese exports would have been stopped dead in its tracks.

China current account to GDP

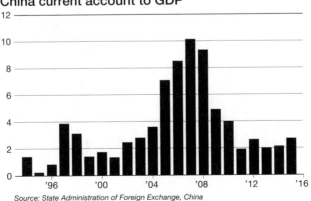

Source: State Administration of Foreign Exchange, China

At the end of the day, central banker palaver about the world's alleged "savings glut" refers to nothing more than the inherent accounting identity in world trade. Mercantilist policy makers that choose to swap the sweat of their workers' brows (China and East Asia) and the bounty of nature buried in their energy and mineral resources (the petro-states) for paper IOUs end up with current-account surpluses; the net issuers of these paper debts accumulate the net deficits.

It has nothing whatsoever to do with too much savings from real incomes. It's a consequence of the rampant money printing that has saddled the world economy with $225 trillion of unrepayable debt and massive excess production capacity that will result in deflationary pressures and low growth for years to come.

Indeed, the world's 200 central bankers have wandered so deep into the rabbit hole of monetary crankery that they no longer even know the difference between honest savings from household incomes, business profits and government surpluses and fiat credits generated ex nihilo by central banks and the financial institutions that they enable.

Accordingly, the global economy has been saddled with a historically aberrational run of malinvestments and surplus capital expenditure (CapEx) that at length has now triggered a sweeping global deflation and collapse of profits in the primary industries and capital goods.

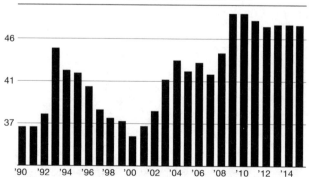

Chinese investment as % of national GDP

Stated differently, lunatic levels of CapEx in China and its supply-chain satellites during the last two decades were not a function of workers' coming out of the rice paddies in their hundreds of millions and saving too much from the 60 cents per hour they were paid in wages. Instead, the economic insanity displayed in the following chart is on central bankers and their foolish $20 trillion emission of fiat credit over this period.

And that gets us to the endgame mendacity of Bernanke, Yellen and most especially Draghi. The blithering fool Draghi answered the valid German complaints about his savage war on European savers with this gem:

> "there is simply not enough demand for capital elsewhere in the world to absorb that excess saving without declining returns," Mr. Draghi said . . . In such an environment, low central bank interest rates were not the enemy, but exactly what was needed to boost demand for investment. "If central banks did not do this, investing would be unattractive," Mr. Draghi said. "So the economy would stay in recession."

What absolute tommyrot!

If there is "not enough demand for capital," then why did the European Central Bank find it necessary to finance the Eurozone governments' borrowing needs through the backdoor or QE? By scarfing up $1 trillion of government and business debt during the last 14 months it was actually supplanting private demand for investment securities.

But then again, the European Central Bank's purpose all along was to suppress yields and the cost of borrowing in pursuit of the hoary Keynesian theory that the debt-saturated Eurozone can borrow its way to prosperity. That is, by punishing savers and rewarding debtors through falsification of interest rates, Draghi claims central banks can magically generate growth and wealth.

As The Donald might say, not a chance!

In fact, the world is likely to face a CapEx depression during the years ahead owing to the massive overhang of excess capacity that has resulted from the cheap-credit boom of the last two decades.

But that baleful condition was caused by central bankers and is baked into the cake of the global economy. It means that no imaginable amount of additional zero-cost credit will generate productive investments in the face of that profit-killing overhang.

EU central bank balance sheet

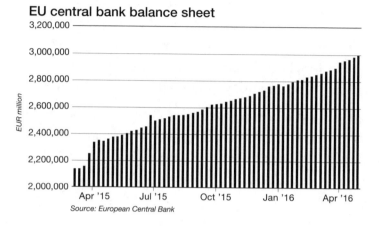

Source: European Central Bank

So the Big Lie about the "savings glut" is especially heinous. Central bankers are using it as a pretext to brutally punish savers for the consequences of their own epic errors.

CHAPTER 17:

———

Fannie Mae's Swell New Palace— Why the Imperial City Must Be Sacked

To HEAR THE ESTABLISHMENT MEDIA TELL IT, YOU WOULD THINK THAT Attila the Hun was fixing to sack the Imperial City. Would that Donald Trump were that bold or dangerous.

Then again, he is a showman of no mean talents. So if there is a maquette of Fannie Mae's planned new $770 million headquarters somewhere around Washington, D.C., he could start the sacking right there. Hopefully, he would not hesitate to shatter it with a fusillade of tweets—or even take a jackhammer to it while wearing a Trump hard hat.

Fannie Mae is surely a monument to crony-capitalist corruption, and living proof that massive state intervention in credit markets is a recipe for disaster. But rather than shut it down after it helped bring the nation's financial system to the edge of ruin, the Beltway pols have come up with an altogether-different idea.

To wit, they plan to move Fannie from her already-luxurious Northwest Washington headquarters to this hideous new glass palace to be built in the heart of Washington, D.C. Could there be a bigger insult than this to the 15 million families who lost their homes to foreclosure owing to the crash of the giant housing bubble that Fannie Mae and the crony-capitalist crooks who ran it helped perpetuate?

And that's to say nothing of the $180 billion of taxpayer money that was pumped into Fannie Mae and the other government-sponsored enterprises (GSEs) after the house of cards came tumbling down in August

2008. In fact, while the politicians on Capitol Hill have dawdled for eight years without any statutory changes or mandates for even minor reforms, Fannie Mae's management and its phalanx of K Street lobbies showed exactly who rules in the Imperial City.

It is the larcenous rule of these syndicates of Beltway racketeers, in fact, that has put Donald Trump's name on the presidential ballot.

So let it be granted that his manners and policy knowledge often appear to be on the meager side. Yet it is malodorous tales like that of Fannie Mae's swank new palace and the crony-capitalist history of plunder behind it that demonstrate why a disrupter on horseback is exactly what the Imperial City deserves.

FREDDIE AND FANNIE—CRONY-CAPITALIST FRAUDS FROM THE BEGINNING

In truth, the government housing-guarantee programs at Fannie Mae and Freddie Mac have been an abomination from the very beginning.

Not only did they inappropriately subsidize home mortgages by upward of $60 billion annually—most of which went to affluent middle class households not entitled to taxpayer help in the first place—but they were also based on the kind of Washington artifice upon which today's rampant crony capitalism thrives.

Namely, the specious claim is that the GSEs are unique, creative "public-private partnerships" that enable a "secondary market" for home mortgages, and thereby remedy the alleged failure of the free market to provide cheap 30-year housing loans to the public.

In fact, the so-called secondary market for mortgages was no such thing. Freddie and Fannie have always been a de facto branch office of the U.S. Treasury, and their securities have been just another variant of Treasury bonds. That finally became official when the U.S. Treasury threw them a $180 billion lifeline on the eve of the 2008 financial crisis.

The reason that became necessary, of course, is that the GSEs had been minting fabulous book profits over several decades by drastically under-reserving for losses, confident that Uncle Sam would bail them out if a crisis ever came.

In fact, when the mortgage meltdown did come, Freddie and Fannie had virtually no accumulated reserves and capital and would have exposed investors to tens of billions of losses.

Needless to say, the implicit "call" on the U.S. Treasury that had always been embedded in the below-market rates on Freddie/Fannie paper was instantly exercised by Wall Street's then plenipotentiary in Washington, former Goldman CEO and U.S. Treasury Secretary Hank Paulson.

To be sure, the proper course would have been to force investors ranging from the sovereign wealth fund of China to Norwegian fishing villages and Wall Street hedge funds to take their lumps for not reading the indentures, which contained no U.S. legal guarantee. And the next order of business would have been to prosecute Freddie and Fannie and their executives for blatant and monumental accounting fraud.

But the accounting fraud was never even acknowledged, let alone prosecuted, owing to the Beltway fiction that the GSEs are "off-budget" public-private partnerships.

This convenient scam was first invented by Lyndon Johnson to magically shrink his "guns and butter" fiscal deficits. But since then it has metastasized into a giant business fairy tale—namely, that behind the imposing brick façade of Fannie Mae's soon-to-be-superseded headquarters, there is a real company generating value-added services that are the source of its reported profits.

In fact, there is nothing behind those walls except a stamping machine that embosses the signature of the American taxpayer on every billion-dollar package of securitized mortgages it guarantees and on all the bonds it issues to fund a giant portfolio of mortgages and securities from which it strips the interest.

That's right. It is the unwitting taxpayers of Flyover America who underwrite Fannie's balance sheet and enable the racketeers who run it and feed off its massive money-shuffling operations to live high on the hog.

Here's how the scam works. Fannie and Freddie typically book upward of 90% gross profit margins owing to the fact that they have essentially no cost of production beyond the trivial expenses of their automated underwriting systems and highly computerized back-office operations. Their true cost of goods would be the large accounting charges for future losses that would be required were they not wholly guaranteed by the U.S. Treasury.

Indeed, the pointlessness of their faux financial statements can be easily demonstrated by the contrafactual. That is, if we wanted to have honest socialist mortgage finance, a handful of GS-14-level civil servants could run Freddie and Fannie out of a small corner of the U.S. Treasury building.

Civil servants could emboss the taxpayers' guarantee on every family's home mortgage just as proficiently as the make-believe business executives who populate Fannie Mae and the other GSEs today; and in the process we could dispense with the sheer waste involved in applying GAAP accounting to the operations of a mere government bureau.

THE POST-CRISIS HEDGE FUND SCAM

We laid this out more fully in *The Great Deformation: The Corruption of Capitalism in America*. Yet the mythology about Fannie and Freddie is virtually immune to these obvious truths. Indeed, the Beltway discourse has been so corrupted that a whole new crony-capitalist scam has been launched by speculators who bought up their worthless securities after the 2008 collapse and subsequent bailout.

What happened was that a passel of hucksters led by hedge fund operatives Bruce Berkowitz, Bill Ackman, Perry Capital and others attempted to pilfer upward of $40 billion from U.S. taxpayers via a raid on Fannie Mae's busted preferred stock.

These were the securities issued at $25 per share to shore up the tottering housing-finance agencies just before Hank Paulson's "bazooka" sputtered in August 2008.

Not inappropriately, when the Republican White House nationalized Freddie and Fannie shortly thereafter these preferred shares plunged to 25 cents—their true value all along.

Like in so many other cases during the post-crisis aftermath, however, these hedge funds scooped up the worthless Fannie stock at pennies on the dollar, expecting it to soar as the Fed's tsunami of liquidity rekindled speculative appetites and its free carry-trade financing buoyed the markets for risk assets.

In this particular case, the potential jackpot was to be powerfully augmented by an expected legislative or judicial ruling that owners of these beaten-down equities were entitled to their pro rata share of the surging but entirely phony accounting "profits" of Fannie and Freddie.

So three years ago came the patented crony-capitalist rush. At the peak of the speculation in early 2014, the equity shares of Freddie and Fannie had risen from 10 cents to $6, and the preferreds had erupted from $0.25 per share to $12, meaning that some speculators had garnered paper returns of 4,500–6,000%!

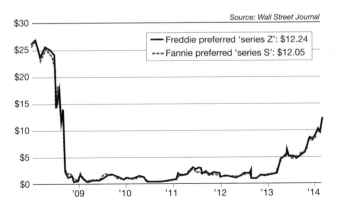

Source: Wall Street Journal

— Freddie preferred 'series Z': $12.24
--- Fannie preferred 'series S': $12.05

And why did this revival miracle transpire?

Quite simply because Berkowitz's Fairholme Capital and his posse of punters had taken turns bidding up the paper, and then laying the legal and political groundwork for overturning the Obama Administration's correct decision to ensure that these bogus securities should remain worthless.

Indeed, in short order Berkowitz and company were in full-on Washington-lobby mode, pounding the table for a bailout of the remnants of the last bailout!

To its credit, the Obama Administration had previously recognized that absent Uncle Sam's bailout of the roughly $6 trillion of Freddie/Fannie mortgage guarantees and debentures, the junior-equity securities in their capital structures (preferred and common stock) would have been worthless.

In fact, at the time the GSEs were essentially nationalized by the Bush Administration in September 2008, the thin layer of equity represented by these shares had been leveraged at approximately 100X. They would have been obliterated in a proper bankruptcy.

Accordingly, the Obama folks had simply decided to treat the remnants of Freddie/Fannie as a wholly owned government investment fund, and sweep back to the U.S. Treasury 100% of the phony "book profits" posted each quarter.

To be sure, the White House wasn't so righteous, either. After all, the Freddie/Fannie profits sweep to the U.S. Treasury itself amounted to an off-budget accounting scam.

What happened is that the U.S. Treasury rented its credit card to Fannie and Freddie for a pittance and then booked the resulting "profits" as government revenue. That is only a tiny step removed from issuing Treasury bonds, and then booking the proceeds minus a modest service charge as income!

Needless to say, the Treasury Department did not enter any offsetting debit for the risk being incurred down the road when the next mortgage crisis inexorably comes. Consequently, this classic Beltway budgetary scam has permitted the Obama Administration to book more than $200 billion of phony deficit reductions since 2009—even as it has attempted to fight off the hedge fund raiders who wanted the loot for their own accounts.

The whole thing stunk to high heaven, but it did not slow down the crony-capitalist hucksters by one whit. During the peak of their lobbying campaign, they even postured themselves as the benefactor of America's middle class homeowners.

> *"There is no viable alternative,"* to Fannie Mae and Freddie Mac, Ackman said today in a Bloomberg Television interview with Stephanie Ruhle after the Sohn presentation. *"Preserving the 30-year prepayable fixed-rate mortgage—it's like the bedrock of the housing system—is critical. We think the only way to do it is by preserving Fannie and Freddie . . .* Ackman said mortgage rates would jump without the government-sponsored enterprises.

Oh, c'mon!

If evidence was ever needed that massive statist interventions like Washington's subventions for homeownership end up generating random income distributions and windfalls to the politically mobilized, the recent hedge fund campaign to "rescue" Fannie and Freddie is surely it.

WHY FREDDIE AND FANNIE ARE NOT NEEDED

In an alternative political universe not corrupted by crony-capitalist mythology about the elixir of homeownership, of course, there would be no need for a Treasury Bureau of Home Mortgage Finance. The decision to own or rent would be made by 115 million American households based on their best lights, not the inducements and favors of the state.

Markets would clear the interest price of mortgage debt and set credit terms and maturities consistent with the risks involved. Undoubtedly, rates would be a few hundred basis points higher and 30-year fixed-rate mortgages quite rare.

Likewise, homeownership rates might end up far different than the 69% level reached during the heyday of the mortgage boom or even the current postcrisis level of 63%. In fact, in the prosperous land of Germany homeownership currently stands at just 53%, and in the equally affluent precincts of Hong Kong and Switzerland it is 51% and 44%, respectively.

So what? The true wealth and prosperity of society is not a function of the homeownership rate, and especially not one selected by pandering politicians of the type who pinned the disastrous 70% ownership goal on the wall during the Clinton-Bush era.

At the end of the day, having 40 million renter households and 25 million mortgage-free owner households provide (in their capacity as taxpayers) trillions of subsidized credit to upward of 50 million mortgage-encumbered households is unfair and arbitrary in the extreme.

To be sure, this perverse arrangement could be dismissed as just another expression of the capricious and random shuffling of income among American citizens that is the tradecraft of the Washington puzzle palace.

Unfortunately, as underscored by this latest attempted hedge fund raid on the Treasury, the reality is not so anodyne. In order to hide this random-redistribution mischief, what amounts to the Treasury Bureau of Home Mortgage Finance has been gussied up to form the simulacrum of a profit-making enterprise.

In that posture, the GSEs have been repeatedly plundered by insiders like Franklin Rains, the $90 million CEO who drove Fannie off the cliff.

Likewise, fast-money stock speculators during the halcyon days at the turn of the century piled into the stock of both companies, driving the combined market cap of Freddie and Fannie to the lunatic level of $140 billion.

These punters took their profits and ran, of course, long before the stocks went to zero. In a similar manner, Wall Street dealers and so-called fund managers milked tens of billions from the spread on GSE securities. That is, they inventoried billions of GSE securities, and then essentially scalped profits from the economically pointless spread between regular Treasury bond yields and the slightly higher GSE variant of the same thing.

All of these hundreds of billions were pocketed by adept cronies and speculators in the various debt, equity and preferred securities of the GSEs during the decades culminating in the 2008 financial crisis. Given the trauma of those events, Secretary Paulson's desperate and ill-disguised nationalization of Freddie and Fannie should have put an end to the plunder.

But it hasn't because there is no end to the zero-cost-of-goods carry trades by which speculators scoop up and fund financial assets—busted and not—during the Fed's money-printing marathons. That's what has been happening since the Fed went all-in on ZIRP and QE in 2009, and this play on the busted securities of Fannie and Freddie is a perfect example.

Likewise, there is also no end to crony-capitalist marauders like Berkowitz, who have the temerity to demand make-wholes from the state. Nor is there any shortage of K Street hirelings—lawyers, accountants and consultants—who are skilled at the manufacture of specious public policy rationalizations for outright thievery.

FIG LEAF OF RATIONALIZATION FOR RAIDING THE TAXPAYERS

Yes, they had a fig leaf of rationalization for their raid on the Treasury. Berkowitz and his sharpies blathered that Freddie and Fannie have now returned $230 billion to the U.S. Treasury, thereby repaying the original $180 billion drawdown, with some change to spare.

But what hay wagon do they think even the clueless officialdom of Washington rides upon?

Roughly $50 billion of that was for writing up a "tax asset" that had earlier been written down eight years ago, owing to the fact that absent nationalization the GSEs had no prospect of booking even accounting income in the future.

And the remaining $170 billion represents dividends paid to the Treasury since 2009 based on the accounting scam described above—that is, using Uncle Sam's credit card to issue the bonds and guarantees that fund the assets from which these so-called GSE profits and dividends are scalped.

Fortunately, a courageous U.S. district judge recently threw a monkey wrench into the works—at least on the judicial front. But the hedge funds are not done, and will now surely revive a legislative drive to accomplish their egregious plunder of America's innocent and unaware taxpayers.

During the peak of their campaign to fleece the nation's taxpayers for the second time around, the leader of the hedge fund gang, Bruce

Berkowitz, appeared on CNBC demanding that Washington exercise its "fiduciary responsibility" to distribute to him and his cronies billions in paper profits that have not been earned and are not owed.

Indeed, so shameless are Wall Street's princes of plunder that Berkowitz told a skeptical CNBC questioner that "we've helped before with AIG" and that he now merely sought a "win-win" to "help with jobs, help with the economy, help with the dream of homeownership"!

In short, the purportedly well-mannered and knowledgeable politicians of the Beltway have sat on their hands for eight years while Wall Street bandits have been launching the blatant raid described above, and while Fannie's management has been fixing to build and occupy the glass palace also shown above.

Hopefully, someone will sack the Imperial City, mannered or not.

Donald Trump might just be the one.

CHAPTER 18:

Red Ponzi Ticking—China and the Dark Side of Bubble Finance

ONALD TRUMP IS ABSOLUTELY CORRECT THAT CHINA IS A GREAT economic menace. But that's not owing to incompetence at the State and Commerce Departments or the U.S. Trade Representative in cutting bad trade deals.

Nor is it even primarily due to the fact that China egregiously manipulates its currency, massively subsidizes its exports, wantonly steals technology, chronically infringes patents and hacks proprietary business information like there is no tomorrow.

If that were the extent of China's sins, a new sheriff in the White House wielding a big stick and possessing a steely backbone—attributes loudly claimed by The Donald—might be able to reset the game. After hard-nosed negotiations, he might even obtain a more level and transparent playing field, thereby eventually reducing our current debilitating $500 billion import flow from China and retrieving at least some of the millions of jobs that have been offshored to the far side of the planet.

But as we demonstrated in Chapter 5, the world fundamentally changed in the early 1990s when Mr. Deng and Chairman Greenspan jointly initiated the present era of Bubble Finance. The latter elected to inflate rather than deflate the domestic U.S. economy and to thereby export dollar liabilities in their trillions to the rest of the world.

At the same time, having depreciated the yuan by 60%, Mr. Deng's discovered that to keep China's nascent export machine booming he needed to run the printing presses in the basement of the People's Bank of China (PBOC) red hot, thereby sopping up the massive inflow of Greenspan's dollars and keeping China's exchange rate pegged to the greenback.

In so doing, Beijing kept domestic wages and prices cheap and turned China into an export powerhouse by draining its vast rice paddies of history's greatest warehouse of untapped industrial labor. In fact, in less than two decades it mobilized more new industrial workers than had existed in the United States, Europe and Japan combined at the time in the early 1990s when Mr. Deng proclaimed that it was glorious to be rich.

Unfortunately, that wasn't the half of it. Greenspan's dollar profligacy was inherently contagious. By the 1990s, the governments of most of the developed world were run by statists and socialists who were loath to see their exchange rates soar in the face of Greenspan's epic flood of surplus dollars.

So rather than harvesting social gains from the cheap American exports Greenspan had on offer, the new European Central Bank and the Bank of Japan reciprocated with monetary expansion designed to keep their exchange rates down and protect domestic industries and labor.

Old-fashioned economists were wont to call this a race to the currency bottom, and surely it was that. But what it really did was unleash a global tsunami of credit expansion and an economic race of another sort—namely, to today's nearly universal malady of Peak Debt.

As we documented earlier, the combined central banks of the world have expanded their balance sheets from $2 trillion to $21 trillion, or by 10X during the past two decades. In so doing they drove the price of credit and capital to the subterranean zones of economic history and rationality, but they did not abolish the laws of economics entirely.

To wit, the more you subsidize an economic resource, the more of it you get. That's what happened with credit and capital when China and its global supply chain ran their printing presses fast enough to keep up with the Fed and its developed-world counterparts.

Accordingly, and as we documented previously, in less than two decades, public and private debt outstanding in the world rose sixfold—from $40 trillion to $225 trillion. On paper that represented a gain that was nearly 4X greater than the global GDP expansion during that period, but in fact it was far worse.

That's because as the global credit spree reached its apogee in recent years, malinvestment and wasteful, inefficient fixed-asset investment became rampant. In effect, the central banks of the world were enabling the "printing" of GDP that wasn't wealth, wasn't sustainable and wasn't the fruit of genuine capitalist enterprise; it was only transient GDP ledger entries destined to become future year write-offs, losses and white elephants.

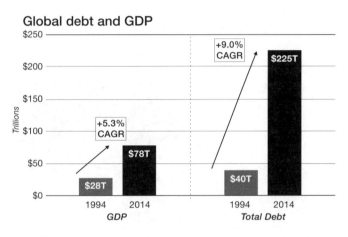

The world's central bank–driven credit binge had a dual impact. In the developed world and especially the United States it resulted in a vast inflation of household debt and leverage—or the equivalent of an internal leveraged buyout as we saw in Chapter 6. Accordingly, the aging households of the developed world were able to live beyond their means or level of current production and income for nearly two decades, boosting mightily the call on exports from China and its emergent supply chain from South Korea and Taiwan to the Persian Gulf and Brazil.

At the same time, booming global trade and export demand in combination with red hot central bank printing presses in China and the emerging markets engendered the greatest capital-expenditure (CapEx) boom in world history. Much of it occurred in China, but also in its satellite resource and mining colonies such as Australia and Brazil and in the global shipping and materials-processing industries, most especially energy.

Needless to say, there is no possible scenario in which global CapEx could have grown from an already-elevated $1 trillion annual rate in the year 2000 to $3 trillion barely a decade later in a world of honest money and market-priced capital. Instead, the world's central banks enabled what old-fashioned liberal economics a century ago called a crack-up boom.

As is evident from the chart, rampant gains in global CapEx are now over and done, and a long era of falling investment and payback has begun. In the interim, however, there is relentless deflation—the natural consequence of massive excess capacity and the lapse into variable-cost pricing by firms desperately seeking cash flow to service their gargantuan debts.

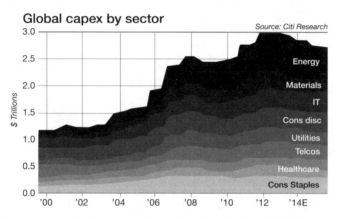

Needless to say, China was the epicenter of this global crack-up boom. Unrestrained by any traditions of sound money or even vestigial mechanisms of market discipline and financial controls, the Communist Party apparatchiks who inherited Mr. Mao's epic mess let loose a credit-driven construction and investment mania like the world has never before seen.

But as we document below, it amounted to a veritable Red Ponzi. That's the real menace.

If a prospective President Trump wants to shut it down, he need not appoint Carl Icahn as the nation's chief trade negotiator or even bother with dumping the TPP or reforming the WTO (World Trade Organization). He only needs to tell the Fed to get its foot off the neck of U.S. savers and retirees and allow U.S. dollar interest rates to rise to market-clearing levels.

That would also clear out the Red Ponzi in a New York minute, and start the world on the long path back to capitalist prosperity.

SOMETHING ROTTEN IN THE STATE OF DENMARK

But as of now, there is something really rotten in the state of Denmark. And we are not talking just about the hapless socialist utopia on the Jutland Peninsula—even if it does strip assets from homeless refugees, charge savers 75 basis points for the deposit privilege and allocate nearly 60% of its GDP to the welfare state and its untoward ministrations.

In fact, the rot is planetary owing to the crack-up boom described above. At this late stage of the great credit deformation there is unaccountable, implausible, wacko-world stuff going on everywhere, but the frightful part is that most of it goes unremarked or is viewed as par for the course by the mainstream narrative.

The topic at hand, therefore, is the looming implosion of China's Red Ponzi, and, more specifically, the preposterous Wall Street and Washington presumption that it's just another really big economy that overdid the "growth" thing and is now looking to Beijing's firm hand to effect a smooth transition. That is, an orderly migration from a manufacturing, export and fixed-investment boom land to a pleasant new regime of shopping, motoring and mass consumption.

Would that it could. But China is not a $10 trillion growth miracle with transition challenges; it is a quasi-totalitarian nation gone mad digging, building, borrowing, spending and speculating in a magnitude that has no historical parallel.

In so doing, It has fashioned itself into an incendiary volcano of unpayable debt and wasteful, crazy-ass overinvestment in everything. It cannot be slowed, stabilized or transitioned by edicts and new plans from the comrades in Beijing. It is the greatest economic train wreck in human history barreling toward a bridgeless chasm.

And that proposition makes all the difference in the world. If China goes down hard the global economy cannot avoid a thundering financial and macroeconomic dislocation—and not just because China accounts for 17% of the world's $80 trillion of GDP or because it has been the planet's growth engine most of this century.

In fact, China is the rotten epicenter of the world's two-decade-long plunge into an immense central bank–fostered monetary fraud and credit explosion that has deformed and destabilized the very warp and woof of the global economy.

But in China the financial madness has gone to a unfathomable extreme because in the early 1990s a desperate oligarchy of despots who ruled with machine guns discovered a better means to stay in power: that is, the printing press in the basement of the PBOC—and just in the nick of time (for them).

Print they did. As indicated above, they bought in dollars, euros and other currencies hand over fist in order to peg their own money and lubricate Mr. Deng's export factories.

In so doing, the PBOC expanded its balance sheet from $40 billion to $4 trillion during the course of a mere two decades. That's a 100X gain. There is nothing like that in the history of central banking—nor even in economists' most febrile imaginings about its possibilities.

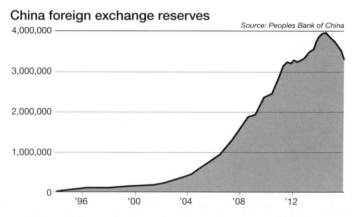

China foreign exchange reserves
Source: Peoples Bank of China

The PBOC's red-hot printing press, in turn, emitted high-powered credit fuel. In the mid-1990s China had about $500 billion of public and private credit outstanding—hardly 1X its rickety GDP. Today that number is $30 trillion or even more, and 3X the size of its vastly inflated GDP accounts.

Yet nothing in this economic world, or the next, can grow at 60X in only 20 years and live to tell about it—and most especially not that treacherous economic commodity called debt. And even more especially, not in a system built on a tissue of top-down edicts, illusions, lies and impossibilities, and which sports not even a semblance of financial discipline, political accountability or free public speech.

THE RED PONZI—A WITCH'S BREW OF KEYNES AND LENIN

In short, China is a witch's brew of Keynes and Lenin. It's the financial tempest that will slam the world's great bloated edifice of central bank–fostered faux prosperity.

So the right approach to the horrible danger at hand is not to dissect the pronouncements of Beijing in the manner of the old Kremlinologists. The occupants of the Kremlin were destined to fail in the long run, but they at least knew what they were doing tactically in the here and now. So it was worth the time to parse their word clouds and seating arrangements at state parades.

By contrast, and not to mix a metaphor, the Red suzerains of Beijing have built a Potemkin village economy. But they actually believe it's legitimate because they do not have even a passing acquaintanceship with the requisites and routines of a real capitalist economy.

Ever since the aging oligarchs who run China were delivered from Mao's hideous dystopia by Mr. Deng's chance discovery of printing press prosperity, they have lived in an ever-expanding bubble that is so economically unreal that it would make "The Truman Show" envious. Any rulers with even a modicum of economic literacy would have recognized long ago that the Chinese economy is booby-trapped everywhere with waste, excess and unsustainability.

Here is but one example. Somewhere near Shanghai, credit-crazed developers built a replica of the Pentagon on 100 acres of land. This was not intended as a build-to-lease deal with the People's Liberation Army. It's a shopping mall that apparently has no tenants and no customers!

One of the more accurate things I have ever said is that the United States' Pentagon was built on a swampland of waste. That is, I do take my antistatist viewpoint seriously and therefore firmly believe that the warfare state is every bit as prone to mission creep and the prodigious waste of societal resources as is the welfare state and the bailout-breeding backrooms of Washington.

But America's Pentagon at least has a public purpose and would return some benefit to society were its mission to be shrunk to honestly defend the homeland. By contrast, China's "Pentagon" gives waste an altogether-new definition.

Projects like the above—and China is crawling with them—are a screaming marker of an economic doomsday machine. They bespeak an inherently unsustainable and unstable simulacrum of capitalism where the purpose of credit is to fund state-mandated GDP quotas, not finance efficient investments with calculable risks and returns.

Accordingly, the outward forms of capitalism are belied by the substance of statist control and central planning. For example, there is no legitimate banking system in China—just giant state bureaus posing as super-banks that are effectively run by party operatives.

Their modus operandi amounts to parceling out quotas for national GDP and credit growth from the top, and then water falling them down a vast chain of command to the counties, townships and villages below.

There have never been any legitimate financial prices in China. All interest rates and foreign exchange (FX) rates have been pegged and regulated to the decimal point; nor has there ever been any honest financial accounting either—bank loans have been perpetual options to extend and pretend.

And needless to say, there is no system of financial discipline based on contract law. China's GDP has grown by $10 trillion dollars during this century alone—that is, there has been a boom across the land that makes the California gold rush appear pastoral by comparison.

Yet in all that frenzied prospecting there have allegedly been almost no mistakes, busted camps, empty pans or even personal bankruptcies. When something has occasionally gone wrong with an "investment," the prospectors have gathered in noisy crowds on the streets and pounded their pans for relief—a courtesy that the regime has invariably granted.

Indeed, the Red Ponzi makes Wall Street look like an ethical-improvement society. Developers there built an entire $50 billion replica of Manhattan Island near the port city of Tianjin—complete with its own Rockefeller Center and Twin Towers.

But the developers of this marvel neglected to tell their lenders and investors that no one lives there. Not even bankers!

CHINA'S MASSIVE WHITE ELEPHANT—1.4 BILLION TONS OF STEEL CAPACITY

Stated differently, even at the peak of recent financial bubbles in London, NYC, Miami or Houston they did not build such monuments to sheer economic waste and capital destruction. But just consider the case of China's mammoth steel industry.

Annual production grew from about 70 million tons in the early 1990s
to 825 million tons in 2014. Beyond that 12X gain, it is the capacity build-up
behind the chart below that tells the full story.

To wit, Beijing's tsunami of cheap credit enabled China's state-owned
steel companies to build new capacity at an even more fevered pace than
the breakneck growth of annual production. Consequently, annual crude-
steel capacity now stands at nearly 1.4 billion tons, and nearly all of that
capacity—about 65% of the world total—was built in the last 10 years.

Needless to say, it's a sheer impossibility to expand efficiently the
heaviest of heavy industries by 17X in a quarter century. And especially so
when, as outlined below, China's long-run sustainable demand for steel is
on the order of 400 million tons, or one-third of its current capacity.

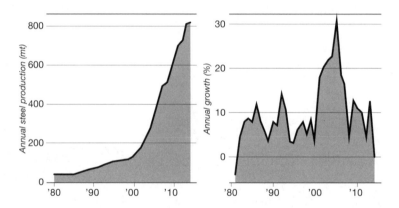

Indeed, what actually happened is that China's aberrantly massive
steel industry temporarily created a significant increment of demand for
its own products.

That is, in order to build up 1.4 billion tons of capacity, it needed massive amounts of plate, structural and other steel shapes that go into blast
furnaces, basic-oxygen-furnace works, rolling mills, fabrication plants and
iron-ore loading and storage facilities. It also needed enormous amounts
of plate and other steel products to expand shipyards where new bulk
carriers were built and also for the huge amounts of equipment and infrastructure used at the iron-ore mines and ports.

That is to say, the Chinese steel industry has been chasing its own tail, but the merry-go-round has now finally stopped. For the first time in three decades, steel production in 2015 was down 2–3% from 2014's peak of 825 million tons and is projected to drop to 750 million tons next year, even by the lights of the China miracle believers.

MASSIVE MALINVESTMENT AND AN EPIC IMPENDING MARGIN CALL

In short, the flip side of the China's giant credit bubble was the most massive malinvestment of real economic resources—labor, raw materials and capital goods—ever known. Effectively, the countryside pig sties have been piled high with copper inventories and the urban neighborhoods with glass, cement and rebar towers that can't possibly earn an economic return, but all of which has become "collateral" for even more "loans" under the Red Ponzi.

So China has been on a wild tear heading straight for the economic edge of the planet—that is, monetary terra incognita—based on the circular principle of borrowing, building and borrowing, and then even more building and borrowing. In essence, it is a giant rehypothecation scheme where every borrower's "debt" becomes the next investor's "asset."

Local city and county governments, for example, have meager incomes, but vastly bloated debts based on the collateral of stupendously overvalued inventories of land—valuations that were established by earlier debt-financed sales to developers.

Likewise, coal-mine entrepreneurs face not only collapsing prices and revenues, but also soaring double-digit interest rates on shadow-banking loans collateralized by overvalued coal reserves. Shipyards have empty order books, but vast debts collateralized by soon-to-be-idle construction bays.

So too, commodity speculators have collateralized massive stockpiles of copper and iron ore at prices that are already becoming ancient history.

So China is on the cusp of the greatest margin call in history. Once asset values start falling, its pyramids of debt will stand exposed to withering performance failures and meltdowns. Undoubtedly the regime will struggle to keep its printing press prosperity alive for another few months or quarters, but the fractures are now gathering everywhere because the credit rampage has been too extreme and hideous.

It is downright foolish, therefore, to claim that the U.S. economy is decoupled from China and the rest of the world. In fact, it is inextricably bound to the global financial bubble and its leading edge in the form of Red Capitalism.

WHY THE CHINA BUBBLE IS GLOBAL

Bubble vision's endlessly repeated mantra that China doesn't matter because U.S. exports to it account for less than 1% of GDP is a non sequitur. It does not require astute observation, for example, to recognize that Caterpillar did not export its giant mining equipment just to China; massive amounts of it went there indirectly by way of Australia's booming iron-ore provinces—that is, until the global CapEx bust was triggered by two years of crumbling commodity prices. Caterpillar's monthly retail sales reports, in fact, are a slow motion record of this unprecedented crash.

Overall, Caterpillar's global retail sales posted a massive 16% drop at the end of 2015 compared to the prior year—a result tied for the worst annual decline since the financial crisis. And that came on top of the 12% decline the prior year, another 9% drop in 2013 and a 1% decline in 2012.

Moreover, four consecutive years of declines is not simply a Caterpillar market-share or product-cycle matter. Its major Asian rivals have experienced even larger sales declines. Komatsu is down, for example, by 80% from its peak sales levels.

In the heavy-machinery sector, therefore, the global CapEx depression is already well underway. There has been nothing comparable to this persisting plunge since the 1930s.

Likewise, the United States did not export oil to China, but China's vast, credit-inflated demand on the world market did artificially lift world oil prices above $100 per barrel, thereby touching off the U.S. shale boom that is now crashing in Texas, North Dakota, Oklahoma and three other states. And the fact is, every net new job created in the United States since 2008 is actually in these same six shale states.

Caterpillar dealer retail sales

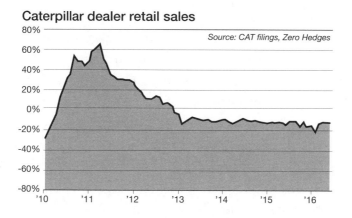

Source: CAT filings, Zero Hedges

Indeed, the rot that was introduced into the global economy by the world's convoy of money-printing central banks extends into nearly unimaginable places, owing to the false bubble prices for crude oil, copper, iron ore, aluminum, nickel and countless other raw materials that were temporarily inflated by the global credit boom.

Indeed, the deformation spread like a tidal wave across the entire planet. Notwithstanding a 33% increase in oil exports last year, Iraq is now so broke, for example, that it is petitioning the IMF for a bailout. Yet as recently as a year ago plans were proceeding apace to build the world tallest building at its oil-country center at Basra.

That right. The Bride of the Gulf now has tin cup in hand and is heading for an IMF rescue. The monstrosity below will likely never be built, but it does succinctly symbolize the trillions that have been wasted around the world by lucky reserve-owning companies and countries during the false boom that emanated from the Red Ponzi.

The planned Bride of the Gulf building in Basra, at a height of 1,152 meters would outdistance even the Jeddah Tower being built in Saudi Arabia.

Similarly, U.S. exports to Europe have tripled to nearly $1 trillion annually since 1998, while European exports to China have more than quintupled. Might there possibly be some linkages?

In short, there is an economic and financial train wreck rumbling through the world economy called the Red Ponzi. In all of economic history there has never been anything like it. It is only a matter of time before it ends in a spectacular collapse, leaving the global financial bubble of the last two decades in shambles.

So forget the orderly-transition myth. What happens when the iron-ore ports go quiet, the massive copper stockpiles on the pig farms are liquidated, the coal country turns desolate, the cement trucks are parked in endless rows, the giant steel furnaces are banked, huge car plants are idled and tens of billions of bribes emitted by the building boom dry up?

What happens is that giant economic cavities open up throughout the length and breadth of the Red Ponzi.

Industrial profits as a whole are already down 5% on a year-over-year basis, but in the leading sectors have already turned into red ink. In a few quarters China's business sector, in fact, will be in the throes of a massive profits contraction and crisis.

Likewise, tens of millions of high-paying industrial and construction jobs, and the consumer-spending power they financed, will vanish. Also, the value of 65 million empty apartment units that had been preposterously kept vacant as a distorted form of investment speculation will plunge in value, wiping out a huge chunk of the so-called savings of China's newly emergent affluent classes.

So where are all the promised new consumers of services supposed to come from? After Peak Debt and the crash of China's vast malinvestments, there will be no surplus income to recycle.

Most importantly, as the post-boom economic cavities spread in cancer-like fashion and the crescendo of financial turmoil intensifies, the credibility of the regime will be thoroughly undermined. Capital flight will become an unstoppable tidal wave as the people watch Beijing lurch from one make-do fix and gimmick to the next, as they have during the stock market fiasco of the past two years.

In short, China will eventually crash into economic and civil disorder when the Red suzerains go full retard with governance by paddy wagons, show trials, brutal suppression of public dissent and a return to Chairman Mao's gun barrel as the ultimate source of Communist Party power

Self-evidently, the Maoist form of rule did not work. But what is now becoming evident is that Mr. Deng's printing press has a "sell by" date too.

RED PONZI LURCHING

The specious notion that the rules of Beijing can deliver a soft landing has been refuted time after time in recent months by spasms of disorder and dysfunction. These events and symptoms are intensifying, and self-evidently can't be patched over with expedients and new credit infusions indefinitely.

One night in February 2016, for example, the red-chip casino took another one of its patented 6.5% belly flops. In fact, more than 1,300 stocks in Shanghai and Shenzhen fell by 10%—the maximum drop permitted by regulators in one day—implying that the real decline was far deeper.

That renewed carnage was the worst since, well, the prior 6% drop in late January. It also meant that the cumulative meltdown from the June 2015 stock market high was pushing 45% or nearly $4 trillion.

Moreover, this red-chip mayhem did not come at an especially propitious moment for the regime, as the *Wall Street Journal* explained:

> It comes at an awkward moment for the Chinese government, which is hosting the world's leading central bankers and finance ministers starting Friday. China has been expected to use the G-20 meeting to address global anxiety about its economy and financial markets. Worries about China's economic slowdown and the volatility of its markets have weighed on investment decisions around the world.

But if we are remarking on "awkward," here's awkward. The G-20 central bankers, finance ministers and IMF apparatchiks who descended on Shanghai in late February should have taken an unfiltered, eyes-wide-open view of the Red Ponzi fracturing all about them, and then made a petrified mad dash back to their own respective capitals. There was nothing more for the G-20 to talk about with respect to China except how to get out of harm's way, fast.

In fact, China is a monumental doomsday machine that bears no more resemblance to anything that could be called stable, sustainable capitalism than did Lenin's New Economic Policy of the early 1920s. The latter was followed by Stalin's gulag and it would be wise to learn the Chinese word for the same, and soon.

The regime is in a horrendous bind because it has played out the greatest credit spree in world history. As we indicated above, this cycle of undisciplined, debt-fueled digging, building, spending and speculating ballooned its collective debt balance by a 60X gain in debt over just two decades in an "economy" that has no legitimate honest financial markets, no legal system and no tradition of bankruptcy and financial discipline.

Its banking system that functions as an arm of the state, cascading credit down from the top in order to "print" an exact amount of GDP each month on the theory that anything that can be built should be built in order to hit Beijing's targets.

If an economy and its ruling regime were an animate being you could call it a "fatal addiction" and be done with it. These folks are on the deadliest strain of financial heroin known to mankind and have no chance of surviving; it's a dead economy walking.

Look no further than the hideous debt gains reported for the early months this year. Total social financing rose at a $6 trillion annualized rate, or by 55% of GDP. And that was on top of the tottering $30 trillion debt tower it already had.

By now China's businesses—especially the giant state-owned enterprises—are drowning in excess capacity and unpayable debt that amounts to upward of 180% of GDP (compared to 70% in the United States). But never mind. New loans to the business sector were up by 73% over the prior year.

Worse still, it is evident that a high share of the lunatic rate of credit expansion in early 2016 was devoted to paying interest on the existing monumental debts of China's businesses and so-called local-government financing vehicles.

Even the Beijing authorities concede that more than 60% of new debt issuance in recent years has been used to pay interest. They are chasing their tail ever more furiously; they are strapped on to a debt whirligig they can't and won't get off . . . until it finally explodes.

In truth, China's economy is no more efficient, productive, stable or prosperous than was Stalin's five-year-plan GDP. The latter, by the way, grew at fully double-digit rates the West envied for more than a decade during the 1930s.

The only difference is that the Red suzerains of Beijing seem to have learned about the advantages of using a printing press and "bankers" to carry out their central-planning schemes rather than tonnage quotas and commissars; and also that swapping quasi-slave labor in their export factories for IOUs from its customers in the United States and Europe could temporarily relieve the misery and poverty that Mao had consigned to the hundreds of millions trapped in China's collectivist rice paddies.

Needless to say, having built a massive Potemkin economy, China's rulers have no clue about how to contain the incendiary pressures that are now building to the ignition point.

Indeed, there are no possible economic mechanisms or even viable half-assed statist schemes to stabilize the $30 trillion mountain of debt that sits precariously on its fracturing hothouse economy, or to relieve it of its fatal debt addiction. So Beijing will soon have no alternative but to rule by the brute force of paddy wagons and even firing squads.

The days during which a giant daisy chain of ever-inflating lending and spending was raising all boats is over and done. There is nothing ahead except a collapsing credit bubble that will be sinking the great Red Ponzi boat and its 1.3 billion passengers—and along with it, a worldwide

economy and financial system afflicted with the kind of plenary misrule
that was recently brought to Shanghai by the G-20.

A POTEMKIN ECONOMY BURIED IN CEMENT

No wonder the Red Ponzi consumed more cement during three years (2011–
13) than did the United States during the entire 20th century. Enabled by
an endless flow of credit from its state-controlled banking apparatus and its
shadow-banking affiliates, China went berserk building factories, warehouses,
ports, office towers, malls, apartments, roads, airports, train stations, high-
speed railways, stadiums, monumental public buildings and much more.

If you want an analogy, the 6.6 gigatons of cement consumed by China
during 2011–13 was the equivalent of 14.5 trillion pounds. By comparison,
the Hoover Dam used about 1.8 billion pounds of cement.

So in three years China consumed enough cement to build the Hoover
Dam 8,000 times over—160 of them for every state in the union!

China used more cement in the last three years than the U.S. used in the entire 20th century.

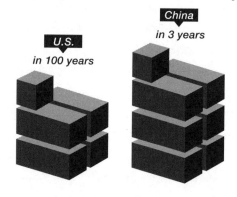

Having spent recent time in China, I can well and truly say that the
Middle Kingdom is back. But its leitmotif is the very opposite to the splendor
of the Forbidden City.

The Middle Kingdom has been reborn in towers of preformed concrete. They rise in there tens of thousands in every direction on the horizon. They are connected with ribbons of highways that are scalloped and

molded to wind through the endless forest of concrete verticals. Some of them are occupied. A lot, not.

The "before" and "after" contrast of Shanghai's famous Pudong waterfront is illustrative of the illusion.

The top picture on the next page is from about 1990, at a time before Mr. Deng discovered the printing press in the basement of the People's Bank of China and proclaimed that it is glorious to be rich and that if you were 18 and still in full possession of your digital dexterity and visual acuity it was even more glorious to work 12 hours per day six days per week in an export factory for 35 cents per hour.

Whether or not this image is precisely accurate as to vintage, by all accounts the glitzy skyscrapers of today's Pudong waterfront did ascend during the last 25 years from a rundown, dimly lit area of muddy streets on the east side of Huangpu River. The pictured area was apparently shunned by all except the most destitute of Mao's proletariat.

But the second picture I can vouch for. It's exactly what you see from the Peninsula Hotel on the Bund, which lies directly across on the west side of the Huangpu River.

Today's Pudong district does look spectacular—presumably a 21st-century rendition of the glory of the Qing, the Ming, the Soong, the Tang and the Han—all rolled into one.

But to conclude that would be to be deceived. The apparent prosperity is not that of a sustainable economic miracle; it's the front street of the greatest Potemkin village in world history.

The heart of the matter is that output measured by Keynesian GDP accounting—especially China's blatantly massaged variety—isn't sustainable wealth if it is not rooted in real savings, efficient capital allocation and future productivity growth. Nor does construction and investment that does not earn back its cost of capital over time contribute to the accumulation of real wealth.

Needless to say, China's construction and "investment" binge manifestly does not meet these criteria in the slightest. It was funded with credit manufactured by state-controlled banks and their shadow affiliates, not real savings.

It was driven by state-initiated growth plans and GDP targets. These were cascaded from the top down to the province-, county- and local-government levels—an economic process that is the opposite of entrepreneurial at-risk assessments of future market-based demand and profits.

China's own GDP statistics are the smoking gun. During the last 15 years fixed-asset investment—in private business, state companies, households and the "public sector" combined—has averaged 50% of GDP. That's per se crazy.

Even in the heyday of its 1960s and 1970s boom, Japan's fixed-asset investment never reached more than 30% of GDP. Moreover, even that was not sustained year in and year out (they had three recessions), and Japan had at least a semblance of market pricing and capital allocation—unlike China's virtual command-and-control economy.

A CREDIT-DRIVEN MADHOUSE

The reason that Wall Street analysts and fellow-traveling Keynesian economists miss the latter point entirely is because China's state-driven economy works through credit allocation rather than by tonnage-toting commissars.

The Gosplan is implemented by the banking system and, increasingly, through China's mushrooming and metastasizing shadow-banking sector. The latter amounts to trillions of credit potted in entities that have sprung up to evade the belated growth controls that the regulators have imposed on the formal banking system.

For example, Beijing tried to cool down the residential real estate boom by requiring 30% down payments on first mortgages and by virtually eliminating mortgage finance on second homes and investment properties. So between 2013 and the present more than 2,500 online peer-to-peer lending outfits (P2P) materialized—mostly funded or sponsored by the banking system—and these entities have advanced more than $2 trillion of new credit.

That's right. A new $2 trillion credit channel erected virtually overnight.

The overwhelming share went into meeting "down payments" and other real estate speculations. On the one hand, that reignited the real estate bubble—especially in the Tier I cities where prices have risen by 20% to 60% during the last year.

At the same time, this P2P credit eruption in the shadow-banking system has encouraged the construction of even more excess housing stock in an economy that already has upward of 65 million empty units.

In short, China has become a credit-driven economic madhouse. The 50% of GDP attributable to fixed-asset investment actually constitutes the most spectacular spree of malinvestment and waste in recorded history. It is the footprint of a future depression, not evidence of sustainable growth and prosperity.

Consider a boundary-case analogy. With enough fiat credit during the last three years, the United States could have duplicated China's cement-consumption spree and built 160 Hoover Dams on dry land in each and every state.

That would have elicited one hellacious boom in the jobs market, gravel pits, cement-truck assembly plants, pipe and tube mills, architectural and engineering offices and so on. The profits and wages from that dam-building boom, in turn, would have generated a secondary cascade of even more phony "growth."

But at some point, the credit expansion would stop. The demand for construction materials, labor, machinery and support services would dry up; the negative multiplier on incomes, spending and investment would kick in; and the depression phase of a crack-up boom would exact its drastic revenge.

In fact, that's exactly the kind of crack-up boom that has been underway in China for the last two decades. Accordingly, it is not simply a little overdone, and it's not in some Keynesian transition from exports and investment to domestic services and consumption. Instead, China's fantastically overbuilt industry and public infrastructure embodies monumental economic waste equivalent to the construction of pyramids with shovels and spoons and giant dams on dry land.

When the credit pyramid finally collapses or simply stops growing, of course, the pace of construction will decline dramatically. In turn, as we suggested above, the collapse of its construction boom will leave the Red Ponzi riddled with economic air pockets and negative spending multipliers.

THE MOTHER OF ALL MALINVESTMENTS

Take the simple case of the abandoned cement-mixer plant pictured below. The high wages paid in that abandoned plant are now gone; the owners have undoubtedly fled, and their high-living extravagance is no more. Nor is this factory's demand still extant for steel sheets and plates, freight services, electric power, waste hauling, equipment replacement parts and on down the food chain.

And, no, a wise autocracy in Beijing will not be able to offset the giant deflationary forces now assailing the construction and industrial heartland of China's hothouse economy with massive amounts of new credit to jump-start green industries and neighborhood recreation facilities. That's because China has already shot its credit wad, meaning that every new surge in its banking system will trigger even more capital outflow and expectations of FX depreciation.

Moreover, any increase in fiscal spending not funded by credit expansion will only rearrange the deck chairs on the Titanic.

Indeed, whatever borrowing headroom Beijing has left will be needed to fund the bailouts of its banking and credit system. Without massive outlays for the purpose of propping up and stabilizing China's vast credit Ponzi, there will be economic and social chaos as the tide of defaults and abandonments swells.

Empty factories like the one pictured above—and China is crawling with them—are a screaming marker of an economic doomsday machine. They bespeak an inherently unsustainable and unstable simulacrum of capitalism where the purpose of credit has been to fund state-mandated GDP quotas, not finance efficient investments and future productivity.

The relentless growth of China's aluminum production is just one more example. It now exceeds US output by 10X. So, when China's construction and investment binge finally stops, there will be a huge decline in industry wages, profits and supply-chain activity.

China's unending production of aluminum stamps out U.S.

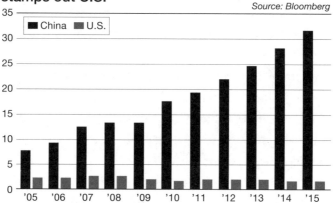

Source: Bloomberg

But the mother of all malinvestments sprang up in China's steel industry, as we outlined above.

And that's where the pyramid-building nature of China's insane fixed-investment spree comes in. China's humungous iron and steel industry is not remotely capable of "rationalization" as practiced historically in the developed-market economies. Even Beijing's much ballyhooed 100–150-million-ton plant closure target is a drop in the bucket—and it's not scheduled to be completed until 2020 anyway.

To wit, China will be lucky to have 400 million tons of true sell-through demand—that is, ongoing domestic demand for sheet steel to go into cars and appliances and for rebar and structural steel to be used in replacement construction once the current one-time building binge finally expires.

For instance, China's construction and shipbuilding industries consumed about 500 million tons per year at the crest of the building boom. But shipyards are already going radio silent and the end of China's manic eruption of concrete, rebar and I-beams is not far behind. Use of steel for these purposes could easily drop to 200 million tons on a steady-state basis.

By contrast, China's vaunted auto industry uses only 45 million tons of steel per year, and consumer appliances consume less than 12 million tons. In most developed economies autos and white goods demand accounts for about 20% of total steel use.

Likewise, much of the current 200 million tons of steel that goes into machinery and equipment, including massive production of mining and construction machines, rail cars and the like, is of a one-time nature and could easily drop to 100 million tons on a steady-state replacement basis.

So it's difficult to see how China will ever have recurring demand for even 400 million tons annually, yet as I indicated above that's less than one-third of its massive capacity investment.

In short, we are talking about wholesale abandonment of a half billion tons of steel capacity or more—that is, the destruction of steel-industry capacity greater than that of Japan, the European Community and the United States combined.

Needless to say, that thunderous liquidation will generate a massive loss of labor income and profits and devastating contraction of the Chinese steel industry's massive and lengthy supply chain. And that's to say nothing of the labor-market disorder and social dislocations that will occur when China is hit by the equivalent of dozens of burned-out Youngstown's and Pittsburgh's.

And it is also evident that it will not be in a position to dump its massive surplus on the rest of the world. Already trade barriers against last year's 110 million tons of exports are being thrown up in Europe, North America, Japan and nearly everywhere else.

This not only means that China's half-billion tons of excess capacity will crush prices and profits, but, more importantly, that the one-time steel demand for steel industry CapEx is over and done. And that means shipyards and mining equipment too.

VANISHING ORDER BOOKS IN CHINA'S GIANT SHIPBUILDING INDUSTRY

That is already evident in the vanishing order book for China's giant shipbuilding industry. The latter is focused almost exclusively on dry-bulk carriers—the very capital item that delivered into China's vast industrial maw the massive tonnages of iron ore, coking coal and other raw materials.

But within in a year or two most of China's shipyards will be closed as its backlog rapidly vanishes under a crushing surplus of dry-bulk capacity that has no precedent, and which has driven the Baltic shipping-rate index to historic lows.

Still, we now have the absurdity of China's state shipping company (COSCO) attempting to compensate for the loss of dry-bulk carrier orders at state-owned shipyards by ordering 11 massive containerships. Yet it can't possibly need this new finished-goods shipping capacity since China's year-to-date exports are down 20% and will be heading lower as the global economy eventually succumbs to outright recession:

> China's waning appetite for raw materials have come around to bite the country's shipbuilders, raising the odds that more shipyards will soon be shuttered.

> About 140 yards in the world's second-biggest shipbuilding nation have gone out of business since 2010, and more are expected to close in the next two years after only 69 won orders for vessels last year, JPMorgan Chase & Co. analysts Sokje Lee and Minsung Lee wrote in a January report. That compares with 126 shipyards that fielded orders in 2014 and 147 in 2013.

> Total orders at Chinese shipyards tumbled 59 percent in the first 11 months of 2015, according to data released Dec. 15 by the China Association of the National Shipbuilding Industry. Builders have sought government support as excess vessel capacity drives down shipping rates and prompts customers to cancel contracts. Zhoushan Wuzhou Ship Repairing & Building Co. last month became the first state-owned shipbuilder to go bankrupt in a decade.

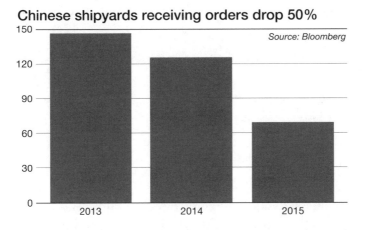

Chinese shipyards receiving orders drop 50%

Source: Bloomberg

It is not surprising that China's massive shipbuilding industry is in distress and that it is attempting to export its troubles to the rest of the world. Yet subsidizing new builds will eventually add more downward pressure to global shipping rates—rates that are already at all-time lows. And as the world's shipping companies are driven into insolvency, they will take the European banks that have financed them down the drink, as well.

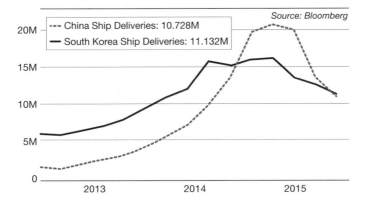

Source: Bloomberg

- - - China Ship Deliveries: 10.728M
— South Korea Ship Deliveries: 11.132M

Still, the fact that China is exporting yet-another downward deflationary spiral to the world economy is not at all surprising. After all, China's shipbuilding output rose by 11X in 10 years!

MADNESS IN THE AUTO ZONE TOO

Nor is the loss of its own tail the only market shrinkage facing China's core steel industry. Even more fantastic has been the growth of China's auto-production capacity. In 1994, China produced about 1.4 million units of what were bare-bones Communist-era cars and trucks. Last year it produced more than 23 million mostly western-style vehicles, or 16X more.

And yes, that wasn't the half of it. China has gone nuts building auto plants and distribution infrastructure. It is currently estimated to have upward of 33 million units of vehicle-production capacity. But demand has actually flattened and will likely head lower after temporary government-tax gimmicks—which are simply pulling forward future sales—expire.

The more important point, however, is that as the China credit Ponzi grinds to a halt, it will not be building new auto capacity for years to come. It is now drowning in excess capacity, and as prices and profits plunge in the years ahead the auto industry CapEx spigot will be slammed shut. too.

Needless to say, this not only means that consumption of structural steel and rebar for new auto plants will plunge. It also will result in a drastic reduction in demand for the sophisticated German machine tools and automation equipment needed to actually build cars.

Stated differently, the CapEx depression already underway in China, Australia, Brazil and much of the emerging markets will ricochet across the global economy. Cheap credit and mispriced capital are truly the father of a thousand economic sins.

HERE COME THE PADDY WAGONS

The worst thing is that just as the Red Ponzi is beginning to crack, China's leader is rolling out the paddy wagons and reestablishing a cult of the leader that more and more resembles nothing so much as a Maoist revival.

As Mr. Xi said while making the rounds of the state media recently, its job is to

> reflect the will of the Party, mirror the views of the Party, preserve the authority of the Party, preserve the unity of the Party and achieve love of the Party, protection of the Party and acting for the Party.

The above proclamation needs no amplification. China will increasingly plunge into a regime of harsh, capricious dictatorship as the Red depression unfolds. And that will only fuel the downward spiral that is already gathering momentum.

During the first eight months of 2016, for example, China's export machine has buckled badly. Exports are now down 20% year over year and show no signs of reviving.

Likewise, local economies in its growing rust belt, such as parts of Heilongjiang, in far-northeast China, have dropped by 20% in the last two years and are still in free fall. Coal prices in those areas have plunged by 65% since 2011 and hundreds of mines have been closed or abandoned.

The next picture below is epigrammatic of what lies behind the great Potemkin village that is the Red Ponzi.

While pictures can often tell a thousand words, sooner or later the numbers are no less revealing. The fact is, no economy can undergo the fantastic eruption of credit that has occurred in China during the last two decades without eventually coming face-to-face with a day of reckoning. And a Bloomberg analysis of the shocking deterioration of credit metrics in the nonfinancial sector of China suggests that day is coming fast.

THE COMING DEBT-SERVICE CRUNCH IN THE BUSINESS SECTOR

Overall interest-expense coverage by operating income has plunged dramatically, and virtually every major heavy industrial sector of the Red Ponzi is underwater with a coverage ratio of less than 1X.

But that's not the half of it. What is evident from the following Bloomberg data below is that the overwhelming share of this year's massive new corporate borrowings are being allocated to pay interest on existing debt because debt service is not being covered by current operating profits.

> Firms generated just enough operating profit to cover the interest expenses on their debt twice, down from almost six times in 2010, according to data compiled by Bloomberg going back to 1992 from nonfinancial companies traded in Shanghai and Shenzhen. Oil and gas corporates were the weakest at 0.24X, followed by the metals and mining sector at 0.52X.

> The People's Bank of China has lowered benchmark interest rates six times since 2014, driving a record rally in the bond market and underpinning a jump in debt to 247 percent of gross domestic product. Yet economic growth has slumped to the slowest in a quarter century and profits for the listed companies grew only 3 percent in 2015, down from 11 percent in 2014. "We will likely see a wave of bankruptcies and restructurings when the interest coverage ratio drops further," said Xia Le, chief economist for Asia at Banco Bilbao Vizcaya Argentaria SA in Hong Kong.

Massive borrowing to pay the interest is everywhere and always a sign that the end is near. The crack-up phase of China's insane borrowing and building boom is surely at hand.

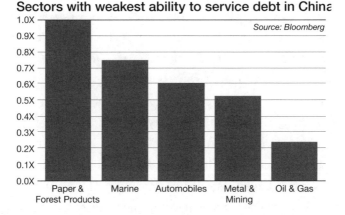

Sectors with weakest ability to service debt in China

Source: Bloomberg

Another warning sign of this dead end is found in the "payables stretches" now happening throughout the Red Ponzi. Struggling under $30 trillion of unpayable financial debt accrued during what amounts to a historical heartbeat of frenzied borrowing, China's businesses are now coping with the inexorable morning-after deflation by means of a time-tested maneuver of last resort.

To wit, they are attempting to pay their bankers by stiffing their suppliers.

As shown below, payables now average an incredible 192 days in China's business system. And that's why its whole house of cards is likely to collapse with a bang, not a Beijing-managed whimper.

At some point, this daisy chain of billions of unpaid claims will far exceed even the capacity of China's state-deputized bankers and its growing fleet of paddy wagons to keep in line.

Indeed, this surge in payables has two untoward implications. The first is that the myth of Beijing's capacity for omniscient and unfailing economic governance will be shattered. All along, it has been a case of mistaken identity—a failure by Wall Street propagandists of "growth" to understand that doling out trillions of credit through a state-controlled banking system merely funds recordable spending and delivers fixed assets; it does not generate efficient growth or sustainable wealth.

But the Red suzerains of Beijing are already proving in spades that when the music of credit expansion finally must stop, they will have no clue about what to do or capacity to execute if they did. In that respect, it now appears that in the first quarter China's banking system generated new credit at an annual rate of nearly 40% of GDP.

In turn, China's so-called "iron rooster" was given a new lease on life as a result of even more artificial demand for capital investment and infrastructure that is already massively overbuilt. Accordingly, during March, China's steel production hit an all-time high, causing prices to temporarily rise and closed mills to reopen.

So much for the credit restraint promised by China's central bank and for the 150 million tons of capacity closures announced by the apparatchiks in Beijing a few months back. In latching itself to Mr. Deng's printing presses, the Chinese Communist Party made a pact with the financial devil. But now it is far too late to stop the Ponzi, meaning that another central bank–driven debt implosion is fully scheduled and waiting to happen.

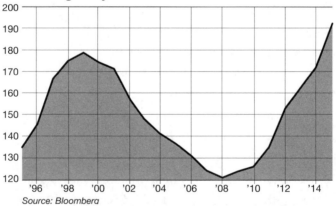

Record high days for China Inc. to convert cash

Source: Bloomberg

GAMBLING LIKE NEVER BEFORE IN THE RED CASINO—ITS BALEFUL GLOBAL IMPLICATIONS

In the heyday of its incredible credit and construction boom, China was building two world-scale utility plants each week and opening up a new airport every day. Economic-fiction writers like Goldman's Jim O'Neill, chief propagator of the BRICs myth, declared the Red Ponzi to be the very Second Coming of capitalism.

Now, by contrast, a Chinese billionaire goes missing practically every day, as a recent *Washington Post* article explained:

> That's what happened last year when China's richest man—at least on paper—lost half of his wealth in less than half an hour. It turned out that his company Hanergy may well just be Enron with Chinese characteristics: Its stock could only go up as long as it was borrowing money, and it could only borrow money as long as its stock was going up. Those kind of things work until they don't.

The gentleman in question, Li Hejun, has had quite the financial spill. About 500 days ago in April 2015, according to Forbes, he was worth $32.7 billion. Then on May 20 last year, when the stock of Hanergy Thin Film Power Group (HTF), in which he had a 81% stake, plunged by 47%, $14 billion of that disappeared in minutes. And since then, all the rest of it has vaporized as well.

Our purpose here is not to jitterbug on the corpse of another riches-to-rags story from the Red Ponzi. The fact is, Li Hejun and his Hanergy caper is China writ large.

Like Hanergy, China is an incendiary cauldron of financial madness that is destined to have a spectacular demise. And it will take the global economy and the gambling dens of Wall Street, London, Tokyo and the rest down with it.

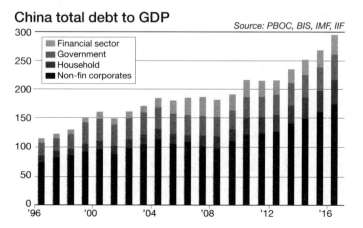

China total debt to GDP

Source: PBOC, BIS, IMF, IIF

Yet the punters continue to frolic in the shallow waters of the market's daily chart-driven undulations, as if oblivious to the great Red Shark fast approaching. Then again, having missed Fannie Mae, Freddie Mac, Lehman and AIG there is apparently no sign obvious enough to empty the financial beaches in a world of central bank–driven Bubble Finance.

Still, consider a little more detail about the Hanergy caper because it represents not an extreme outlier, but the actual central tendency of the Red Ponzi. The *Washington Post* account summarizes the pure madness as well as can be done whilst keeping a straight face:

> The first thing to know about Hanergy is that it's really two compa-
> nies. There's the privately owned parent corporation Hanergy Group,
> and the publicly traded subsidiary Hanergy Thin Film Power (HTF).
> The latter, believe it or not, started out as a toymaker, somehow
> switched over to manufacturing solar panel parts, and was then
> bought by Hanergy Chairman Li Hejun. And that's when things re-
> ally got strange. The majority of HTF's sales, you see, were to its
> now-parent company Hanergy—and supposedly at a 50 percent net
> profit margin!—but it wasn't actually getting paid, you know, money
> for them. It was just racking up receivables. Why? Well, the question
> answers itself. Hanergy must not have had the cash to pay HTF. Its
> factories were supposed to be putting solar panels together out of
> the parts it was getting from HTF, but they were barely running—if
> at all. Hedge-fund manager John Hempton didn't see anything going
> on at the one he paid a surprise visit to last year. It's hard to make
> money if you're not making things to sell.
>
> But it's a lot easier to borrow money and pretend that you're making
> it. At least as long as you have the collateral to do so—which Ha-
> nergy did when HTF's stock was shooting up. Indeed, it increased
> 20-fold from the start of 2013 to the middle of 2015.

And then it came crashing back to earth on May 20 when the ruse got exposed. That is, its market cap had gone from $5 billion to $42 billion in about five months, and then it was all given back in five minutes.

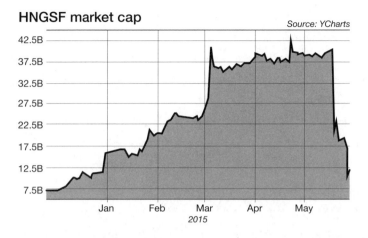

HNGSF market cap

Source: YCharts

In fact, the company presently has no market cap at all. It has been "suspended" from trading since last summer.

Nevertheless, it is not just the the phony 8X gain at the beginning of 2015 that reveals the incendiary underside of the Red Ponzi. The more fantastic side of the story is how this stock was levitated by upward of $35 billion in such a brief span of time.

As the *Washington Post* story further explained, it all happened in the last 10 minutes of trading every day!

> Suppose you'd bought $1,000 of HTF stock every morning at 9 a.m. and sold it every afternoon at 3:30 p.m. from the beginning of 2013 to 2015. How much would you have made? Well, according to the *Financial Times*, the answer is nothing. You would have lost $365. If you'd waited until 3:50 p.m. to sell, though, that would have turned into a $285 gain. And if you'd been a little more patient and held on to the stock till the 4 p.m. close, you would have come out $7,430 ahead. (Those numbers don't include the stock's overnight changes).

That's some pattern. And there's almost no way it could have been the result of chance. The most reasonable explanation is that someone was deliberately moving the stock up and up so that he could borrow more and more against it. Nobody knows who was behind it—at least not yet, but it's clear who benefited from high share prices the most: Hanergy Chairman Li Hejun.

It turns out that China's very richest man at the time was posting his HTF shares as collateral for loans from the giant state-owned banks and shadow-banking lenders.

He did some of it through offshore subsidiaries, but when even that loan gravy train ran out there was no place to hide. Lenders were forced to sell the company's shares that had been pledged for the loans, and in a matter of minutes the stock crashed and was subsequently suspended.

As the *Post* finally explained,

> there isn't much of a company left. HTF has lost four times as much money as it's taken in over the past year, it can't even pay the rent for all of its offices, let alone its bonds, and Li just unloaded some of his shares on the private market for 97 percent less than they were worth at their peak.

We have contended that China's so-called banking system is just an extension of the Beijing-based state command-and-control machinery. It has virtually nothing to do with legitimate banking, and, in fact, is just a giant financial waterfall through which fiat credit is sluiced into the economy on a top-down basis.

Surely, the billions that were being pumped into the Hanergy Ponzi—in the face of what even a lending-officer trainee could see was a stock-rigging operation—leaves no other conclusion.

In fact, the parallel surge of the Shanghai stock market during approximately the same period was funded in exactly the same manner. During the period between July 2014 and June 2015, when the Shanghai index soared by 150%, margin lending exploded from $100 billion to $500 billion.

Relatively to China's ostensible GDP, that was in the same ballpark as the eruption of margin lending that preceded the 1929 stock crash in New York.

Indeed, at the peak of the stock frenzy last June, Chinese gamblers had opened 389 million stock-trading accounts—one for every man, woman and child in America with 60 million left over. And on top of conventional broker margin loans, the number of online P2P-lending operations had surged, as discussed above, from 100 in 2013 to upward of 2,500 by last year.

The point is, after $30 trillion of debt issuance in less than two decades China has turned itself into a giant mob of speculators and gamblers.

The place is dangerous, and not because it bought a rusted-out used aircraft carrier from the Ukraine a few years back, and not because it cheats in world trade, as The Donald so loudly and correctly insists.

The Red Ponzi threatens the world by virtue of a printing press that is so white hot that an implosion that will shake the global financial system is only a matter of when, not if.

CHAPTER 19:

The Apotheosis of Bubble Finance— the Coming Crash of Tesla and the FANGs

THE INEXORABLE EFFECT OF CONTEMPORARY CENTRAL BANKING IS SERIAL financial booms and busts. With that comes increasing levels of systemic financial instability and a growing dissipation of real economic resources in misallocations and malinvestment.

At length, the world becomes poorer.

Why? Because gains in real output and wealth depend upon efficient pricing of capital and savings, but the modus operandi of today's central banking is to deliberately distort and relentlessly falsify financial prices.

As we have seen, the essence of ZIRP and NIRP is to drive interest rates below their natural market-clearing levels so as to induce more borrowing and spending by business and consumers.

It's also the inherent result of massive QE bond buying where central banks finance their purchases with credits conjured from thin air. Consequently, the central banks' big fat thumb on the bond market's supply/demand scale results in far higher bond prices (and lower yields) than real savers would accept in an honest free market.

The same is true of the hoary doctrine of "wealth effects" stimulus. After being initiated by Alan Greenspan 15 years ago, it has been embraced ever more eagerly by his successors at the Fed and elsewhere ever since.

Here, the monetary transmission channel is through the top 1% that own 40% of the financial assets and the top 10% that own upward of 85%. To wit, stock prices are intentionally driven to artificially high levels by means of "financial easing." The latter is a euphemism for cheap or even free finance for carry-trade gamblers and implicitly subsidized hedging insurance for fast-money speculators.

As the stock averages rise and their Fed-subsidized portfolios attain ever-higher "marks," the wealth-effects operators supposedly feel, well, wealthier. They are thereby motivated to spend and invest more than otherwise, and to actually double down on these paper-wealth gains by using them as collateral to obtain even more cheap funding for even more speculations.

The trouble is, financial prices cannot be falsified indefinitely. At length, they become the subject of a pure confidence game and face the risk of shocks and black swans that even the central banks are unable to offset. Then the day of reckoning arrives in traumatic and violent aspect.

Exactly that kind of Lehman-scale crisis is now descending on global markets. In fact, it's even worse. Speculative excesses that are even more fantastic than during the dot-com era mania have now infested the technology and social media stocks.

So once again the end result of today's massive central bank intrusion in financial markets will be yet another thundering crash of the highfliers and a resulting financial crisis of unprecedented extent.

THE FOLLY OF THE FANGS

Needless to say, there have been some spectacular rocket ships in the market's melt-up during the last several years. But if history is any guide this is exactly the kind of action that always precedes a thundering bust.

To wit, the market has narrowed down to essentially four explosively rising stocks—the FANG quartet of Facebook, Amazon, Netflix and Google—that are sucking up most of the oxygen left in the casino.

At the beginning of 2015, the FANG stocks had a combined market cap of $740 billion and combined 2014 earnings of $17.5 billion. So a valuation multiple of 42X might not seem entirely outlandish for this team of racehorses, but what has happened since then surely is.

At the end of August 2016, the FANG stocks were valued at $1.3 trillion, meaning they have gained $570 billion of market cap or nearly 80%

during the previous 19 months. Not only has their combined PE multiple escalated further to 50X, but even that's almost entirely owing to Google's far more sober PE at 30X.

By contrast, at the end of August 2016, Netflix was valued at 300X its meager net income of $140 million, while Amazon was valued at 190X and Facebook at 60X.

In a word, the gamblers are piling on to the last trains out of the station. And that means, look out below!

An old Wall Street adage holds that market tops are a process, not an event. A peak under the hood of the S&P 500 index, in fact, reveals exactly that.

On the day after Christmas 2014, the total market cap of the S&P 500 including the FANG stocks was $18.4 trillion. By contrast, it closed at $19.0 trillion in August, reflecting a tepid 4% gain during a 19-month period when the stock averages were spurting to an all-time high.

Needless to say, if you subtract the FANGs from the S&P 500 market-cap total, there has been virtually no gain in value at all; it was still $17.7 trillion.

So there you have it—a classic blow-off market top in which 100% of the gain over the last 19 months was owing to just four companies.

Actually, there is growing deterioration down below and for good reason. Notwithstanding the FOMC's stick save at nearly every meeting during the past two years, each near miss on a rate hike reminded even Wall Street's most inveterate easy-money crybabies that the jig is up on rates.

Sooner or later the Fed will just plain run out of excuses for ZIRP, and now, after 93 straight months on the zero bound, it clearly has.

And at the most inopportune time. As we demonstrated earlier, the world economy is visibly drifting into stall speed or worse, and corporate earnings are already in an undeniable downswing. As we have also indicated, reported earnings per share for the S&P 500 during the LTM ended in June 2016 came in at $87 per share, or 18% below the $106 per share reported in September 2014.

So the truth is, the smart money has been lightening the load during much of the last two years, selling into the mini-rips while climbing on board the FANG momentum train with trigger finger at the ready.

CHASING THE LAST MOMO STOCKS STANDING— AN OLD WALL STREET STORY

Needless to say, this narrowing process is an old story. It famously occurred in the bull market of 1972–73 when the impending market collapse was obscured by the spectacular gains of the so-called Nifty Fifty. And it happened in spades in the spring of 2000 when the Four Horsemen of Microsoft, Dell, Cisco and Intel obfuscated a cratering market under the banner of "this time is different."

But it wasn't. It was more like the same old delusion that trees grow to the sky. At its peak in late March 2000, for example, Cisco was valued at $540 billion, representing a $340 billion, or 170%, gain from prior year.

Since it had earned $2.6 billion of net income in the most recent 12-month period, its lofty market cap represented a valuation multiple of 210X. And Cisco was no rocket ship startup at that point, either, having been public for a decade and posting $15 billion of revenue during the prior year.

Nevertheless, the bullish chorus at the time claimed that Cisco was the monster of the midway when it came to networking gear for the explosively growing internet, and that no one should be troubled by its absurdly high PE multiple.

The same story was told about the other three members of the group. During the previous 24 months, Microsoft's market cap had exploded from $200 billion to $550 billion, where it traded at 62X reported earnings. In even less time, Intel's market cap had soared from $200 billion to $440 billion, where it traded at 76X. And Dell's market cap had nearly tripled during this period, and it was trading at 70X.

Altogether, the Four Horsemen had levitated the stock market by the stunning sum of $800 billion in the approximately 12 months before the 2000 peak.

That's right. In a manner not dissimilar to the FANG quartet during the past year, the Four Horsemen's market cap had soared from $850 billion, where it was already generously valued, to $1.65 trillion, or by 94%, at the time of the dotcom bubble peak.

There was absolutely no reason for this market-cap explosion except that in the final phases of the technology and dot-com bull market, speculators had piled onto the last momentum trains leaving the station.

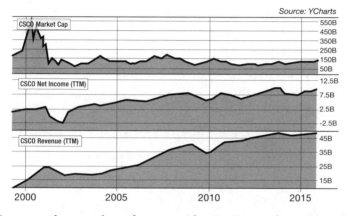

But it was a short and unpleasant ride. By September 2002, the combined market cap of the Four Horsemen had crashed to just $450 billion. Exactly $1.0 trillion of bottled air had come rushing out of the casino.

Needless to say, the absurdly inflated values of the Four Horsemen in the spring of 2000 looked exactly like the FANG quartet today. The ridiculously bloated valuation multiples of Facebook, Amazon and Netflix speak for themselves, but even Google's massive $550 billion market cap is a sign of the top.

Despite its overflowing creativity and competitive prowess, Google is not a technology company that has invented a rocket ship product with years yet to run. Nearly 90% of its $82 billion in LTM revenues came from advertising.

But the current $575 billion worldwide advertising spending is a 5% growth market in good times, and one that will slide back into negative territory when the next recession hits. Even the rapidly growing digital-ad subsector is heading for single-digit land; and that's according to industry optimists whose projections assume that the business cycle and recessions have been outlawed.

The fact is, Google has more than half of this market already. Like the case of the Four Horsemen at the turn of the century, there is no known math that will allow it to sustain double-digit earnings growth for years into the future and therefore its 30X PE multiple.

Likewise, Amazon may well be effecting the greatest retail revolution in history, but it's been around for 25 years and still has never posted more than pocket change in profits. More importantly, it is a monumental cash-burning machine that one day will run out of fuel.

During the LTM period ending in June 2016, for example, it generated just $6.3 billion of operating free cash flow on sales of $120 billion. It was thus being valued at a preposterous 58X free cash flow.

So here's the thing. The Four Horsemen last time around were great companies that have continued to grow and thrive ever since the dot-com meltdown. But their peak valuations were never remotely justified by any plausible earnings-growth scenario.

In this regard, Cisco is the poster child for this disconnect. During the last 15 years its annual revenues have grown from $15 billion to nearly $50 billion, and its net income has more than tripled to nearly $10 billion per year.

Yet its market cap today at $150 billion is just 25% of its dot-com bubble peak. In short, its market cap was driven to the absurd height recorded in March 2000 by the final spasm of a bull market, when the punters jumped on the last "momo" trains out of the station.

This time is surely no different. The FANG quartet may live on to dominate their respective spheres for years or even decades to come. But their absurdly inflated valuations will soon be deFANGed.

FACEBOOK'S BICOASTAL BUBBLE BINGE—
THE ONCE AND FUTURE "FACEPLANT"

Indeed, the so-called social media stocks represent the very essence of the bicoastal Bubble Finance prosperity of Wall Street and Silicon Valley.

The truth is, Facebook—along with Instagram, WhatsApp, Oculus VR and the 45 other testaments to social media drivel that Mark Zuckerberg has acquired with insanely inflated Wall Street play money during the last few years—is not simply a sinkhole of lost productivity and low-grade self-indulgent entertainment. It is also a colossal valuation hoax, and one that is heading for another "Faceplant" when the third great financial bubble of this century comes crashing down.

Why? Because at bottom, Facebook (FB) is just an internet billboard. It's a place where people idle their time—especially millennials in or out of their parents' basement. Whether they grow tired of Facebook remains to be seen, but one thing is certain.

To wit, FB has invented nothing, has no significant patents, delivers no products and generates no customer subscriptions or service contracts. Its purported 1.8 billion monthly average users are fiercely devoted to free stuff in their use of social media.

Therefore, virtually all of its revenue comes from advertising. But ads are nothing like a revolutionary new product such as Apple's iPhone, which can generate tens of billions of sales out of nowhere.

The pool of advertising dollars, by contrast, is relatively fixed at about $175 billion in the United States and $575 billion worldwide. And it is subject to severe cyclical fluctuations. For instance, during the Great Recession, U.S. advertising spending declined by 15% and worldwide spending dropped by 11%.

And therein lies the problem. Due to its sharp cyclicality, the trend growth in U.S. ad spending during the last decade has been about 0.5% per annum. Likewise, global ad spending increased from about $490 billion in 2008 to $575 billion in 2015, reflecting a growth rate of 2.3% annually.

Yes, there has been a rapid migration of dollars from TV, newspapers and other traditional media to the digital space in recent years. But the big shift there is already over.

Besides that, you can't capitalize a one-time gain in sales of this sort with even an average market multiple. And that's saying nothing about the fact that FB's recent $360 billion market cap represented a preposterous multiple of 225X its $1.6 billion of March 2016 last-12-months (LTM) free cash flow.

For the June 2016 LTM period, in fact, its multiple was infinite because its free cash flow was actually negative $1.5 billion.

In any event, the digital share of the U.S. ad pool rose from 13.5% in 2008 to an estimated 32.5% last year. But even industry optimists do not expect the digital share to gain more than a point or so per year going forward. After all, television, newspapers, magazines, radio and highway billboards are not going to disappear entirely.

Consequently, there are not remotely enough advertising dollars in the world to permit the endless gaggle of social media entrants to earn revenue and profits commensurate with their towering valuations and the sell side's hockey-stick growth projections. In social media alone, therefore, there is more than $1 trillion of bottled air.

In fact, in a milieu built around the concept of free stuff, the massive amount of speculative venture capital that has entered the social media space is certain to drive customer-acquisition and customer-service costs ever higher and margins to the vanishing point.

The fact is, none of the social media competitors, not even Facebook, have a permanently defensible first-mover advantage. That is evident in the current tally of 140 so-called venture capital "unicorns." Each has a private pre-IPO "valuation" of $1 billion or more, or at least did until recently when the drought of IPOs has begun to puncture the fantasy. Even then, the group is still "valued" at $500 billion in the rarefied precincts of Silicon Valley.

But the unicorns are doing two things that will eventually eviscerate FB's massively bloated valuation.

First, they are hatching new competitors like there is no tomorrow.

Secondly, and more importantly, they are burning venture capital by the tens of billions attempting to find "users" and customers and attain business viability by buying mobile advertising from . . . yes, Facebook!

As we learned from the dot-com bust, when freshly minted companies start taking in each other's laundry in Silicon Valley things get way out of whack. Capital morphs into revenue and "burn babies" temporarily and deceptively appear to be a booming new customer base.

That is, until the bubble implodes, new capital flows dry up, startups disappear en masse and revenue from their purchases of equipment, services (for example, Amazon's cloud services) and advertising vanishes.

And that gets us to the ludicrous hockey sticks on which FB's current valuation is based—even as the end-of-bubble handwriting is already on the wall.

Startup-company space, for example, is being vacated all over the place in San Francisco, and real-world consumer-products companies like the mighty Proctor & Gamble have already decided to stop paying exorbitant rates for Facebook's ineffective targeted mobile advertising.

Nevertheless, Merrill Lynch is currently projecting that Facebook's $16.6 billion of ad revenue in 2015 will grow by 84% to $30.5 billion by 2017.

But what would happen if it turns out that the central banks have not abolished the business cycle after all?

Assume that the growing signs of global recession are not irrelevant and that a downturn materialize between now and then, and that it results, for example, in an ad spending decline about half as severe as the Great Recession.

Accordingly, this time world ad spending would drop by only 5%, not 10–15%, to about $545 billion. Furthermore, assume optimistically that the digital ad share gains another two points per year, rising from 26% of global ad spending last year to 30% by 2017.

Under those perfectly sober assumptions, digital spending would rise by about $15 billion over the next two years from the $150 billion level achieved in 2015. And in the non-search segment where FB competes— that is, the portion outside of Google's near monopoly—the gain would be about $7.5 billion.

In short, the Wall Street hockey stick brigade is essentially projecting that FB will pick up 200% of the available new ad dollars that would likely materialize under an even moderate global-recession scenario.

But that isn't even the half of it. Even a hint of recession would knock the props right out from under the monumentally bullish financial-market bubble that has been fueled by the Fed and other central banks since the 2008 crisis.

History leaves little doubt about what happens then. The massive amount of venture capital pouring into Silicon Valley and the social media space would dry up in no time; and the "burn baby" ad spending by the unicorns and other startups would quickly vanish.

So instead of growing at 40% per year, there is a very distinct possibility that FB's sales will slump to the single-digit range not too many quarters down the road.

Stated differently, Facebook is a valuation train wreck waiting to happen. It is spending tens of billions on acquisitions of companies that do not even have revenues and ramping up its internal operating costs at staggering rates of gain.

This means that when ad spending hits the recessionary skids in the months ahead—look out below. Its stock price will crater.

In short, Bubble Finance hype is the sum and substance of Facebook's crazy valuation and its modus operandi. But its founder, controlling shareholder and CEO, the brash young Mark Zuckerberg, is no Bill Gates. Not by a long shot.

Gates was a true business genius who created an essential component—desktop operating systems—of the internet age. By contrast, Zuckerberg happened to be hanging around a Harvard dorm room just as the central bankers of the world were cranking up their printing presses to warp speed.

The hallucinatory sense of grandeur that accompanied Facebook's IPO eight years later in May 2012 has been on display ever since. But Zuckerberg's madcap M&A frenzy—culminating in the insane WhatsApp deal—may well become the defining moment for the third and final bubble of this century.

To wit, Zuckerberg paid the stunning sum of $22 billion for a social media outfit that had just $10.2 million of revenue. The purchase price thus amounted to 2,150X sales.

And while you are at it, just forget about the fact that WhatsApp actually lost half of a billion dollars during the year prior to the deal's close in October 2014.

Then again, the way you lose such staggering amounts of money on virtually no sales is quite simple. That is, you adopt a business model that even the most intellectually challenged hot dog–stand operator would not have contemplated before the age of Bubble Finance.

Namely, plow headlong into a huge business operated by the biggest telecom companies in the world—in this case, one that generates $20 billion in annual billings for the wireless carriers. And the key to grabbing market share in that brutal neighborhood: offer your service for free!

That's right. WhatsApp is just a text-messaging service that challenged the paid SMS services of AT&T, Sprint, Verizon and the rest by reducing the transmission charge from $10–$20 per month to, well, nothing.

The CEO of a competitor succinctly explained why this tactic works:

> "It always comes down to the economics," said Greg Woock, the chief executive of Pinger. "Free is a compelling price point."

Yes, it is. Not surprisingly, WhatsApp's free messaging service had gone from a standing start in 2009 to 400 million users by 2014. Now that's the kind of "growth" that social media bubble riders can get giddy about.

But it amounted to this: Facebook paid $55 per user for a business that had 13 cents per user of revenue.

But never mind. Having virtually his own legal printing press—FB issued $17 billion of freshly minted stock to pay for most of the deal—Zuckerberg explained it this way:

> Our strategy is to grow and connect people. Once we get to 2–3 billion people there are ways we can monetize.

In fact, WhatsApp now has nearly 1 billion users, but still no revenue and has actually eliminated a minor annual user charge. If this sounds vaguely like the dot-com mania in early 2000, it is and then some.

TESLA—BONFIRE OF THE MONEY PRINTERS' VANITY

But the social media billionaire brats are not the half of it. The central bank money printers have transformed Wall Street into a nonstop casino that has showered a tiny slice of hedge funds and speculators with unspeakable windfalls from the likes of monstrosities such as Valeant and hundreds of similar momentum bubbles.

Just consider the shameless mountebank who has conjured the insane valuation of Tesla from the gambling pits of Goldman Sachs and Wall Street. The company has never made a profit, never hit a production or sales target and has no chance whatsoever of becoming a volume auto producer.

Indeed, at this late stage in the bubble cycle, the Wall Street casino is festooned with giant deadweight losses waiting to happen. But perhaps none is more egregious than Tesla—a crony-capitalist con job that has long been insolvent, and has survived only by dint of prodigious taxpayer subsidies and billions of free money from the Fed's Wall Street casino.

Not surprisingly, the speculative mania on Wall Street has reached such absurd lengths that Tesla is being heralded and valued as the Second Coming of Apple and its circus-barker CEO, Elon Musk, as the next Henry Ford. Indeed, so raptured were the day traders and gamblers that in the short span of 33 months between early 2012 and September 2014 they ramped up Tesla's market cap from $2.5 billion to a peak of $35 billion.

That's a 14X gain in virtually no time—and it's not due to the invention of a revolutionary new product like the iPad.

Instead, we're talking about 4,600 pounds of sheet metal, plastic, rubber and glass equipped with an electric-battery power pack that has been around for decades and that is not remotely economic without deep government subsidies.

Beyond that, the various Tesla models currently on the market carry price tags of $75k to more than $130k. So they are essentially vanity toys for the wealthy—a form of conspicuous consumption for the "all things green" crowd.

But notwithstanding all the hype on Wall Street, there had been nothing remotely evident in its financials that justified Tesla's market cap of $35 billion at its peak, and which still floats in the financial stratosphere at $29 billion.

Net sales for the LTM period ended in June 2016 amounted to $4.6 billion, meaning that speculators were putting a Silicon Valley–style multiple of 6X sales on a 100-year-old industrial product—and one sold by a fly-by-night company distinguished from its auto-company peers, which trade at 0.5X sales, only by marketing hype and a high-cost power plant that could be made by any of a dozen global car companies if there was actually a mass-market demand for it.

Needless to say, Tesla's meager LTM sales were not accompanied by any sign of profits or positive cash flow. June's LTM net income clocked in at -$1.13 billion. Worse still, its cash flow from operations of $333 million was further compounded by CapEx of $1.32 billion.

Altogether, then, its operating free cash flow for the last 12 months amounted to -$1.7 billion, and that was on top of $4 billion of red ink during the previous five years.

Unless you are imbibing the hallucination-inducing Kool Aid dispensed by Goldman Sachs, which took this red-ink machine public in 2009 and has milked it via underwritings, advisories and early-stage investments for billions ever since, Tesla's valuation was patently absurd.

Yet the gamblers had earlier piled in based on the utterly improbable assumption that oil would remain at $115 per barrel forever; that a mass market for electric-battery autos would soon develop; and that none of the powerhouse marketing and engineering companies like BMW, Toyota or even Ford would contest Tesla for market share at standard-industry profit margins.

The truth is, there is massive excess capacity in the global auto industry owing to government subsidies, bailouts and union protectionism that keep uncompetitive capacity alive; and that chronic condition is now especially pronounced due to the wildly soaring growth of excess production capacity in China.

This means, of course, that the global economy is literally saturated with expert resources for auto engineering, design, assembly, machining and component supply.

Consequently, if a mass market were to develop for battery-powered vehicles these incumbent industry resources would literally swarm into Tesla's backyard. In so doing, they would eventually drive margins to normal levels, sending Elon Musk's razzmatazz up in the same cloud of smoke that has afflicted many of his vehicles.

Here is the simple proof. There is no reason to think that any long-term mass-market player in the auto industry could beat Toyota's sustained performance metrics.

In the most recent period, its net profits amounted to 7.5% of sales and it traded at 11X LTM net income. So even if you take as granted the far-fetched notion that in a world of $2–$3 per gallon gasoline—which is likely here for a sustained duration—that a mass market will develop for electric-battery vehicles, Tesla would still need upward of $50 billion of sales at Toyota profit rates and valuation multiples to justify its current market cap.

So, given Tesla's $4.6 billion of LTM sales you would need to bet on an 11X gain in sales over the next few years, and also that today's rag-tag startup manufacturing operation could achieve levels of efficiency, quality and reliability that it has taken Toyota 60 years to perfect.

Yet take one hard look at Tesla's historical financials and it is blindingly evident that there is no reason for such an assumption whatsoever. It is not a Toyota in the making.

To the contrary, it's a Wall Street scam in plain sight. It has been a public filer for nine years now, and here are the horrific figures from its financial statements.

Since 2007 it has booked cumulative sales of just $12.5 billion, and that ain't much in Autoland. In fact, it amounts to about two weeks of sales by Toyota and four weeks by Ford.

Likewise, its cumulative bottom line has been a net loss of $2.9 billion, and the losses are not shrinking—having totaled nearly $1.5 billion in the last six quarters alone.

More significantly, during its entire nine years as a public filer, Tesla has failed to generate any net operating cash flow (OCF) at all, and has, in fact, posted red ink of $1.1 billion on cash flow from operations. During the same nine-year span ending in Q2 of 2016, its CapEx amounted to a cumulative $3.9 billion.

There is obviously no need to "go figure." Combining OCF and CapEx you get a balance sheet hemorrhage of $5 billion. The real question, therefore, is not why Tesla was worth $35 billion at its recent peak, but why it wasn't bankrupt long ago.

The answer is that it was and it should be now. Tesla would not have even made it to its Goldman-led IPO without a $500 million bailout by Uncle Sam.

That the hard-pressed taxpayers of America were called upon to underwrite a vanity toy for the wealthy—and one peddled by a serial milker of the public teat—is surely a measure of how deep crony-capitalist corruption has penetrated into the business system of America.

But even these egregious windfalls do not begin to compare with the gifts showered on Elon Musk by the money printers in the Eccles Building.

Tesla has stayed alive only because it has been able to raise billions of convertible debt in the Wall Street casino at yields that are the next-best thing to free money. In short, it has been burning massive dollops of cash for years and replenishing itself periodically in capital markets that are rife with momentum speculators flying high on cheap carry trades and the Fed's buy-the-dip safety net.

In truth, Tesla's true losses are even greater than its accounting statements suggest. For instance, it has booked upward of $500 million of revenue and profits owing to zero-emissions vehicle credits. The latter were invented by Al Gore after he finished inventing the internet, and amount to nothing more than bottled air—clean or not.

Also, Tesla's affluent customers pocket about $10,000 per vehicle of federal and state tax credits, meaning that taxpayers have fronted another $800 million or so to stimulate Tesla sales.

Finally, Tesla's marketing machine has even converted itself into a repo man for the wealthy. That is, Tesla guarantees a large share of its customers that it will buy back their vehicles at no loss after three years.

So how does it possibly make a profit deploying this blatant rent-a-car for free gimmick? Ask its accountants. In their wisdom and clairvoyance, they have undoubtedly assumed that the residual value of these vehicles will be levitated by the same juice that fuels Tesla's stock price.

Yes, Tesla is a bonfire of the central bank vanities. In due course, the bubble will collapse and billions will have been wasted—much of it with taxpayer money—on things like its ballyhooed gigafactory in Nevada. But that's what happens when central bankers destroy honest price discovery and turn capital markets into a gambling casino.

Yet the scam artist behind it has no compunctions at all, and will surely lead the punters in his stock straight over the cliff. Thus, after posting another wider-than-expected $293 million loss in its June 2016 quarter, which was 60% higher than last year's red ink, Elon Musk doubled down on his snake oil offering.

His previous promise that Tesla would finally become cash flow positive in 2016, after burning through the above-mentioned $5 billion in cash since 2007, was abruptly declared inoperative in classic Nixonian fashion.

Instead, Tesla will do another giant dilutive capital raise in order to fund an acceleration of the Model 3 so that it can deliver 500,000 vehicles in 2018.

That's a con job worthy of the seediest used-car lot in America. In auto-production land, today is already 2018 in the case of a mass-production vehicle that has barely been designed and that has not yet been production engineered, tooled, tested or sourced for components and materials.

Indeed, the idea that a company that produced only 57,000 vehicles in the last 12 months can scale up to 10X that volume virtually overnight on a production line and supply system that does not even exist is a laughable fiction.

But what isn't laughable is that the Wall Street casino is so blinded by speculation, greed and Fed puts and liquidity pumping that it is enabling dozens of circus barkers like Elon Musk to inflate spectacular bubbles just like Tesla.

And these financial deformations will end up destroying the Main Street homegamers who fall for them just like the previous two times this century—even as they dissipate loads of scarce capital in the process.

AUGUST 2007 REDUX

Nearly everywhere on the planet the giant financial bubbles created by the central banks during the last two decades are fracturing. If this is beginning to sound like August 2007, that's because it is. And the denials from the casino operators are coming in just as thick and fast.

Back then, the perma-bulls were out in full force peddling what can be called the "one-off" bromide. That is, evidence of a brewing storm was spun as just a few isolated mistakes that had no bearing on the broad market trends because the Goldilocks economy was purportedly rock solid.

Thus, the unexpected collapse of Countrywide Financial was blamed on the empire-building excesses of the Orange Man (Angelo Mozillo) and the collapse of the Bear Stearns mortgage funds was purportedly owing to a lapse in supervision.

So it boiled down to an injunction of "nothing to see here." Just move along and keep buying.

In fact, after reaching a peak of 1,550 on July 18, 2007, the S&P 500 stumbled by about 9% during the August crisis, but the dip buyers kept coming back in force on the one-off assurances of the sell-side "experts." By October 9 the index was back up to the pre-crisis peak at 1,565 and then drifted lower in sideways fashion until September 2008.

The bromides were false, of course. Upon the Lehman event the fractures exploded, and the hammer dropped on the stock market in violent fashion. During the next 160 days, the S&P 500 plunged by another 50%.

The supreme irony of the present moment is that the perma-bulls insist that there is no lesson to be learned from the Great Financial Crisis. That's because the single greatest risk-asset liquidation of modern times, it turns out, was also, purportedly, a one-off event.

It can't happen again, we are assured. After all, the major causes have been rectified, and 100-year floods don't recur, anyway.

In that vein it is insisted that U.S. banks have all been fixed and now have "fortress" balance sheets. Likewise, the housing market has staged a healthy recovery, but remains lukewarm and stable without any signs of bubble excesses. And stock market PE multiples are purportedly within their historic range and fully warranted by current ultralow interest rates.

This is complete day traders' nonsense, of course. During the past year, for example, the core CPI has increased by 2.20% while the 10-year Treasury recently penetrated its all-time low of 1.38%. The real yield is effectively -1%, and that's ignoring taxes on interest payments.

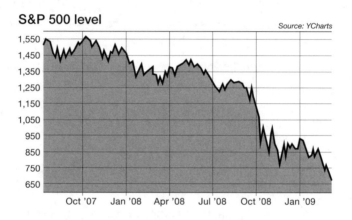

The claim that you can capitalize the stock market at an unusually high PE multiple owing to ultralow interest rates, therefore, implies that deep negative real rates are a permanent condition, and that governments will be able to destroy savers until the end of time.

The truth of the matter is that interest rates have nowhere to go in the longer run except up, meaning that the current cap rates are just plain absurd. Indeed, at the end of this summer's melt-up rally, as we indicated earlier, the S&P 500 was trading at 25.2X LTM reported earnings.

Moreover, the $87 per share reported for the period ending in June 2016 was actually down by 18% from the $106-per-share peak recorded in September 2014. So in the face of falling earnings and inexorably rising interest rates, the casino punters were being urged to close their eyes and buy the dip one more time.

And that's not the half of it. This time is actually different, but not in a good way. Last time around during the post–August 2007 dead-cat bounce LTM reported earnings for the S&P 500 peaked at $85 per share, meaning that on the eve of the 2008 crash the trailing multiple was only 18.4X.

That's right. After the near-death experience of 2008–9 and a recovery so halting and tepid as to literally scream out that the Main Street economy is impaired and broken, the casino gamblers have dramatically upped the valuation ante yet again.

There is a reason for such reckless obduracy, however, that goes well beyond the propensity of Wall Street punters and robo-traders to stay at the tables until they see blood on the floor.

Namely, it is their failure to understand that the current central banking regime of Bubble Finance inherently and inexorably generates financial boom-and-bust cycles that must, and always do, end in spectacular crashes.

THE BALEFUL LEGACY OF BUBBLES— ALAN GREENSPAN

And that brings us back to the father of Bubble Finance, former Fed Chairman Alan Greenspan. In a word, he systematically misused the power of the Fed to short-circuit every single attempt at old-fashioned financial-market corrections and bubble liquidations during his entire 19-year tenure in the Eccles Building.

That includes his inaugural panic in October 1987 when he flooded the market with liquidity after Black Monday. Worse still, he also sent the monetary gendarmes of the New York Fed out to demand that Wall Street houses trade with parties they knew to be insolvent and to prop up stock prices and other financial valuations that were wholly unwarranted by the fundamentals.

Greenspan went on to make a career of countermanding market forces and destroying the process of honest price discovery in the capital and money markets. Certainly, that's what he did when he slashed interest rates in 1989–90, and when he crushed the justified revolt of the bond vigilantes in 1994 with a renewed burst of money printing.

The same was true when he bailed out Long-Term Capital and goosed the stock market in the fall of 1998—a maneuver that generated the speculative dot-com bubble and subsequent collapse.

And then he applied the coup de grace to what remained of honest price discovery on Wall Street. During the 30 months after December 2000, he slashed interest rates from 6.25% to 1.0% in a relentless flood of liquidity. The latter, in turn, ignited the most insane housing-market bubble the world had ever seen.

During the second quarter of 2003, for example, as rates were brought down to a previously unheard of 1.0%, the financial system generated mortgage financings at upward of a $5 trillion annual rate. Even a few years earlier, a $1 trillion rate of mortgage financing had been on the high side.

Needless to say, housing prices and housing-finance costs were systematically and radically distorted. The crash of 2008–9 was but the inexorable outcome of Greenspan's policy of financial-asset price falsification—a policy that his successor, Bubbles Ben, doubled down upon when the brown stuff hit the fan.

So as we sit on the cusp of the third Bubble Finance crash of this century, now comes Alan Greenspan to explain once again that he knows nothing about financial bubbles at all. According to the unrepentant ex-maestro, it's all due to the irrationalities of "human nature."

Why, central banks have nothing to do with it at all!

The 2000 bubble collapsed. We barely could see a change in economic activity. On October 19, 1987, the Dow Jones went down 23% in one day. You will not find the slightest indication of that collapse of that bubble in the GDP number—or in industrial production or anything else.

So I think that you have to basically decide what is causing what. I think the major issue in the financial models has got to be to capture the bubble effect. Bubbles are essentially part of the fact that human nature is not wholly rational. And you can see it in the data very clearly.

No, you can't!

As the astute student of 30 years of Bubble Finance, Doug Noland, recently observed:

Had the Greenspan Fed not backstopped the markets and flooded the system with liquidity post the '87 Crash, Credit would have tightened and bursting Bubble effects would have been readily apparent throughout the data. Instead, late-eighties ("decade of greed") excess ensured spectacular Bubbles in junk debt, M&A and coastal real estate. It's been serial Bubbles ever since.

Noland is completely correct. During the early part of the Bubble Finance era, the Main Street economy was goosed time and again by cheap credit, which induced household and business spending from the proceeds of steadily higher leverage.

But now the households of Flyover America are stranded at Peak Debt. Yet the Fed keeps hammering their real incomes via its specious 2% inflation target and their savings by its lunatic adherence to ZIRP.

Accordingly, and as we have previously demonstrated, the massive liquidity emissions of the Fed and other central banks never get beyond the canyons of Wall Street—where they fuel ever more incendiary financial excesses and ever more traumatic crashes.

Now comes another.

PART 3

IMPERIAL WASHINGTON AND
ITS GLOBAL DEPREDATIONS

CHAPTER 20:

Imperial Washington—
Why There is Still No Peace on Earth

FTER THE BERLIN WALL FELL IN NOVEMBER 1989 AND THE DEATH OF the Soviet Union was confirmed two years later when Boris Yeltsin courageously stood down the Red Army tanks in front of Moscow's White House, a dark era in human history came to an end.

The world had descended into a 77-year global war, incepting with the mobilization of the armies of old Europe in August 1914. If you want to count bodies, 150 million were killed by all the depredations that germinated in the Great War, its foolish aftermath at Versailles, and the march of history into World War II and the Cold War that followed inexorably thereupon.

Upward of 8% of the human race was wiped out during that span. The toll encompassed the madness of trench warfare during 1914–18; the murderous regimes of Soviet and Nazi totalitarianism that rose from the ashes of the Great War and Versailles; and then the carnage of WWII and all the lesser (unnecessary) wars and invasions of the Cold War including Korea and Vietnam.

At the end of the Cold War, therefore, the last embers of the fiery madness that had incepted with the guns of August 1914 had finally burned out. Peace was at hand. Yet 25 years later there is still no peace because Imperial Washington confounds it.

In fact, the War Party entrenched in the nation's capital is dedicated to economic interests and ideological perversions that guarantee perpetual war. These forces ensure endless waste on armaments; they cause the inestimable death and human suffering that stems from 21st-century high-tech warfare; and they inherently generate terrorist blowback from those upon whom the War Party inflicts its violent hegemony.

So there was a virulent threat to peace still lurking on the Potomac after the 77-year war ended. The great general and President, Dwight Eisenhower, had called it the "military-industrial complex" in his farewell address. But that memorable phrase had been abbreviated by his speechwriters, who deleted the word "congressional" in a gesture of comity to the legislative branch.

So restore Ike's deleted reference to the pork barrels and Sunday-afternoon warriors of Capitol Hill and toss in the legions of Beltway busybodies who constituted the civilian branches of the Cold War armada (CIA, State, AID and the rest) and the circle would have been complete. It constituted the most awesome machine of warfare and imperial hegemony since the Roman legions bestrode most of the civilized world.

In a word, the real threat to peace circa 1990 was that the American Imperium would not go away quietly in the night.

In fact, during the past 25 years Imperial Washington has lost all memory that peace was ever possible at the end of the Cold War. Today it is as feckless, misguided and bloodthirsty as were Berlin, Paris, St. Petersburg, Vienna and London in August 1914.

A few months after the slaughter had been unleashed 100 years ago, however, soldiers along the western front broke into spontaneous truces of Christmas celebration, song and even exchange of gifts. For a brief moment they wondered why they were juxtaposed in lethal combat along the jaws of hell.

The truthful answer is that there was no good reason. The world had stumbled into war based on false narratives and the institutional imperatives of military mobilization plans, alliances and treaties arrayed into a doomsday machine and petty short-term diplomatic maneuvers and political calculus. Yet it took more than three-quarters of a century for all the consequential impacts and evils to be purged from the life of the planet.

The peace that was lost last time has not been regained this time, and for the same reasons. Historians can readily name the culprits from 100 years ago.

These include the German general staff's plan for a lightning mobilization and strike on the western front called the Schlieffen Plan; the incompetence and intrigue in the court at St. Petersburg; French President Poincare's anti-German irredentism owing to the 1871 loss of his home province, Alsace-Lorraine; and the bloodthirsty cabal around Winston Churchill who forced England into an unnecessary war, among countless others.

Since these casus belli of 1914 were criminally trivial in light of all that metastasized thereafter, it might do well to name the institutions and false narratives that block the return of peace today. The fact is, these impediments are even more contemptible than the forces that crushed the Christmas truces one century ago.

IMPERIAL WASHINGTON—THE NEW GLOBAL MENACE

There is no peace on earth today for reasons mainly rooted in Imperial Washington—not Moscow, Beijing, Tehran, Damascus, Mosul or even Raqqa. Imperial Washington has become a global menace owing to what didn't happen in 1991.

At that crucial inflection point, Bush the Elder should have declared "mission accomplished". So doing, he should have slashed the Pentagon budget from $600 billion to $200 billion (2015 $); demobilized the military-industrial complex by putting a moratorium on all new weapons development, procurement and export sales; dissolved NATO and dismantled the far-flung network of U.S. military bases; reduced the United States' standing armed forces from 1.5 million to a few hundred thousand; and organized and led a world-disarmament and peace campaign, as did his Republican predecessors during the 1920s.

Unfortunately, George H. W. Bush was not a man of peace, vision or even middling intelligence. He was the malleable tool of the War Party, and it was he who single-handedly blew the peace when he plunged America into a petty argument between the impetuous dictator of Iraq and the gluttonous emir of Kuwait. But that argument was none of George Bush's or America's business.

By contrast, even though liberal historians have reviled Warren G. Harding as some kind of dummkopf politician, he well understood that the Great War had been for naught, and that to ensure it never happened again the nations of the world needed to rid themselves of their huge navies and standing armies.

To that end, he achieved the largest global-disarmament agreement ever during the Washington Naval Conference of 1921, which halted the construction of new battleships for more than a decade. And even then, the moratorium ended only because the vengeful victors at Versailles never ceased exacting their revenge on Germany.

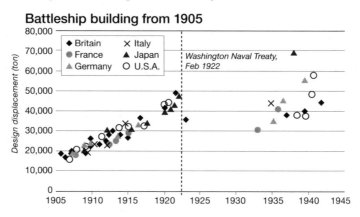

And while he was at it, President Harding also pardoned Eugene Debs. In so doing, he gave witness to the truth that the intrepid socialist candidate for president and vehement antiwar protestor, who Wilson had thrown in prison for exercising his First Amendment right to speak against U.S. entry into a pointless European war, had been right all along.

In short, Warren G. Harding knew the war was over and the folly of Wilson's 1917 plunge into Europe's bloodbath should not be repeated, at all hazards.

But not George H. W. Bush. The man should never be forgiven for enabling the likes of Dick Cheney, Paul Wolfowitz, Robert Gates and their neocon pack of jackals to come to power—even if he has now denounced them in his doddering old age.

Even more to the point, by opting not for peace but for war and oil in the Persian Gulf in 1991 he opened the gates to an unnecessary confrontation with Islam and nurtured the rise of jihadist terrorism that would not haunt the world today save for forces unleashed by George H. W. Bush's petulant quarrel with Saddam Hussein.

We will momentarily get to the 45-year-old error that holds the Persian Gulf is an American lake and that the answer to high oil prices and energy security is the Fifth Fleet. Actually, the answer to high oil prices everywhere and always is high oil prices—a truth driven home in spades last winter when the world oil price plunged below $30 per barrel.

But first it is well to remember that there was no plausible threat anywhere on the planet to the safety and security of the citizens of Springfield MA, Lincoln NE or Spokane WA when the Cold War ended.

The Warsaw Pact had dissolved into more than a dozen woebegone sovereign statelets; the Soviet Union was now unscrambled into 15 independent and far-flung republics from Belarus to Tajikistan; and the Russian motherland would soon plunge into an economic depression that would leave it with a GDP about the size of the Philadelphia MSA.

Likewise, China's GDP was even smaller and more primitive than Russia's. Even as Mr. Deng was discovering the People's Bank of China's printing press, which would enable it to become a great mercantilist exporter, an incipient Chinese threat to national security was never in the cards.

After all, it was the 4,000 Wal-Marts in America upon which the prosperity of the new Red Capitalism inextricably depended and upon which the rule of the Communist oligarchs in Beijing was ultimately anchored. Even the hardliners among them could see that in swapping militarism for mercantilism and invading America with tennis shoes, neckties and home textiles the door had been closed to any other kind of invasion thereafter.

NO ISLAMIC TERRORIST OR JIHADI THREAT CIRCA 1990

Likewise, in 1990 there was no global Islamic threat or jihadi terrorist menace at all. What existed under those headings were sundry fragments and deposits of Middle Eastern religious, ethnic and tribal histories that were of moment in their immediate region, but no threat to America whatsoever.

The Shiite/Sunni divide had coexisted since A.D. 671, but its episodic eruptions into battles and wars over the centuries had rarely extended beyond the region, and certainly had no reason to fester into open conflict in 1990.

Inside the artificial state of Iraq, which had been drawn on a map by historically ignorant European diplomats in 1916, for instance, the Shiite and Sunni got along tolerably. That's because the nation was ruled by Saddam Hussein's Baathist brand of secular Arab nationalism, flavored by a muscular propensity for violent repression of internal dissent.

Hussein championed law and order, state-driven economic development and politically apportioned distributions from the spoils of the extensive government-controlled oil sector. To be sure, Baathist socialism didn't bring much prosperity to the well-endowed lands of Mesopotamia, but Hussein did have a Christian foreign minister and no sympathy for religious extremism or violent pursuit of sectarian causes.

As it happened, the bloody Shiite/Sunni strife that plagues Iraq today and functions as a hatchery for angry young jihadi terrorists in their thousands was initially unleashed only after Hussein had been driven from Kuwait in 1991 and the CIA had instigated an armed uprising in the Shiite heartland around Basra.

That revolt was brutally suppressed by Hussein's republican guards, but it left an undertow of resentment and revenge boiling below the surface. That was one of many of George H. W. Bush's fetid legacies in the region.

Needless to say, when it came their turn, Bush the Younger and his cabal of neocon warmongers could not leave well enough alone.

When they foolishly destroyed Saddam Hussein and his entire regime in the pursuit of nonexistent WMDs and ties with al-Qaeda, they literally opened the gates of hell, leaving Iraq as a lawless failed state where both recent and ancient religious and tribal animosities were given unlimited violent vent.

WHY THE WAR PARTY NEEDED TO DEMONIZE IRAN

Also circa 1990, the Shiite theocracy ensconced in Tehran was no threat to America's safety and security—even if it was an unfortunate albatross on the Persian people. The very idea that Tehran is an expansionist power bent on exporting terrorism to the rest of the world is a giant fiction and tissue of lies invented by the Washington War Party and its Bibi Netanyahu branch in order to win political support for their confrontationist policies.

Indeed, the three-decade-long demonization of Iran has served one overarching purpose. Namely, it has enabled both branches of the War Party to conjure up a fearsome enemy, thereby justifying aggressive policies that call for a constant state of war and military mobilization.

When the Cold War officially ended in 1991, the Cheney/neocon cabal feared the kind of drastic demobilization of the U.S. military-industrial complex that was warranted by the suddenly more pacific strategic environment. In response, they developed an anti-Iranian doctrine that was explicitly described as a way of keeping defense spending at high Cold War levels.

And the narrative they developed to this end is one of the more egregious big lies ever to come out of the Beltway. It puts you in mind of the young boy who killed his parents, and then threw himself on the mercy of the courts on the grounds that he was an orphan!

To wit, during the 1980s the neocons in the Reagan Administration issued their own fatwa again the Islamic Republic based on its rhetorical hostility to America. Yet that enmity was grounded in Washington's 25-year support for the tyrannical and illegitimate regime of the shah, and constituted a founding narrative of the Islamic Republic that was not much different than America's revolutionary castigation of King George.

That the Iranians had a case is beyond doubt. The open U.S. archives now prove that the CIA overthrew Iran's democratically elected government in 1953 and put the utterly unsuited and megalomaniacal Mohammad Reza Shah Pahlavi on the Peacock Throne to rule as a puppet on behalf of U.S. security and oil interests.

During the subsequent decades the shah not only massively and baldly plundered the wealth of the Persian nation; with the help of the CIA and U.S. military, he also created a brutal secret police force known as SAVAK. The latter made the East German Stasi look civilized by comparison.

All elements of Iranian society including universities, labor unions, businesses, civic organizations, peasant farmers and many more were subjected to intense surveillance by the SAVAK agents and paid informants. As one critic described it:

> Over the years, Savak became a law unto itself, having legal authority to arrest, detain, brutally interrogate and torture suspected people indefinitely. Savak operated its own prisons in Tehran, such as Qezel-Qalaeh and Evin facilities and many suspected places throughout the country as well. Many of those activities were carried out without any institutional checks.

Ironically, among his many grandiose follies, the shah embarked on a massive civilian nuclear-power campaign in the 1970s, which envisioned literally paving the Iranian landscape with dozens of nuclear power plants.

He would use Iran's surging oil revenues after 1973 to buy all the equipment required from Western companies—and also fuel-cycle support services such as uranium enrichment—in order to provide his kingdom with cheap power for centuries.

At the time of the revolution, the first of these plants at Bushehr was nearly complete, but the whole grandiose project was put on hold amidst the turmoil of the new regime and the onset of Saddam Hussein's war against Iran in September 1980. As a consequence, a $2 billion deposit languished at the French nuclear agency that had originally obtained it from the shah to fund a ramp-up of its enrichment capacity to supply his planned battery of reactors.

Indeed, in this very context the new Iranian regime proved quite dramatically that it was not hell-bent on obtaining nuclear bombs or any other weapons of mass destruction. In the midst of Iraq's unprovoked invasion of Iran in the early 1980s, Ayatollah Khomeini issued a fatwa against biological and chemical weapons.

Yet at that very time, Saddam was dropping these horrific weapons on Iranian battle forces—some of them barely armed teenage boys—with the spotting help of CIA tracking satellites and the concurrence of Washington. So from the very beginning, the Iranian posture was wholly contrary to the War Party's endless blizzard of false charges about its quest for nukes.

However benighted and medieval its religious views, the theocracy that ruled Iran did not consist of demented warmongers. In the heat of battle they were willing to sacrifice their own forces rather than violate their religious scruples to counter Saddam's WMDs.

HOW WASHINGTON INSPIRED THE MYTH OF IRAN'S SECRET NUCLEAR-WEAPONS PROGRAM

Then in 1983 the new Iranian regime decided to complete the Bushehr power plant and some additional elements of the shah's grand plan. But when they attempted to reactivate the French enrichment-services contract and buy necessary power plant equipment from the original German suppliers they were stopped cold by Washington. And when they tried to get their $2 billion deposit back, they were curtly denied that, too.

To make a long story short, the entire subsequent history of off-again, on-again efforts by the Iranians to purchase dual-use equipment and components on the international market, often from black market sources like Pakistan, was in response to Washington's relentless efforts to block its legitimate rights as a signatory to the Nuclear Nonproliferation Treaty to complete some parts of the shah's civilian nuclear project.

Needless to say, it did not take much effort by the neocon "regime change" fanatics that inhabited Washington's national-security machinery, especially after the 2000 election, to spin every attempt by Iran to purchase even a lowly pump or pipe fitting as evidence of a secret campaign to get the bomb.

The exaggerations, lies, distortions and fear mongering that came out of this neocon campaign are truly deplorable. Yet they incepted way back in the early 1990s when George H. W. Bush actually did reach out to the newly elected government of Hashemi Rafsanjani to bury the hatchet after it had cooperated in obtaining the release of American prisoners being held in Lebanon in 1989.

Rafsanjani was self-evidently a pragmatist who did not want conflict with the United States and the West; and after the devastation of the eight-year war with Iraq, he was wholly focused on economic reconstruction and even free market reforms of Iran's faltering economy.

It is one of the great tragedies of history that the neocons managed to squelch even Bush the Elder's better instincts with respect to rap-prochement with Tehran.

So the prisoner-release opening was short-lived—especially after the top post at the CIA was assumed in 1991 by the despicable Robert Gates. He was one of the very worst of the unreconstructed Cold War apparat-chiks who looked peace in the eye, and elected, instead, to pervert John Quincy Adams' wise maxim. That is, Gates spent the rest of his career searching the globe for monsters to fabricate.

In this case the motivation was especially loathsome. Gates had been Bill Casey's right-hand man during the latter's rogue tenure at the CIA in the Reagan Administration. Among the many untoward projects that Gates shepherded was the Iran-Contra affair that nearly destroyed his career when it blew up, and for which he blamed the Iranians for its public disclosure.

From his post as deputy national-security director in 1989 and then as CIA head, Gates pulled out all the stops to get even. Almost single-hand-edly he killed off the White House goodwill from the prisoner release, and launched the blatant myth that Iran was both sponsoring terrorism and seeking to obtain nuclear weapons.

Indeed, it was Gates who was the architect of the demonization of Iran that became a staple of War Party propaganda after 1991. In time that morphed into the utterly false claim that Iran is an aggressive would-be hegemon and a fount of terrorism dedicated to the destruction of the state of Israel, among other treacherous purposes.

The latter giant lie was almost single-handedly fashioned by the neo-cons and Bibi Netanyahu's coterie of power-hungry henchman after the mid-1990s. Indeed, the false claim that Iran posed an "existential threat" to Israel is a product of the pure red meat domestic Israeli politics that have kept Bibi in power for much of the last two decades.

But the truth is Iran has only a tiny fraction of Israel's conventional military capability. And compared to the latter's 200-odd nukes, Iran never even had a nuclear weaponization program after a small-scale research program was abandoned in 2003.

That is not our opinion. It was the sober assessment of the nation's top 16 intelligence agencies in the official National Intelligence Estimates for 2007, and has been confirmed ever since.

It's the reason that the neocon plan to bomb Iran at the end of George W. Bush's term didn't happen. As Dubya confessed in his autobiography, even he couldn't figure out how he could explain to the American public why he was bombing facilities that all his intelligence agencies had said did not exist. That is, he would have been impaled on WMD 2.0 on his way out of the White House.

Moreover, now in conjunction with a further study arising from the 2015 nuclear accord, which will straitjacket even Iran's civilian program and eliminate most of its enriched-uranium stockpiles and spinning capacity, the International Atomic Energy Agency (IAEA) has also confirmed that Iran had no secret nuclear-weapons program after 2003.

The whole scary bedtime story was false War Party propaganda manufactured from whole cloth.

On the political and foreign policy front, Iran is no better or worse than any of the other major powers in the Middle East. In many ways it is far less of a threat to regional peace and stability than the military butchers who now run Egypt on $1.5 billion per year of U.S. aid.

And it is surely no worse than the corpulent tyrants who squander the massive oil resources of Saudi Arabia in pursuit of unspeakable opulence and decadence to the detriment of the 30 million citizens who are not part of the regime, and who one day may well reach the point of revolt.

When it comes to the support of terrorism, the Saudis have funded more jihadists and terrorists throughout the region than Iran ever even imagined.

MORE WAR PARTY LIES—DEMONIZATION OF THE SHIITE CRESCENT

In this context, the War Party's bloviating about Iran's leadership of the so-called Shiite Crescent is another component of Imperial Washington's 25-year-long roadblock to peace. Iran wasn't a threat to American security in 1991, and since then it has never organized a hostile coalition of terrorists that requires Washington's intervention.

Start with Iran's long-standing support of Bashir Assad's government in Syria. That alliance goes back to his father's era and is rooted in the historic confessional politics of the Islamic world.

The Assad regime is Alawite, a branch of the Shiites, and despite the regime's brutality, it has been a bulwark of protection for all of Syria's minority sects, including Christians, against a majority-Sunni ethnic cleansing. The latter would surely occur if the Saudi-supported rebels, led by the Nusra Front and ISIS, were ever to take full power.

Likewise, the fact that the Baghdad government of the broken state of Iraq—that is, the artificial 1916 concoction of two striped-pants European diplomats (Messrs. Sykes and Picot of the British and French foreign offices, respectively)—is now aligned with Iran is also a result of confessional politics and geo-economic propinquity.

For all practical purposes, Iraq has been partitioned. The Kurds of the Northeast have declared their independence and have been collecting their own oil revenue for the past two years and operating their own security forces. And the western Sunni lands of the upper Euphrates, of course, have been conquered by ISIS with American weapons dropped in place by the hapless $25 billion Iraqi army minted by Washington's departing proconsuls.

Accordingly, what is left of Iraq is a population that is overwhelmingly Shiite and nurses bitter resentments after two decades of violent conflict with the Sunni forces. Why in the world, therefore, wouldn't they ally with their Shiite neighbor?

Likewise, the claim that Iran is now trying to annex Yemen is pure claptrap. The ancient territory of Yemen has been racked by civil war off and on since the early 1970s. And a major driving force of that conflict has been confessional differences between the Sunni South and the Shiite North.

In more recent times, Washington's blatant drone war inside Yemen against alleged terrorists and its domination and financing of Yemen's government eventually produced the same old outcome—that is, another failed state and an illegitimate government that fled at the 11th hour, leaving another vast cache of American arms and equipment behind.

Accordingly, the Houthis forces now in control of substantial parts of the country are not some kind of advanced guard sent in by Tehran. They are indigenous partisans who share a confessional tie with Iran, but who have actually been armed, if inadvertently, by the United States.

And the real invaders in this destructive civil war are the Saudis, whose vicious bombing campaign against civilian populations controlled by the Houthis are outright war crimes if the word has any meaning at all.

Finally, there is the fourth element of the purported Iranian axis—the Hezbollah-controlled Shiite communities of southern Lebanon and the Beqaa Valley. Like everything else in the Middle East, Hezbollah is a product of historical European imperialism, Islamic confessional politics and the frequently misguided and counterproductive security policies of Israel.

In the first place, Lebanon was not any more a real country than Iraq was when Sykes and Picot laid their straight-edged rulers on a map. The result was a stew of religious and ethnic divisions—Maronite Catholics, Greek Orthodox, Copts, Druse, Sunnis, Shiites, Alawites, Kurds, Armenians, Jews and countless more—that made the fashioning of a viable state virtually impossible.

At length, an alliance of Christians and Sunnis gained control of the country, leaving the 40% Shiite population disenfranchised and economically disadvantaged, as well. But it was the inflow of Palestinian refugees in the 1960s and 1970s that eventually upset the balance of sectarian forces and triggered a civil war that essentially lasted from 1975 until the turn of the century.

It also triggered a catastrophically wrong-headed Israeli invasion of southern Lebanon in 1982, and a subsequent repressive occupation of mostly Shiite territories for the next 18 years. The alleged purpose of this invasion was to chase the PLO and Yasser Arafat out of the enclave in southern Lebanon that they had established after being driven out of Jordan in 1970.

Eventually Israel succeeded in sending Arafat packing to North Africa, but in the process created a militant, Shiite-based resistance movement that did not even exist in 1982 and that in due course became the strongest single force in Lebanon's fractured domestic political arrangements.

After Israel withdrew in 2000, the then-Christian president of the country made abundantly clear that Hezbollah had become a legitimate and respected force within the Lebanese polity, not merely some subversive agent of Tehran:

> For us Lebanese, and I can tell you the majority of Lebanese, Hezbollah is a national resistance movement. If it wasn't for them, we couldn't have liberated our land. And because of that, we have big esteem for the Hezbollah movement.

So, yes, Hezbollah is an integral component of the so-called Shiite Crescent, and its confessional and political alignment with Tehran is entirely plausible. But that arrangement—however uncomfortable for Israel—does not represent unprovoked Iranian aggression on Israel's northern border.

Instead, it's actually the blowback from the stubborn refusal of Israeli governments—especially the right-wing Likud governments of modern times—to deal constructively with the Palestinian question.

In lieu of a two-state solution in the territory of Palestine, therefore, Israeli policy has produced a chronic state of confrontation and war with the huge share of the Lebanese population represented by Hezbollah.

The latter is surely no agency of peaceful governance and has committed its share of atrocities. But the point at hand is that given the last 35 years of history and Israeli policy, Hezbollah would exist as a menacing force on its northern border even if the Iranian theocracy didn't exist and the shah or his heir was still on the Peacock Throne.

In short, there is no alliance of terrorism in the Shiite Crescent that threatens American security. That proposition is simply one of the big lies that was promulgated by the War Party after 1991 and that has been happily embraced by Imperial Washington since then in order to keep the military-industrial-security complex alive, and justify its self-appointed role as policeman of the world.

WASHINGTON'S ERRONEOUS VIEW THAT THE PERSIAN GULF IS AN AMERICAN LAKE—THE ROOT OF SUNNI JIHADISM

The actual terrorist threat has arisen from the Sunni, not the Shiite, side of the Islamic divide. But that, in turn, is largely of Washington's own making; and it is being nurtured by endless U.S. meddling in the region's politics and by the bombing and droning campaigns against Washington's self-created enemies.

At the root of Sunni-based terrorism is the long-standing Washington error that America's security and economic well-being depend upon keeping an armada in the Persian Gulf in order to protect the surrounding oil fields and the flow of tankers through the straits of Hormuz.

That doctrine has been wrong from the day it was officially enunciated by one of America's great economic ignoramuses, Henry Kissinger, at the time of the original oil crisis in 1973. The 43 years since then have proven in spades that it doesn't matter who controls the oil fields, and that the only effective cure for high oil prices is the free market.

Every tin pot dictatorship from Libya's Muammar Gaddafi, to Hugo Chavez in Venezuela, to Saddam Hussein, to the bloody-minded chieftains of Nigeria, to the purportedly medieval mullahs and fanatical revolutionary guards of Iran has produced oil—and all they could because they desperately needed the revenue.

For crying out loud, even the barbaric thugs of ISIS milk every possible drop of petroleum from the tiny, wheezing oil fields scattered around their backwater domain that have not yet been bombed to smithereens by Washington. So there is no economic case whatsoever for Imperial Washington's massive military presence in the Middle East, and most especially for its long-time alliance with the despicable regime of Saudi Arabia.

The truth is, there is no such thing as an OPEC cartel—virtually every member produces all they can and cheats whenever possible. The only thing that resembles production control in the global oil market is the fact that the Saudi princes treat their oil reserves not much differently than Exxon.

That is, they attempt to maximize the present value of their 270 billion barrels of reserves, but ultimately are no more clairvoyant at calibrating the best oil price to accomplish that than are the economists at Exxon or the International Energy Agency.

The Saudis overestimated the staying power of China's temporarily surging call on global supply, and underestimated how rapidly and extensively the $100-per-barrel marker reached in early 2008 would trigger a flow of investment, technology and cheap debt into the U.S. shale patch, the Canadian tar sands, the tired petroleum provinces of Russia, the deep waters offshore Brazil and the like. And that's to say nothing of solar, wind and all the other government-subsidized alternative sources of BTUs.

Way back when Jimmy Carter was telling us to turn down the thermostats and put on our cardigan sweaters, those of us in Congress on the free market side of the so-called energy-shortage debate said that high oil prices would bring about their own cure. Now we know.

So the Fifth Fleet and its overt and covert auxiliaries should never have been there—going all the way back to the CIA's coup against Iranian democracy in 1953.

But having turned Iran into an enemy, Imperial Washington was just getting started when 1990 rolled around. Once again in the name of "oil security" it plunged the American war machine into the politics and religious fissures of the Persian Gulf, and did so on account of a local small-potatoes conflict that had no bearing whatsoever on the safety and security of American citizens.

As U.S. Ambassador Glaspie rightly told Saddam Hussein on the eve of Hussein's Kuwait invasion, America had no dog in that hunt.

Kuwait wasn't even a country; it was a bank account sitting on a swath of oil fields surrounding an ancient trading city that had been abandoned by Ibn Saud in the early 20th century.

That's because Saud didn't know what oil was or that it was there; and in any event, it had been made a separate protectorate by the British in 1913 for reasons that are lost in the fog of diplomatic history.

Likewise, Iraq's contentious dispute with Kuwait had been over its claim that the emir of Kuwait was "slant drilling" across his border into Iraq's Rumaila field. Yet it was a wholly elastic boundary of no significance whatsoever.

In fact, the dispute over the Rumaila field started in 1960 when an Arab League declaration arbitrarily marked the Iraq–Kuwait border two miles north of the southernmost tip of the Rumaila field.

And that newly defined boundary, in turn, had come only 44 years after a pair of English and French diplomats had carved up their winnings from the Ottoman Empire's demise by laying a straight-edged ruler on the map. In so doing, they thereby confected the artificial country of Iraq from the historically independent and hostile Mesopotamian provinces of the Shiites in the South, the Sunnis in the West and the Kurds in the North.

In short, it did not matter who controlled the southern tip of the Rumaila field—the brutal dictator of Baghdad or the opulent emir of Kuwait. Neither the price of oil, nor the peace of America, nor the security of Europe nor the future of Asia depended upon it.

THE FIRST GULF WAR—A CATASTROPHIC ERROR

But once again Bush the Elder got persuaded to take the path of war. This time it was by Henry Kissinger's economically illiterate protégés at the National Security Council and Bush's Texas oilman secretary of state. They falsely claimed that the will-o'-the-wisp of "oil security" was at stake, and that 500,000 American troops needed to be planted in the sands of Arabia.

That was a catastrophic error, and not only because the presence of crusader boots on the purportedly sacred soil of Arabia offended the CIA-trained mujahedeen of Afghanistan, who had become unemployed when the Soviet Union collapsed.

The 1991 CNN-glorified war games in the Gulf also further empowered another group of unemployed crusaders. Namely, the neocon national-security fanatics who had misled Ronald Reagan into a massive military buildup to thwart what they claimed to be an ascendant Soviet Union bent on nuclear-war-winning capabilities and global conquest.

All things being equal, the sight of Boris Yeltsin, vodka flask in hand, facing down the Red Army a few months later should have sent the neocons into the permanent disrepute and obscurity they so richly deserved. But Dick Cheney and Paul Wolfowitz managed to extract from Washington's Pyrrhic victory in Kuwait a whole new lease on life for Imperial Washington.

Right then and there came the second erroneous predicate—to wit, that "regime change" among the assorted tyrannies of the Middle East was in America's national interest.

More fatally, the neocons now insisted that the Gulf War proved it could be achieved through a sweeping interventionist menu of coalition diplomacy, security assistance, arms shipments, covert action and open military attack and occupation.

What the neocon doctrine of regime change actually did, of course, was to foster the Frankenstein that ultimately became ISIS. In fact, the only real terrorists in the world who threaten normal civilian life in the West are the rogue offspring of Imperial Washington's post-1990 machinations in the Middle East.

The CIA-trained and CIA-armed mujahedeen mutated into al-Qaeda not because bin Laden suddenly had a religious epiphany that his Washington benefactors were actually the Great Satan owing to America's freedom and liberty.

His murderous crusade was inspired by the Wahhabi fundamentalism loose in Saudi Arabia. This benighted religious fanaticism became agitated to a fever pitch by Imperial Washington's violent plunge into Persian Gulf political and religious quarrels, the stationing of troops in Saudi Arabia, and the decade-long barrage of sanctions, embargoes, no-fly zones, covert actions and open hostility against the Sunni regime in Bagdad after 1991.

Yes, bin Laden would have amputated Saddam's secularist head if Washington hadn't done it first, but that's just the point. The attempt at regime change in March 2003 was one of the most foolish acts of state in American history.

Bush the Younger's neocon advisers had no clue about the sectarian animosities and historical grievances that Hussein had bottled up by parsing the oil loot and wielding the sword under the banner of Baathist nationalism. But shock and awe blew the lid and the de-Baathification campaign unleashed the furies.

Indeed, no sooner had George Bush pranced around on the deck of the Abraham Lincoln declaring "mission accomplished" than Abu Musab al-Zarqawi, a CIA recruit to the Afghan war a decade earlier and small-time specialist in hostage taking and poisons, fled his no-count redoubt in Kurdistan to emerge as a flamboyant agitator in the now-disposed Sunni heartland.

The founder of ISIS succeeded in Fallujah and Anbar province just like the long list of other terrorist leaders Washington claims to have exterminated. That is, Zarqawi gained his following and notoriety among the region's population of deprived, brutalized and humiliated young men by dint of being more brutal than their occupiers.

Indeed, even as Washington was crowing about the demise of Zarqawi, the remnants of the Baathist regime and the hundreds of thousands of demobilized republican guards were coalescing into al-Qaeda in Iraq, and their future leaders were being incubated in a monstrous nearby detention center called Camp Bucca that contained more than 26,000 prisoners.

As one former U.S. Army officer, Mitchell Gray, later described it,

"You never see hatred like you saw on the faces of these detainees," Gray remembers of his 2008 tour. "When I say they hated us, I mean they looked like they would have killed us in a heartbeat if given the chance. I turned to the warrant officer I was with and I said, 'If they could, they would rip our heads off and drink our blood.'"

What Gray didn't know—but might have expected—was that he was not merely looking at the United States' former enemies, but its future ones as well. According to intelligence experts and Department of Defense records, the vast majority of the leadership of what is today known as ISIS, including its leader, Abu Bakr al-Baghdadi, did time at Camp Bucca.

And not only did the US feed, clothe and house these jihadists, it also played a vital, if unwitting, role in facilitating their transformation into the most formidable terrorist force in modern history.

Early in Bucca's existence, the most extreme inmates were congregated in Compound 6. There were not enough Americans guards to safely enter the compound—and, in any event, the guards didn't speak Arabic. So the detainees were left alone to preach to one another and share deadly vocational advice . . .

Bucca also housed Haji Bakr, a former colonel in Saddam Hussein's air-defense force. Bakr was no religious zealot. He was just a guy who lost his job when the Coalition Provisional Authority disbanded the Iraqi military and instituted de-Baathification, a policy of banning Saddam's past supporters from government work.

According to documents recently obtained by German newspaper Der Spiegel, Bakr was the real mastermind behind ISIS's organizational structure and also mapped out the strategies that fueled its early successes. Bakr, who died in fighting in 2014, was incarcerated at Bucca from 2006–08, along with a dozen or more of ISIS's top lieutenants.

The point is, regime change and nation building can never be accomplished by the lethal violence of 21st-century armed forces; and they were an especially preposterous assignment in the context of a land rent with 13-century-old religious fissures and animosities.

In fact, the wobbly, synthetic state of Iraq was doomed the minute Cheney and his bloody gang decided to liberate it from the brutal but serviceable and secular tyranny of Saddam's Baathist regime. That's because the process of elections and majority rule necessarily imposed by Washington was guaranteed to elect a government beholden to the Shiite majority.

After decades of mistreatment and Saddam's brutal suppression of their 1991 uprising, did the latter have revenge on their minds and in their communal DNA? Did the Kurds have dreams of an independent Kurdistan spilling into Turkey and Syria that had been denied their 30-million-strong tribe way back at Versailles and ever since?

Yes, they did. So the $25 billion spent on training and equipping the putative armed forces of post-liberation Iraq was bound to end up in the hands of sectarian militias, not a national army.

In fact, when the Shiite commanders fled Sunni-dominated Mosul in June 2014 they transformed the ISIS uprising against the government in Baghdad into a vicious fledgling state in one fell swoop. It wasn't by beheadings and fiery jihadist sermons that it quickly enslaved dozens of towns and several million people in western Iraq and the Euphrates Valley of Syria.

THE ISLAMIC STATE IS WASHINGTON'S VERY OWN FRANKENSTEIN

To the contrary, its instruments of terror and occupation were the best weapons that the American taxpayers could buy. That included 2,300 Humvees and tens of thousands of automatic weapons, as well as vast stores of ammunition, trucks, rockets, artillery pieces and even tanks and helicopters.

And that wasn't the half of it. The newly proclaimed Islamic State also filled the power vacuum in Syria created by its so-called civil war.

But in truth that was another exercise in Washington-inspired and Washington-financed regime change undertaken in connivance with Qatar and Saudi Arabia.

These princes of the petro-states were surely not interested in expelling the tyranny next door; they are the living embodiment of it. Instead, the rebellion was about removing Iran's Alawite/Shiite ally from power in Damascus and laying the gas pipelines to Europe—which Assad had vetoed— across the upper Euphrates Valley.

In any event, due to Washington's regime change policy in Syria, ISIS soon had even more troves of American weapons. Some of them were supplied to Sunni radicals by way of Qatar and Saudi Arabia.

More came up the so-called ratline from Gaddafi's former arsenals in Benghazi through Turkey. And still more came through Jordan from the "moderate" opposition trained there by the CIA, which more often than not sold them or defected to the other side.

So, that the Islamic State was Washington's Frankenstein monster became evident from the moment it rushed upon the scene 30 months ago. But even then the Washington War Party could not resist adding fuel to the fire, whooping up another round of Islamophobia among the American public and forcing the Obama White House into a futile bombing campaign for the third time in a quarter century.

But if bombing really worked, the Islamic State would be sand and gravel by now. Indeed, as shown by the map below, it is really not much more than that anyway.

The dusty, broken, impoverished towns and villages along the margins of the Euphrates River and in the bombed-out precincts of Anbar province do not attract thousands of wannabe jihadists from the failed states of the Middle East and the alienated Muslim townships of Europe because the caliphate offers prosperity, salvation or any future at all.

What recruits them is outrage at the bombs and drones being dropped on Sunni communities by the U.S. Air Force and by the cruise missiles launched from the bowels of the Mediterranean that rip apart homes, shops, offices and mosques containing as many innocent civilians as ISIS terrorists.

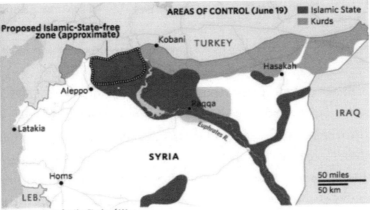

Source: Institute for the Study of War

The truth is, the Islamic State was destined for a short half-life anyway. It was contained by the Kurds in the North and East and by Turkey with NATO's second-largest army and air force in the Northwest. And it was surrounded by the Shiite Crescent in the populated, economically viable regions of lower Syria and Iraq.

So absent Washington's misbegotten campaign to unseat Assad in Damascus and demonize his confession-based Iranian ally, there would have been nowhere for the murderous fanatics who pitched a makeshift capital in Raqqa to go. They would have run out of money, recruits, momentum and public acquiescence in their horrific rule in due course.

But with the U.S. Air Force functioning as their recruiting arm and France's anti-Assad foreign policy helping to foment a final spasm of anarchy in Syria, the gates of hell have been opened wide. What has been puked out is not an organized war on Western civilization as Hollande so hysterically proclaimed in response to the recent episodes of mayhem in Paris.

It was just blowback carried out by that infinitesimally small contingent of mentally deformed young men who can be persuaded to strap on a suicide belt.

Needless to say, bombing won't stop them; it will just make more of them.

Ironically, what can stop them is the Assad government and the ground forces of its Hezbollah and the Iranian Revolutionary Guard allies.

It's time to let them settle an ancient quarrel that has never been any of America's business anyway.

But Imperial Washington is so caught up in its myths, lies and hegemonic stupidity that it cannot see the obvious.

And that is why a quarter century after the Cold War ended, peace still hasn't been given a chance, and it is the reason that horrific events like last November's barbarism in Paris still keep happening.

Even the so-called "inspired" terrorists, like the pair who attacked San Bernardino and the wackjob who besieged the Orlando night club, emerge episodically because the terror that the American military visits upon Muslim lands is, apparently, what finally triggers their underlying pathologies.

After all, whatever the Koran has to say about purging the infidel, it inspired no attacks on American soil until Imperial Washington went into the regime-change and military-intervention business in the Middle East after 1990.

ANOTHER FALSE DEMON—PUTIN'S RUSSIA

At the end of the day there now exists a huge irony. The only force that can effectively contain and eventually eliminate the Islamic State is the so-called Shiite Crescent—the alliance of Iran, Baghdad, Assad and Hezbollah. But since they are allied with Putin's Russia, still-another unnecessary barrier to peace on earth comes into play.

The fact is, there is no basis whatsoever for Imperial Washington's relentless campaign against Putin, and Washington-NATO's blatant intervention in Ukraine.

Contrary to the bombast, jingoism, and shrill moralizing flowing from Washington and the mainstream media, America has no interest in the current spat between Putin and the coup that unconstitutionally took over Kiev in February 2014.

As we outline below, for several centuries the Crimea has been Russian; for even longer, the Ukraine has been a cauldron of ethnic and tribal conflict, rarely an organized, independent state, and always a meandering set of borders looking for a redrawn map.

Like everything reviewed above, the source of the current calamity-howling about Russia is the warfare state—that is, the existence of vast machinery for military, diplomatic and economic maneuvers that is ever on the prowl for missions and mandates and that can mobilize a massive propaganda campaign on the slightest excitement.

The post-1991 absurdity of bolstering NATO and extending it into Eastern Europe, rather than liquidating it after attaining "mission accomplished," is just another manifestation of its baleful impact. In truth, the expansion of NATO is one of the underlying causes of America's needless tension with Russia and Putin's paranoia about his borders and neighbors.

Indeed, what juvenile minds actually determined that America needs a military alliance with Slovenia, Slovakia, Bulgaria and Romania, and now Montenegro!

So the resounding clatter for action against Russia emanating from Washington and its house-trained media is not even a semi-rational response to the facts at hand; it's just another destructive spasm of the nation's warfare state and its Beltway machinery of diplomatic meddling, economic warfare and military intervention.

Not only does Washington's relentless meddling in the current Russian-Ukrainian food fight have nothing to do with the safety and security of the American people, it also betrays woeful disregard for the elementary facts of that region's turbulent and often-bloody history.

MEMO TO WASHINGTON: IT'S THEIR RED LINE

In fact, the allegedly "occupied" territory of Crimea was actually annexed by Catherine the Great in 1783, thereby satisfying the longstanding quest of the Russian czars for a warm-water port. Over the subsequent ages Sevastopol then emerged as a great naval base at the strategic tip of the Crimean Peninsula, where it became home to the mighty Black Sea Fleet of the czars and, at length, the commissars.

For the next 171 years Crimea was an integral part of Russia—a span that exceeds the 166 years that have elapsed since California was annexed by a similar thrust of "Manifest Destiny" on this continent, thereby providing, incidentally, the U.S. Navy with its own warm-water port in San Diego.

While no foreign forces subsequently invaded the California coasts, it was most definitely not Ukrainian rifles, artillery and blood that famously annihilated the Charge of the Light Brigade at the Crimean city of Balaclava in 1854; these stalwart patriots were Russians defending the homeland from Turks, Europeans and Brits.

And the portrait of the Russian "hero" hanging in Putin's office is that of Czar Nicholas I—whose brutal 30-year reign brought the Russian Empire to its historical zenith, and who was revered in Russian hagiography as the defender of Crimea, even as he eventually lost the 1850s war to the Ottomans and Europeans.

At the end of the day, it's their red line. When the enfeebled Franklin Roosevelt made port in the Crimean city of Yalta in February 1945, he—unlike Obama and the neocon claque that has bamboozled him—did at least know that he was in Russia!

Moreover, Washington's current historical ignorance is actually worse. That's because Crimea became part of the Ukraine in recent times only by the caprice of the long-gone Soviet empire.

To wit, maneuvering to cement his control of the Kremlin in the intrigue-ridden struggle for succession after Stalin's death a few years later, Nikita Khrushchev allegedly spent 15 minutes reviewing his "gift" of Crimea to his subalterns in Kiev in honor of the decision by their ancestors 300 years earlier to accept the inevitable and become a vassal of Russia.

Self-evidently, during the long decades of the Cold War, the West did nothing to liberate the "captive nation" of the Ukraine—with or without the Crimean appendage bestowed upon it in 1954. Nor did it draw any red lines in the mid-1990s when a financially desperate Ukraine rented back Sevastopol and the strategic redoubts of the Crimea to an equally pauperized Russia.

In short, in the 65 years before America got its Pacific port in 1848 and in the 166-year interval since then, its national security has depended not one whit on the status of the Russian-speaking Crimea.

That the local population of Crimea has now chosen fealty to the grand thief in Moscow over the ruffians and rabble who have seized Kiev is their business, not ours.

The real threat to peace is not Putin, but the screeching sanctimony and mindless meddling of Susan Rice, Samantha Power and Victoria Nuland. Obama should have sent them back to geography class long ago—and before they could draw any more new red lines.

The one in the Ukraine has been morphing for centuries among the quarreling tribes, peoples, potentates, patriarchs and pretenders of a small region that is none of our damn business.

The current Ukrainian policy farce emanating from Washington is not only a reminder that the military-industrial-beltway complex is still alive and well, but also demonstrates why the forces of crony capitalism and money politics that sustain it are so lamentable.

The fact is, the modern warfare state has been the incubator of American imperialism since the Cold War, and is now proving itself utterly invulnerable to fiscal containment, even in the face of a $20 trillion national debt.

So 102 years after the Christmas truces along the Western Front there is still no peace on earth.

And the long-suffering American taxpayers, who foot the massive bills generated by the War Party's demented and destructive policies, have no clue that Imperial Washington is the principal reason.

CHAPTER 21:

A Peace Deal for the Donald—
Go to Tehran, Bring Home the
American Troops

NY HOPE OF ARRESTING THE NATION'S DRIFT TOWARD FISCAL CALAMITY must start with a Peace Deal. That's the right thing from a national security standpoint, but it's also the secret to unlocking Washington's intractable budget gridlock—a destructive paralysis that has essentially been in place since 1982.

Back then, megascale budget deficits exploded for the first time in peacetime history on the heels of a collapsing economy and the giant tax cuts enacted during Reagan's first year. In theory the desperate need to curtail the hemorrhage of red ink—still a frightful development at the time—provided the greatest opportunity since the New Deal to shrink the welfare state, and especially the middle class social-insurance entitlements.

But the White House's modest assault on the welfare state got stopped stone cold by a revolt of middle-of-the-road Republicans and conservative Democrats. They simply couldn't countenance the simultaneous eruption of military appropriations for the Reagan defense buildup while taking the carving knife to food stamps, Social Security and every manner of benefits in between.

And Ronald Reagan's defense buildup was truly a fiscal eruption. The plan was to increase military spending from Jimmy Carter's outgoing budget of $140 billion to $350 billion within four or five years. While the buildup was eventually slowed down slightly and stretched out into the future, one thing never changed.

To wit, an invincible coalition of military hawks, pork barrel politicians and social-welfare liberals found a modus vivendi that kept the welfare state virtually intact, while the defense spending climbed steadily higher and never looked back, and for an ironic reason.

The rationale for Reagan's defense buildup was the Soviet Union's purported nuclear first-strike threat—a chimera that was vastly exaggerated and lied about by the president's neocon advisers in the early 1980s. But since there was no real strategic nuclear threat to counter, 85% of the massive buildup over the next decade went to the conventional forces.

That is, the 600-ship Navy, the M1 tank program, upward of 10,000 new helicopters and conventional aircraft, vastly augmented capacities for air- and sealift and logistical support, and cruise missiles and smart munitions of every type.

In short, the Reagan defense buildup morphed into a conventional-warfare armada. Accordingly, it was irrelevant to the nonexistent Soviet strategic nuclear threat and too late to harry a Soviet conventional military that, in any event, was sold for scrap when the Soviets disappeared from the pages of history.

But it was a godsend to the Bush and Clinton clans in their pursuit of regime change and wars of intervention and occupation. Without Reagan's mistaken conventional-warfare machine, there would have been no Gulf War in 1991, no crusader (American) boots on the holy lands of Arabia and no spring-training interventions in Bosnia and Serbia/Kosovo.

That's because no Congress would have voted for the massive new conventional-force procurements that enabled these pointless interventions. Once the Soviet Union was no more, even the porkers of Capitol Hill would have seen that they had nothing to do with the security and safety of the citizens of Lincoln NE and Springfield MA.

But once the tank-, ship- and aircraft-production lines had been opened in congressional districts across the land, it was an altogether different political dynamic. The congressman from the Lima, Ohio, M1 tank line, for example, was more than eager to repudiate John Quincy Adams' injunction about not searching the earth for monsters to destroy; to get more tanks and jobs at home, he needed to find more monsters abroad.

At length, the monsters materialized, and as we have seen they were of Washington's very own making.

As we indicated in Chapter 20, Osama bin Laden was the leader of the mujahideen fighters that Washington recruited, transported, trained, armed and provisioned to fight in Afghanistan in the 1980s. Afghanistan was surely none of our business—crumbling Soviet empire or no—but the mujahideen quickly morphed into al-Qaeda when 500,000 U.S. forces entered the lands of Arabia in 1991.

The fluke catastrophe of 9/11 followed, and the real wars of invasion and occupation erupted from Afghanistan to Iraq, Libya, Syria and beyond, but once again enabled by Ronald Reagan's grand conventional armada.

At length and after decades of pointless wars Reagan's armada had metastasized unrecognizably. Obama's third budget, in fact, brought defense and security spending to $750 billion, or 2.5X Jimmy Carter's last budget in inflation-adjusted dollars.

So now in the fullness of time, Barack Obama—the "peace candidate" of 2008—is leaving office with a $20 trillion national debt. Jimmy Carter, of course, left one of less than $1 trillion. And what happened in the interim is the reason why a peace deal is so urgently needed.

THE GLOBAL FISCAL CRUNCH AND A NEW CHANCE FOR PEACE

A peace deal would permit at least $200 billion to be wacked out of the defense budget. In turn, that would break open the post-1982 fiscal deadlock, paving the way for entitlement reform and revenues, too. It would also close the doors to future neocon-style interventions and adventures abroad.

A propitious opportunity for peace, in fact, is emerging worldwide owing to the Great Deflation. This historic reversal of the great credit boom of 1995–2015 is shaking the very foundations of China's Red Ponzi already and is administering the coup de grâce to Russia's third-rate energy-, mineral- and wheat-based economy.

At the same time, the next U.S. administration will be grappling with recession-generated trillion-dollar annual deficits while the socialist enclaves of European NATO face fiscal burial in a renewed eruption of public debts that already average nearly 100% of GDP.

The key to a global peace deal is renunciation of Washington's encroachment on Russia's backyard in Ukraine and the former Warsaw Pact nations. As we indicated in the last chapter, it would open the door to a Russian/ Washington/Shiite alliance to encircle the Islamic State and enable Muslim fighters from Syria, Iran, Iraq and Hezbollah to finish off the butchers of the mutant Sunni caliphate.

The NATO-renunciation part of the deal is in Donald Trump's wheelhouse because he thinks he can make a deal with Putin anyway, and has had the common sense to see that NATO is obsolete. What he needs to further understand is that Russia—with a GDP about the size of the New York City metro area—is incapable of threatening Europe and has no designs to do so.

Moreover, it is Washington, not the Europeans, who insisted on the pointless expansion of NATO. And it was Washington that betrayed George H. W. Bush's sensible promise to Gorbachev in 1989 that in return for his acquiescence to the reunification of Germany, NATO would "not be expanded by a single inch."

There is even a bonus presidential-debate point for The Donald on the latter matter. The betrayal of Bush the Elder's pledge was initiated by none other than Bill Clinton in the midst of his political crisis during the blue-dress affair. The Donald needs to put that one straight to Hillary.

A LEAF FROM EISENHOWER'S NOTEBOOK—TRUMP SHOULD PLEDGE A TRIP TO TEHRAN

Likewise, Trump is already halfway there on the ISIS threat. Unlike the neocon adventurists of Washington, he has welcomed Putin's bombing campaign against the jihadist radicals in Syria and recognizes that the enemy is headquartered in Raqqa, not Damascus.

So it is to be hoped that he somehow comes to understand that Imperial Washington considers Iran to be part of the axis of evil for one principal and wholly invalid reason. Namely, because the neocons leading the Never Trump movement put Tehran in that box 25 years ago, as outlined in Chapter 20, in order to justify their imperial agenda.

The true history is far different. As we have explained, the Iranians have a justified grudge against Washington for its historic support of the shah's plunder and savage repression; for CIA aid to Saddam's brutal chemical warfare against Iran during the 1980s war; for Washington's subsequent demonization of the regime and false claims that it is hell-bent on nuclear weapons—a charge that even the nation's top 16 intelligence agencies debunked more than a decade ago; and most especially for the brutal but pointless economic sanctions that were imposed on the Iranian people by Washington's imperial bullies.

So Donald Trump needs to declare the neocons' revisionist history inoperative. In fact, the way out of the bloody mess in Iraq, Syria, Yemen and Libya—all of which are projects bearing Hillary's support and even inspiration—is a rapprochement with Iran's able and moderate states-man, President Hassan Rouhani, who has just received another wave of political reinforcement in the recent elections.

Someone needs to tutor The Donald on the great General Eisenhower's campaign pledge to go to Korea and make peace immediately after the 1952 election, which is exactly what he did. Likewise, the GOP candidate should pledge to go to Tehran to "improve the deal," and this time Trump even has the plane!

"Improving" the deal, of course, might be positioned as somehow strengthening Obama's "bad deal" on the nuclear accord, but that would be a diplomatic fig leaf for domestic political consumption.

The far-broader purpose would be to bury the hatchet on decades of confrontation between the United States and Iran. In its place would come an agreement to secure Rouhani's leadership role in the above-ref-erenced Muslim-led ground campaign to extinguish ISIS and liberate the territories now controlled by the Islamic State.

Such an "I will go to Tehran" pledge by Trump could electrify the entire Mideast policy morass and pave the way for early U.S. extraction from its counterproductive and wholly unaffordable military and political intrusion.

The fact is, the Islamic State is on its last legs because of U.S. and Russian bombings, $40 oil and its own barbaric brutality. These forces are rapidly drying up the Islamic State's financial resources, and without paychecks its "fighters" rapidly vanish.

Indeed, ISIS is now so financially desperate that its fighters are literally disappearing. That is, it is shooting its wounded and selling their organs on the black market.

Needless to say, no army of fighters has ever prevailed or even survived by harvesting its own flesh. And especially not when confronted by an opposing force of better-trained, better-equipped fighters motivated by an equal and opposite religious fanaticism.

PATH TO PEACE—A TRUMP-PUTIN-ROUHANI ALLIANCE

Accordingly, a Trump-Putin-Rouhani alliance could very readily celebrate the liberation of Raqqa and Mosul by July 4 next year. That could be accompanied by a history-reversing partition agreement to cancel the destructive Sikes-Picot boundaries of 1916.

The latter would be superseded by Shiite, Sunni and Kurdish states, respectively, in their historic areas of Iraq, and a shrunken state of Alawites, Christians and other non-Sunni minorities in western Syria, with protectorates in the North for Kurds and the East for Sunnis.

At that point, a President Trump could stage his own "mission accomplished" pageant by bringing home every last American military personnel now stationed in the Middle East, either overtly or covertly and wearing boots on the ground or not.

And he could do so from the deck of an aircraft carrier that had been withdrawn from the Persian Gulf as part of the comprehensive peace deal with Putin and Rouhani. The Persian Gulf would be an American lake no more.

The Donald might even be positioned to collect his Nobel Peace Prize on the way home.

Before then, however, he would also be in a position to collect some giant domestic political plaudits that could be married with the defeat of ISIS and the winning of peace in the Middle East and Europe. To wit, Trump should promise to sign legislation day one permitting families of the victims of 9/11 to sue the Saudis for their losses.

Nothing could better bring closure to the vastly exaggerated domestic terrorist threat than the simultaneous eradication of the Islamic State by other Muslims, and by multihundred-billion-dollar lawsuits against the alleged 9/11 puppeteers hitting the headlines day after day.

Also, nothing would do more to provide political cover and impetus for the balance of the peace deal. That's because the indigenous terrorist threat in Europe is not sponsored, supported or funded in any manner by the nations of the Shiite Crescent.

Instead, it is an extension of the mutant jihadism of radical Sunni and Wahhabi clerics—mostly based in Saudi Arabia and heavily funded by the cowardly, gluttonous oligarchs who surround the throne in Riyadh.

Needless to say, even the unspeakably corrupt and arrogant princes of the House of Saud would get the message when the 5th Fleet steams out of the Persian Gulf for the last time and the Trump/Putin/Rouhani alliance takes out the Saudis' jihadist proxies in Syria and the Islamic State itself.

In short, the financial lifeblood of terrorism would dry up—whether the Saudi royals remained in Riyadh or decamped to Switzerland.

The essence of the great Peace Deal required to save the American economy is an end to procurement and R&D spending by the Pentagon and a drastic demobilization of the 2.3 million troops in the regular armed forces and national guards. And that can happen under the auspices of a global military "build-down" agreement and freeze on all further weapons exports.

Bankrupt governments in a world where NATO has been decommissioned, the jihadi terrorist threat quelled and the Middle East stabilized will absolutely be interested in a defense "build down" and global arms-re-duction agreement.

And there is no one better qualified to lead a sweeping military cost "restructuring" deal among bankrupt nations than Donald Trump, who knows a thing or two about exactly that.

CHAPTER 22:

In Praise of Ignorant Politicians—
Unschooled in Beltway Delusions

THE IMPERIAL CITY DESERVES TO BE SACKED BY INSURGENT POLITICIANS of a very "ignorant" kind—that is, outsiders unschooled in its specious groupthink and destructive delusions of grandeur.

That's why Donald Trump's challenge to the Beltway's permanent bipartisan ruling class is so welcome. He is largely ignorant of the neocon and war hawk catechisms and sophistries propounded by establishment joints like the Council on Foreign Relations.

But owing to his overweening self-confidence, he doesn't hesitate to lob foreign policy audibles, as it were, from the presidential campaign's line of scrimmage.

It is these unpredictable outbursts of truth and common sense, not his bombast, bad manners and alleged bigotry, that has the Acela Corridor in high dudgeon. The Donald's establishment betters are deathly afraid that he might confirm to the unwashed electorate of Flyover America what it already suspects.

Namely, it suspects that Washington's hype-interventionism and ungodly expensive imperial footprint all around the globe has nothing at all to do with their security and safety, even as it saddles them with massive public debts and the threat of jihadist blowback to the homeland.

The fact is that most of Trump's wild pitches—the Mexican wall, the Muslim ban, waterboarding—are basically excesses of campaign rhetoric that would likely get fashioned into something far more palatable if he were ever in a position to govern. His evolution, and even flip-flopping, on these hot button issues on the campaign trail says as much.

By contrast, the fundamental consensus of our bipartisan rulers is a mortal threat to peace, prosperity and democratic rule.

THE FOLLY OF CURRENT NATO PROVOCATIONS ON RUSSIA'S DOORSTEP

Worse still, the Beltway consensus is so entombed in groupthink that the machinery grinds forward from one folly to the next with hardly a peep of dissent. Nothing could better illustrate that deleterious dynamic, in fact, than the NATO warships recently trolling around the Black Sea.

For crying out loud, the very thought that Washington is sending lethally armed destroyers into the Black Sea is an outrage. That Eurasian backwater harbors no threat whatsoever to the security and safety of the citizens of America—or, for that matter, to those of Germany, France, Poland or the rest of NATO, either.

The shrunken remnants of the Russian Navy—home ported at Sevastopol on the Crimea, as it has been since Catherine the Great—could not even uncork the Dardanelles with war-making intent. Not in the face of the vast NATO armada implacably positioned on the Mediterranean side of the outlet.

So what is possibly the point of rattling seaborne cruise missile batteries on Russia's shoreline? It assumes a military threat that's nonexistent and a hostile intent in Moscow that is purely an artifact of NATO propaganda.

In truth, these reckless Black Sea naval maneuvers amount to a rank provocation. With one glance at the map, even the much-maligned high school–educated voters who have rallied to Trump's cause could tell you that much.

The same can be said for the 31,000 NATO troops recently conducting exercises in Poland and the Baltic republics right alongside the border with Russia. These are not isolated cases of tactical excess or even far-fetched exercises in "deterrence." Instead, they directly manifest Imperial Washington's hegemonic raison d'état.

Indeed, these utterly pointless maneuvers on Russia's doorsteps are just a further extension of the same imperial arrogance that stupidly initiated a fight with Putin's Russia in the first place by igniting a Ukrainian civil war on the streets of Kiev in February 2014.

IMPERIAL WASHINGTON'S HISTORICAL IGNORANCE ON THE UKRAINE FAR EXCEEDS THE DONALD'S

Washington not only sponsored and funded the overthrow of Ukraine's constitutionally elected government, but did so for the most superficial and historically ignorant reason imaginable. To wit, it objected to the decision of Ukraine's prior government to align itself economically and politically with its historic hegemon in Moscow.

So what?

There is nothing at stake in the Ukraine that matters. During the last 700 years, as I indicated in Chapter 20, it has been a meandering set of borders in search of a country. In fact, the intervals in which the Ukraine existed as an independent nation have been few and far between.

Invariably, its rulers, petty potentates and corrupt politicians made deals with or surrendered to every outside power that came along. These included the Lithuanians, Turks, Poles, Austrians, czars and commissars, among others.

Indeed, in modern times Ukraine functioned as an integral part of Mother Russia, serving as its breadbasket and iron and steel crucible under czars and commissars alike. As we noted previously, Crimea itself actually became Russian territory in 1783, when Catherine the Great purchased it from the Turks; and it remained so until the mid-1950s, when in a fit of drunken stupor the newly ascendant Khrushchev gifted it to his Ukrainian compatriots.

Given this history, the idea that Ukraine should be actively and aggressively induced to join NATO was just plain nuts. You might wonder what bantam brains actually came up with the scheme.

Then again, that is only until you recall that NATO itself has been a vestigial organ since 1991. It's now in the business of self-preservation and concocting missions, not securing the peace of anyone, anywhere on the planet.

The Ukraine intervention has already caused NATO, the IMF and Washington to pony up more than $40 billion of aid, which has gone straight down the proverbial rat hole. The part that wasn't stolen by the thieving oligarchs Washington installed in Kiev has been used to prosecute a horrific civil war that has killed and wounded tens of thousands of civilians caught in the cross fire and destroyed what is left of the Ukrainian economy.

Indeed, it was the neocon meddlers from Washington who crushed Ukraine's last semblance of civil governance when they enabled ultra-nationalists and crypto-Nazis to gain government positions after the February 2014 putsch. In one fell swoop, that inexcusable stupidity reopened Ukraine's blood-soaked modern history.

That includes Stalin's re-population of the eastern Donbas region with "reliable" Russian workers after his genocidal liquidation of the kulaks in the early 1930s. It also encompasses the large-scale collaboration by Ukrainian nationalists in the West with the Nazi Wehrmacht as it laid waste to Poles, Jews, gypsies and other "undesirables" on its way to Stalingrad in 1944.

And then there was the equal and opposite spree of barbaric revenge as the victorious Red Army marched back through Ukraine on its way to Berlin.

What Beltway lame brains did not understand that Washington's triggering of "regime change" in Kiev would reopen this entire bloody history of sectarian and political strife?

Moreover, once they had opened Pandora's box, why was it so hard to see that an outright partition of Ukraine with autonomy for the Donbas and Crimea, or even accession to the Russian state from which these communities had originated, would have been a perfectly reasonable resolution?

Certainly that would have been far preferable to dragging all of Europe into the lunacy of the current anti-Putin sanctions and embroiling the Ukrainian factions in a suicidal civil war.

After all, the artificial country of Czechoslovakia, created on a political whim at Versailles, was peacefully and inconsequentially devolved into its separate Czech and Slovakian nations a few years ago. The same is true of Yugoslavia—a polyglot federation that has now devolved into six nations.

In that instance, the partition was partially owing to American bombers that forcibly separated Kosovo from its Serbian parent. And even then, this Washington-sanctioned partition ended up in the hands of a criminal mafia in Kosovo that makes Putin appear sainted by comparison.

In short, the current spate of NATO saber-rattling exercises on Russia's borders is living proof that Washington is in thrall to a permanent ruling class of educated fools and power-obsessed apparatchiks.

Is it any wonder, therefore, that the Imperial City continues to squander scarce fiscal resources on the obsolete machinery of NATO and the bloated Cold War military establishments of its members that have no legitimate purpose?

WAR PARTY HARRUMPHING AT TRUMP'S COMMON SENSE

No wonder Trump's establishment betters scolded and harrumphed when he had the temerity to suggest that NATO was too expensive and possibly obsolete.

But of course it is!

Its mission ended 25 years ago when Boris Yeltsin mounted a Soviet tank, vodka flask in hand, and stood down the Red Army. The very geopolitical earth parted right there and then.

Two years earlier, as we previously explained, Bush the Elder and his able secretary of state, James Baker, had promised Gorbachev that in return for acquiescing in the reunification of Germany, NATO would not be expanded "by a single inch."

Time and again that promise has been betrayed for no good reason except imperial aggrandizement. Now a military alliance that had no purpose other than to contain 50,000 Soviet tanks on the central front—which were long ago melted for scrap and parts—has been joined by the likes of Albania, Croatia, Latvia, Slovakia, Slovenia and Bulgaria too.

Has the ascension of these microstates added to the security and safety of the citizens of Lincoln NE or Springfield MA?

No, it hasn't. It has actually subtracted from national security by threatening Russia, which is a third-rate power with a GDP no larger than that of the New York MSA and an annual defense budget amounting to less than 30 days of Pentagon spending.

As to the necessity of the current naval maneuvers, even the leaders of Bulgaria—a nation cheek by jowl with Russia's Black Sea fleet—have demurred, pointing out the obvious.

To wit, the Black Sea is a place for sailboats and vacationers, not NATO warships.

In fact, that point is so obvious that it is no wonder the Beltway elites are frothing at the mouth about Donald Trump. He just might mobilize the country against the threadbare predicates of their ruinous rule.

As its prime minister, Boiko Borisov, observed about the Black Sea,

> *it should be a place for holidays and tourists, not war . . . I always say that I want the Black Sea to see sailboats, yachts, large boats with tourists and not become an arena of military action . . . [T]o deploy destroyers, aircraft carriers near [the resort cities of] Bourgas or Varna during the tourist season is unacceptable.*

That's the beginning of good sense. Disbanding NATO would be the next rational step forward. And while it lasts, getting them to pay a fair share, as Trump has so sensibly suggested, shouldn't even be debatable.

CHAPTER 23:

Hillary Clinton—Class President of a Failed Generation

HILLARY CLINTON HAS ALWAYS BEEN AT THE HEAD OF HER CLASS. THAT includes being among the leading edge of the 80-million-strong baby boom generation that first started arriving in 1946–47.

She did everything they did: got out for Barry Goldwater in high school; got upwardly mobile to Wellesley and social liberation during college; got "Clean for Gene" and manned the antiwar barricades in the late 1960s; got to Washington to uplift the world in the 1970s; got down to the pursuit of power and position in the 1980s; joined the ruling class in the 1990s; and has helped make a stupendous mess of things ever since.

The baby boom generation, which started with so much promise when it came of age in the 1960s, has ended up a colossal failure. It has turned America into a bloody imperial hegemon abroad and a bankrupt spy state at home where financialization and the 1% thrive, half the population lives off the state and real Main Street prosperity has virtually disappeared from the land.

Quite a deplorable legacy, that. And all the while Hillary has been our class president. God help the world if she becomes our nation's president. She has betrayed all that was right about the baby boomers in the 1960s, and has embraced all the wrong they did during their subsequent years in power.

THE CHANCE FOR PEACE IN 1968

It starts during our defining moment when peace finally had a chance in the spring of 1968. We drove a sitting president from office, and, at that, one whose megalomaniacal will to power was terrifying.

In so doing, we called bull on the Cold War hysteria that had once put us under our desks at school and now falsely claimed that peasants in far-off rice paddies threatened our security. We stopped the Vietnam War cold, dented the Cold War deep and put the whole warfare-state apparatus on the run—the Pentagon, the CIA, the generals and admirals, the military-industrial complex. Within a few years the warfare-state budget was down by 40% in constant dollars.

So it was an epochal chance to break the deadly cycle of war that had started a half century earlier in the bloody trenches of northern France during the Great War; that had been rebooted for a future reprise in the vengeful folly of Versailles; that had been made inexorable by the rise of nationalism, statism, autarky and militarism during the 1930s; and that had been unnecessarily and dangerously extended by the clash of military machines that both victors refused to demobilize after they won the peace in 1945, supplanting the silence of the German and Japanese war guns with the nuclear Sword of Damocles of the Cold War.

True enough, the defeat and retreat of the American Imperium by the idealism and defiance of the baby boomers was interrupted by the Reagan defense build-up and Cold War revival. But that historical error is what makes the Clintons all the more culpable.

As we argued in *The Great Deformation: The Corruption of Capitalism in America*, by 1981 the Soviet Union was already in terminal economic decline. America even then was safe behind its nuclear deterrent.

THE NEOCONS' PHONY CASE AGAINST A DYING SOVIET UNION IN 1981

At the dawn of the 1980s, the Soviet empire was dying under the weight of its statist economic yoke; its militarized "state within the state" was sucking the larger society dry. What the United States needed to do at that juncture was to wait it out—safe behind an ample strategic retaliatory force of Minuteman missiles and Trident submarines. That this more benign course—upon which history had already firmly embarked—was denied at the 11th hour can be blamed on the neocons primarily.

While there were clues and signs everywhere of Soviet industrial decay, the neocon branch of the military-industrial complex trumpeted a new version of the phony missile gap that John Kennedy had promoted during the 1960 campaign.

But the neoconservative version of the alleged "gap" in military capabilities was portrayed as pervasive, ominous, and intensifying. They even claimed the Soviet Union was hell-bent on acquiring nuclear-war-winning capabilities.

In truth, this Soviet nuclear-war-fighting strategy never really existed. Moreover, the huge U.S. military buildup mounted to counter it allocated almost nothing to strategic weapons and countermeasures.

Instead, the Pentagon poured hundreds of billions into equipping and training a vast conventional armada: land, sea, and air forces that were utterly irrelevant to the imaginary Soviet nuclear first strike.

Ironically, the Reagan conventional-force buildup was still cresting when Boris Yeltsin, vodka flask in hand, mounted a tank and stood down the enfeebled Red Army. Future presidents were thus equipped to launch needless wars of invasion and occupation, mainly because owing to the Reagan armada they could.

Indeed, immediately thereafter two American political dynasties arose, and both of them did just that.

The elder Bush was born with a cloak and dagger and christened "Magog" by the Yale Skull and Bones. So maybe he did honestly think there was a difference between the corpulent, tyrannical emir of Kuwait and Saddam Hussein that made worthwhile the spilling of American blood and treasure in Gulf War 1.0. We now know there wasn't.

WHY THE CLINTONS ARE CULPABLE

But you can't exonerate the Clintons, and that includes Hillary, who even in 1993 was not baking cookies in the White House mess. It was their job as the first baby boom co-presidents to finish the work of 1968, and by the time they entered the White House it was a lay-up. The Soviet Union was no more, and Mr. Deng had just declared that to get rich is glorious.

Their job was to have at least the vision of Warren G. Harding. After all, he did demobilize the U.S. war machine completely, eschewed the imperial pretensions of Woodrow Wilson and actually launched a disarmament movement that resulted in the melting down of the world's navies and the Kellogg-Briand treaty to outlaw war.

Yet the opportunity at the Cold War's end was even more compelling. There was absolutely no military threat to American security anywhere in the world.

The Clintons could have drastically reduced the defense budget by mothballing much of the navy and air force and demobilizing the army. They should have cancelled all new weapons programs and dismantled the military-industrial complex.

They could also have declared "mission accomplished" with respect to NATO and made good on Bush's pledge to Gorbachev by actually disbanding it. And, as legatees of 1968, they were positioned to lead a global disarmament movement and to end the arms export trade once and for all.

That was their job—the unfinished business of peace. But they blew it in the name of political opportunism and failure to recognize that the American public was ready to end the century of war, too.

So they capitulated to the pork barrel politics of the Pentagon, plunged into the lunacy of the Balkan wars, launched the misbegotten project to expand NATO, failed to bring Iran back into the community of nations when its leaders reached out to Washington, and kept America in harm's way by keeping our war machine in the Persian Gulf and extending the pointless campaign against Saddam Hussein that could only open the gates to hell in Baghdad.

Needless to say, all of this betrayal did not pacify the neocons and Republican Right. It just egged them on to full-throated imperialism, and enabled the madness of Cheney-Bush to be put into operation without the political inconvenience of raising a war budget.

The great sin of the Clintons was that they left the Reagan conventional armada of invasion and conquest intact and ready to roll.

To wit, at the height of the Cold War in 1961 Eisenhower had left in place a defense budget of $380 billion in constant dollars (2005 $) and a speech warning about the military-industrial complex. The Clintons left behind a budget of $400 billion a full decade after the Cold War ended after having capitulated to the very forces that Ike warned about.

What the only general to lead the nation during its century of war thought was more than enough at the peak of Soviet power, the Clintons did not even bother to challenge at a time when the Kremlin was occupied by a harmless drunk.

And you can't let Hillary off the hook on the grounds that she had the health care file and Bill the bombs and planes. On becoming senator she did not miss a stride betraying the opening for peace that had first broken through in 1968.

She embraced Bush's "shock and awe" campaign in Iraq and was thereby complicit in destroying the artificial nation created by Sykes-Picot in 1916. In so doing, Clinton helped unleash the furies of Islamic sectarian conflict that eventually led to the mayhem and brutality of the Shiite militias and the rise of the ISIS butchers on the backs of the dispossessed Sunni tribes and the demobilized officer corps of Saddam.

WAR HAWK HILLARY

Tellingly, Hillary Clinton made a beeline for the Senate Armed Services Committee, the domain of the Jackson "war Democrats", not the Foreign Affairs Committee, where Frank Church had exposed the folly of Vietnam and the treacherous deeds of the CIA. Undoubtedly, this was to burnish her commander-in-chief credentials, but it spoke volumes.

By the time Hillary got to the seat of power, the idealism and defiance of the warfare state that had animated her and the baby boomers of 1968 had dissipated entirely. For her and most of them, it was now all and only about getting and keeping power. In that respect, Hillary's term at the State Department was a downright betrayal.

Whether by accident or not, Barack Obama had actually been elected as the "peace candidate" by echoing the rhetoric of 1968 that he had apparently read in a book but had been too young to actually hear.

What this untutored and inexperienced idealist needed to hear from his secretary of state was a way forward for peace and the dismantlement of a war machine that had wreaked havoc on the world, left behind 4 million damaged and disabled veterans who had sacrificed for no good reason and a multitrillion-dollar war tab that had bloated the national debt.

What he got was Hillary the Hawk. When Obama took Bush's already-bloated $650 billion war budget (2005 $) to a level that was almost 2X Eisenhower's, Hillary was completely on board.

When Obama was bamboozled into a "surge" of forces in the godforsaken expanse of the Hindu Kush, Hillary busied herself rounding up NATO support. When her neocon and R2P (responsibility-to-protect) advisers and administration compatriots urged making peace by starting wars in Syria, Libya and the Ukraine, Hillary led the charge. All of them have been disasters for their citizens and a stain on America's standing in the world.

When the deep state began lining up the next enemy, Hillary joined the gumming brigade, warning about the China threat. My god, were the Red Capitalists of Beijing to actually bomb 4,000 Walmarts in America, their system would collapse in six months and their heads would be hung from the rafters in the nearest empty Foxconn/Apple factory.

Here's the thing. Hillary Clinton's selling out to the warfare state is not just about war and peace—even as it fosters the former and precludes the latter. It's also about the nation's busted fiscal accounts, its languishing Main Street economy and the runaway gambling den that has taken over Wall Street.

The one thing that I learned during my time on both ends of Pennsylvania Avenue is that the defense budget, and the military-industrial complex that perpetuates it, is the mother's milk of fiscal irresponsibility.

One of Hillary's predecessors, Alfonse D'Amato, who was known as "Senator Pothole," symbolized it succinctly. There was not a weapons system made in Georgia, Texas, California or Washington that he wouldn't support if he could trade his vote for another pothole appropriation for New York.

Since the time of Reagan there has been no fiscal responsibility in Washington because there is no longer a party of fiscal rectitude. The GOP spends half its political capital defending the defense budget and the neocon agenda of permanent war and the other half pretending that deficits don't matter or that they are solely caused by too many Democrats in Washington or too little growth on Main Street.

And so the Clinton Democrats have had a free political ride. Unlike Tip O'Neill of circa 1980, they do not fear a political attack from the right on the issue of deficits, debt and big spending. So nothing is done to defuse the generational time bomb known as social insurance—even though means testing the wealthy recipients of Social Security and Medicare would ameliorate much of the problem.

Likewise, nothing is done to put in place a 21st-century consumption tax that could pay the nation's bills before it is too late or, in the alternative, permit the elimination or sharp reduction of the jobs-destroying payroll and corporate income taxes before the U.S. economy grinds to a complete halt.

As it is, the day of fiscal reckoning is being forestalled by an artificial, destructive and unsustainable monetary regime that has drastically lowered the true cost of the national debt and monetized trillions of public debt with central bank credit plucked out of thin air.

After all this time, however, Hillary doesn't get any of this. She thinks war is peace; deficits don't matter; the baby boom is entitled to the social insurance they didn't earn; and the Fed's serial bubble machine is leading the nation back to prosperity.

Actually, it's leading to the greatest financial bubble in human history. After 93 months of ZIRP and a decade of Wall Street coddling and subsidization by the Fed, the windfalls to the 1% have become unspeakable in their magnitude and illegitimacy.

But none of this troubles Hillary Clinton. She rose to fame delivering an idealistic commencement address at the beginning of her career. But like the generation she represents, she has betrayed those grand ideals over a lifetime of compromise, expediency, self-promotion and complacent acquisition of power, wealth and fame.

She doesn't deserve another stint at the podium—let alone the bully pulpit.

CHAPTER 24:

A Lesson for The Donald—
Barack, We Hardley Knew Ye

"With your drums and guns and guns and drums, hurroo, hurroo
With your drums and guns and guns and drums, hurroo, hurroo
With your drums and guns and guns and drums
The enemy nearly slew ye
Oh my darling dear, Ye look so queer
Johnny I hardly knew ye."

THIS MEMORABLE STANZA FROM THE CLASSIC ANTIWAR SONG COULD NOT be more apt with respect to Barack Obama. He became president because he campaigned across the land draped in the garlands of peace. Yet he has now spent his years in the White House smearing his face with war paint and strutting around the Imperial City marshaling its "drums and guns and guns and drums."

And let's be clear. The president's so-called counterterrorism campaign—that special kind of violent eruption that isn't a "war"—is not really about punishing some barbarians who have beheaded innocent civilians and who have also recruited perhaps a dozen not-so-innocent Americans to join their bloodthirsty ranks.

Civilized adults just do not start a war on the other side of the world on account of such thin gruel, as horrific as the actions involved might be.

So it is to be hoped that The Donald learns from Obama's giant errors before he too falls prey to the War Party's self-defeating cycle of retaliation, provocation and blowback.

WOODROW WILSON OBAMA

Barack Obama's stated reasons for Washington's renewed war in Iraq and an extended war in Syria and now Libya too—beheadings and venomous rhetoric and barbaric rule of some dusty backwater towns and villages on the Upper Euphrates—reverberate with failed history. To wit, the nation's 44th president has been on the same slippery slope that Woodrow Wilson stood on when he sent 2 million American GIs into the senseless slaughterhouse of northern France 99 years ago.

Back then, it was to vindicate the freedom of Americans to sail into war zones, even on armed belligerent ships.

In the cold light of history, Wilson's misbegotten crusade on behalf of an utterly untenable principle accomplished nothing more than to prolong a war that was already over in the spring of 1917 due to the mutual exhaustion and bankruptcy of both sides.

In so doing, as we suggested in Chapter 20, Wilson spawned the Bolshevik tyranny in Russia, the punitive peace treaty of Versailles, the revanchist evil of Nazi Germany and the world wars and cold wars that followed.

That was "blowback" writ large—a chain of repercussions that shaped the very warp and woof of the entire next century. Yet in 1917, the safety and security of citizens in Lincoln NE or Spokane WA could not have been enhanced in the slightest by plunging into a pointless war in Europe to secure "freedom of the seas" during its final hours of carnage.

Likewise, in 2016 the case for a war on the ancient battlegrounds of the Shiite/Sunni divide and numerous related tribal and ethnic enmities to avenge the murder of journalists, humanitarians, tourists and Western officials who knowingly ventured into a zone of vicious civil war, anarchy and barbarism is no more compelling or rational.

What Obama's Iraq War 2.0 is really about, therefore, is the capacity of the American warfare state to co-opt any and all dissenting views and to transform cruel doings from virtually anywhere on the planet into a casus belli.

Accordingly, Obama's recurring patter from the Oval Office about the administration's plan to "degrade" and "ultimately destroy" ISIS is just so much Beltway pettifoggery; it's the kind of verbal smokescreen that the chattering politicians temporarily bivouacked along Pennsylvania Avenue are pleased to deploy as they go about implementing—unwittingly or otherwise—the agenda of Washington's permanent imperial machinery.

IRAQ WAR 2.0—AN EXERCISE IN FUTILITY

So here's the thing that Donald Trump needs to understand. Either Washington means to eradicate the Islamic State root and branch in a Normandy-style invasion and occupation of the Sunni-Euphrates valley, or it's just inviting vengeance and blowback that will cause to pale in significance that which has occurred to date.

Dropping bombs from high-altitude aircraft, or launching Tomahawk missiles from distant ships or dispatching drone payloads via video consoles in Nevada, may kill a few ISIS warriors and leaders along with thousands of innocent Sunni civilians in the territories they now occupy. But in the end it will amount to jabbing a hornet's nest with a short stick.

As we indicated in Chapter 21, a far-better alternative would be to evacuate the inferno of rubble and carnage that constitutes the so-called Islamic State caliphate, and leave it to the Shiite Crescent to finish off the barbaric and bloodthirsty regime of their mortal enemies.

After all, do ISIS' menacing oratory and graphic videos really constitute a clear and present danger to the American homeland that can't be handled with increased domestic vigilance and police protections?

Does a regime that materialized almost overnight from the madness of Iraq 1.0 provide sufficient cause for launching hell-fire from the skies on a territory bigger than the state of New Jersey and occupied by roughly 5 million Sunni Arabs who in the main are not at all fond of the "indispensable nation" that has appointed itself to rescue them from their new rulers?

Notwithstanding the president's vaporous rhetoric, double-talk and self-contradiction, the Department of Homeland Security has testified on Capitol Hill that it still has no hard evidence that the Islamic State is planning an attack on U.S. territory. To the contrary, there is no evidence that it has even a semblance of the logistical capacity to accomplish one.

The closest Washington's vaunted $80-billion-per-year intelligence octopus has come to identifying a tangible ISIS threat is chatter on Twitter. Indeed, even the recent horrific incidents of ISIS-"inspired" attacks in San Bernardino and Orlando involved no organizational link to the Islamic State at all.

Likewise, it is breathtaking in the extreme that in the blood-soaked wreckage of the non-nation of Syria, which was scribbled on a map by dandies in the British and French foreign offices in 1916, Washington is now attempting to eliminate two regimes at the same time.

Never mind that the Assad-Alawites in the Southwest and West and the ISIS-Sunni caliphate in the North and East between them control 90 percent of Syrian territory. At least Donald Trump has been sensible enough to see that playing monkey in the middle borders on insanity.

He also seems to recognize that American boots on the ground to secure the dusty villages, bleak desert expanses and other pointless redoubts controlled by the Islamic State is pointless.

Hopefully, he will not succumb instead to the Pentagon fallacy, as did Barack Obama, that the Islamic State can be bombed back into the Stone Age by a purely aerial campaign—and that the "moderate" opposition can be recruited, organized, trained, equipped and provisioned to do the job of killing off the stragglers.

That's right. The silly, naïve man in the Oval Office signed up to a bombing campaign that simply enraged the hordes of medieval butchers encamped in the Islamic State, while destroying much of what was left of civil society and killing innocent men, women and children in their thousands as "collateral" damage.

Worse still, he spent upward of $500 million training a rag-tag bunch of 60 buccaneers who lasted not even a week on the actual Syrian battlefield. As we previously described, within days of deployment, their commander and his deputy were captured by the jihadists, a dozen or more were killed and the rest fled—either leaving their U.S.-supplied weapons behind or selling them to the highest bidder.

IN A SANE WORLD, OBAMA'S ISIS STRATEGY WOULD BE IMPEACHABLE MADNESS

In a sane world, this would be considered an impeachable madness. In today's Washington, however, Barack Obama's ludicrous "no boots, all air" strategy passes for mainstream wisdom. And so does the preposterous idea that Washington is once again enabling the Iraqi government and its so-called army to liberate their own homeland.

But that is worse than a pipe dream. The reason that there will be no Iraqi government and war-capable Iraqi army, of course, is that there is no Iraqi nation—just the Sykes-Picot borders.

Yet the latter were long ago irreparably shattered by the Bush war of shock and awe against the last dictator who had been able to corral the Sunni, Shiite and Kurds into a temporary polity at the end of a sword.

As we have seen, the truth is that the brief and vanished nation of Iraq is already partitioned. The Kurds have already created a de facto Kurdistan in the Northeast, while the Shiite South is already a de facto province of Iran.

So be it. The greater Shiite polity on the North and East of the Persian Gulf is a more certain barrier to Islamic State expansion than any imaginary coalition of the unwilling that Washington might concoct.

But here's the giant flaw in Obama's Iraq War 2.0 strategy. The Peshmerga can be counted upon to ferociously defend Kurdistan against ISIS encroachment, and the Shiite militias will doubtless accomplish the same in their own territories.

But no one with a modicum of historical knowledge would think it sane to send the Shiite militias up into the Sunni lands of the Euphrates valley to mop up after the American bombs, missiles and drones; they would commit genocide if given half the chance.

In short, if Washington were to double down on Obama's evident failure in a full bombs-away mode there would be no force of moderate rebels nor any reconstituted Iraqi army to finish the job. And the idea of meaningful Sunni boots on the ground from a regional coalition among the enmity-ridden nations of Turkey, Jordan, Saudi Arabia, Qatar and the UAE is too preposterous to even merit discussion.

So what Obama actually launched two years ago was Operation Blowback—Washington's stupidest military campaign yet from among a long list that stretches back through two previous wars in Iraq, countless Cold War coups and interventions and grand disasters like Vietnam.

Needless to say, there is a better way. The best safeguard and only real protection against the theoretical threat of the Islamic State is vigilance and enhanced public security at home. And coupled with it, an end to pointless bombing campaigns in Muslim lands that mainly succeed in destroying American tanks, artillery pieces and other equipment left behind in earlier delusional campaigns.

So, yes, let the Islamic State try to govern 5 million people in the dusty villages and impoverished desert expanse of the Euphrates valley by means of the sword and medieval precepts of Sharia law.

The eventual flight, sabotage and revolt of the long-suffering peoples of the ISIS-occupied lands will do more for the safety and security of the American people than all the drones and bombers that Washington could send to forge still more puppet nations within the Syrian and Iraqi "borders"—nations that have already been deposited in the dustbin of history.

The peace candidate of 2008 might have seen the sensibility of that course of action.

But after nearly eight years at the throne of power in the Imperial City it might be well and truly said by the world's war-weary everywhere that Barack, we hardly knew ye.

CHAPTER 25:

The Aspen Strategy Group—
Hillary's War Cabinet in Waiting

THIS FAIR SUMMER CAMP FOR THE (VERY) FORTUNATE GOT DOUBLE whammyed by the War Party during a weekend of "big think" last August.

First there was a "debate" about whether ISIS should be "contained" or "defeated." That was followed by a glowing progress report from General John Allen. He was President Obama's special envoy for the Global Coalition of the Unwilling and Unable (to fight ISIS), and the gist of his speech was that 6,000 airstrikes since the previous August had been winning droves of hearts and minds in the Upper Euphrates valley.

Well, that number is up to 11,000 now, and there is scant sign of hearts and minds being won.

Still, General Allen's speech was all for the edification of the pooh-bahs of the foreign policy establishment who had been in town for the annual Aspen Strategy Group conclave. The latter bills itself as "a bipartisan foreign policy group that includes legislators, experts, journalists, policy practitioners, members of academia, and business leaders."

No, it's not. It's an off-campus exercise in mendacity, vapid groupthink and narcissistic self-glorification by the perpetrators of Washington's endless foreign policy catastrophes. Once a year they come to admire each other and split hairs about pointless tactical differences.

DEBATING A BIPARTISAN FOLLY

The debate about "containing" versus "defeating" ISIS proved that in spades. In fact, the "exterminate ISIS" team embodied an exact caricature of the bipartisan folly that has congealed in the Washington War Party.

Not surprisingly the #2 chair in the duo was occupied by an out-and-out neocon warmonger, Professor Philip Zelikow. He was an architect of the Bush wars on WMD and head of the 9/11 Whitewash Commission. His case boiled down to shouting vehemently that the Islamic hordes are heading for Times Square.

So America needs to obliterate the 200,000 citizens of Raqqa, Syria, before they get us. Never mind that there is not one iota of evidence that the self-appointed enforcers of Islamic purity who occupy a few dusty desert towns in the Upper Euphrates have any real capacity to mount a military attack on the fleshpots of Broadway and 42nd.

But the neocons are taking no chances. To nearly every last armchair warrior, led by Robert Kagan, they are lining up behind Hillary.

Apparently, they fear Donald Trump might make a deal with Putin to unleash President Assad and his Shiite Crescent allies. In short order that would put the Islamic State out of business and close the Syrian theatre of the neocon war game, too.

But what was dispositive about last summer's confab was that the #1 chair on the perpetual-war team was occupied by Michèle Flournoy.

That's right. She was Obama's #2 at the DOD and was ostensibly a legatee of what was once the Democratic Party's left-leaning peace wing.

No more. Ms. Flournoy has climbed Washington's slippery pole of power by growing a heavy plume of hawkish feathers.

Accordingly, she presented not a single coherent argument about how ISIS is a military threat to the safety and security of the citizens of Lincoln NE or Springfield MA. Her case amounted to nothing more than a glib recitation of ISIS' murderous brutalities, beheadings and benighted barbarisms.

But as John Quincy Adams so profoundly observed, America's security does not require that it search the world for monsters to destroy.

HILLARY'S WAR HAWKS—WHY TRUMP DESERVES A CHANCE

Apparently, Hillary Clinton thinks otherwise.

Her secretary of defense designate is none other than Michèle Flournoy. Both share an obliviousness to Adams' profound truth because they are credentialed members of the Washington War Party.

And as a team, they are as good a reason as any to give Donald Trump a shot at the commander–in-chief job.

After all, he has not spent a lifetime in the Imperial City looking for monsters to destroy abroad. He has even had the good sense to suggest that the vast network of U.S. bases used for this purpose should be sharply curtailed.

Defend America at home, first, he says. And why not? The Washington Imperium has failed virtually everywhere, and its bombs, drones and occupations have hatched far more terrorists than they have killed.

Nor is Trump a paid-off supplicant of the military-industrial-congressional complex that Eisenhower warned about, and which since the demise of the Soviet Union has done exactly as he predicted.

To wit, it has never stopped inventing enemies, provocations and threats designed to justify a massive, costly and obsolete Cold War military machine.

As we indicated in Chapter 20, the whole military-industrial complex, NATO and the international-security apparatus should have been disbanded when the Cold War ended for lack of a genuine industrial-state enemy.

Instead, searching for monsters to destroy has been the very raison d'être of American foreign policy. And it has surely been the source of the endless catastrophes that have ensued.

As we previously demonstrated, in the great wash of history it didn't really matter to America which tyranny—that of the brutish Saddam Hussein or the repressive Sharia-law-based regime of Sheikh al-Sabah—controlled the oil fields on the Kuwait/Iraq border.

As we have insisted, the answer to oil shortages everywhere and always is high prices, not the 5th Fleet. This truth has been demonstrated over and over in the last half century—not the least in the current cycle.

High oil prices at $150 per barrel lasted a few months in 2008 and tottered above $100 a few years thereafter, but have now been buried as far as the eye can see by an outpouring of shale, tar sands and other lower-grade or costly-to-extract hydrocarbon supplies from provinces all over the planet. And that's to say nothing of the vast upwelling of alternative energy and conservation responses to higher prices.

In fact, OPEC is no more. One day—perhaps soon—the opulent princes of the Persian Gulf will even be scrambling to fuel up their 747s for a final bon voyage.

Stated differently, economics will out, and whatever sovereign controls the bounty of Mother Nature buried beneath the desert sands of the Persian Gulf and North Africa will produce all of it they can.

Every dictator of the last half century proved that—from Muammar Gaddafi, to Saddam Hussein, to the mullahs of the Iranian Republic.

Indeed, the politically induced shortages have all been the work of the War Party's perennial sanctions and embargoes. So the slight "shortages" that did occur from time to time were actually cooked up by the denizens of the Aspen Strategy Group, not bloodthirsty men in black turbans.

STILL WRONG AFTER 25 YEARS

Needless to say, as the Aspen Strategy Group carried on its simulacrum of debate and analysis, the original grey-haired perpetrators of the Persian Gulf oil-security myth were all there to cheer them on, including Brent Scowcroft, who had advised Bush the Elder to draw a pointless line in the Kuwaiti sand.

Yet, as we now know, what actually got implanted in the sand were the boots of the American army in Saudi Arabia. It was Washington's spurious meddling in the $40 billion dispute between Saddam and the greedy princes of Riyadh over who owed what from their joint war on Iran during the 1980s that resurrected a Wahhabi fanatic named Osama bin Laden.

As we have seen, the latter had been left in obscurity and unemployment after his CIA-funded mujahideen work in Afghanistan ended with the collapse of the Soviet Union.

That senseless revival, in turn, ultimately enabled the fluke calamity of 9/11.

As bin Laden ranted in his famous "Declaration of War Against the Americans Occupying the Land of the Two Holy Places,"

> *The latest and the greatest of these aggressions, incurred by the Muslims since the death of the Prophet (ALLAH'S BLESSING AND SALUTATIONS ON HIM) is the occupation of the land of the two Holy Places [Mecca and Medina] -the foundation of the house of Islam, the place of the revelation, the source of the message and the place of the noble Ka'ba, the Qiblah of all Muslims- by the armies of the American Crusaders and their allies. (We bemoan this and can only say: "No power and power acquiring except through Allah")*

But once bin Laden's tiny cohort of fanatical jihadists—never numbering more than a few thousands according to the CIA itself—was unleashed, the War Party proceeded to add insult to injury. It mistook the U.S. military's easy time of shooting Saddam's ducks in a barrel on the Kuwaiti desert as evidence of Washington's war-winning prowess, and the popularity of CNN's first-ever live-action war games as an endorsement of the American people's appetite for foreign adventurism.

So under the clueless authority of Bush the Younger, the denizens of the Aspen Strategy Group added lies and dissimulation to the sin of false pride. That is, they carried out an unprovoked shock-and-awe invasion of a country that had never, ever threatened America, had no capacity to harm the American people, and had no connection whatsoever to the fanatical sect that pulled off 9/11 against all odds.

Stated differently, 9/11-style terrorism was a domestic public-safety and policing challenge back then, and it remains so today. The remote threat of an ISIS terrorist attack or even an ISIS-inspired copycat attack in any given American city or town has not been reduced by an iota owing to the random bombing and droning campaigns being carried out in the Upper Euphrates valley by the Washington War Party.

So Imperial Washington had it wrong from the beginning. Fighting terrorism was never an appropriate mission for the Pentagon's conventional war machine—a lethal armada of tanks, planes and ships that had been mistakenly built by Ronald Reagan to fight an industrialized enemy like the Soviet Union, which was no more.

OPENING THE GATES OF HELL

Yet once the American war machine was unleashed on the fragile polity that Saddam had stapled together with machine guns and canisters of deadly gases, the furies of historical grudges and sectarian grievances were inexorably unleashed

The truth is, Washington midwifed ISIS by hanging Saddam and destroying a brutal but serviceable regime that had at least been based on the secularist tenets of Baathist nationalism. Saddam had a penchant for brandishing rifles and liquidating dissidents, but he did not cotton to beheading infidels.

That was the modus operandi of the Shiite militias who got a free hand once Saddam was gone. And it was these vengeance seekers who ran riot over the land between the two rivers after the American people properly elected a peace candidate pledged to extricate Washington from its grizzly mayhem in Iraq.

Likewise, the reason more than anything else that the Sunni lands of western Iraq fell to the butchers of ISIS during the summer of 2014 was that they offered a shield of protection against the vengeance of the Shiite vigilantes and the monumental corruption and theft of the Shiite government in Baghdad.

Even then, however, their lightning conquest was made in Washington. As we have seen, ISIS conquered its territories not by the "sword" of Sunni fundamentalism at all, but owing to the massive arsenal of tanks, Humvees, field artillery, lethal weaponry and ammunition and advanced paraphernalia of 21st-century warfare that had been deposited there by the departing American military.

Indeed, during the debate about "containment" versus "rollback" that Sunday afternoon there occurred a moment of clarity that explains why the War Party's abominations go unchecked.

David Petraeus, the disgraced general whose misbegotten "surge" campaigns caused the pointless deaths of more than 1,000 American servicemen in Iraq and Afghanistan and whose egomaniacal strutting led him to drop the CIA's black book of secrets on Paula Broadwell's pillow, had the cheek to stand up and explain that it was Obama who blew his victory in Anbar province.

Yes, that's exactly what the man said!

Did the audience give the ex-general the Bronx cheer he deserved, or did the moderator call foul ball?

No, they did not. The moderator invited him to star in the next debate, and the audience welcomed the blithering nonsense he offered in the guise of a question.

Well, here's the real question. Whose infinitely dumb idea was it to spend $25 billion purportedly training and equipping an "Iraqi" army in what by 2007 was an utterly failed state, rent asunder by sectarian strife that was beyond recall?

Yes, it was David Petraeus and his congressional sponsors like the rabid warmongers Senators McCain and Graham who did exactly that.

The only reason that there was even a debate about the proper anti-ISIS strategy during this Aspen confab was because the War Party in its wisdom left behind in Sunni lands 2,300 Humvees, 74,000 machine guns, 40 Abrams tanks, and countless more accouterments of war with what was, in fact, a Shiite militia wearing Iraqi uniforms—uniforms they instantly shed when it came to defending Sunni towns against the descending hordes of ISIS.

Needless to say, the War Party learns nothing and never quits. Thus, its debate team of ISIS eradicators had yet another scheme. By their lights, "containment" of ISIS in its pitiful desert redoubts is not enough. Channeling Barry Goldwater's 1964 campaign slogan, they claimed that America can settle for no less than "victory" over ISIS.

Yes, and that is to be accomplished with no American boots on the ground. The eradication is to be carried on by the Sunnis themselves.

WHERE'S THE SUNNI WALDO?

Say what?

Would that be the Sunni nation of Turkey, equipped as it is with NATO's best 1,000 planes, 5,000 tanks and a professional military of 500,000? Well, that all depends on what Sultan Erdogan intends to do now that he has made himself dictator.

Besides, there are complications due to the Kurdish issue and the obsession of the Sultan with liquidating the Syrian Kurdish allies of his own insurgent population of 15 million Kurds before getting around to vanquishing the Sunni caliphate.

Indeed, most of the cross-border bombing campaigns carried out by Turkey in the past year have really been a thinly disguised cover to make war on the Kurdish enclaves of northern Syria and Iraq.

Why? The better to stir up anti-Kurdish venom among the Turkish populace. Nothing could better serve Erdogan's evident plan to extend his current emergency powers to rule by decree or to eventually amend the nation's constitution to make himself presidential dictator for life.

The next Sunni candidate, of course, is the real irony. The only great Sunni tribe that has shown itself willing and able to fight ISIS is the Kurds. But Kurdistan—a nation of 30 million—doesn't even have an army because it was the one large tribe that came back from Versailles empty-handed and without a nation of its own.

So its people remained scattered among hostile Shiite governments in Iraq and Iran, and bombed and prosecuted by a newly installed dictatorship in Ankara. The only boots the Kurds will be leaving on the ground are the ones felled by the Turkish air force.

Likewise, to the south is the 88-million-strong Sunni nation of Egypt. But it goes without saying that General al-Sisi, its newly legitimized dictator by way of Washington's renewed $1.5 billion flow of aid and weapons, will not be sending his army to the Upper Euphrates. He needs the entirety of his 469,000-man military to keep the population of Egypt subdued.

In the case of the vast Sunni population of Saudi Arabia (about 25 million), the prospects of raising an anti-ISIS fighting force under the auspices of the government in Riyadh are between slim and none. The House of Saud knows full well that if it sends its army to Syria it will defect to the Sunni jihadists' side in short order.

So whence cometh the Sunni boots on the ground that will be needed to eradicate the purported 20,000 ISIS fighters? After all, we have already demonstrated what happened last time Washington got itself busy identifying, recruiting, vetting, training and deploying the proverbial "moderate" Syrian rebels who, purportedly, want to take back their country from the jihadists.

To wit, after years of jabbering and a half-billion dollars spent, Washington was finally able to field a force of 60 soldiers, but within days of deployment its commander and deputy were captured by the Nusra Front, several members were killed and the balance defected or disappeared into the rubble of the former Syrian state.

Yes, this is beyond pathetic. But here's the thing. The opposing side in the Aspen Strategy Group debate was at least sober enough to advocate "containment" rather than indulging in the juvenile game of Where's the Sunni Waldo.

But they never did say how long the United States would have to "contain" ISIS by bombing the 81,000 square miles it controls, or whether this would constitute taking it back to the Stone Age or merely recognizing that it was already essentially there.

THE ISLAMIC STATE THAT ISN'T

Notwithstanding that Ramadi, Fallujah, Mosul and Raqqa were once respectable centers of civilization and commerce, the truth is there is next to nothing left there after years, even decades, of U.S.-instigated warfare.

So the so-called Islamic State is no state at all—it's just a backwater dystopia that is utterly incapable of ever mounting a military threat to America's security.

Indeed, now that oil is down to $40 per barrel and most of the motley array of Syrian oil wells have been decimated, the Islamic State has apparently discovered a new method of revenue raising. As we previously indicated, they are reportedly harvesting and selling the body parts of their wounded.

Stated differently, the blood-thirsty fanatics who run the Islamic State are killing the commerce, the population and even the flocks and fields on which these quasi-subsistence villages once depended. For crying out loud, according to General John Allen himself, the whole joint was being run on revenue of less than $1 billion per year; and now that its oil revenues are going dry, its funds are down to a small fraction of even that.

Don't these Washington geniuses know that when it comes to recruiting even soldiers of Allah, the rule of "no ticky, no washy" applies, and in spades?

And what kind of crackpots really think that as abhorrent as ISIS is—that a real state with a modern military capability can finance itself on the slave trade of young women, the body parts of the wounded, hostage taking and punitive taxation of a nearly starving population in its shrunken areas of control?

This is nuts! The War Party's futile effort to "contain" ISIS by relentless droning and bombing of the unfortunate towns and villages caught up in it snare is accomplishing only one thing—and it amounts to a monumental self-inflicted setback.

Namely, it provides horrific, living-color video proof that the crusaders are still visiting mayhem on the innocent and Allah-fearing peoples of the putative caliphate. And it is the overpowering magnet that brings new recruits to join the fight against the Great Satan in Washington.

A BETTER WAY FORWARD

As we have indicated, the way to stop ISIS is to ground the bombers and drones; send home the spotters, trainers and other infrastructure of intervention; forget about who controls the oil—it will be produced by someone; and recognize that American has no dog in the 1,300-year-old fight between Sunnis and Shiites.

Indeed, the elephant in the room during the Aspen debate was the Shiite Crescent—that is, the 100 million Shiite citizens of Iran; the rump of Iraq in Bagdad and the South; the Alawite/Shiite minority of the Assad regime in Syria; and the Hezbollah/Shiite fighters who represent 40% of Lebanon and constitute its largest political party.

All of them have been condemned to the sword as apostates by the ISIS caliphate, and at the end of the day they are the one force that can keep the latter bottled up in its miserable territories until its bloody regime collapses of its own inhumanity.

Alas, when it comes to the Shiite Crescent—a group of Islamic nations no better or worse than the brutal tyranny of Egypt or the gluttonous obscenity of the Persian Gulf sheikdoms—the War Party cannot see straight.

The Aspen Strategy Group, Hillary Clinton, Michelle Flournoy and the rest are utterly clueless as to why the Iranian regime has been so hostile to the American Imperium's plans for a better world.

So we must reiterate. The CIA did overthrow Iran's elected government in 1953 for the sin of nationalizing the nation's oil fields. Washington did stand 100% behind the shah's 25-year reign of plunder and helped him organize and operate the brutal SAVAK.

The neocons of the Reagan White House did tilt toward Iraq after its unprovoked attack on Iran, and they went so far as to use the CIA's spy satellites to act as spotters for Saddam's chemical-weapons attacks.

And their successors in the administration of Bush the Elder did identify the Iranian Republic as the new enemy to replace the fallen Soviets, thereby keeping the military-industrial complex and CIA surveillance state alive and funded at its accustomed levels.

Likewise, they did induce Bush the Younger to identify Iran as part of the axis of evil in his 2002 State of the Union address. That is, they proclaimed Iran among the nations slated for the cleansing force of a Washington-orchestrated "regime change" and that its leaders, like Saddam, would be disposed of at the end of a hangman's rope.

So they don't like us—profoundly so. Yet the leaders in Tehran have had the good sense to bend over and accept Obama's humiliating deal to exchange a nonexistent nuclear-weapons program and 15 years of an international nuclear-inspection proctology for the right to re-enter world commerce and the community of nations.

Even then, they will fight and contain ISIS because their survival depends upon it.

ASPEN WAR GAMES AND THE GHOST OF GENERAL WESTMORELAND

None of these realities penetrated last summer's Aspen war games, nor Hillary's war cabinet in waiting.

Indeed, as General Allen droned on during that occasion—and, yes, the man was droning profusely—about the scores of godforsaken Syrian border towns that have been allegedly liberated from ISIS, the police forces that have been stood up, the fresh recruits that have joined the so-called Iraqi Army, the thousands of ISIS fighters who have been sent to a better world, the thousands of teachers and medics who have been put into the field, I closed my eyes.

I then did hear the voice of General William C. Westmoreland echoing over the decades. We are winning the hearts and minds of the Vietnamese people, he intoned; we are Vietnamizing the conflict; the strategic hamlet program has become a swell success; we are building schools and clinics in the rice paddies; the body count of dead Viet Cong is swelling by the day.

It was all one giant tapestry of BS, of course, which temporarily camouflaged the catastrophe of LBJ's war and the genocidal destruction that it inflicted on an innocent people.

Still, General Allen's completely bogus progress report reminded me why I was a peacenik way back then; of how profoundly Hillary and her War Party have betrayed the cause; and why even an untutored and often-uncouth showman like Donald Trump cannot possibly do worse than the pretentious armchair warriors of the Aspen Strategy Group.

CHAPTER 26:

In Praise of the Iran Nuke Deal—
A Chance for Peace If We Can Keep It

NEAR THE END OF HIS TERM IN OFFICE, BARACK OBAMA FINALLY STOOD up to the War Party. That could mark a decisive turning point in rolling back Washington's destructive interventionism and imperial pretensions in the Middle East and, indeed, around the world.

Yet this chance for peace is fragile. If Donald Trump is elected, it is to be hoped that he will prove to be sensible enough to jettison his campaign rhetoric about Obama's "horrible" nuclear deal, and, instead, board a plane for Tehran as outlined in Chapter 21.

The fact is, there is nothing "horrible," deficient or weak at all about the Iranian nuclear agreement. To the contrary, it is a decisive refutation of the War Party's hoary claim that Iran is hell-bent upon obtaining nuclear weapons.

As we explained earlier, this deafening but untruthful narrative was long ago debunked by the 2007 National Intelligence Estimates (NIEs). These authoritative findings were issued by the nation's 16 top intelligence agencies in November 2007, and they held that what had possibly been a small-scale Iranian weapons-research effort was abandoned in 2003 and never restarted.

That NIE verdict has been reiterated several times since then, and has now been revalidated by the International Atomic Energy Association (IAEA), as well.

WMD 2.0

As we previously recalled, even the Great Decider ultimately threw on the towel. In his memoir he confessed that it would have been hard to explain to the American public why he was launching another war to eliminate an alleged Iranian WMD threat when his own intelligence agencies had just concluded it did not even exist!

Indeed, the war drums about Iran's alleged nuclear-weapons program were then being beaten loudly by the very same crowd—Cheney, Wolfowitz, Bolton, Feith and the like—that had falsified the WMD claims against Saddam Hussein.

And, as we also described previously, they had resorted to the same kind of falsified intelligence that the first time around had generated the infamous "curveball" pictures of Saddam's alleged biological-weapons labs that turned out to be pasteurized-milk plants.

This time it was a bunch of falsified drawings and nuclear weapons plans mysteriously found on a laptop computer that had been turned over by a Iranian dissident group called the MEK. The latter, ironically, had long been allied with Saddam Hussein and had been on the State Department terrorist list from 1997 to 2012.

So it needs to be shouted from the rafters that all the arm waving and screeching against this deal by the GOP warmongers and the Israeli lobby is grounded in a Big Lie. The whole Iran-is-after-the-bomb narrative is just WMD 2.0.

Indeed, the War Party has been so shrill and unrelenting in promulgating this trumped-up story that the other side of the equation is hardly known to the American public. Yet as we documented in Chapter 20, the overwhelming weight of the evidence over more than three decades—including information obtained by the IAEA during the course of extensive investigations—is that Iran's primary aim has been to obtain enrichment capacity for its civilian reactors.

In fact, when its incipient weapons-research program was shut down in 2003, the Ayatollah Khamenei took a decisive step to remove all doubt inside the Iranian government. He issued a fatwa (ban) against the possession of nuclear weapons by the Islamic Republic.

This anti-WMD edict was in keeping with a similar fatwa against biological and chemical weapons issued by his predecessor, the Ayatollah Khomeini, in the midst of Iran's war with Iraq in the 1980s. As we indicated in reviewing that episode, Saddam was then dropping those horrific weapons on Iranian battle forces with the spotting help of CIA tracking satellites and the concurrence of Washington.

So in the context of all of that history we now have a solemn international agreement that's designed to ensure that the nuclear-weapons program that the CIA has never found and that the Iranians say they never had and that their supreme leader has forbidden—does, in fact, never happen.

That's not only a very good thing; it's also an overwhelmingly sure thing by the light of any rational analysis.

NOT EVEN HOUDINI COULD BREAK OUT OF THE NUKE AGREEMENT'S CONTAINMENT CHAINS

After all, why would a nation purportedly motivated by a fiendish desire to get the bomb ever agree to a network of restrictions, controls, roadblocks and handcuffs from which not even Houdini could escape? All of this containment machinery would keep the Iranian regime many steps— nay, many miles—removed from anything even remotely resembling an A-bomb capability.

In fact, the agreement is designed to virtually suffocate even the civilian nuclear industry that Iran has proclaimed to be its purpose all along. And needless to say, that is something that it is entitled to—including uranium-enrichment capabilities—as one of the 193 signatories of the Nuclear Nonproliferation Treaty. The latter, of course, is most definitely a nonexclusive club—since it includes every nation on the planet except India, Pakistan, South Sudan and Israel.

Under any rational assessment of the agreement, therefore, suffocation of its incipient civilian nuclear-power industry is exactly what Iran has embraced. It has done so in the name of ending the wholly unnecessary confrontation with the West over its mythical nuclear-weapons program and to thereby gain relief from the sadistic regime of sanctions that have so drastically and unfairly punished its 77 million innocent citizens.

To wit, Iran will eliminate 98% of its existing stockpile of mostly low-enriched uranium and convert the limited number of centrifuges at its one truly hardened site (Fordow) to non-uranium research activities.

Further, it will cut the number of centrifuges at its large Natanz facility from 20,000 to 5,060 units, and this absolutely minimal capacity will be restricted to three-decade-old, slow, inefficient first-generation technology. Not even research on more advanced enrichment technologies may be undertaken for the next eight years.

Moreover, the centrifuges that it will be permitted to operate will be restricted to enriching uranium to only 3.67% purity, meaning that Iran will not be remotely capable of producing the 90% purity material needed for bomb making.

It will also dismantle the core of its heavy water reactor at Arak, which would produce plutonium as a by-product. Although such waste material cannot be used to make a bomb without a reprocessing plant, which Iran does not have and could not likely get, Iran has agreed to replace the current core with an alternative non-weapons capable reactor technology.

Finally, wrapped around all of these limited capacities for civilian enrichment will be a cradle-to-grave inspection regime covering its entire nuclear fuel cycle. This will put inspectors on the ground and sophisticated monitoring equipment in place at its uranium mines, milling plants, storage and transportation facilities, processing plants, centrifuge operations, civilian reactors, waste-handling and -processing stations and all the supporting services and equipment supply and maintenance activities along the entire route.

In short, Iran has agreed to put what will be a tiny civilian nuclear-power and uranium-enrichment industry into a wholly transparent fishbowl. The inspection and monitoring system will be so exhaustive and intrusive that it will resemble the lockdown in a high-security federal prison, and, in fact, will make Iran's entire sovereign territory subject to inspection demands "anytime and anywhere"—including its military facilities.

Yes, in the case of suspected sites not on the primary inspection system it will require a request by the international inspectors. And if the Iranian authorities say no, it will go to a resolution panel where the majority of the members will represent the United States and the other Western signatories to the agreement. But the key thing is all of this must happen within 24 days.

Can anyone in their right mind really believe that Iran could build an illicit facility with tens of thousands of unauthorized centrifuges and all the rest of the bomb cycle equipment that would be required to stage a "breakout" and that this could escape discovery by U.S. intelligence satellites?

And then, if found out, be dismantled and have every trace removed within 24 days?

A GIANT TISSUE OF LIES IS NOW EXPOSED

Here's the thing. The fulminations of Senators McCain, Graham and the rest of the GOP War Party, along with the hysterical bellowing of Prime Minister Netanyahu and his legions of lobbyists on the Potomac, have nothing to do with the actual nation of Iran and the actual leaders who signed the agreement.

The War Party is attacking a giant fiction and tissue of lies of its own making—an untruthful narrative that is grounded in pure politics, not the security interests of the citizens of either America or Israel.

Indeed, the three-decade-long demonization of Iran has served one overarching purpose. Namely, it has enabled both branches of the War Party to conjure up a fearsome enemy, thereby justifying aggressive policies that call for a constant state of war and military mobilization.

As we described earlier with respect to the Washington branch, when the Cold War officially ended in 1991, the Cheney crowd in the George H. W. Bush White House feared the kind of drastic demobilization of the U.S. military-industrial complex that was warranted by the suddenly more pacific strategic environment. In response, they developed an anti-Iranian doctrine that was explicitly described as a way of keeping defense spending at high Cold War levels.

Yet, as we also saw in Chapter 20, the narrative they developed to this end is one of the more egregious Big Lies ever to come out of the Beltway.

The story is the same for the Israeli branch of the War Party, as we have also seen.

In lieu of a two-state solution in the territory of Palestine, Israeli policy has aimed to produce a chronic state of war with Hezbollah and its Iranian ally.

And that goes to the heart of Netanyahu's Big Lie. His relentless claim that Iran is out to annihilate Israel and by implication liquidate its Jewish population is a preposterous distortion and exaggeration of Iran's policy, as articulated by its supreme leader himself.

The real issue is the Palestinian question and the gross injustices that the Palestinian diaspora outside of Israel's current borders, and the occupied populations pinned inside the massive settler communities of the West Bank, has suffered for decades.

But even then, Iran does not propose to seek redress for the Palestinians by dropping nuclear bombs on Israel or sending in its own feeble military or even hordes of hired terrorists.

No, the Ayatollah Khamenei has proposed to vote the present sectarian state of Israel out of existence by referendum, not A-bombs!

In one of his most recent pronouncements on the topic in March 2012, in fact, he said the following during a Friday prayer sermon calling for a multi-religious secular state in Palestine:

> *Holding a referendum in Palestine among the Palestinians, and all those that became refugees—if, of course, they want to return to Palestine—is a rational solution [to the problem]. Those [Palestinians], who live in Lebanon, Kuwait, Jordan, Egypt, and elsewhere, can return home. I am not advocating forcible return of anybody. Then, [Palestinians should] hold a referendum among these who were living there before 1948, when the illegitimate state of Israel was formed, whether Muslim, or Jew or Christian, which will then decide the type of government that must be formed there.*

This is democracy. Why is democracy good for others, but not for the Palestinians? Why it is that all the people of the world can decide their own fate, but not the Palestinians? There is no doubt that the present regime [Israel] took over through deception, trickery, and force. Thus, the people there have an imposed regime.

Fine! Let the people of Palestine hold a referendum to choose the type of the government that they want for themselves. That regime and that government should form and then decide what to do with the people who moved there after 1948. Whatever decision it made, that would also be the fruit of people's vote, as well as democracy, respect for human rights, and in line with the world's present rationale. This is a good solution that must be implemented.

Needless to say, the wizened old man who rules Iran for the time being has no right or authority to call for a referendum among peoples outside his own borders. But that he preaches the doctrine of a secular-state solution that was accepted by much of the civilized world as a plausible answer to the Palestinian question only 40 years ago is surely not evidence that Iran is led by fiendish men who plan another Holocaust.

So what is at stake in the nuclear agreement is of truly epochal importance. The Iranians have signed the agreement in good faith and have locked up any potential for development of a nuclear weapon that they do not want, and have thrown away the key.

Look at the jubilation on the streets of Iran that came after the announcement. It was owing to the prospect that the West's brutal sanctions will be lifted, and that their country now has a pathway back into the community of nations.

Once prosperity and self-respect return to the ancient land of Persia—not this ayatollah nor any other will ever be in a position to do anything more harmful to Israel than what is embodied in the quoted paragraph above. That is, preach vainly about a history that might have been.

In the interim, Israel ought to thank its lucky stars that two flawed but inspired politicians—Barack Obama of the United States and Hassan Rouhani of Iran—found it possible to transcend 30 years of lies and enmities on both sides in order to give peace a chance.

More importantly, as Iran comes back into the community of nations and re-enters global commerce it will give the citizens of Israel an opportunity to see that they have been betrayed and jeopardized by the terrible lies, bullying, megalomania and insuperable will to power of Bibi Netanyahu.

The path to a better, safer future for Israel's citizens does not lie in the repeal of this agreement on the floor of the U.S. Congress during the next administration, whether it is led by Hillary or The Donald.

A better future lies, instead, in a resounding repudiation of the Netanyahu government the very next time the Israeli voters have the chance to go to the polls.

INDEX